SUPER-LEARNING 2000

SUPER-LEARNING 2000

by Sheila Ostrander and Lynn Schroeder
with Nancy Ostrander

Delacorte Press

Published by
Delacorte Press
Bantam Doubleday Dell Publishing Group, Inc.
1540 Broadway
New York, New York 10036

Library of Congress Cataloging in Publication Data

Ostrander, Sheila.
    Superlearning 2000 / by Sheila Ostrander & Lynn Schroeder,
  with Nancy Ostrander.
       p.   cm.
  Sequel to: Superlearning. c1979.
  ISBN 0-385-31274-1
    1. Learning, Psychology of.   2. Educational acceleration.
  I. Schroeder, Lynn, 1935–   . II. Ostrander, Nancy.
  III. Ostrander, Sheila. Superlearning.   IV. Title.
  LB1060.O88   1994
  370.15'23—dc20   94-6402
                                               CIP

Manufactured in the United States of America
Published simultaneously in Canada

September 1994

10 9 8 7 6 5 4 3 2 1

BVG

To the pioneers worldwide, many of whom are mentioned in these pages, who with vision, passion, and courage are venturing to set free that "imprisoned splendor" that waits in us all.

Acknowledgments

Thanks are owed to the many men and women who have shared their thoughts and their work with us. A special word of gratitude to: Charles Adamson, Ivan Barzakov, Al Boothby, Janalea Hoffman, Patricia Joudry, Michael Lawlor, Toni Maag, Mayumi Mori, Pamela Rand, Robina Salter, Dyveke Spino, Bruce Tickell Taylor, John Wade, Hartmut Wagner, Rosella Wallace, Win Wenger. And what would we have done without the support of Donna MacNeil and Christina Vandenboorn, who kept our Superlearning base afloat through bad times and good times. Finally, our thanks to Richard Gallen and John McCaleb for their support and negotiating skills.

Contents

SECTION TWO
HOW-TO HANDBOOK OF SUPERLEARNING

SECTION THREE
EXERCISES

SECTION FOUR

What Is Superlearning?

These are the Superlearning core techniques that vastly accelerate learning and brighten performance. Techniques that can help you take charge of change.

- Get into a stress-free, "best" mindbody state for what you are doing
- Absorb information in a paced, rhythmic way
- Use music to expand memory, energize the mind, and link to the subconscious
- Engage your whole brain, your senses, emotions, and imagination for peak performance
- Become aware of blocks to learning and change, then flood them away

Not even a multiple personality would want to use all the exercises and ploys offered in this book. The idea is to give you a choice. You don't need to pick up very many to flesh out the basic Superlearning protocols. First and foremost, Superlearning involves a new sense of your self and your possibilities, a new perspective—a twenty-first-century point of view.

Section One

HOW FAR CAN YOU REACH? HOW FAST CAN YOU GO?

1
A New Edge

"If the only tool you have is a hammer, every problem looks like a nail," remarked Abraham Maslow. It's time to reach into a bagful of new tools and stop hammering out the same old solutions. It's time to give up horse-and-buggy learning. Time perhaps to tune in to a curious melody circling the world, special music that is helping people learn faster than they ever imagined, helping them change with a grace and ease they never thought possible.

In Herrenberg, Germany, middle-aged IBM employees close their eyes and heave a sigh of relief as the soothing strains of Vivaldi begin to play. Halfway around the world, on St. Lawrence Island in the frozen Bering Strait, Vivaldi's "Winter" seems particularly apropos as a gang of feisty Eskimo teens close their eyes, too, and settle in for the day's lesson between whaling stints. In Indiana a bright sixth-grader sets the music playing. She checks her graphs to see how the music has influenced her classmates' test scores. In Montreal a would-be champion feels his body relax to the wonderful music as vivid images of a tough karate match pivot in his mind.

Would you like to learn two to five times faster *without* stress? And remember what you've learned? You can. That's what the people wrapped in the special music were doing. They are engaged in a new way to learn that we call Superlearning. They are using it to tap in to that ocean of potential that experts keep saying lies waiting in each of us. "I never knew learning could be so much fun!" exclaimed one German IBM employee, echoing the exhilaration that often springs as learning accelerates and talents open up.

Being able to soak up facts, figures, and high-tech data two to five times faster than before can help put you on the fast track to new opportunities and higher earnings. It's proven to save enormous amounts of time and money in job training or retraining, and in learning the languages of the global economy. That's part of the underreported good news. But it's only half of the story.

Something else is important to all of us. Change isn't an option anymore. The option now is to become an agent of change, not a victim of change. As never before, we need to be flexible, to know how to take charge of change without terrible-struggle. As never before, we need the know-how to bring more of our abilities on line—that supposed 90 or 95 percent of human potential we don't usually connect with. A hundred years ago William James calculated we use only about five percent of our innate ability.

"It's more like three percent. Few of us use even five percent of our capacity," insists Dr. Raymond Abrezol, who has trained hundreds of Olympic stars.

How far might we reach? "The ultimate, creative capacity of the brain may be, for all practical purposes, infinite," says writer-educator George Leonard. That's a quote from our first Superlearning book, published in 1979. It always sounds so good, so wide open. But then what do you do? How do you wake up and not see the same old person in the mirror in the same old groove every morning? Here are some new quotes from individuals who've found one way to begin to bring more of themselves alive.

"Besides increased facility in learning, Superlearning has been the starting point of profound and highly beneficial changes in my personality," writes Montreal neurologist Christian Drapeau.

Another Canadian, the well-regarded writer Robina Salter, says simply, "My acquaintance with the new approach created a paradigm shift in my life."

"Again and again teachers, trainers, and learners say that the courses have changed their lives," reports Gail Heidenhain, director of Delphin, a German business training company that uses the new techniques. "It is one thing to say that everyone has much hidden potential, but how much more powerful to actually discover that *I* have potential I never dreamt I had. Only then does theory come to life."

"After thirty years of teaching, I *knew* there had to be a better way," says Californian Bruce Tickell Taylor. "Superlearning has changed my life for the better and that of my students too."

Dr. Mayumi Mori, a pioneering Japanese educator, heard these comments from her accelerated learning class: One student wrote, "I felt as if I had touched upon something very deep and essential as a human being." Another marveled, "Who could even imagine that one could be moved so deeply in lessons like English conversation!" From Yokohama to New York to Heidelberg, something is stirring as people begin to sense their own possibilities. Most are surprised how easy it is to connect with new talents—once they know how. Except for one young man. His passion to realize the dreams pushing up inside him became a life or death challenge.

On the cloudy night of September 10, 1976, Ivan Barzakov waded away from the Bulgarian shore into the choppy Aegean Sea and began to swim. He was swimming for America. First stop would be the marshy Yugoslavian coast almost seven miles across open, shark-infested water. Barzakov wasn't a champion swimmer, just a good one, when he wasn't fighting off asthma, a frequent fight in Bulgaria, where needed medication was rarely available. Ivan Barzakov had one thing going for him. He was a teacher trained in a new form of learning developed by the Bulgarian M.D. Georgi Lozanov, a method that is the taproot of all Western Superlearning systems.

"I had the kernels of the mental technology," Barzakov says, and he used it to relax and keep stroking when the unremitting cold almost paralyzed him. He summoned it to block two incipient asthma attacks. Stroking farther and farther out, "I had to use the mental technology to block memories of death. On several occasions in the sea I have almost been chased by death. Years before, I'd tried to escape by swimming to Turkey, but the cold forced me back."

Swim, Ivan, swim for America . . . arm-wearying stroke after stroke. About the time he realized he'd never swum so far before, "I heard noises, I thought the Yugoslavs must be dumping something in the sea—then suddenly the water all around me shifted. It seemed to boil! Later I learned it was the moment of the great earthquake in Trieste." But Ivan kept swimming. He made it through the treacherous Yugoslavian marshes, across the border to Italy, and into a refugee camp—the sort with one shower for five hundred people.

Today Ivan Barzakov with his American wife, Pamela Rand, another innovative teacher, leads OptimaLearning Systems in Novato, California. He's nurtured those kernels of mental technology into full-blown techniques to help others find the freedom of enhanced performance. In 1992 a seemingly impossible full circle closed. Barzakov was invited to bring his expertise back to Bulgaria to help his countrymen navigate the treacherous turbulence of changing from police state to free economy.

What propelled Barzakov to commit himself so completely to the black Aegean waves? "The number one issue was to be free of the oppressive Communist yoke," he told us recently. Then he added another goal "no less important."

"I had the privilege to work with Dr. Lozanov's experimental education, and I knew these ideas were just at the beginning. We were accelerating language learning and memory. But I felt there was something more, much more. It's what so attracted people in your first Superlearning book, a feeling for the enormous potential of human beings, the excitement of our capacities. . . . With this technology I *knew* we could touch a profound source within us. But that could only happen in the West, particularly in America."

A Wake Up Call

A global wake up call has been ringing for quite a while. Presidential candidate Bill Clinton resonated to it during the TV debates when he said, "To keep doing the same thing over and over and expect a different result is a form of insanity." It's a good quote, from personal-development coach Tony Robbins. Candidate H. Ross Perot almost seemed to be echoing us as he repeatedly insisted, "We have to learn *how* to learn." That's been the rallying cry of Superlearning since its beginning.

"The horizon leans forward offering you space to place new steps of change," Maya Angelou said on the cold, clear high noon of the inauguration of the forty-second president of the United States. She looked out at the listening women, men, children thronging the Capitol Mall. She looked farther to the vast land, and the long drum roll of history unfurled behind them. "Give birth again to the dream," Angelou prodded. "Now, finally awakening, say, 'Good morning.' "

In what may go down as the do-it-yourself decade, you'll have to say "Good morning" on your own. Our establishments, reared by the old status quo, aren't going to do it for you—which may be why we so quickly tire of our leaders. They haven't made everything all right again. As change hits like shock therapy, no one quite knows how the pieces are going to rearrange themselves. It's becoming clear that if we are going to flourish, it's time to stop nattering about solutions and potentials and actually start becoming the free-ranging, accomplished human beings we are designed to be.

The know-how to set you on your way is growing. You can find a lot of it in Superlearning. You can find, too, that it doesn't matter where you are in life, whether you're old or young or what your past encounters with education have brought. The beauty of it is you can finally take a deep breath and relax. Instead of adding pressure in the push to do, do, learn, keep up, accomplish, excel, Superlearning drains stress away. You can learn how to learn through the circuitries of pleasure. Does it sound too good to be true? We thought so too.

A Better *Bulgarian* Way?

It was the end of the sixties, the bad old days in Eastern Europe, when we received an unexpected invitation to Moscow's First (and last) All Soviet Conference on Parapsychology. Before you could say "Intourist," we were roller coasting through a three month adventure trying to grab hold of the Communists' well funded, hard science study of the far reaches of human potential. Some of it seemed to be reaching a little too far. BULGARIANS BREAKTHROUGH TO SUPERMEMORY! chorused Communist dailies. WORKERS LEARN 500 FOREIGN WORDS A SESSION. AND

IMPROVE HEALTH AT THE SAME TIME! Even staid old *Pravda* joined in the hyperventilating, trumpeting, YOU CAN LEARN A LANGUAGE IN A MONTH! It had to be propaganda.

As we sat in Georgi Lozanov's sunny office in the state-funded Institute of Suggestology in Sofia, we knew we were talking with Bulgaria's only psychiatrist, its leading parapsychologist, and the mastermind of Suggestology—an eclectic bag of techniques Lozanov used to conjure seemingly miraculous cures of the sick and the psychotic, anticipating by decades the flowering of alternative medicine. The doctor had discovered a new malady, "didactogenic syndrome"—sickness caused by poor teaching methods—and set his sights on healing it with Suggestopedia. He aimed, he said, "to open the greatest resource a country has—the untapped resources of the human mind."

If the studies that Lozanov's staff showed us were true, tiny Bulgaria stood to become to mental resources what the Arab Emirates have become to natural ones. (For the intriguing story of Lozanov's breakthrough work and of the intrepid educators who seeded the system in the West, see *Superlearning*, Delacorte, 1979.) Lozanov was a charmer, a man with a warm, all embracing laugh and an electric shock of hair that made him look like the stereotypical genius. We still didn't buy most of the "Bulgarian Breakthrough." But we began to wonder "what if . . . ?" If even half the wild and woolly claims were true, we realized, as Barzakov later did, that a big story was breaking in obscure Bulgaria. Not news of Superlearning math or French but the big story of the talents so-called average people can ignite once they know how. It's a story still only in the opening chapters.

Five pages, that's all we devoted to Lozanov learning when we wrote about our Communist odyssey. (See *Psychic Discoveries Behind the Iron Curtain,* 1970; updated and to be republished, 1995.) Inquiries roared in from everywhere, even the Pentagon's Institute of Defense Analysis. Western mind-groupies rushed Sofia, while a handful of pioneering educators began the hard work of adapting the Communist learning system to North America.

A genuinely powerful new way to learn, to expand memory, to excel began to emerge in Des Moines, Toronto, Atlanta. By the late

1970s an innovative psychologist, Dr. Donald Schuster of the University of Iowa at Ames, founded the Society for Accelerative Learning and Teaching (SALT). Now there are professional societies in a dozen countries, including the very international Society for Effective Affective Learning (SEAL) in England. At the time only a few professionals had moved outside of establishment lines. What about all the other people who always wanted to color outside the lines? We took what was proven and devised something that wasn't: a do-it-yourself system, Superlearning®, open to everyone. The generic name is accelerative or *accelerated learning*.

Basic Superlearning draws from Lozanov and his sources, ancient ones like Raja Yoga, contemporary ones like Soviet science, which often took very different turns from ours. And we got lucky. We came across another "ology": Sophrology, "the science of harmonious consciousness," a cornucopia of routes to excellence, still almost unknown in America, developed by Alfonso Caycedo, a Spanish M.D. every bit as innovative as Lozanov. If you're interested in healing, you might want to know that over two thousand European doctors use Sophrology to give patients the know-how to help heal themselves. If you're an athlete, you might want to discover how Sophrology has powered hundreds of Olympic medal winners.

Heading into the 21st century, you are no longer a mind and a body; you're mindbody. Almost 80 percent of what is known about how that single system works has popped up since people began Superlearning, bringing a rush of insight about how to make it even more effective. And there's a bumper crop of new, at times mind boggling ways to wake up potential: high-frequency sound and other psychoacoustic breakthroughs, supernutrition, interactive TV, "dynamic" memory, mind machines, underwater contemplation. . . .

If you want to open up full-throttle, it helps to realize that the accelerated way is first and foremost a *new perspective* embodying a *core set of techniques* you can select, rearrange, shrink, or expand to fit your circumstances. That's why it's blossoming in such diverse places: businesses and the military, kindergartens and colleges, wellness centers, even float tanks. That's why Superlearning is working successfully for individuals of all sorts, from sanitation foremen to neurologists.

"A Great Work Upon Myself"

Can you really accelerate learning on your own? After thirteen years of feedback we can give you a confident yes. Of all the people who've told us of their do-it-yourself success, the one whose story is a writer's dream come true for us is that of neurologist Christian Drapeau. Stressing that he usually doesn't talk about his accomplishments so baldly, this Canadian wanted us to know what he'd done "all on my own."

In 1980 a shy, fifteen-year-old with few friends, Drapeau came upon the French edition of *Superlearning* in a Montreal bookstore. "I have always been interested in the fantastic faculties of the brain," he says. "I've always had, as long as I can remember, a certainty that man has the potential to do whatever he wants and that his limits are those he decides to set for himself." Still . . . it was a pricey book for a teenager. "After one week of going every day to contemplate the book, I bought it."

Drapeau first put his investment to work on what seemed a matter of survival. "In high school I was terribly insecure when I had to speak to people or in front of the class. I was very easily intimidated by anyone." He began using the Superlearning relaxation and mental rehearsal techniques. It worked. Within a summer he "gained a kind of self-mastery" and became an outgoing young man. Today Drapeau is sought after as a conference speaker and as a guest on radio shows.

In high school Drapeau took up Tae Kwon Do, Korean style karate. Rigorous training brought his brown belt. "Just before I won my black belt, I began to tire of the intensive practice." Then Drapeau learned that the 1981 North American Games, which included Tae Kwon Do, would be held in the neighboring province of Ontario. "I saw this as an opportunity for an interesting challenge. I totally stopped physical training. Instead I trained mentally every day using the Superlearning methods." Sixteen-year-old Drapeau arrived at the games in Kitchener, Ontario, permeated with self-confidence.

"Fighting among the black belts, facing people much older than I, in one weight category *above* my own, I won the contest."

In college Drapeau's grasp of Superlearning—the use of special

Baroque music, suggestion, relaxation—allowed him to spend much of his energy composing a rock opera instead of hunching over science texts. "There wasn't much time to study, and I rarely spent more than an hour reviewing for exams. Yet I graduated with an 87% in science." Next he became one of only six students from Quebec accepted into McGill University's neurophysiology program.

On graduation Drapeau plunged into memory research at the Montreal Neurological Institute and in his spare time created tape courses that soon had friends learning at an accelerated clip. He felt the best way to help society is to give children techniques that help them become self-confident and allow them to learn easily, and he set up experimental accelerated classes in six private schools.

"It was the Superlearning techniques that allowed me to do what I conceive of as a great work upon myself," Drapeau remarks. "I was a North American Tae Kwon Do champion. I have a master's degree in neurology and neurosurgery, have composed music, studied and published a book on philosophy, written another on nutrition. I am engaged in full-time research and am making an in-depth study of religion. I am now twenty-seven years old."

The Superlearning techniques Drapeau used to accomplish his "great work" are detailed later. The point here is—you can do it yourself. With many techniques you *have* to do it yourself.

Horse-and-Buggy Learning Isn't Going to Cut It

"A teacher from 1890 could step out of a Winslow Homer painting and feel right at home in a 1990 classroom," says Ellen Dempsey, president of Teachers Network. "What other business could remain in existence exactly the same way for one hundred years?"

It's a marginal business. As director of Project Renaissance, Dr. Win Wenger remarks, "Considering the state of education today, virtually *any* system that works could be considered accelerated." In his accelerated training Wenger often asks executives to imagine fitting new heads over their old ones. A new head, a new perspective, that's what will summon the best from our schools, he insists, not the bureaucratic mating call "More money." That money is not a magic fix-it is excruciatingly obvious in a state like New York, which spends far above the national norm per student. Yet tens of thousands of New York kids, particularly minorities, are sinking or sunk. It isn't just a teenage disaster. Until just decades ago a society could flourish with most workers needing only a strong back and capable hands. Today even if we do it well, those who stick with horse-and-buggy learning are going to be shoved to the shoulder, if not run over, on the new information superhighways. The old way won't cut it for wage earners of the 21st century. "People can't be trained as cogs anymore," warns Secretary of Labor Robert Reich. "The next economy will rely on workers capable of fast learning." Those who get up to speed will enjoy the new wealth that all the wrenching changes will bring, riches as hard for us to foresee as it was for preindustrial people to imagine how wide their horizons would soon become.

"The U.S. has a Third World labor force," reported "60 Minutes" in an exposé of America's skills gap with Germany. Thirty percent of U.S. kids drop out of school. Canada has a 30 percent failure rate, too, even though it spends $44 billion a year, second highest in the world, on education. It's not time just to retool but to rethink—and to look around.

Germany seems to be hatching a 21st century workforce right now. Germans work smarter with quality skills for high wages and generous vacations. What's their secret? In part the remarkable continuing-education networks set up by industry across the nation, that offer on-the-job learning in a host of specialties, from robotics to language learning. There's another secret at the heart of many German training centers. For years they have used Superlearning techniques. Old style education, many realize, is out of sync with high tech. By the time a new system is learned, another is invented. Trainees can't keep up. Superlearning filled the breach, thanks in part to Dr. Hartmut Wagner.

Skeptical yet challenged, Wagner, a teacher, set out to see if the new method offered steak as well as sizzle. Today he heads the SKILL-Training Institute in Heidelberg with a staff of thirty-four, who've taught over a thousand trainers and continually work with executives, including those excited IBM employees listening to Vivaldi in Herrenberg, Germany. Siemens, Audi, Phillips, Rank, Xerox, Opel—

the blue chips have jumped on the accelerated wave in Germany because it pays a double dividend: high skills at high speed and, as employees will tell you, better mental and physical health.

If learning know-how is survival equipment in the corporation, it's even more imperative for the majority of us. The largest U.S. job category in the next millennium, forecasters say, will be "knowledge workers"—technicians, service specialists, and entrepreneurs who will increasingly work in small teams or on their own, freelance. What is required for success now, Ronnie Sandroff warns in *Working Woman,* is the skill "to transform ourselves into quick change artists who can turn on a dime, shrug off past success and failures and frequently reinvent ourselves to fill the new roles that suddenly replace the old." Exhilarating if you know how, terrifying if you don't. How can we school our children and ourselves with the flexibility to thrive? One answer is the shift in perspective that Dr. Charles Adamson made.

An American working in the very high pressure cooker of Japanese colleges, Adamson took to Superlearning with gusto. When his conservative colleagues at the Shizuoka Science and Technical Institute got wind of what was going on in his classroom, they sniffed, "That is not teaching."

"I decided they were right," Adamson says. "No more teaching in my classes, just learning."

From hard experience most of us think education means cramming something in, as if you were stuffing a sausage or a Strasberg goose. Which is why we often view lifelong learning with the enthusiasm reserved for flossing our teeth. But the literal meaning of *education* is to "draw out from." That's what Superlearning systems are designed to do, draw out a wealth of innate talent and, though you may not think so, the vast store of knowledge you already possess. It's not a new idea but rather the rebirth of a very old one. On their way to becoming the glory that was Greece, the archetypal teacher Socrates; his best student, Plato; and many of the other ten thousand citizens of Athens operated on the principle that we all have innate genius, that we are all connected to infinite knowledge. They worked with the whole person to draw that genius out. They understood a secret: It's hard to stop people from learning for a lifetime if it's synonymous with adventure and the pleasure of discovery. (The elite in many ancient cultures knew the secret. Lozanov drew some of his best ideas from them.) To shape the future closer to the heart's desire, we need to bring learning back inside ourselves and again sense it as a natural process, ongoing, fascinating, and as limitless as life itself.

"You Aren't Going to Change, Kid!"

If you want to unfold your wings, you have picked the best moment in history. You don't have to become an initiate of a secret society guarding the perennial wisdom. Ways to expand capability are appearing constantly. The times demand. The times may also be helping.

"Amid all the chaos without and chaos within, there is a very real change happening in the psyche," declares the eminent Jungian Marian Woodman, who is in a position to look deeply into many psyches. Her clients "are finding a new energy is being released in their bodies." And Woodman hears it expressing as "We want our inner freedom!"

Good Jungian that she is, Woodman also hears, "we want to be free of the old Mother and old Father"—not one's own parents but two enormous complexes in the collective mind. We are becoming conscious of the old Mother of deadening security, who wants to keep us in place, and of the old Father of law and tradition, that holds our lives in outworn patterns. This is the duo that says, "You're not going to change, kid!" They may finally be proved wrong, Woodman believes. She sees that new energy increasingly propelling people to proclaim, "I *want* to be free. I *want* to take responsibility for my own life." We may finally have grown to the point where it's time to leave home and stretch out in our own expanded digs.

The chaos in our world and in ourselves that Woodman addresses is fearful. It may also be a once in a millennium opportunity. As structures collapse, possibilities are freed, openings appear. The accelerated systems aren't a panacea, though they certainly seem part of many solutions. Superlearning isn't a magic pill for individuals, either, though it occasionally acts like one. You will learn faster and greatly enhance your memory. Accelerated learning can work that "magic" for just about anyone. At best, though, the new way is global learning, a passport to the whole world of yourself. It is one way you can move toward what Abraham Maslow, the father of Humanistic Psychology, called self-actualization, what some call wholeness, what business psychologist Marsha Sinetar calls "a 21st century mind." That's the sure footed route to conjuring a better way out of the chaos, for as Aldous Huxley knew, "There's only one corner of the universe you can be certain of improving and that's your own." Why just sit in your corner when you can pick up the know-how to claim a galaxy of just-over-the-horizon possibilities?

2
Supermemory?

How fast can you learn? There may not be a speed limit. At the moment people of every stripe and background—third-graders in Alaska, Filipino nuns, AT&T technicians—find they can relax and cruise through the material they need to know two to five times faster than before. Occasionally people sizzle along ten times faster and still remember what they've learned.

The most straightforward, elegant use of Superlearning, one that's proved endlessly successful, is to lean back and learn facts, figures, and languages quickly, at any age. Imagine how you would feel with a solid grasp of a necessary subject if you could do it without crowding your time. Or the kick of finally getting a handle on something you've always wanted to know. Mastering subjects is like a practical form of firewalking—once you prove to yourself what you are capable of, old limitations can fall across the board. How would you accelerate learning science, for instance, or math? You can do it the way university students did in Japan, or you can do it, home alone, as Brian Hamilton does in the States.

In a large lecture hall at Japan's University of Tokai, four hundred engineering students sat breathing in sync. A soft tone sounded to pace the gentle rise and fall of their breath as their professor recited the day's lecture in an unusual rhythm. He drew from his own textbook, *Electricity and Magnetism*. Eventually Dr. Hideo Seki put down his notes, the lights lowered and brightly colored diagrams came alive on a large screen. Soft music, Bach's *Air in G*, then Vivaldi's *Four Seasons*, began to play as the colorful slides, too, seemed to march along in a precise rhythm. Not a word was spoken. As the last slide faded, four hundred students let their shoulders slump, felt their arms and legs grow limp and heavy as they closed their eyes and listened to special Baroque music. From a spot of warm comfort within themselves they heard their professor recite the exact same lesson over again, this time above the slow, steady beat of the music.

Dr. Hideo Seki is a wise old man in his eighties, with a twinkle in his spirit as well as in his eye, who invited us on a never-stop-talking lecture tour through Japan from top to bottom. We met his colleagues, leaders in industry and academia, a group with a unique cachet. Like Seki, at the end of World War II they'd been considered special enough for the U.S. government to transplant them for a few years to the best American universities. Engineer and information specialist Seki immediately saw the promise of Superlearning. He ran the first tests in Japan and wrote the first books on accelerating ability and opening the higher octaves of human nature.

At the end of the semester at Tokai University, Seki's published reports revealed "the number of students who scored high grades increased dramatically, while the number of low grades decreased." He proved even very large groups can Superlearn.

New Yorker Brian Hamilton proved to himself that it works rather smartly, too, for one person alone in his apartment. Ten busy years had passed since Hamilton won his master's degree in social work and became a therapist. Now he was back in school taking a tough pre-med course at Columbia University. "I felt a little rusty, sort of out of the rhythm of studying," Hamilton admits. "I was getting B-minuses, but I wanted to do better. Two weeks before midterms, *Superlearning*, which I'd bought but never read, literally fell off the shelf at my feet. I went through it all in one night and thought, why not?" Hamilton made himself some trigonometry tapes focusing on "identities," something he had to know for his exams. (For step-by-step instructions of how to create a Superlearning program, see Chapter 24.)

During study sessions Hamilton took a few minutes to get into a "best state" for learning facts and figures. He relaxed his body to a place of deep comfort, calmed and centered his mind using full-sensed imagination; then he gave himself a few rousing positive suggestions. Ready to learn, he switched on his tape. Hamilton heard information pulsing to him in a specific rhythm: four seconds of data, four seconds of silence, four seconds of data, four seconds of silence. He breathed along in sync. He held his breath when something was said, breathed in and out during the pauses. Adding to the rhythmic effect, information was spoken in three different voice intonations—normal; soft and conspiratorial; loud and commanding—cycling over and over. Once through, Hamilton put down the script he'd been following and turned on a Superlearning Music tape.

He stretched out and closed his eyes. Then he heard the exact same lesson over again, this time backed with special 60-beat-a-minute Baroque. As soothing string sounds flooded around him, Hamilton let his mind float easily between trigonometry and the tightly structured harmonics of Bach. That was it.

Get in the right state of body and mind for whatever you're doing. Imbibe data in a suggestive, highly rhythmic way backed by very specific music. This is the heart of Superlearning that pumps much of the spectacular speed-up. Some people just relax and listen to the music while they read or hear data. That brings good results too, but you probably have to beat with the full rhythm of the system to unfold supermemory.

The first time we heard of supermemory beyond tabloid ads, it was whistling along under its scientific name, *hypermnesia*. Hypermnesia, the fascinating opposite of amnesia, was the big attractor of Lozanov's breakthrough in Communist lands. For years Soviets dogged this elusive potential, practically dismantling memory superstars, like the famous Veniamin, "the man who could remember everything." If one person can do it, maybe others can be trained to it, they insisted. Why? Because the Soviets saw world-class memory as the royal road to the untapped and, in the farthest reaches, still unknown resources of your mind.

Hypermnesia, Lozanov style, allows the world-class memory you already possess to emerge. Everything that's ever happened to you lives in you somewhere. The trick is to retrieve what you've perceived. One way to tempt memory into consciousness is to feed it data in a specific, rhythmic, musical way; another is to build bridges to your subliminal mind.

Pumped-up memory sparks all accelerated systems. *You learn faster because you remember better.* Have you ever had to go back dozens of times to catch the conjugation of a Russian verb, to remember that theorem or bit of sports trivia? Superlearning is designed to fix information in memory with few repetitions. Experience shows, too, that as you learn specific subjects, over time the effect globalizes and your whole memory strengthens.

What happened to Brian Hamilton's memory with his home-made tapes and special music? "In just two weeks of Superlearning I went from B-minuses to A's," Hamilton says. Here-for-the-exam and gone-tomorrow learning? "You might say my retention is almost too good," Hamilton says with a grin. "Sometimes when I go to Carnegie Hall and hear Vivaldi, trigonometry identities start reeling off in my head." Hamilton soon became a pre-med student by weekday, Superlearning teacher on the weekends.

Global Learning

Our lives dance in an extraordinary web of global communication. Billions of people together eyewitness the rooftop flash of a Scud missile, a hand reaching out to close around a long-desired Oscar. At the same time scientists are revealing a ceaseless buzz of communication, every bit as complex, inside of us. Thoughts and emotions translate into rushing chemical messages, brain signals speed to organs, organs shoot back replies, while the mobile immune system, like an executive on a cellular phone, exchanges the latest news with far-flung realms of body and brain. Mindbody, we've come to know is one interdependent system, like humanity and the good earth that supports us.

Superlearning taps global communication, both outside and inside. Mainline education still speaks mostly to your logical, so-called left brain. The accelerated way engages your whole brain, your conscious and unconscious minds, your imagination, senses, emotions—and that vital component usually overlooked in education, your body. As you use Superlearning to remember better, you are also literally re-membering yourself, putting back together all the different parts of you that have been ignored or repressed in traditional learning. If you involve your whole self, you ante up your chances of accomplishing any goal, quickly and well. It's like striking out free-stroke for the far shore instead of bobbing along in the waves with one arm and two legs trussed up.

Often called the musical memory method, Superlearning is designed to keep your abilities playing together, supporting each other in concert. Why let two thirds of your exquisite equipment—your senses, your emotions—sit idle or noodle off on their own distracting agenda while you're trying to learn or perform? Make your emotions part of the team and, for one thing, you'll find your memory is greatly enhanced.

Learning as a source of better health? Built-in stress reduction is a major plus in Superlearning. And there are more subtle benefits. The new approach stimulates more areas of your brain than traditional learning does; that's vital as you age, insists French brain specialist Dr. Monique Le Poncin. If brain cells are underutilized through overspecialization or lack of challenge, "strategic mobility" is lost, Le Poncin finds. This makes it difficult to change and keep up in middle age. This is what brings serious deficiencies in old age. You can also gain finesse in relaxation, visualization, and imaginative rehearsal—the current big three in ventures into mental healing.

And you can flush away toxins—mental toxins. Your entire life experience rides along in your memory, and as mounting research reveals, we all carry baggage we've never been consciously aware of—maybe a traumatic birth, almost certainly immobilizing suggestions ("Change is frightening," "Girls aren't good at math") that have seeped in silently from the environment. We carry words and opinions, too, long ago, forgotten words such as "Are you dumb!" that live on in us as unnoticed as colonies of bacteria. The suggestive power of negative subterranean memories goes a long way toward explaining why we only run on a fraction of ourselves. "Helping clients overcome their unconscious scripts is one of the surest ways to open high achievement," says accelerated teacher Dr. Tatiana Radonjic-Matano. As you open up circuits to memory, you have an open sesame to conscious change, to dissolving blocks. When circuits connect, you may also be surprised to find that you really do know a lot more than you think you do—something Al Boothby proved to a sagging group of high school failures.

A college instructor and high school teacher in the Sacramento school district, Boothby signed up for a stress reduction workshop. "The instructor, an L.A. Police Department psychologist, held up a book with flame-orange lettering on black that proclaimed, 'Superlearning.' " Over the weekend Boothby went through the book twice. Fortuitously. On Monday he was asked to tackle summer classes for high school seniors who'd failed to graduate. Why not try Superlearning?

To get diplomas, eighteen students needed to pass U.S. history. Before plunging into text, they listened on multichannel headphones to taped relaxation instructions, then heard Boothby speaking in the rhythmic Superlearning format telling them exactly what they'd be required to know. "I told them that not only would they remember the subject matter, they would also be able to add all of the information that they had accumulated in their lifetime about that particular event in history. The purpose of the text, I said, was to help them understand what they already knew. Thank God! It worked to perfection."

Boothby led his class through imaginative exercises; he had them call back the past to get a feeling for the vividness and reach of their memories. His students became so absorbed in their work that, just to see what would happen, he rolled a metal wastebasket the length of the room. Not a single reader stopped or looked up. Part of the final was oral. "Amazing to me," Boothby told us, "though they hadn't passed history before, they gave complete, precise and enriched answers. The enrichment did not come from the text. Somewhere, somehow, they had all acquired a store of knowledge about the United States and were now able to relate it and explain it. They'd learned how to put information into their memories and how to draw information out. Skeptics turned into true believers."

Believers in themselves. Boothby reports many are in fine jobs now as a result of continuing their education. "They'd discovered that they could learn just about anything they wanted to." And Al Boothby had discovered that drawing out what is already there and igniting innate ability can turn F's into A's more handily than stuffing students.

An Unreported Revolution

If you join the learning revolution, you'll be part of a phenomenon that doesn't recognize national boundaries any more than seeds riding the intercontinental winds. The seeds seem to thrive anyplace—in the crowded avenues of Mexico City or in Vanuatu, a dot of an island so tiny on the map that a pin obliterates it. And then there's Finland. Imagine the outcome if an entire country shifted into accelerated. That's what's been happening in state schools in Finland for the past decade, with results that have moved outside professionals to exclaim "stunning," "inspiring," . . . "Super-Finns!"

Shift to 21st century learning and you'll hook up, in spirit at least, with all the others who know that the great press is on. We have to accelerate knowledge of the outside world—but, equally important if we are to shake the destruction of the past, we must accelerate knowledge of our own inner worlds.

"We are at a unique place at a unique time in the history of this planet," teacher Bruce Tickell Taylor reminds his self-built worldwide network of accelerated mavens. His global perspective is probably genetic. Born to a British actress and an American mining engineer in Seoul during the twenties, a time of sharp repression by the Japanese overlords, Taylor immediately began a life of high adventure with his delivery into a bed with a secret. The outlawed Korean Declaration of Independence was hidden under his mother's mattress.

To have a future, Taylor believes, the global community has to learn to pull together. It's not a matter of changing human nature, "but we do need to change the unconscious beliefs resulting from childhood conditioning. The ability to change the unconscious through affirmation and inner imagery is a very important point that many involved with accelerated learning are well aware of, though most of the population is not. *We are in a unique position to help.*"

Like many others around the world, Mayumi Mori sees it too. She believes the need to learn how to learn is greater than ever. "Gaining the ability to interact with fellow human beings on a different 'energy level' and developing 'noble aims' is paramount now," says Mori, founder of the Japanese Society for Accelerative and Integrative Learning (SAIL).

As a better way proliferates, so have its names. Apart from Superlearning, there's OptimaLearning, Power Learning, The Lind Institute, Sound Learning, Inner Track Learning, Project Renaissance, Super Study, to list a very few, and not to mention a slew of organizations with *Accelerated* in their title, enough so that we sometimes long for a memory tape to tell them apart. They are all branches of the same tree. One cautionary: *Superlearning 2000* is *not* a directory. Beyond those mentioned, there are plenty of top-notch others putting a better way to good use. Good uses are as multiple as needs. Once you know how, learner or teacher, you can go almost anywhere you want.

What Can You Do?

The basics. We've got to get back to the basics. Vocabulary, spelling, grammar, arithmetic—if they're not already second nature, Superlearning can really help. Or if you want to assist others, it might even help you win a government grant as Dr. Mary Harris of Atlanta did from the Defense Department. Her project: Superlearning SAT Vocabulary tapes to give kids in Junior ROTC the academic equipment to keep marching forward. At the other end of the spectrum, individuals far along the road to accomplishment make their own tapes to loft over a variety of professional hurdles; to get real estate licenses; to pass foreman, civil service, and bar exams. Rocklin, California, teacher Ruth James, for one, put together tapes to prepare for a tough state exam that would credential her as a language development specialist. So pleased was James with the results, she's arranged to use the Superlearning Music and now markets a "Stress-Free Success for the LDS" cassette.

Some people have taken off into the wild blue yonder on their own. The most intrepid we know is novelist George Guthridge, who teaches for a living. In 1982 he landed in Gambell, an Eskimo village on St. Lawrence Island, a piece of earth about the size of Delaware, thirty-seven miles from Siberia. Guthridge, who'd gotten his new job over the phone, walked into a school with virtually no library or lab equipment. What it did have was an extremely aggressive group of kids.

"Four days in, one guy threatened to throw me through the window when I asked him to read." These islanders were used to warring; they'd been fighting the Siberians for four thousand years. Many of Guthridge's students had never set foot on the mainland, never seen a hotel or ridden in an elevator. Some showed up in class with traces of the animal they'd just skinned clinging to their hands. His predecessor, kids said, simply flipped on the movie projector and let it run until spring. But Guthridge had gotten wind of Superlearning from his cousin, physicist Don Lofland. Lofland was surprising people in community colleges up and down California with how fast they could pick up science data and languages.

Guthridge decided to make Superlearning the foundation of his own unique learning method, Reverse Instruction. Aggression flashed into a new channel, academic contests. In 1983 Guthridge's rough-hewn kids entered the prestigious National Problem Solving Competition. Up against 15,500 schools, including some of the best in the country, they made the finals by spring 1984. That's when a wonder seemed to happen.

High school students, including two who didn't even know what a cell was a few months before, grabbed the national championship by solving a problem in genetic engineering, a problem tough enough, Guthridge says, to have the judges phone an expert for advice. Guthridge's younger students soared to the occasion, too, capturing first prize in the Junior High Problem Solving Competition. For the first time one school swept both championships. A school in Gambell, St. Lawrence Island.

The full story of the transformation Guthridge wrought in many classes sounds as unbelievable as those hyper Bulgarian headlines. Still, in 1987 George Guthridge became the Alaskan winner of the

Department of Education's $25,000 Christa McAuliffe Fellowship. (For more on Guthridge's Reverse Instruction, see Chapter 30.)

Parlez-vous almost anything. From New South Wales to Singapore to Siberia, people are shedding stress and picking up just about every language you can think of—Japanese, Russian, Mandarin Chinese, Indonesian, Zulu—and some you probably won't think of, like Esperanto, the universal tongue, and computer language.

If you've ever taken a language in school, you'll feel a pang of empathy for British reporter Caroline Mead. She'd aced French. So in France, Mead sat down to dinner and confidently ordered a succulent-sounding lamb pastry. Soon a little foil packet arrived in a cloud of steam. "When that cleared, I realized that what was on my plate was clearly not lamb at all, let alone in pastry. It was calf's brain." Gustatory disaster, Mead says, sprang from the traditional parrot-fashion method by which she was taught. "Knowledge stays just long enough to sweep you through exams." She looked into French taught the accelerated way in England by Geoffrey Pullen for vocabulary that lingers to bring fond food memories.

Peabody Award–winning journalist Charlayne Hunter-Gault is often in the thick of real disasters. A regular on "The MacNeil/Lehrer NewsHour," she was headed toward yet another hot spot in Central America. Bobbing and weaving through a hectic schedule, Hunter-Gault took a little time out to plug in to her Superlearning Spanish tapes. Tension melted away as she imagined herself gliding down an escalator through a rainbow of colors: red, orange, yellow, green, blue, indigo, ultraviolet. She relaxed on a minivacation, felt the sun baking her shoulders, sand crunching between her toes and took long, slow breaths of fresh salt air as she watched the glistening blue waves rolling to shore. She could learn Spanish easily, she suggested to herself, quickly and easily. In the right state to learn, she heard, "Can you tell me? . . . *¿Puede usted decirme?*"—phrases pulsed to her in the special, rhythmic format backed by Baroque.

"I started using Superlearning for Spanish," she says. "But once I mastered the exercises, I found they improved my interviewing, my writing, speech making, and just about everything else involving my memory."

You might have been surprised by what happened to your memory if a few years ago you'd been one of the more than one hundred students crowded into Dr. Don Schuster's class at the State University of Iowa to learn Pascal, the computer language. You probably would have been relieved, too, at semester's end to find that your accelerated class scored slightly higher than three groups learning the usual way—because *you'd done it in half the class hours*. On Schuster's accelerated schedule you didn't even have to go to class on Fridays.

"I was burned out, but now I'm not"—or, as it sometimes sounds, "But now I'm saved"—is a common refrain from teachers who take up accelerated learning. "Half my students were failing, most didn't seem to care about learning chemistry," says Leo Wood, who realized he was a potential burnout after twenty-four years teaching in Tempe, Arizona. Then he found Ivan Barzakov's workshop.

First he woke up his own memory by playing the special music while reading. "Now I can remember things I never could before." Wood tried the better way in his chemistry classes. Before, only twenty-five percent of the class got A's, B's, C's. Now "ninety-three percent of my students receive A's, B's, and C's. My dropout rate has fallen from forty-eight percent down to seven percent. Which is fabulous for me," says Wood, adding that now he can hardly wait to go to work, it's so "exhilarating."

Salespeople use Superlearning to fix a product line in mind. Others learn Morse code. People who have to speak in public, from the boardroom to the PTA, use it to feel secure in their topics. Birders memorize the characteristics of their quarry; trivia mavens pick up sports stats. Actors become super-quick studies. And Cantor Richard Silverman of Temple Israel in Westport, Connecticut, a Superlearner ignited by Brian Hamilton, is bringing the new mind tech to an ancient ritual. Bar Mitzvah is a time of great celebration, but also one of hard study and often great anxiety for Jewish teens. Cantor Silverman realized that whole-brain learning could help keep this most important rite of passage on the joyous side. Consulting with Hamilton, he's created a soon to be published Bar Mitzvah prep program—complete with stress reducing, right-state-for-learning routines, and Baroque behind the necessary Hebrew.

"I guess Superlearning can sometimes work automatically,"

Hamilton called to say. "I never heard Hebrew prayers until I worked with the cantor. I happened to stay at the beach with a Jewish friend. 'Oh, it's Friday,' she said one day, 'I should at least light a candle.' She did, then fumbled for a prayer. Out of the blue I began chanting the prayers in perfect Hebrew. I don't know which one of us was more surprised."

Fast, stress-free factual learning works. As you'll see in coming chapters, you can use the same techniques to enhance creativity and performance—violin playing, speaking, writing, or sprucing up your tennis, basketball, or golf game. And to pick up a different set of basics, equipment to handle what Alvin Toffler calls "too much change in too little time": future shock.

The core techniques work on their own. But if you put them all together, you might find yourself unfolding like a Christian Drapeau or realizing, like employees of the international electronics giant Siemens, "I can learn anything!"

3
The Right State = The Right Stuff

Do you find it hard to let the words *joy* and *learning* flow trippingly off your tongue in the same sentence? If so, you're a prime candidate for the Joy of Learning exercise. It's become one of the most effective, popular Superlearning techniques, after people got over their initial guffaws. Even the copy editor who checked the first Superlearning book queried Joy of Learning. "Isn't that too much hype? Can those two really go together?" he asked. Today, instead of laughing, a lot of people are grinning with a new feel for self-mastery. This ploy will put you in a good mood. And it will do something more important. It will put you in a "best" state for learning, performing, accomplishing.

Relax, get comfortable, close your eyes. Think of a time when you felt really good about yourself, when you were riding high with success, when all systems were go. It might be when you gave a socko report at a business meeting, played the tennis game of your life, or when the girl of your dreams said yes. The farther back you can go in time, the better. How about when you finally got your driver's license, learned to ride your bike on your own, or the day the kindergarten teacher chose your picture for a place of honor on the wall and you went home with a great big gold star?

Find a time when you felt terrific about yourself, and be there. Summon the setting, remember who was there. How were they acting toward you? What were they saying? Was there applause or a kiss from your mom? Summon the sights, sounds, smells, everything connected with your triumphant moment. As you live in the memory, notice how you feel inside—warm, tingling, light, or heavy. How did your legs feel? your thighs? your belly? What about your shoulders; how were you breathing? Were you smiling—on the outside, on the inside? Revel in this state, feel the joy. Then cross two fingers. Tell yourself you'll be able to summon this great feeling state whenever you cross those fingers. Ride with the feeling for a bit, then slowly return to the present.

Practice until you can easily bring this memory wholly alive before tackling any challenge: announcing for councilwoman, learning spelling or statistics, plotting a new sales campaign, taking up wind surfing, or entering the local bridge tournament. If time's lacking for the whole exercise, cross those fingers to fire up your "best" primed-for-success state. This is called triggering, a shortcut successfully exploited by countless doers, particularly those trained in Neurolinguistic Programming (NLP).

Relive your memory of success and you'll be in the right state— body, mind, emotions, spirit—for achievement. All of these elements live in a vivid memory. A vivid memory . . . once you get a handle on what's really going on in a vivid memory, you have a key, perhaps *the* key to conscious change. The mysterious, shaping power of memory is that elusive something beneath the usual Superlearning techniques that now and then kicks in to bring remarkable change and transformation, the sort of thing that sparked a Christian Drapeau. It took us a while to figure out how it works.

What is your memory? Data bank? Storehouse? Some days all of us would agree with the small boy who explained, "My memory is the thing I forget with." The idea that memory is a reservoir holding everything that's happened to you has always been the good news of Superlearning. It's all there. But there's a flip side to memory as data bank, an X-factor, as necessary to our lives as water to a trout. It is *dynamic memory*. And right now it's determining who you are and what you are capable of accomplishing.

Moment by moment your dynamic memory pulls together strands of feeling, thoughts, behavior, insults of the past, hopes of the future, meshing them with the ongoing signals of your glands, with far-flung messages from your circulating immune system, to weave a unique pattern: you. It is memory that makes you who you are. Memory lets you say, "There is no one exactly like me in the universe." Why do we so greatly fear losing our memories? Because if we do, as far as the world is concerned, we lose our Self.

Once you realize that memory isn't just something that sits at the bottom of your head like a necessary suitcase, that it's a creative process, you can get leverage. You can begin to make it work *for* you, not against you. You can turn the key and drop the limiting bonds of memory that chain you to the past, you can begin coloring in bright memories of the future. You'll also find new ways to remember things a whole lot better.

What Does a Memory Look Like?

A memory looks like you at the time it was born. To get a feeling of what that means, remember the first time you fell in love. Summon a bright, shimmering time with that wonderful "other." See your lover smile, remember the scent of a special moment, hear "your" song, feel a touch, feel your body, your whole self beginning to glow. . . .

If you did that little exercise, you've pulled off a bit of wizardry worthy of Merlin. You've raised the dead. You've summoned the past alive in the present. You've proved, as one of Faulkner's characters said, "The past ain't dead, it ain't even past."

Everything that was going on outside you and inside of you right down to the flow of your hormones can live in a strong memory. Just as astrologers believe that the universal moment is imprinted on a baby at birth, so a memory can carry a living imprint of the whole moment of its birth. If instead of summoning the warm memory of a first love you'd raised the specter of the worst moment of your life, you could have relived that tightening in your gut, those searing sights, spiraling emotions. When you recall a powerful memory, the whole state you were in will begin to resonate in you. It's like plucking a guitar string in a quiet room—the same string on another guitar comes alive, vibrates, resonates. This is called *state dependent memory, learning, and behavior* and it explains why the Joy of Learning exercise can be so potent, resonating a mindbody chord of success. It explains, too, why negative memories can so massively short-circuit ability.

Do you remember things better when you are in a good mood or in a depressed one? On the road to understanding state dependent memory, Stanford University psychologists discovered it doesn't matter how you feel at the moment. The key is how you felt when the memory was formed. If you were gloomy, you'll recall that memory more quickly and clearly when you're depressed. If you were feeling great, feel great again to best summon memory. States resonate with each other.

"Where did I leave my coat?" boozers ask in the sober dawn. "My briefcase? My wife?" Pursuing state dependent memory and learning, researchers asked volunteers to chug enough vodka to get a buzz on. Under the influence, subjects memorized vocabulary words. When sobriety returned, they had little memory of what they'd learned. But when they were once again given a good jolt of vodka, the words came back with the buzz. (Is that where "try a little hair of the dog" came from?) Their memory, their learning, was tied to their state. News of the dynamics of state dependent memory is still coming in. It's a major, though little known, breakthrough in the brainmind sciences. Getting a handle on it will give you a master key to accelerate learning and change.

The Best States to Live In

Having the right stuff may really boil down to being in the right state. Why is it that we only use one, two, ten percent of our supposed potential? Why is it, as Soviet scientists long maintained, that even 35 to 45 percent of our physical capabilities remain untapped? The circuits seems to be there. Maybe it's because we don't know how to get into the states where these abilities connect and light up.

U.S. Olympic pentathlete Marilyn King says flatly, "Potential is a state of mind." King's insight was forced upon her by an injury. Confined to bed in the months leading to the Olympic trials, King knew she had to keep training, so she did in her imagination. Back on her feet, she won second in the pentathlon. Now, as president of Beyond Sports, King uses "applied Olympic thinking" to coach adults in power states of mind, to help kids become world-class learners. "Once a negative self-fulfilling prophecy begins to be replaced by a new script, a new film loop—watch out," she says.

That's state shifting, getting into the right place to access the right stuff. One crowd has always known their work state was something else again. "The poet is two people," explains the Russian poet Andrei Voznesensky. "One is an insignificant person, leading the most insignificant of lives. But behind him, like an echo, is the other person who writes poetry." Artists have forever petitioned their muse to lift them into that other person, that other state.

A less lofty, but no less magical state as far as other teachers were concerned, was one Al Boothby evoked in a class of boyz 'n the hood types. Boothby retired to work double time, troubleshooting for the Sacramento Board of Education, and stepped right into an archetypal problem class. "These kids, seniors, came from incredible poverty, abusive homes," he says, "some of the saddest cases I've seen. They'd given up on school, on themselves."

Boothby's six feet seven inches lent authority when he said the unexpected. "You can learn," he told his problem cases. "And you can do it easily." Guiding them through relaxation and into the Superlearning routine, he let them prove it to themselves. Quickly, easily, they mastered ten words in Portuguese. The kids were surprised, the observing teachers came closer to astonishment. The sort of class you don't turn your back on had suddenly become focused, quiet, cooperative for the whole session. "I wanted the faculty to learn, too," Boothby admits, "that Superlearning is fun and allows everyone to learn."

No matter what your goal, you'll realize it faster if you seek states that enable and avoid those that shackle. Feeling competent, totally adequate, empowered—these are life-giving, change-bringing states. Whenever you feel inadequate, unworthy, not in control of your life, you're in a minus state, one that drains away your best shots at realizing innate abilities. It drains your vitality too. You can learn how to mentally and emotionally step away from minus states and into plus states. It's not a matter of battling circumstances or "gaining control over the minds of men." It's simply a matter of learning how to shift your inner weather at will.

Entertainment or Enlightenment?

"You can't *have* too much fun in a Superlearning class!" enthused one English teacher. That still sounds a touch seditious, to some, foolishly permissive. After all, most of us were taught, "Learning is serious business." Yet high seriousness doesn't really get the life juices flowing and would be a tough state to maintain for a lifetime of learning. "Serious" education almost always builds stress.

Scientific data has caught up with common sense: You're going to do better at something that doesn't make you feel terrible. If the state you are in lives in a memory, why would you want to resonate a state of boredom, fear, anxiety? Why wouldn't you unconsciously tend to blank out the memory of that state along with the learning attached to it? "Education," it's said, "is what you have left over after you forget everything you've learned." Most of us do forget over 90 percent of what we've imbibed in twelve, sixteen, or more years of school. That's why Superlearners strive for states that help the resonance linger on. Are those states "just fun"?

"If a kid goes to a Michael Jackson concert, he'll be entertained. If you made him go every night for a month, the fun would fade," points out teacher/novelist George Guthridge. "But if you give him the means to learn well and keep on learning, he's on the road to enlightenment with excitement that can last a lifetime." Which is a good definition of the joy of learning. Eric Booth, an educational innovator inside the establishment, would agree. Children are natural learners, he says, "however, for a growing majority, schooling, at best sends this instinct to learn largely underground, and at worst strangles it. There is no more important responsibility in education than nurturing the pleasure of learning." That's true for any age.

Just as the horse that pulled the buggy was urged on by a flick of the whip, not too long ago, learning was often powered by pain, information pounded into students with the cane or the strap. Today we know there are very basic reasons to combine pleasure and learning, as basic as your neurotransmitters, your brain's chemical messengers. Pleasure-producing ones are intricately involved with consolidating learning. Those evoked by pain damp down your memory. As a raft of data accumulates, it's getting obvious that pleasure, not dutiful plodding; that exhilaration, not pressure; will be the 21st century fast lane to unfolding accomplishment.

A Super State

Mind alert, body relaxed. That's a "best" state Superlearners achieve before leaning back to learn facts, figures, languages. Simple breathing and relaxation routines can get you there. So can the special Superlearning music, which helps keep you there. You can also opt for a little vacation before soaking up new data.

Close your eyes and listen. Can you hear the seagulls cry as they wheel high above you in an infinite blue sky? . . . Can you sense the sun warming your shoulders, feel the sand crunching between your toes, smell the salt air as you watch the long waves rolling rhythmically, breaking, foam flying on the beach? . . . Superlearners have improved on the old Scotsman who, rather than pay for a vacation, stayed home and let his mind wander. They take a few minutes to restore themselves by traveling in their mind's eye to a beautiful spot in nature. You can go anywhere—stroll through a meadow bursting with wildflowers and birdsong or bundle up in cozy down clothes and breathe in the fragrance of a pine forest deep in glistening snow. If you're so inclined, you can lie down in green pastures beside still waters or for a few moments join a host of golden daffodils in a favorite poem. The only requirement is to find a place of natural beauty. After you've relaxed, suggest to yourself that learning astronomy or how to swim will be just as easy and pleasant as strolling on the beach.

Once you get the hang of it, you can give yourself a break and in very little time stretch out in your restorative place. Superlearners call this "mind calming," one more simple but powerful technique that can give you an edge as you set out to learn or perform at your best.

Shake, Rattle, and Shift

"We are just about as happy in life as we decide to be," said Abe Lincoln. A Sioux proverb goes farther: "The first thing people say after death is, 'Why was I so serious?' " One thing Superlearners often carry away from class is the novel idea that they can choose what state they're in. Success at state shifting led to the seemingly weird evaluations students at the University of Toronto gave Professor Jane Bancroft after she taught them with Superlearning.

"I've gotten over my sinus headaches." "I'm not afraid of exams anymore." "I hardly ever fight now with my parents." Really nice, Bancroft thought, but it certainly didn't tell her much about the French course she'd given. (But exams did. Students had learned faster and showed "definitely improved memory.")

If you want to enjoy life more (and learn more), check the pulse of the state you're in. Some Japanese firms check electronically with the Nap-Ban, devised to keep office workers in an alert state. Employees wear a ring on their index finger. If that necessary digit doesn't move for a certain amount of time, they're jolted wide awake by a 105-decibel alarm on their wrist. There are other ways. Feeling drowsy? Get out of your chair, jump up and down, and shout, "Hallelujah, I'm one smart dude! Hallelujah, I'm one clever cookie!" You'll probably wake up a lot of other people too. A tenet of Superlearning is: head learning or any single mode of learning is best done in short cycles of twenty to thirty minutes. To break a pattern, interrupt it. Be outrageous, make a real interrupt. Why not?

As Burt Reynolds says, "You can only hold your stomach in for so many years." Rather than plugging along in low-voltage states resonating gray memories, jog, jump rope, swim, walk, walk, walk. Exercise combats depression. Feeling anxious? Put on your favorite music and dance away. Mad as hell? Fill the bathroom sink with water, put your head under, and shout out what you think of those so-and-sos. When it comes to shifting into specific learning states, as you'll see in later chapters, music, sound, and almost-21st-century mind machines can speed you on your way.

It's established now that your level of self-esteem greatly affects your level of performance. If you need to feel more adequate, even healthier, summon happy memories. Sophrology M.D.'s report excellent gains in mental and physical health with this simple technique. Remember the joy you felt as a child waking up the morning of your birthday, ready for parties, games, gifts? Or the long ago joy of just waking up on a summer morning with a whole day before you to fill with adventure? Kid stuff. Yet, do you ever wonder where has all the joy gone? If there's one emotion many us would like to feel more often, it's that simple joy that came so spontaneously as a kid. If only we could enjoy what we're doing as adults as much as we did doing almost anything as a child. And listen to them—the mega-successful adults: "I love what I do. I'd do it even if no one paid me." Noel Coward said it all: "Work is much more fun than fun." That's kid stuff at work. Just as you can reexperience a state of high accomplishment when you need to do your best, you can also summon full-sensed imagining such as the joy of long ago sunny days, "the splendor in the grass, the glory of the May," to reconnect with nurturing emotions. The child in you can delight again in the anticipation of Christmas Eve or whatever holiday made you glow. That delight can carry you to new ease in accomplishing any goal.

Well before it became popular to make friends with your inner child, accelerated learning teachers, following Lozanov's instruction, were weaving their workshops to help you learn like a kid. Part of the reason for dancing, singing, painting and playing games in Superlearning classes is to break through the adult ice and resuscitate the child, a natural Superlearner. If you can recapture the joy of exploration, the open mind, and the fresh senses of a child, the curiosity, you'll find learning becomes second nature at any age. "Except you become like a little child"—maybe it's an another old idea we're getting around to using.

No matter what's coming down on the outside, you don't have to live by the law of averages. You can do something about your inner weather. There are dozens of quick tricks for shifting out of low-voltage states, one place to find some is in NLP, particularly in the books of its cofounder Richard Bandler. Bandler's the kind of man who, when a client walks into his office and says, "I'm depressed," extends his hand and replies, "And I'm Richard." That's pattern interrupt. Tony Robbins, another masterful power-state coach, has a gambit that will make you laugh. Look in a mirror, smile, grin at yourself like a crazy fool. Then practice laughing—the belly laugh, the sly laugh, the nerdy Jerry Lewis laugh, hiccup-and-giggle laughs. You'll set up "smile circuits," little physical memories that become easier and easier to access. When British prime minister John Major was feeling as low as his ratings in the polls, his doctor prescribed what one reporter dubbed transcendental chuckling. Sit cross-legged and just laugh for a few minutes. Some cardiovascular experts report that three minutes of roaring laughter is worth many more minutes of aerobic exercise. "And," as Phyllis Diller said, "I'd rather have the laughs!" Lately evidence has appeared that you can laugh your immune system into better shape.

Self-reliance

Hand in glove with the empowering knowledge that you can change your state is taking responsibility for your state. It's easy, once you shift perspective from "out there" to "in here." From the old viewpoint it's the lousy "out there" that's sent you into a stew: the late bus, the dreary teacher, the unfair boss. If you stop and think, you really do know you can't control what goes on out there. But you can always choose what goes on inside you. If you're really good at it, that's *always*, even in Dachau.

Trapped in Dachau, the eminent psychologist Viktor Frankl noted that often it wasn't the young and brawny who survived the unthinkable; it was those who grabbed hold of "the last freedom left," the freedom to choose one's response, one's state. Frankl chose love. Continually he summoned the whole, breathing, pulsing memory of his beloved wife, sensing her in exquisite detail. "I saw her smile, her encouraging look, it was more luminous than the sun about to rise." Living in full-bodied memory, Frankl sidestepped despair and lived not just to tell the story but to become a great and wise teacher.

"It helps no one, least of all the students, if they blame other people or events when things go wrong," John Wade tells his "super-students" across Australia. Wade, a longtime member of the board of the Accelerative Learning Society of Australia, is a masterfully inno-vative teacher with a stellar sense of humor whose book *Superstudy* is the Australian best seller on the new way of learning.

Wade is a strong believer in self-reliance. Allowing yourself to feel victimized, making it your view of life, as some do, is one of the surest ways to stultify learning, change, growth. At school, Ward points out, victims say things such as "This question is too difficult." "I'll try to be clearer on my next essay." "I shouldn't have a beer before I finish studying." An easy way to slip out of the victim state, Ward finds, is to use the power of language.

"You've said the question is too difficult? Take charge by elim-inating the 'too.' Change the last word into 'challenging.' See what a difference it makes when you avoid giving your power away. Instead say 'This question is challenging,' " Wade advises.

You're going to *try* to be clearer on your essays? Going to "try" to do anything implies failure. You either try or you *do*. Commit your-self, says Ward: "I will be clearer on my next essay."

"I shouldn't have a beer before I finish studying." Saying *shouldn't* implies there's some invisible force outside of you trying to stop you from doing something. It's your decision. Ward councils super stu-dents, "*Always acknowledge your power to choose.*" Say either "I will have" or "I won't have" a beer. Language shapes, particularly when it comes to self-talk. Taking conscious control of inner chat can act like a magic wand to shift you to more competent states of being. (For more on self-talk, see Chapter 14.)

Our Fate Lies Not in Our Hats

Another way to shift states is with triggers. Professor Charles Adam-son built one out of a few square feet of space in his classroom at the Shizuoka Institute of Science and Technology in Fukuroi, Japan. Adamson set triggers for his students, not for himself.

Adamson's students shied away from asking questions in En-glish. How could he encourage them? When his science majors did ask a few questions, he went to a spot where he didn't normally stand. Whenever questions came up, he went to that few feet of space, "the rest of the time I avoided it like the plague." Soon, to evoke the "questioning state" in his class, he simply moved to the question spot. You can set triggers for others or yourself in infinite ways, Adamson says, using gesture, voice, position, even clearing your throat.

Triggers didn't burst alive with the advent of NLP. Watch the home-run hitter tap his bat on the ground precisely three times before stepping to the plate. Or look at the artistic pros: the famous German dramatist Friedrich von Schiller once confided he could not put down a decent phrase unless he had rotten apples on his desk. The smell, he said, evoked his muse.

To get an inkling of why superstitions pay off enough to persist, look through the eyes of state dependent memory. You brought down the house at a sales meeting, played the tennis game of your life, solved a tough engineering problem. What was different? Casting about, the mind can light on anything associated with the moment. Superstition is believing it really is your hat—gee, and it looked like all the others in the store—that causes you to shoot the winning hoop or ace the exam. Being smart is knowing you can use your hat or any trigger to help bring back the all-signals-go state you were in when you hit, when you soared above your norm.

State dependent memory can bring light to the minor mysteries of superstition. It has just begun to open one of the major mysteries of this or any other time. The mysteries of sickness and health. The sometimes mystery of who gets better and who stays sick. The mysterious, awesome power of the placebo. What state does it trigger, how? Can we one day discover enough to get into a really super kind of learning, learning to heal?

Curiously there already are people who can shift states and banish ailments in an instant. The electrifying power of Voznesensky's muse to transform him into another person, a poet, is meek compared to the shifts these unhappy souls trigger. They do turn into other people, lots of them. You may have read about the three faces of Eve, the sixteen faces of Sybil, the seventeen people living in Billy Millikin, the more than one hundred personalities sighted in Trudi. Alter egos are cases of state dependent memory taken to the over-the-edge extreme. Different states or personalities come with their own world of memory.

The shifting states of a full-blown multiple personality hold clues to accessing potential. Many exhibit a range of learning that makes the rest of us seem retarded. But there is something more unbeliev-able, something profound going on in multiple personality. What does it mean that one personality breaks out in hives when he drinks orange juice but another personality in the same body does not? Or that a personality turns red-eyed and sneezy within yards of a cat, yet with no ill effect her alter ego can take over the body and play with a lapful of kittens? When various alter egos take over, they also show different biochemical patterns in the brain just as separate people do, according to Dr. Robert DeVito at Loyola University. Different personalities may result, he speculates, from a "biochemical switch process involving the complex phenomenon of memory." The last decade has brought heavy research on multiple personality; cases abound of patients' bodies shifting in and out of various ailments including diabetes and heart and eye problems as they change personalities, change states, change memories.

Most of us can swallow the idea: Shift your memories and change your mental state. But *change your memories and change your body?* That sounds like tales of paradise regained. It gives a primal meaning to dynamic memory, to "memory makes you who you are." Today very intricate webs of research are tracing the hard science of the mind's effect on body mediated by the filter of memory. One day this may go down as "the big one," the breakthrough that finally begins to let humanity lift above pain and disease—even aging.

It's already shaking loose some stunning remarks. Sophrologist Dr. Raymond Abrezol puts it simply: "*All disease is memory,*" he told us. And there's endocrinologist Deepak Chopra, a member of the National Institute of Health's Advisory Panel on Unconventional Med-ical Practice. Like any M.D., Chopra knows that our cells change constantly; your entire stomach lining, for instance, changes every four days. Why is a lesion or a tumor still there, why does it build back in? Chopra points to an answer: "What is a cell? A memory that has built some matter around itself. Your body is just the place your memory calls home." Chopra, a man who drew over thirty thousand inquiries when he appeared on "Oprah," speaks, too, of exceptional healings that can occur if you can shift wholly into a very special state—bliss.

The tantalizing link between state dependent memory and

health may well turn out to be a matter of learning. If you're interested in a fascinating detective story in progress and the references, see our book *Supermemory: The Revolution* (Carroll & Graf, 1991).

Rise and Shine

Do you hit the deck in the morning, or does it feel like the deck hits you? Does a rush of worry, anxiety, must-do things jostle you awake? The thoughts and emotions that climb out of bed with us can set the tone, our state, for the day. That is why traditional societies have morning rituals. Just as the Joy of Learning is a good all-purpose ploy to get you into the right state for accomplishment, you can craft your own morning routine to set you up to make the most of any day. It takes little extra time.

As soon as you awaken, think "thanks" for the extraordinary gift of life. Gratitude is one of the most powerful plus states and does good things for body and mind. Once you're upright, take a deep breath or two. Then imagine a brilliant sun a few feet above you. Take four quick, deep breathes to begin pumping the bright, sparkling light beams of that sun down through a warm spot on the top of your head. Enjoy the pure, energizing light filling your head, flowing into your neck, your shoulders, running down to your hands, cascading through your torso to your feet, filling your body with light to overflowing. Let that overflowing brilliance beam out through your heart and create a great sphere of light around you. Tell yourself you'll walk in clarity in this light all day long.

Next you're probably off to the only sanctuary any of us have these days, the bathroom, a great place to do mental work. Try something Tony Robbins suggests, ask yourself empowering questions. "What am I looking forward to? Or what could I look forward to?" (If you can't come up with an answer, insert the word *could*, and something will come.) "What do I like about myself?" "What makes me feel good?" "Who do I admire as a role model?" "Who do I love?" "What am I committed to?"

Then reach to your goals, as Lisa Curtis instructs in her Seven-Minute Stress Busters (see Chapter 5). Stretch up toward your goal of the day. Imagine you touch it, and feel it accomplished. Again, reaching higher, stretch to your goal for the year. And once more, stretching way, way up to your goal for the decade. That's it. If you're doing affirmations, seize the opportunity and sing them out in the shower or catch your own eye in the mirror.

Every year *Money* prints a list of the best places to live. Perhaps one day they'll list the inner states as well as the outer; certainly many of the accomplished men and women they feature live in states that streamline and fuel their efforts. Learn to shift states just as you shift steps when the music changes, and you'll be in rhythm with accomplishment.

4
Learning with the Subliminal Memory

"Your conscious mind is very intelligent and your subconscious is a hell of a lot smarter," quipped the eminent medical hypnotist Milton Erickson. Superlearning draws much of its voltage from that smart but shadowy powerhouse, the subliminal memory. Unlike traditional education, all accelerated systems address both your conscious and your unconscious minds. Working on the "double plane," Lozanov called it.

When the work is done skillfully, you can be turned around without even noticing it, as one Japanese man who "didn't like English at all" discovered. He entered Dr. Mayumi Mori's class in Yokohama because "in my mind I wanted to speak English, but . . . I had complex feelings against it." Then he became immersed in Mori's seamless teaching, which flooded over the barrier. She employed things like music, imagery, pleasure to communicate with his subliminal as well as his conscious mind. "I didn't have a moment to even remember my preconceptions," the once-reluctant student later wrote in English. "I was totally involved and English came into me just so naturally."

As hypnosis and brain probes show, it's your subliminal mind that remembers the names of your first-grade classmates; remembers what the surgical team said when you were out cold on the operating table, and knows how many red lights you stopped for en route to the office. Your subliminal mind can—but you usually can't—pick up data by glancing at a page for one second. As long as your brilliant second self is privy to everything that's going on, why not pay attention to its nature? When you know how, you can befriend this lusty powerhouse and travel comfortably together. One example of what cooperation can bring shows in something curious about accelerated learning. It snowballs. You often remember more the fourth day than the second, the third week than the first. What's happening, experiments reveal, is that information "taught" to your subliminal mind is gradually rising into consciousness. Superlearning is user-friendly to the unconscious. It attends to little things, like avoiding the static of mixed messages going to your two minds.

That can be as simple as a teacher saying "I know you're going to be a good student" while his body language is radiating "One more loser." You may not notice, but your subliminal mind does. It notices, too, if you're told, "Education is one of the most important things in life," as you sit in a shabby, paint-peeling room where nothing very valued could be going on. Superlearners know the subliminal mind learns from what you pick up out of the corner of your eye. And learns, too, from things you don't consciously pick up at all. Pictures and sayings posted on the walls, the arrangement of furniture, the way positive suggestion is embedded in oral instructions— everything in an accelerated learning class is orchestrated to keep signals flowing in the right direction.

If you're learning on your own, the foot-dragging effect of mixed messages often springs from inner, not outer dissonance. You decide to learn how to fly. That idea shivers your unconscious like finger-nails running down a blackboard. It sets vibrating a bunch of old suggestions: "Don't dare too much, don't fly too high, the world's a dangerous place, look out you'll fall!" You'll find a lot of techniques in this book to exorcise those old spooks. One Superlearning aficionado has come up with a way to have a late-night chat with your unconscious.

Until recently professor of business at the University of Alaska, then a special assistant to the governor, Dr. Teri Mahaney has led white-water rafting trips, facilitated dozens of executive workshops, and mothered a teenage daughter. Mahaney also took time to bring forth a fruitful new shoot from the Superlearning root. She read *Superlearning* and also came across "What You Don't Know Can Help You—or Hurt You," a report we'd written on decades-long scientific research of subliminal suggestion. Mahaney put two and two together and came up with something more than four—intriguing subliminal tapes in the powerfully suggestible Superlearning format. Called *Change Your Mind*, they are helping people do just that with good speed. A practical route to energizing any kind of change, this approach can quickly dissolve blocks to learning and performance.

"All my life I've been curious about why some people make it and others don't," Mahaney admits. I looked into subliminals, into the suggestions in the unconscious that keep us from making it. When I saw what happened when people dissolved the negatives, the puzzle clicked into place." Now, she declares, "I expect everyone to make it."

You can craft Mahaney's techniques to your own needs, to be rid of habits that dampen your chances at work, tangle relationships, or slow down learning. They can give a feeling of resourcefulness as you become an agent of desirable change in yourself. If you do, you're going to give yourself a rather shocking suggestion. To make sense of it, first you have to know a little about the intriguing research of the late Dr. Lloyd Silverman of New York University, for years the premier U.S. investigator (outside of closely wrapped government scientists) of subliminal suggestion. A subliminal suggestion—usually visual or audio—is one that comes to you below the level of conscious perception.

Silverman and Dr. Rose Bryant-Tucker chose a tough milieu to test what subliminal suggestion can do for learning. At a special school in Peekskill, New York, they asked sixty-four emotionally troubled, generally delinquent teenagers to look through a light device called a tachistoscope three times a week. Kids peered through the eyepiece: flash! a bright light blinked. That was it. A sentence was embedded in that light, but it flashed too fast for the conscious mind to perceive it. No one knew the message.

After some weeks of flashes the kids took the standard California Achievement Reading Test. All of a sudden they were reading better. They scored significantly higher than a control group. More good news: Their math grades inexplicably rose, too, and so did the amount of homework they did. Even their behavior outside class shaped up.

Adults studying business law at Queens College, New York, also put their eye to the tachistoscope to experience Silverman's pregnant flash. Their professor, Dr. Kenneth Parker, adamantly refused to reveal the message even after finals. He waited four more weeks to test for long term retention. Parker found his law students had gotten the secret message in more ways than one. They remembered more of what they learned than a control group lacking subliminal prompting. They also scored ten grade points higher for the course.

A nice surprise, but nothing compared with the shock students got when Parker revealed the message their deep minds had embraced: "*Mommy and I are one.*" Embarrassing, preposterous— maybe, but that childlike sentence can have a thunder-and-lightning transformative effect on the unconscious. Ever since Silverman conjured her over twenty-five years ago, Mommy has been trotting through scientific literature, helping out everywhere: boosting weight loss, dart throwing, math scores; a universal mommy who works in other cultures too. If you call this unconscious trigger Mother or Mom, Daddy or Professor, it can work, but not so potently as Mommy. As you can guess, psychologists have papers full of reasons why *Mommy* is such a mover. But she also seems to resonate levels beyond psychology, realms of wholeness and unity. (If steam is coming out of your ears at the mere thought of becoming one with Mommy—you really didn't like yours—research suggests the gambit will be particularly helpful for you.)

Boffo performer though she is, *Mommy*'s only one small part of the simmering world of subliminal suggestion. For over seventy years now, scientists worldwide have been reaching into people's minds with subliminal suggestion, generally through sight or sound. The Soviets long ago learned how to use subliminal touch to set conditioned reflexes in people. Working under tight laboratory conditions, subliminals can influence almost any part of your body, from heartbeat to stress factors in the blood. They can influence your choices, cure phobias, and seed meaning. You could spend days plowing through the scientific literature, which remains strangely unknown to the public even though media philosopher Marshall McLuhan went out of his way to warn people there might be more meaning in the message than they suspected. And sometimes more harm.

McLuhan strongly supported Dr. Wilson Key, who has done more than anyone to expose subliminals in advertising. "What would you do if you wanted to use suggestion, subliminal and otherwise, to bring down a society?" a film writer once asked Key. "Just what we're doing," Key replied, "feed endless suggestions of violence and pornography to the populace." Does Superlearning, based in part on Suggestology, make you more suggestible? Careful European studies found accelerated learning makes you *less* suggestible. Greater awareness, better communication with all parts of your self, is probably why. Rather than arguing over censorship today it might be more effective to make part of the learning agenda an exploration of the powers of suggestion.

If you do look into the scientific literature, you'll know that when an "expert" says subliminal suggestion is a fantasy, he's either ignorant or up to something. Teri Mahaney has been up to something for over five years and she's doing her best to share it with business and government professionals, students, air-traffic controllers, even IRS employees.

Making Tapes to Talk with Your Unconscious

It occurred to Mahaney that if you mate the powerful Superlearning Music and paced format with *Mommy* and other subliminal suggestions, you might get a dynamite catalyst for change. The music and timed rhythmic repetition engage the subliminal mind on their own to open a clear channel for suggestion. Mahaney began weaving custom made tapes for individuals. Then one of her business classes got wind of her subliminal performance boosters. Could she help them with test taking? "I prepared a subliminal tape suggesting they were relaxed, understood questions easily and quickly, remembered the answers instantly, and so on," Mahaney remembers. These business students took two tests before and two after listening to the tape. Subliminal prompting made them quicker and smarter—at least at taking tests. On average they finished their exams in 20 percent less time than before. Even better, average scores rose by 20 percent. Unbeknownst to the students, Mahaney gave *Mommy* an extra task. She added some general positive suggestions aimed at time management, goal setting, health. "For the next few weeks students kept coming up to me saying, 'Something has changed. I'm feeling much better and have started . . .' and would tell a story of how they were doing something different around time management, health, or goals."

Making a subliminal tape to help a friend's daughter in college, Mahaney expanded on the oneness idea. "English literature and I are one. Chemistry and I are one. . . ." The young woman's grades rose to A's and B's across the board. Tellingly the girl's roommate, who was often around when the Superlearning Music with the unheard suggestions played, also began getting A's and B's, but only in the subjects they were both taking.

As a professor of business, Mahaney is more keenly aware than most that we have already hurtled to a day when people will have seven or eight different careers in a lifetime, a day when a primary job skill will be the ability to quickly let go of the structures of the past and open to accelerating opportunities of the present. She's upped the accessibility of her technique. Tapes are now subliminal in the sense that you "listen" as you sleep or as you drift off. As the voice is audible, it's easy for anyone to make his own. Use the Superlearning Music and the basic Superlearning paced format. Repeat suggestions three times in intonations if you desire. For content, Mahaney uses an empty-the-glass, fill-the-glass approach: Flush out the negatives, then pour in the positives. To get rid of the toxic waste of a lifetime, Mahaney finds a heavy dose of forgiveness helps.

The bare bones of a script might read like this: "Mommy and I are one. I forgive Mommy for _____ ." (Fill in the blank, for instance, "expecting too much of me.") Follow that with: "I forgive Mommy for not expecting much of me. I forgive myself for expecting too much of me. I forgive myself for not expecting much of me. I transcend expecting too much of me." You can run through the authority figures of your life, becoming one with and forgiving. When Mahaney found herself conflicted about full time teaching and frustrated by the university's good-old-boy system, she became one with teaching, with the School of Business, the dean, the old-boy network, and a list of others, forgiving, releasing, transcending.

An award-winning insurance salesman discovered the importance of emptying the cup. Soon after he'd been singled out for his achievement, this man suddenly stopped selling. He couldn't force himself to make cold calls. "A little digging revealed he was the son of a minister in a very traditional religion. He had been raised not to stand out," Mahaney says. After his subliminal memory heard a tape that cleared away the unhappy idea that standing out was against his religion and family, he again made his daily quota of calls effortlessly.

After you've emptied the glass of the old, fill your subliminal mind with oneness and strong positive suggestions. Mahaney puts as many as two hundred suggestions on a tape, figuring some are bound to click. She finds it takes ten nights of playing the tape for your deep mind to process suggestions, to rearrange itself and begin prompting more satisfying behavior.

If you want help with specific learning, like Spanish, Mahaney suggests you use Superlearning while you're awake. Then while you drift to sleep, become one with Spanish, suggest to yourself that speaking Spanish is fun. Say, "I learn Spanish easily, effortlessly, I hear the intonations of Spanish, I mimic the flow of Spanish, I speak fluently," and so on. Mahaney finds this double whammy lifts people over the hurdles of CPA exams, bar exams, all sorts of professional tests with ease.

Making your own tapes lets you aim at your specific needs. And your unconscious will hear a voice it's very attached to—yours. (Mahaney finds that if another voice is used, the unconscious will generally accept a female voice more readily than a male one.) If you want more guidance, Mahaney, head of Supertraining Inc., has some excellent scripts in her book *Change Your Mind* and now produces ready-made tapes. If you want to know more about the ongoing adventure of subliminal probing by contemporary scientists like Dr. Eldon Taylor, who ran the first state-supported subliminal program in a penitentiary, see *Supermemory: The Revolution*.

Commercial subliminal tapes enjoyed a trendy romp recently. We know subliminal suggestion does work in the lab. Whether any particular commercial tape works is a moot point. "Just suggestion" is how many people dismiss them—an A-one example of why many people don't come up with seminal ideas like Lozanov did. Lozanov researched sleep learning, a technique brought to high effectiveness in the Soviet bloc. Young Communists did do significantly better in class after their lessons played along with their dreams at night. They kept right on doing better even after Lozanov secretly switched off the nightly recording. He could have muttered, "Just suggestion." Instead he said, "Aha!" and plunged into a comprehensive exploration of the all pervasive, powerful effects of suggestion. Whether we like it or not, and usually whether we know it or not, suggestion shapes our lives. Why not grab hold of it and purposefully use subliminal, semiliminal, and conscious suggestion to access capability? Lozanov became the first in modern times to orchestrate all levels of suggestion to deliver a blockbuster new way to heal with Suggestology, and to learn with Suggestopaedia. (For the ground rules of positive suggestion, see Chapter 10.)

"Beneath all the Superlearning techniques, I think it's the suggestive elements that do the most to propel people to greater achievement by dissolving blocks," says Dr. Tatiana Radonjic-Matano, whose Speed Learning courses in New York City are filled with graduate students, doctors, high achievers of every kind. They're already good learners, she says, but like most people who want to be really successful, they're looking for ways to develop further—but without burning out. A high achiever herself, Radonjic-Matano didn't always have the answer. Armed with a fine background, a doctor of philosophy specializing in cognitive science at the University of Paris, she still felt something was lacking in her efforts to open creativity and first rate thinking in her students. She found the missing pieces in the holisitic accelerated approach, particularly the orchestrated, practical use of suggestion. Radonjic-Matano uses a spectrum of suggestion, from conscious goal setting to self-suggestion and imaginative rehearsal, to help clients let go of negative scripts and leap to the next plateau.

She also introduces them to "George," a gambit created by SALT founder Don Schuster. Another way to talk with your unconscious is to personalize it as George. You can talk to George, get his suggestions, and once you get his attention, consciously turn problems over—and let George do it. During an exam, for instance, Schuster suggests that after you put down all the answers you do know, close your eyes, take eight slow, deep breaths, and ask George to float needed answers into consciousness.

Every day a barrage of suggestions feeds into your mind. You don't have to be a random number living by the laws of chance, an average who trundles along picking up some helpful, some damaging suggestions. Choosing the suggestions you use to reach out to your subliminal mind, taking care that suggestion works for you, not against you, is basic to Superlearning. It can power you, right now, into more expansive dimensions.

5
Befriending Your Body

Imagine how Atlas felt, rooted to the spot, the world's horrendous weight grinding ever downward into his shoulders. That's heroic—old style. As the rigid symbols of the old world exit, the body is beginning to dance free. Even somersaulting through the urban hustle, we're paying attention to the body's care and feeding. In the military, in companies small and big, and certainly in Superlearning classes individuals practice techniques to liberate themselves from the physical negatives of stress.

Today learning to let go isn't a luxury like steam baths for movie moguls. It's a necessity to avoid being ground down in the tectonic shifts of this territory and that. *Scramble* is the refrain Walter Kiechel III chose when he wrote the *Fortune* cover story "How We Will Work in the Year 2000." As the corporate ladder is relegated to the recycling bin—*scramble*. As global competition heats—*scramble*. As more and more jobs are freelance—*scramble*. It will be the defining activity of the era, Kiechel thinks. "Scrambling even to carve out moments of tranquility under a banner blazoned FIGHT STRESS, a banner flapping like a Tibetan prayer flag in the gales of change." Then again, Kiechel doesn't count on the flexibility of a super learner. Know how to turn scramble into new vitality and you'll live smarter in more ways than one.

A classic study at Georgetown University found that piled up stress can affect even eight-year-olds, lowering IQ by as much as ten points. Training in stress reduction has almost universally shown enhanced performance in the learning disabled, the gifted, and everyone in between. In Atlanta the Wholistic Stress Control Institute brought its defusing ways to an area elementary school with the highest poverty rate and lowest academic scores. Violent behavior dropped by half, school suspensions by 40 percent. A 1993 poll revealing that 100,000 U.S. kids carry weapons to school, mostly for defense, gives a clue to how pressed many children, even very young ones, feel. The Wholistic Institute, an Afro-American community group, provides children with what may be the most important head start of all. Their Pre-School Stress Relief Project won the 1990 National Exemplary Program Award, from the Office of Substance Abuse Prevention. The earlier one knows how to cope in nondestructive ways, these programs show, the better one's chances to learn and grow and, in some places, to survive. The ability to cope can prove vital to anyone's survival, according to a recent report in *Epidemiology*. People suffering heavy psychological stress at work, researchers find, are at increased risk of colon cancer. If aggravation has lasted a decade or more, the risk is over five times greater than usual.

The ability to relax the body at will is a Superlearning core technique. The reason it's such a central skill became clear when the prestigious Addiction Research Foundation of Ontario ran an unusually fine-comb test of Eli Bay's stress management course. Founding director of Toronto's Relaxation Response Ltd., Bay has helped ease anxiety, lower the use of painkillers and sleeping pills, and lifted the sense of self-mastery for thousands of bureaucrats, business people, and teachers across Canada. A soft spoken man with the calm geniality of an affable Buddha (he does hanker after Chinese food), Bay has also brought thousands of people into the right state for learning on the basic Superlearning tape.

How would 170 men and women, big city, white collar workers respond to Bay's "Beyond Stress," a program also seen on TV? Researchers rolled in the big guns: batteries of tests charting everything from anxiety to feelings of hostility and paranoia, from perception of life experience to alcohol, tranquilizer, and coffee consumption. After fifteen hours of relaxation training, a large majority of these business people moved toward more healthy norms. And they did it pretty much across the board. "Relaxation appeared to be the key that provided access to a variety of other changes," researchers reported. It is this overall unlocking effect that makes relaxation such a valuable skill. Researchers called it "a leaven of well being that activates one's ability and will to break out of the vicious cycles of deleterious habits that otherwise tend to reinforce each other endlessly." Relaxing at will "permits the possibility of at least some measure of self-reintegration at a happier, healthier level."

Interestingly, many of the Toronto business people felt as strained when life changed for the better as when it slid downhill. Change itself was nerving them up—something else that dissipated when Bay showed them how to shift beyond stress.

When you stop carrying the world around, you can begin to tune in to the many things the body knows. New Yorker Elizabeth Reudy is an articulate, Swiss trained mathematician who works accelerated wonders helping mathephobes pass tough academic exams. She's also a memory expert. "Check your body," she says, when you're searching for that word or name almost on the tip of your tongue. "Start making guesses even if they're far afield. When you feel your body take a deeper breath, you're getting close, or you've got it."

Your body can speak for your intuition. High achievers, from hotel magnate Conrad Hilton to archeologist Iris Love, readily credited intuition with being a major factor in their success. Often that all important hunch comes as a body signal, a gut feeling. Something feels right, it fits, or, as Robert Wilson, founder of Holiday Inn, often said, contradicting the "facts" when choosing new sites for his motels, "It just doesn't smell right."

If you're feeling like the kid who complained, "The hurrier I go the behinder I get," you may think you don't have time to befriend your body. But those who do, enjoy a paradox. Slow down and go faster. As blood pressure, heartbeat, and breathing slow, the metabolism of time seems to slow down too. You accomplish more, handily, in fewer hours. "Of all the Superlearning techniques, I think the real key is being in the right state to learn," says Brian Hamilton. Like Christian Drapeau, when Hamilton became involved with Superlearning, he focused first on becoming well grounded in relaxation to shift his inner state and learn to imagine with all his senses. "During vacation I practiced one or even two hours a day." One of the best investments you can ever make, one that doesn't cost a cent, is to learn to relax and shift your body states at will. You'll add new dimensions to your life and probably some years. You may also be adding a marketable skill; training others to manage stress is a growing job opportunity. There are a lot of ways to shift your body state, even by jiggling your belly button. As an innovative German doctor proved, when it comes to body balancing, you can definitely do it yourself.

Self-Birthing

Self-birthing—it certainly sounds like the ultimate in self-mastery. Perhaps that's why German M.D. Johannes Schultz chose the name Autogenics, literally *self-birthing,* for an unusual new "prescription" he concocted. Though a medical man, Schultz, as long ago as the 1930s, sought something more primary than symptom-based pills and surgeries to cure his patients' woes, and devised formulas to teach them to relax and control their bodies at will. After patients became adept at shifting into healthy body states, Schultz gave them more formulas to help them make the most of their states of mind. So the self-birthing began. His patients stopped feeling pushed out of shape by external circumstances; they assumed control. And a great many of them got better—with only positive side effects.

"My arms are heavy and warm"—this first step of the autogenic formula seems simple enough. Yet world medical literature is crammed with case histories of autogenic practitioners overcoming everything from diabetes to bed wetting to heart disorders. Beyond the closely monitored medical world, all manner of people now summon autogenics to triumph over things like forty foot ocean waves, nosedive Alpine ski runs, the vagaries of weightlessness in space—and even more exceptional today, to triumph over the rupturing costs of health insurance (see page 363).

Hannes Lindeman, another German M.D., bet his life on the

power of autogenics to support stunning performance. He determined to achieve what over a hundred adventurers before him had failed to do: to travel solo from the Canary Islands to the New World in a canvas sailing canoe. Seventy-two days after push off, Lindeman hopped ashore on St. Maarten in the Caribbean. Though forced to sit upright the whole way, as his picture smiling from the cover of *Life* showed, Lindeman was amazingly fit. He suffered neither saltwater sores routine on such a trip, nor experienced the hallucinations that often accompany long distance solo sailors. How had he kept body and mind in such robust good health? "It is to autogenic training that I owe my success," Lindeman declared.

Bets are you don't want to take a canvas canoe to Europe. But you might want to learn to control your body states for other show-boat performances. Sophrologist Dr. Raymond Abrezol uses a modified form of autogenics to train European athletes to ski, play hockey, swim, run, box. His trainees are world-class athletes who so far have garnered over one hundred Olympic medals, fourteen of them gold. Alphonso Caycedo, the M.D. father of Sophrology, uses autogenics interwoven with strands of Zen and Qi Gong to lift people from addictions as well as physical ailments. Caycedo has seen his methods come close to raising the dead when they rescued the supposedly irredeemable, drugged-out street urchins of Colombia. We met three of Caycedo's "irredeemables" at a Sophrology conference in Lausanne, born again, it seemed, as clear eyed, clean cut college students.

In the old Soviet Union the pursuit of excellence, for a few favored groups, was state policy. Seemingly limitless funds and effort poured into the search for ways to nurture high flying performance. Not surprisingly Soviet athletes, ballet dancers, and cosmonauts all trained in autogenics. The autogenic routine that the teenage Christian Drapeau picked up from Superlearning to control his physical state at will is one originally designed for Soviet cosmonauts. Now a full grown neurologist, Drapeau remarks that "even after a few years of meditating and a year spent teaching yoga, I have never reached a more profound state of relaxation than I did then with autogenics." It is an elegant, proven, flexible system, that's why we recommended it for Superlearning. If you want to excel or just plain feel better, try it. (For instructions, see page 370.)

Autogenics accelerates learning, Ukrainian psychologist Vladimir Stefanishin recently wrote to tell us. Not a surprise. Spanish Sophrologists have long used modified autogenics to catapult students over disabilities of all kinds and quicken learning. What was surprising is that Stefanishin had a microfilm of *Superlearning,* a book not permitted under the old regime.

At university Stefanishin became expert in autogenics and began a career of probing ways to use different states of being to open new facets of mind. Now a "teacher of self-education" at the Kiev Palace for Youth, he trains teens in self-birthing to enhance both learning and health. "Autogenics allows students to increase their memory of foreign vocabulary by three to four times," he reports. "It also reduces the time needed to learn factual information, poems and so on."

Though it takes eight weeks to learn, once you've got autogenics, you can shift into a balanced mindbody state in a short time. Charles Adamson, led by Superlearning to train his Japanese students in autogenics, found another plus. Practiced in a group, it brings the state of individuals closer together; sometimes even their breathing will synchronize. Students report feeling a helpful rapport; teachers are able to work with a cohesive group. Adamson worked with one thousand students and twelve teachers in his autogenic program at Trident College, in Nagoya. Given the option of dropping the exercise, almost 100 percent of the students voted to continue. All but one of the teachers gave autogenics unqualified support.

Of course you don't have to master autogenics to Superlearn. Autogenics is just one of a smorgasbord of techniques that Eli Bay offers (see Section Three). Remember too, mindbody is one system. Just as letting go of muscle tensions will relax the mind, so guided imagery or mind calming can drain physical stress. So can twenty minutes of chanting mantras or meditating. The point is to find a way to befriend your body and guide it into healthy, powerful states. If taking twenty-minute breaks isn't your cup of tea, relax. Lisa Curtis may have just the ticket for you.

Seven-Minute Stress Busters

Years ago Lisa Curtis had a dream. She was climbing Jacob's Ladder. Mounting swiftly up and up into the brightening sky, suddenly she was frozen in mid-step by a commanding voice. "Get back down there, you're supposed to be helping out."

Ever since, this vivacious woman with her trademark green-rimmed glasses has been helping out in the conversion business, energy conversion. As the prime exponent of Sophrology in the United States, she knew a lot about relaxation. As a New York PR woman, she understood "no time!" People on the run, she reasoned, need quick ways of converting pent-up pressure back into free-flowing energy.

Curtis' Seven-Minute Stress Busters have pumped new energy into fast moving Venezuelan oil executives, just as they worked for the American Dowsers Society and the very specialized dentists of the International Congress of Oral Implantologists. Still, after one of Curtis' workshops, a friend with a taste for marketing said, "Lisa, it's too simple!" That's the point. "I want to give people techniques that they will really use, not tell them to spend thirty minutes doing this, then thirty-five minutes doing that. No one has time." Simple enough for a school-girl, effective enough for a CEO, Curtis' stress busters are first aid when you're struck with overload. Practiced regularly, New Jersey columnist Tony Carlyle found, "It really boils down to a gift of life."

Belly breathing is a simple, age-old technique that Curtis advises.

> Standing, feet slightly apart, inhale through your nose while imagining you're drawing the air in through your toes inflating a giant balloon in your belly. Do this for eight slow beats. Hold that great balloon of air four beats, then exhale, flattening your balloon to the count of eight. Remain empty for four beats. Relax, then repeat four or five times. Do this anytime, anyplace to quickly shed tension.

Curtis has also come up with a breath of her own she dubbed "How Eagles Fly," which makes use of the minor chakras, or energy centers, in the palm and the armpit.

Stand, feet hip-width apart, arms loosely at your sides. Or sit in a chair, feet flat on the floor, palms up on your lap. Mouth closed, inhale through your nose while focusing on the palms of your hands. Draw breath up from your palms to your armpits to the count of four. (With practice you'll begin to feel an energy flow.) Hold for two beats, then exhale for six imagining the air flowing down from your armpits and out of your palms. Hold your lungs empty for two beats and repeat. Do it a while and you'll feel lighter, lifted.

"Joy is the feeling generated," Curtis says, "the joy of being, the joy of flying. Considering how little joy many of us experience, that can be a gift."

The Eagle Breath can also buoy you up while walking, particularly hiking.

Omit breath holding. Breathe in up through the palms for two steps, then out down the arms for two steps, making sure you step left leg forward with right arm, right leg with left arm. It's a simple way to enhance coordination and raise vitality. Curtis also summons the "eagle" to lift her out of bed when the alarm rings early. Lying on your back, breathe in as usual, but instead of holding your breath, imagine it flowing right on up to your eyes before the exhale.

Some of Curtis' techniques are even more simple. When you're stuck on an exam, when you hit a moment of contention or a knotty problem at work, pause. Press your fingertips together like hands in prayer. That's all. It helps you relax and center.

The Yes/No exercise is another do-anywhere stress buster Curtis recommends when your overload light flashes, or before making an important decision. Take a deep breath, inhaling through your nose, hold it, and move your head forward and backward four times as if nodding yes. Exhale. Take another deep breath and do a slow-motion no four times. Turn your head left, try to see what's behind you. Then to the right.

Easy as pie, but as Curtis remarks, "It not only relaxes muscle tension, but it stimulates the thyroid, and the carotoid arteries that carry blood—oxygen—to the brain." Your brain is an oxygen guzzler. Add to the flow and brighten the lights.

If you're the sort who likes to experiment with a couple from column A and a couple from column B, here are other quickies to bring your body into balance, a little at first, more as they become second nature.

Just follow your breathing. That's the oldest relaxation ploy around. Don't try to regulate your breath or change it. Attend to your breathing, in and out, in and out. A friend of ours, versed in stress management, had to undergo angiograms and open heart surgery. She reported the only way she could escape the horrors of the moment, the only exercise she could focus on, was following her breath.

What's better than twenty winks? Maybe a six-second relaxer named the Quieting Reflex (QR) by its creator, New York psychiatrist Charles Stroebel, who came up with QR as a last resort to conquer his excruciating headaches. Practice QR as you go through the day, he says. You'll perform better and still have enough pizzazz left to get a kick out of the evening. QR has six steps.

Become aware that you are tense. Say to yourself, "Alert mind, calm body." Smile, sparkle inwardly to relax your face. Relax your jaw. Inhale to the count of three, imagining the air coming up through the soles of your feet, through your legs, into belly and stomach. Exhale, letting jaw, tongue, shoulders go limp, feeling heaviness leave the body.

The ease of QR is deceptive, contends Stroebel, who wrote a whole book on the successes of his six-second technique. He cautions it may take half a year's practice to get the full health benefits. Worth six seconds now and then, for the stress lines are getting clearer; Japanese scientists recently revealed the first evidence that psychological stress can even damage DNA.

Exercising Chi

Apart from relaxation there are other shortcuts to getting your body into optimal learning states. To energize his super students, John Wade mined the wealth of experience racked up in the Orient by millennia-long practice of mindbody systems. Chinese medicine sees you whole, mind and body as one system vitalized by subtle *chi* energy. As Wade points out, though it may be considered "alternative" in Australia or the United States, to one billion Chinese it's our medicine that's alternative. Recently the Chinese government ordered the army to help the masses in countryside clinics with Qi Gong, an ancient system of manipulating vital energy (see Section Three). Wade draws on this vast tradition to help his super students fine tune with acupressure. The idea is to work on energy flowing along acupuncture meridians carrying information to and from the brain.

Getting familiar with the *shenque* acupoint, which is on your bellybutton, can help reading comprehension, according to Ward. Press a finger—it's okay to do it through clothing—on your navel and massage it, jiggle it. At the same time, using the thumb and finger of your other hand, massage two points "that are the slight depressions just below the bumps at the inside ends of your collarbones." After a few seconds, reverse hands and jiggle and massage a bit longer.

The *renzhong* point is squarely between the bottom of your nose and the center of your upper lip. Before giving a talk or tackling a writing assignment, Wade says press and jiggle the point with one finger. At the same time use a finger from your other hand and rub the bony end of your spine. Again after a few moments reverse hands and repeat. This can look weird to passersby, Wade admits, and advises a brief retreat to the restroom.

American teacher William Phillips uses a finely orchestrated Chinese regimen to help students of all ages get in touch with themselves. A dark haired, middle-aged guy with a ready grin, Phillips comes across as a paradox. He has the inner poise of a wise old man, but radiates the energy of a very young man. Which is as it should be. Apart from teaching high school English in New York City and lecturing at Kingsborough Community College, Phillips is a longtime student and teacher of Tai Chi Chuan.

If you're looking for a physical routine to accompany lifelong learning, it would be hard to find a better companion than Tai Chi

("Supreme Ultimate"). Here and there, accelerated learning teachers are adding the graceful, slow motion movements of this ancient Chinese system to their repertoire. "Because it doesn't require a lot of strength, you can do Tai Chi at almost *any* age," Phillips says, "even if you can only lift your foot an inch off the floor." Lifting that foot can pay off with a bevy of benefits as you get older. One medical study, for instance, found Tai Chi cut the incidence of osteoporosis almost in half.

Watching a master like Phillips move through a Tai Chi cycle is an aesthetic experience worlds removed from watching a workout. But the real glory of Tai Chi is experienced from the inside. Even a few months' practice will give you a taste of the richness of this ancient art. Like a prize gem, it has many highly polished facets to release the light within.

The basis of the martial arts (Phillips holds a fifth-degree black belt in Shotokan Karate), Tai Chi balances and strengthens the body; it calms, focuses, and develops the mind, including the ability to visualize. It can be a form of moving meditation. Tai Chi is a system of Chinese medicine, both curative and preventative, and it is a premier way to enhance and direct chi energy. In the East chi is seen as intimately involved with memory, as the "stuff" or carrier wave of memory.

In Japan Dr. Mayumi Mori speaks from this tradition when she says the master teacher must know how to orchestrate the whole learning procedure in order to allow chi to flow. "Once this is achieved, memory and learning ability increase naturally as a by-product." If you're interested in a one-stop self development package, the Patience Tai Chi Association, which Phillips founded and heads, offers a free referral system to Tai Chi teachers nationwide.

Phillips has created organized play drawn from Tai Chi "to help grammar school children develop balance, flexibility, sensitivity to their body and its relationship to the environment."

Attached Arms—Detached Arms gives an understanding of the paired opposites of movement. "Let's see who can hold their arms out in front of themselves, palm up at a right angle as though flat against a wall, rigid and strong," Phillips says to the kids. "Now can you walk around like that?

"Can you imagine what an opposite kind of movement would be like? How about this. Hold your right arm out. Pretend your hand's against a wall. Walk up to it. Don't pull if off the wall, don't push it through. Walk back and forth to that hand." The teacher can hold a child's wrists so that the student can feel his elbow joint being forced to open and close as he moves smoothly toward and away from his hands. Like much of Tai Chi this is a little lesson in flexibility, in keeping balance by rolling with the punches of life. Phillips has other simple exercises, like the Slow Walk, which challenges kids to become wholly focused on "slooow," smooth steps that give a taste of the concentration and sense of connectiveness that can flow from Tai Chi.

Rochester, New York, psychologist Dr. Deborah Sunbeck has developed a "walk," too, one she believes can help you step into "unlimited potential." When Sunbeck took on her first learning-disabled client, fourteen-year-old Michael DeLuca, in trouble since first grade, she won his confidence with a confession. As a child, she too had trouble moving between the rustling, magical world of her favorite woods, where she felt so alert, into the dizzying world of books, letters, and figures that too often set her adrift in a reference-less fog. "My brain feels fuzzy most of the time," Mike admitted. Working with him, Sunbeck developed the concepts of the Infinity Walk to mend the gaps in Mike's functioning. A hobbled mind "broke free." Mike made the honor roll, won a seat on the student council and a college scholarship.

Sunbeck has a fresh way of viewing the body-mind-world connection. We move, she says, from one-dimensional unity in the womb to the three-dimensional natural, sensual world. Suddenly we're plunged headlong into a two-dimensional world, the social world of symbols, language, reading, writing, figures. Some have trouble making the two-dimensional connections. Others do it so well, they lose connections to the 3D or 1D worlds. The flow of peak performance springs from coordination of worlds with integrated circuits and brain rhythms.

Sunbeck checks the three major ways you process information: sight, hearing, touch. Which is your dominant eye? Is your left or right ear dominant (which do you usually press to the phone)? Are you a rightie or leftie? Often dominance is split between sides. You might be left eyed, right eared and handed, which can be an advantage for verbal fluency but cause static in reading and physical coordination. Glitches in brainbody circuits can arise with all eight possible combinations, according to Sunbeck. Not to fret. You can walk yourself right out of that static with the Infinity Walk. "Infinity"—because greater integration opens into optimal functioning, but also because you walk a large figure eight, the infinity symbol. It's ideal preparation for Superlearning, Sunbeck says.

Stop reading and walk a figure eight right now, Sunbeck would say. How did you feel? Were the loops of the eight balanced? Did you have to stare at the floor? Now you know where you're starting from. Practice eights daily, arms swinging rhythmically from your shoulders, in sync with the opposite leg, shoulders even and relaxed, elbows and hands relaxed but not limp, feet meeting the floor solidly heel first, breathing easily, rhythmically. Sunbeck adds even more refinements to strengthen neural circuits including those shorted by emotional blocks.

When people can walk their eights with grace, Sunbeck brings in visual, auditory, even problem-solving activities (see her book *Infinity Walk: Preparing Your Mind to Learn*). Swinging along through figure eights can bring rewards quickly—and a few extra bonuses: Sunbeck uses it to break TV addiction.

Pressure on the Inside

Maybe you're the sort who shrugs off outside stress with a "no sweat!" Some people thrive on arduous schedules; they enjoy responsibility for an emergency room full of patients, for steering a school, company, even a country. But they trip up on inner stress, the growing pains, often, of change. As you wake up and smartly shift strategies and goals, you depart from habitual unconscious patterns and beliefs. That's when the inner stress lines begin to show. Physical relaxation helps blow off the tensions of inner dissonance, but to jump to a new level of equilibrium, one must also attend to harmonizing the conscious and subliminal minds. Second Level autogenics is one well used route for forging new options with the aid of the deep mind and by drawing on innate wisdom—the wise woman, the guide, the guardian angel. (For other ways of getting your "heads" together and resolving, in particular, the often intense tensions of change in the workplace, see Chapters 10 and 14.)

Simply doing Superlearning can lift a chronic form of inner stress. Geoff Pullen, a friendly-looking, bearded man who teaches languages at Britain's Brighton Polytechnic, runs his special brand of accelerated learning workshops in England and recently in Eastern Europe. "I have adapted my French teaching seminars to fit a twenty-hour weekend format that suits local businessmen," Pullen says. "After using accelerated techniques, students come out more energized on Sunday than when starting on Friday." A chance to take a deep breath and be wrapped in soothing music no doubt tones up the British businessmen. But something else can add a spring to their step as they exit Pullen's class: the lift that comes from finally connecting with oneself.

Underuse of one's ability is an overlooked, pernicious form of inner stress. It takes a lot of effort to sit on yourself, day after day, year after year. Do it long enough and you may be swamped with free-floating anxiety, repressed rage, addictions of all kinds. At least you'll never be bored if you take a chance, damn the torpedoes, and let yourself loose.

In some Superlearning venues, like sports, your body takes the lead. In others it plays a supporting role. But no matter what you're up to, you can lighten up and light up. Remember those light bulbs going off over the heads of comic strip characters? When your abilities move together coherently, you have something more like laser power that can cut to the heart of almost any matter and make tangible invisible possibilities the way a laser plucks a full-bodied hologram out of seeming nothingness. Ease your body online and you'll make a best friend pulling with you, not against you.

6
Superlearning Music

Sixth-grader Jamee Cathcart wondered what the judges at the 1991 Northwestern Indiana Science Fair at Purdue University would think of her entry. Experiments with Baroque music weren't exactly common in the biology division of science fairs. She was in the running against many older students, the cream of the state's entire northwest region. She remembered how she blended her love of music with scientific method . . .

"I just want you to listen to some special music," she told twelve classmates at Long Beach Elementary School. "It's called Baroque music. All you have to do is let me check your test results before and after listening."

Twelve sixth-graders listened to the harmonious string sounds of special Baroque regularly for four weeks. Jamee kept testing. Eleven out of twelve of Jamee's classmates showed remarkable improvement on test scores—scores that Jamee graphed in stand-out colors. The "after" graph showed half of them had shot right up to almost the top of Jamee's chart.

Results were so clear-cut and impressive, Jamee pasted up a brightly colored exhibit called "Baroque Brain Booster" showing her test procedure, results, and the all-important graphs. Now she was in the Purdue University competition. Judges gave the young but enterprising Jamee's Superlearning Music project an Honorable Mention Award.

"I really enjoyed working on my science project using Superlearning Music," Jamee wrote us. "It works and I had fun proving it! I'm sure everyone will be using it someday," she adds.

Twelve-year-old Jamee joined a distinguished group of researchers who've been showing for three decades that certain kinds of music can enhance mind, memory, and energy. And you can get this remarkable boost as easily as pressing the button of a tape or disc player. The music does it for you effortlessly.

Superlearning music can make you smarter, speed learning, expand memory, relieve stress, help concentration and visualization, and open inner awareness. Plus it's good listening. That sounds like a tall order, maybe even a tall story, but the music comes with a long scientific pedigree.

The revolutionary discovery that music is one key to the kind of fast, stress-free learning so needed today was originally made by scientists in the former Soviet bloc. They discovered that a certain kind of music written by composers of the seventeenth and eighteenth centuries, Baroque composers such as Vivaldi, Telemann, and Bach, has powerful effects on mind and memory. These old masters created music according to very specific formulas supposedly handed down through music guilds since ancient times.

Researchers found it's the *slow tempo section* in Baroque concertos—the largo or andante movement with a restful tempo of about 60 beats a minute—that brings the amped-up learning effect. (Tempo can be 55 to 65 beats a minute.) Baroque composers frequently scored this slow, soothing, serene music for string instruments, the violin, mandolin, guitar and harpsichord, which produce sounds rich in natural high-frequency harmonics. Today these high-frequency sounds are known to literally, physically, impart energy to the brain and the body—a story of its own (see Chapter 8). The largo movement in a concerto is usually very brief, so to experiment, researchers strung several slow movements together.

Then they held "concerts" in the lab. If you'd been one of their concert-goers, hooked up to an array of physiological and medical instruments, you might have found the data printing out on the graphs even more entertaining than the music. As the tranquil largos play, your blood pressure relaxes and lowers and your heartbeat slows to a healthy rhythm. Stress factors in your blood drop, probably enhancing your immune system. At the same time EEG monitors reveal that your brain waves are changing. Your fast, beta waves eventually decrease by 6 percent and the alpha brain waves of relaxation increase by an average of 6 percent. The right and left hemispheres of your brain become synchronized. It seems that slow Baroque is synchronizing your brain and body, too, as they move into harmony at slower, more efficient rhythms. The music has induced a powerful form of *alert* relaxation in you—relaxed body, alert mind—an ideal state for optimal accomplishment. Physiological research shows that in a calm state your body functions *more efficiently on less energy,* which makes more energy available to your brain. The effects of slow Baroque music match many of the physical benefits of mantra meditation, except that unlike chanting mantras or doing relaxation routines, you don't have to do anything. The music does it for you.

Interestingly, studies at the Menninger Foundation in Kansas found that synchronizing the hemispheres of the brain (which Superlearning Music can do in minutes) is at the physical heart of Zen meditation. This synchronization makes your brain's activities coherent, laserlike, and highly productive.

Secrets of Supermemory

What is the secret of supermemory? What makes supergifted people? These questions rang with more than academic interest in the old USSR. It wasn't for nothing that one of the most pervasive Soviet political slogans was "Knowledge is power." Recovering after the devastation of World War II, the Soviets were convinced that accelerated learning was the cure for tough times. With it they could quickly train and retrain, catch up and leap ahead technically, soar to the top in sports and ballet and attract the world to their system. At the height of the Cold War countless well-funded Soviet labs were committed to seeking ways of opening up the reserves of the human being.

How did yogis with hypermnesia (supermemory) manage to have total recall for voluminous ancient texts? They could reel them off, line perfect, often taking several days from start to finish. How did people with the a talent for "instant calculating" total up reams of figures faster than computers? How did individuals with psychic gifts tap into other people's memories? How could they access data that might be invaluable for spies or crime solvers? For years Soviets monitored and studied, probed and prodded, supergifted people of all kinds and in some cases almost dismantled them, using state-of-the-art technology of the time.

One secret of supermemory seems to go against common sense. Supergifted people mentally outdistanced others by *slowing down* brainwave activity to the slower alpha level (7–13 cycles a second) and body rhythms to more restful levels. It was a combination of the hare and the tortoise. The physical moved slowly, the mind shot ahead. By taking your foot *off* the accelerator, you could actually go faster and superperform.

How could average people reach this key state for mental superperformance? Soviet scientists tried dozens of methods. For instance you normally drift through slower rhythms as you fall asleep, and again as you float to awareness in the morning. In scores of Soviet schools and colleges, radios beamed lessons to students in dormitories at key phases in their sleep cycle. Reportedly thousands accelerated their learning of even complex subjects, like math, languages, science.

But there were drawbacks. Sleep learning requires a complicated setup. It can't be done in a classroom. Occasionally, students developed sleep disorders. There was another drawback as far as outsiders were concerned. The Soviets took their quest so seriously that much of the sleep-learning data was classified. (At first, key points in Lozanov learning were also veiled to foreigners.) In the United States at least cold warriors were paying attention, for the

Office of Strategic Services also classified its data on accelerated sleep-learning language courses.

Working in the Soviet milieu, Lozanov investigated a variety of routes to open mental resources quickly and easily: sleeplearning; relaxopedia, using autogenics; hypnopedia, using hypnosis. How else could people reach the all-important optimal state for mind and memory? At Kharkov University in Ukraine, Dr. Lozanov, while working on his doctorate, an exploration of the controlled use of suggestion, delved into the suggestive power of music. He observed that Ukrainian, Bulgarian, and Russian hospitals and sanatariums routinely played special music through speakers set up in each ward to help speed patients' recovery from illnesses and surgery. In some cases it was the major treatment. Checking patients' charts, Lozanov noted that the music appeared to help regulate heartbeat and blood pressure. Pajama-clad patients, seated comfortably in chairs in hospital halls, appeared to be dozing, to be almost asleep, but when he spoke with them, he noticed that they were alert. Much of their stress and anxiety about their illness eased as they were lifted out of themselves with music, while falling into states of deep relaxation.

Ideas began to percolate in Lozanov's mind, to link with other bits of knowledge he'd garnered as an expert hypnotist and longtime practitioner of Raja Yoga, mental yoga. He'd traveled throughout India investigating the most famous yogis of the time who could demonstrate hypermnesia or supermemory. Lozanov was also familiar with classic Indian Vedic texts.

According to the Vedas, *supermemory is a state of consciousness*. In this optimal state, one's ability to retrieve memory is infinite. The Vedas, a major influence on generations of yogis and others who follow mindbody disciplines, teach that memory is not contained within your physical body, but that all our memories are totally recorded within the universe, outside of time. The Vedas view the brain in somewhat the way we think of a radio, as a receiver, an instrument that can tune in to data. In this case, the data is information stored in the collective memory since the beginning of time. Followers of the Vedas don't bother with words to distinguish short term and long term memory. Supermemory is a seamless, natural state, they believe. Supermemory is the optimal state of an individually developed memory. In this belief, they agree with ancient memory masters of the West like Plato and Pythagoras. Raja Yoga contains special exercises for developing this altered state that is supermemory. Mantra yoga, the Vedic science of sound, reveals specific sound frequencies that can elicit altered states.

An expert on Raja Yoga and altered states, Lozanov had also studied music and played the violin. He'd grown up in Bulgaria, long a Turk-dominated crossroads at the gateway to the Orient, a society influenced by esoteric Buddhist and Hindu teachings from Zen, yoga, and the Vedas. One of Bulgaria's legendary healers, nineteenth-century Prince Veniamin (known as Boyan the Magus), had brought back Oriental practices and traveled the country healing people through music, song, incantation, and visualization.

At labs at the Bulgarian Academy of Sciences and Sofia Medical Institutes, Lozanov plunged into music research. He found his genie! What he called "mathematical" slow Baroque music could bring students into a state of *alert* relaxation. Here was the technique he'd been searching for to induce the optimal learning state. This "musical" state could substitute for the sleep in sleep-learning. No longer would accelerated learning have to be tied to bedtime in college dormitories. It could be done anywhere. Moreover students listening to the special music reached the optimal state invisibly—without any observable means—no hypnotist's suggestions, no mechanical induction with flashing lights or clicking sounds, no yoga exercises. A relaxing concert session of slow Baroque music from their own European tradition gave the method entree into a broad range of educational environments where ideological Communists had been quick to call relaxation training "mysticism."

With his longtime friend, educator Dr. Aleko Novakov, Lozanov pieced together a learning system. They added in everything discovered in the decades of research into suggestion, learning acceleration, and sleep-learning. Just like sleep-learning, they broke up data to be learned into four-second sound-bites, sandwiched between four-second pauses. Each "data chunk" was no more than seven or eight words. Memory experiments had shown this to be the optimum length. As in sleep-learning, they used special intonations. They calculated the ideal number of repetitions, lesson length, sequence, and presentation. How much data could students learn per session? Which slow Baroque music gave the very best results? Tests showed music scored for string instruments rich in harmonic overtones produced superior results to music scored for brass, horns or pipe organ. Music with a beat of 60 to 64 per minute gave the best results and helped memory improve globally. Slow Baroque could really be called "Supermemory" Music, they determined. The slow-beat also gave an inner sense of "time expansion."

That's something all of us could use. It's also something that was known and shown in America decades ago. Maybe it's finally time to put it to work. Two well known research doctors, Lynn Cooper and Milton Erikson, set 60 beats-a-minute clicking on metronomes. They, too, found the rhythm slowed mind and body rhythms. In this state people felt as if time had ballooned. The two M.D.'s pushed further and suggested to hypnotized subjects that they had a whole hour to do something, when really they were allowed only five minutes. Tricked out of their usual time frame, people vastly accelerated their thinking and creative processes. In just a tiny amount of clock time, they would come up with things such as designs for a dress or device.

Drs. Robert Masters and Jean Houston later also led people into expanded time, prompting students, for instance, to improve graphic skills that usually take a semester of training, in only a few hours. Freeing people from our apparently learned limits of clock time could certainly accelerate the realization of potential at any age. And what a relief to feel you have more time. It may be an extra little bonus in special Baroque.

Lozanov and Novakov pressed on into other musical territory in their labs. They had a rich heritage of decades of Soviet and Bulgarian music therapy research to guide them. There were still more specific mental and physical benefits to be extracted from classical music. They developed a second concert session, the "active" concert featuring certain classical music that research showed gave extra mindbody benefits. For this "active" concert they used full-length concertos and symphonies by composers like Mozart, Beethoven, and Brahms. They also developed a very elaborate, dramatic way of reading stories and dialogues over this special music. Students listened to the "active" concert while poring over the textbooks and noting key material. Meshing text material with this particular music linked right and left hemispheres of the brain and gave the data a global imprint in memory, Lozanov found. The "active" concert followed by the "passive" slow Baroque concert formed a dynamite combination. Later research in France was to show more reasons why both concert sessions were such powerful brain energizers and balancers. As it turned out, these particular classical and Baroque selections had secret ingredients in them (see Chapter 8).

Soon Lozanov had a fully developed accelerated learning program: Suggestopedia. Soon it was making those wild headlines throughout Communist bloc countries. Soon there was an entire, government funded institute in Sofia devoted to Suggestology, an educational center that held, we discovered, more physiological instruments than books.

As classes began, Lozanov's team found the music might be doing more than they'd anticipated. Adult students arrived at night classes tired after a long day's work. Instead of being even more exhausted after their multihour rapid-learning cram courses, they emerged invigorated. Physiological graphs printed out proof—lower muscle tension, lower blood pressure, slower pulse. The full learning system brought still more healthy benefits. Headaches and other pains vanished. Allergies cleared. As students began operating as a whole, all aspects of personality seemed to strengthen, the researchers found. People felt emotionally upbeat. Creative and intuitive abilities increased. Self-esteem soared. Some learning disabilities vanished. Concentration and attention span improved. It felt, students said, as if their total awareness was expanding. Music was an important, though not the only major factor in this system, a system that apparently opened a window of opportunity for the mind to reach a higher orbit.

Even more important for researchers, students' memories were greatly strengthened. Soon a select group, ages twenty-two to sixty, demonstrated the kind of memory feats previously reserved for famous yogis. After a single day-long class session tests showed they remembered one thousand foreign language phrases, almost half the working vocabulary of a language, and with a 97 percent retention level. All done effortlessly! This was a scientific experiment to see how far one could push the envelope. It was not a teaching technique. Still students wheeled out of the institute feeling they'd just had an encounter of the "nth" kind. But the extra-dimensional beings they'd met were themselves.

"Human memory is virtually limitless," Lozanov asserts. His research into hypnosis showed him we all have supermemory—in our subconscious. "The human mind remembers a colossal quantity of information," he says, "the number of buttons on a suit, steps on a staircase, cracks in a sidewalk, footsteps to the bus stop." It seems that everything that happens to us is recorded in memory. Freed from all distractions that hamper its functioning, the human mind can access and recall all these "unknown perceptions," says Lozanov. Slow Baroque music proved one potent way to lift the conscious mind away from those distractions, and to expand its access to its natural supermemory. At the same time as people discovered how to mobilize their subconscious minds, they were discovering that their "potential quotient" may be limitless too.

7
Going for Baroque

Amid piles of costly records and tapes, stopwatches wearily in hand, many would-be Superlearners were driven to ask, "Can't you make the music part of Superlearning easier? More people could use the system." Quite a number told us they couldn't detect whether a piece was in 4/4 time, let alone if there were 60 beats in a minute. One bewildered soul asked, "Just where do you find this bark music anyway?"

Sheila, who studied with the Royal Toronto Conservatory of Music and the Royal Schools of Music of Great Britain for many years, was elected to produce a tape. After lots of listening research we obtained the rights for specific Baroque selections from major record companies. We chose pieces of slow Baroque performed on string instruments rich in high-frequency sounds, all in 4/4 time with selections sequenced in ascending keys. Three minutes of fast, up-tempo music at the end gave a lift back to the day's activities. The tape featured world-class performances by international soloists and top European orchestras.

Even though *Superlearning*'s first edition had a typo in our office address directing people to a pothole in the middle of New York's

Lexington Avenue, Superlearning Music® seekers ferreted us out. We began to get feedback affirming that this slow tempo, high-frequency music really did revitalize mind and memory, speed learning, banish fatigue, and harmonize the body.

"Superlearning Music is fabulously relaxing—a veritable tranquilizer," reported *The Saga* from Norway. "Superlearning Music brings greater success than all-night, coffee-jag cram sessions do," said Mary Anne Robinson from Newport Beach, California. Jamee Cathcart's grandmother wrote to tell of her young prizewinner's success at Purdue University with the Superlearning tape. There seemed to be more "magic" in the music than we'd anticipated.

Tests at Iowa State University, for instance, found that slow Baroque music alone (without the full accelerated system) speeded up learning by 24 percent and increased memory retention by 26 percent. Teachers working for the Washington State Department of Immigration played the music during English classes for recent arrivals from Cambodia, Laos, and other Asian countries. Teachers reported it eased the trauma these older adults experienced at having to pick up a new language and use it in a very foreign culture. The music also accelerated their learning.

In Alaska, which seems to breed educational innovators, two language teachers, Anne Arruda and Tam Gisler, put Superlearning Music on their Spanish and French study tapes for students at Mears Junior High in Anchorage. At term's end they asked for comments. "On a scale of one to ten, the tapes were a nine," said one teen. "They helped me learn and REMEMBER," another wrote. Classes included a few hyperactive students, who reported they felt more relaxed and could concentrate better. In all, 85 percent found the music-enhanced tapes greatly improved their understanding of French or Spanish. Ninety percent began using the music tapes. Other teachers called the tapes a "miracle."

Inspired, Arruda and Gisler combined Superlearning Music with James Asher's Total Physical Response method of language learning to create full-length Spanish and French courses that have now been published (see Chapter 25).

"Our science unit sounds like the music department," admits Leo

Wood speaking of his chemistry classes in Tempe, Arizona. Actually, Wood has done something for music appreciation. "One of my students, Daniels, had one hundred and fifty rock tapes, many of them acid rock. He discussed them with me after class. Why couldn't he keep using them to relax and study? I asked him to just try Baroque and see what happened. A month later, he popped into my office. 'Guess what, Mr. Wood. I took all hundred fifty of my tapes downtown and traded them in for classical music!' "

Dr. Jane Bancroft, associate professor of French at the University of Toronto's Scarborough College, has bulging files of testimonials from Superlearning students. A great many testify to improved mental and physical health. Bancroft, whose indefatigable worldwide travel and research helped us unravel the secrets of Superlearning Music in the first place, credits music with much of the health benefit. Like Wood, she suggested that students switch from rock to Superlearning Music for studying. Concentration, memory, and marks improved.

Confronted with Baroque, American ingenuity reared its happy head. Soon we heard of other benefits. "I used to need three martinis to unwind," a New York executive wrote in one of our favorite comments. "Now that I listen to Superlearning Music after work, I only need two!" A New Jersey woman blended Baroque art with culinary art. "My family is so happy," she said. "I play the music to keep me calm while I cook and for the first time ever, the whole meal comes out at the same time." A Miami driving instructor remarked, "I play it all the time now in the car. It seems to help the students, but the main thing is that no matter what crazy thing they do, it keeps *my* stress level down." Other drivers report the balanced structure of Baroque helps them jockey and brake through urban traffic without shoulder-clenching tension.

People stretched out on massage and chiropractic tables began hearing the music. To our surprise so did one of us, when drifting in the timeless darkness of a float tank. Athletes play the melodies to heighten and embed mental training in whole-body memory. And for reasons never explained, Superlearning Music got trendy in dentists' offices in Saudi Arabia and the United Arab Emirates. "Please, send the music that will relax my patients," said a number of D.D. letters with exotic stamps. Then there were the letters saying cats and dogs cottoned to the music. They didn't mention if they learned faster— but just maybe they could. Brain investigator Maya Pines years ago reported that slowing down body/mind rhythms in lab animals doubled their rate of learning. People aware of the effects of sound on vegetation also wrote to report that serenading houseplants with Baroque yielded bushy green benefits.

Not only does Baroque help take the pain out of the birth of knowledge, it also helps take the pain out of birth, according to Michelle LeClaire O'Neill, Ph.D., R.N., of the Institute for Noble Birthing in Malibu, California. Dr. O'Neill, who developed the LeClaire Method of natural childbirth, which encompasses visualization, self-hypnosis, and dream analysis, added Superlearning Music to her technique. The comforting, suggestion-heightening largos play as the mothers-to-be go through training sessions. Interestingly the music features high-frequency sounds that babies are able to hear in the womb (see Chapter 8), which may be why some mothers later find that Baroque can quickly soothe a cranky infant.

Dr. O'Neill experimented with playing the music during labor and found it shortens the first stage of labor by 20 percent in addition to easing pain. Minimum pain and maximum control. That's what the combination of relaxation training and slow tempo music can provide. O'Neill recently published her techniques in *Birthing and Beyond*. In her own work O'Neill goes quite a bit beyond birth to the opposite edge of life. She is a staff psychologist at the Simonton Cancer Center in Pacific Palisades, famous for its mental treatment of cancer. The music weaves its spell here, too, as O'Neill guides terminal patients through imagery exercises. Sometimes the beautiful melodies do much more than soothe, O'Neill reports. People are lifted out of their suffering into a sense of oneness with the universe and find new peace.

Setting her sights on people trying to rise to new accomplishment in this world, Dr. Teri Mahaney meshed Superlearning Music with her own unique "Change Your Mind" programs. The combination proved to be dynamite for reaching and repatterning the powerful subconscious mind.

The ability of 60-beat music to help put the conscious and subconscious in touch with each other makes it ideal for use with affirmations, both conscious and subliminal. Our tape series using Superlearning Music along with affirmations directed to the subliminal memory have been helping people ease themselves into positive changes for nearly a decade.

In Hawaii fourth-degree black-belt judo instructor Dr. Lloyd Migita, at the Shobukan Judo Club, played slow Baroque music to tournament players ages eight to seventeen as they did relaxation exercises and affirmations ("I have no fear of any opponent." "I concentrate in matches from start to finish." "I'm unbeatable; I'm a winner."). Not only did this combination produce more judo champions, but parents also noticed a remarkable improvement in academic skills, self-confidence, and attitude.

Marketing magazine reports also struck a familiar note—or beat. If you want to sell more, they said, pipe 60-beat music through your supermarket. Sales increase significantly. Customers spend more time at each display. More than half the high-spending shoppers, on an exit quiz, said they hadn't noticed any music playing.

Contemporary Superlearning Music Composers

One of the first young American musician/composers to look into the powers of 60-beat-per-minute music was registered music therapist Janalea Hoffman, of the University of Kansas. After reading *Superlearning* she began to experiment with 60-beat Baroque. She told *Prevention* magazine that in addition to increasing learning, the music helped lower blood pressure and overcome heart arrhythmias, migraines, and insomnia in a test study with sixty patients. Like the Bulgarians she, too, found that string music worked best. "Brass instruments gave a jangly reaction," she says. Like Dr. Teri Mahaney, she believes that combining 60-beat music with mind programs and visualization helps those techniques work even better.

Hoffman, who began her career as a classically trained musician, started composing 60-beat music in the Baroque style—freshly minted music for piano and orchestra to add to the repertoire of music for Superlearning. Hoffman's series of successful "metered music" tapes and CDs (see page 283) facilitate speed learning of course but also enhance relaxation and body awareness and ease insomnia and high blood pressure.

One of Hoffman's latest, *Deep Daydreams,* starts on side one at 60 to 64 beats a minute, the ideal pace for the human heart at rest. Your body and mind are brought into sync with the beat helping to ease stress. Side two slows to 50 beats a minute, a hypnotic pace, good for mental sports training and getting in touch with inner responses. The music also helps patients with terminal diseases handle pain, Hoffman says. In addition to her work as a stress management counselor and private practice as a music therapist, Hoffman lectures widely to diverse audiences on the benefits of her special metered music, benefits backed by statistical studies published in scientific journals.

At the Kansas University Medical School her music tape, *Mind Body Tempo,* played in the background as nursing students took their most difficult test of the semester. A control group went without the music. Nurses surrounded by the new Baroque had both higher test scores and lower heart rates than controls. Full details of the test were published in the *Journal of Nursing Education,* February 1990. Other Hoffman studies backing up the powers of music on the mind are reported in *The International Brain Dominance Review.*

Hoffman makes her healing rhythms visual in *Rhythmic Medicine,* a video that features her 60-beats-a-minute music, slowing to 50 beats as images move in perfect sync with the music. "Many hypnotists are using it, as well as dentists and some hospitals," she told us. In the corporate world she uses her musical techniques to train employees in stress control in order to cut sickness and insurance claims. Some corporations buy her video in bulk for their people.

"Musical biofeedback" is another Hoffman innovation, which will be featured in her upcoming book. Instead of relying on signals from biofeedback equipment, patients use the strong beat of music as a point of reference for slowing down body rhythms. Portable music is much handier to use to control blood pressure, for instance, than instrumented biofeedback. After practicing musical biofeedback, patients report the approach takes hold full time. Even when tough customers phoned at work, they could simply get in touch with the rhythm of their breathing and sail through the problem instead of tightening up and sending blood pressure soaring.

The innovative Hoffman mixed Baroque with memory in a new way, to speed the dissolving of bad memories that diminish one's ability to learn and live. In therapy Hoffman found the music helped bring even preverbal memories to the surface effortlessly. It makes sense. Music is mainly processed by the right hemisphere of the brain, an avenue to the creative, healing self. One depressed fifty-two-year-old patient, for instance, was helped by the music to release a preverbal memory of abandonment as a tiny infant, a voiceless memory that until then manifested itself as depression. "These preverbal memories are like crystallized energy that stop us from moving on in our lives," says Hoffman. Music also aided visualization to dissolve the toxic memory.

Other patients have tapped into a sense of the transcendental through the 60-beat music. One medical professional felt heightened creativity and an impression of being very elevated from the humdrum of everyday living. It was "a subtle feeling of power . . . so different from usual levels of awareness or consciousness." Janalea Hoffman's freshly composed 60-beat music is a sound addition to the Superlearning repertoire for accelerated learning and high level, healthy performance. (For a list of 60-beat music by both contemporary and famous Baroque composers, see page 283.) Apart from Baroque, the world is full of music, and beats to many rhythms. Some of these can add to your Superlearning prowess too.

"Turning Sound"—
Sophrology Music

Got a backache or a strained leg muscle? Go home and take two tapes! And you won't have to call me in the morning. It's the prescription of Dr. Raymond Abrezol, the Swiss Sophrologist, much sought after as an Olympic sports trainer. It's a prescription he later ordered to take the pain out of memorization too. Involved in an ongoing project that shows mindbody training cuts illness and medical costs, it was natural for Abrezol to seek drugless pain control.

Aware of Baroque's good effects, he developed "Turning Sound," Baroque with certain frequencies electronically altered, plus a rhythmic shifting of the sound back and forth from ear to ear. This shifting back and forth alternately stimulates each brain hemisphere. Listeners also hear a breathing tone, a periodic signal that keeps their breath slow and rhythmic. As an Olympic coach Abrezol saw extra health benefits in using sound and mind training to keep athletes pain-free and at peak performance levels: There would be no drug residues that could show up later in tests and disqualify competitors.

Abrezol had clients—athletes, doctors, and dentists—test his "Turning Sound" tapes. They reported the rhythmic music seemed to lift them into another state, a state where pain didn't hurt. "Turning Sound" has been whiting out pain for years in Europe, not just for sports enthusiasts but also for women practicing natural childbirth. Now it's come to America (see Resources section).

Musical pain control is being documented in U.S. hospitals. At Baltimore's St. Agnes Hospital classical music is played in critical-care units. Dr. Raymond Bahr, head of the coronary care unit, reports, "Half an hour of music produced the same effect as ten milligrams of Valium." At St. Luke's Hospital in Cleveland, patients hear Vivaldi, Mozart, and Brahms before and during surgery to lower the need for sedation and painkillers. Abrezol believes his electronically altered music adds to the pain-relieving effect.

It occurred to Abrezol, an old friend of Superlearning, that his "Turning Sound" created the ideal mind state for accelerated memorization. If you were trying this technique you simply place the data you need to learn in front of you. Then, closing your eyes, you let the "Turning Sound," playing back and forth, back and forth, between the two hemispheres, carry you into that special superreceptive state. You open your eyes and, like a camera taking a slow, steady picture, look at your data for seven or eight seconds. Then close your eyes and sink back into the music for the same amount of time. This process is repeated in a paced, rhythmic way as the data becomes imprinted on your mind.

"That's an all purpose memory technique," Abrezol says. You can use it to speed learning of anything and—this is a plus—in any language. Eventually, Abrezol says, memorizing becomes automatic. Still experimenting, he's currently getting good results using contemporary music as "Turning Sound."

"Sound" Concentration

Ever find your eyes glazing over when you're confronted with deadly dull material that you absolutely *must* ingest? Wake up! You can beat boredom with beats! In fact you can *literally* tap new potentials with the tap, tap, tap of these rhythms. Virginia engineer Robert Monroe found that special rhythmic beats can help you in a galaxy of ways, from reading to drawing, from concentrating in the classroom to weightlifting on your own. They might be an ideal, medication-free way to overcome burgeoning concentration problems.

In Tacoma the sensuous strands of Kitaro's *Silk Road* swirled around sixth-graders learning math. Vangelis' *China* played as third-graders spelled. Down the hall Paul Horn's melodious sounds surrounded first-graders embarked on creative writing. It wasn't just the kids' sudden spurt in performance that was making the teachers feel good. While the special beats embedded in the music were imperceptibly tuning students' brains to bring them into "best" states for concentrating and learning, the teachers were also benefiting from them.

Founder of the Monroe Institute of Applied Sciences and an internationally known consciousness explorer, Bob Monroe developed the use of beat frequencies to lead the brain into synchronized rhythmic patterns. Your brain actually creates a beat frequency. For instance, if you don headphones and a 100 hertz signal is sent to your left ear and a 105 hertz signal to your right ear, your brain comes up with the difference and resonates to 5 hertz. This resonating is a more potent way to entrain the brain than using outside signals and will bring your whole brain into step in seconds. Monroe dubbed his technique Hemi-Sync. It's one more effective way of using sound to expand your reach. You can use Hemi-Sync to select the brain state best suited to what you want to do—learn, image, work out.

"The bane of education!" That's what philosophy professor Dr. Devon Edrington hoped to banish. It's an equal opportunity bane, one we all fall prey to: wandering attention. At Tacoma Community College Edrington fed beat frequencies via headphones to students pursuing a catalog full of subjects. Psych students shifted by Hemi-Sync into a focused, attentive state scored significantly higher on a series of tests than those who tried to concentrate on their own. Odds were only one in ten thousand that they improved by chance.

"Why can't we use this 'beat' in Tacoma public schools?" first grade teacher Jo Dee Owens insisted. Though earphones carry the beat better, Edrington rigged up stereo speakers for her. The boredom-beating beats still worked! Parents, principal, and evalua-tors soon beat a path to the room with the unhearable beats. The first graders had changed. Concentration was way up; so was coopera-tion and ability to learn on their own. Kids completed work on the three Rs and wrote stories while their teacher worked with others. "Then they read their stories," reported Tacoma Public School Sys-tems Evaluator Bruce Anaklev. "They gave one minute talks and answered questions raised by classmates. FIRST GRADERS!"

To help teachers tune their kids into "best" states, Edrington developed the Binaural Phaser, a kind of beat-factory, a synchronizer that lets you mix six different frequency patterns with music. Each can help with a specific concentration need. If kids gallop into class after a hot volleyball game, a teacher can switch to a beat that evokes slow, calming delta brainwaves for a few minutes. Then she turns to another beat to help focus attention on English or biology and yet another for art or geometry. Supposedly after a few months people get the hang of tuning their brain state on their own without beats.

Adults often don't pay attention either. Hans Heinzerling, at the University of Puget Sound, turned on Edrington's synchronizer in hot, humid, summer classes for teachers. The beats took hold, and the teachers came up with high-level attention and rousing participation that delighted Heinzerling. "I would never work without the syn-chronizer if I could help it." At Fort Lewis in Washington State, army teachers put the subtle beats to work in foreign language classes and reported excellent results at national education conferences.

We need citizens who are not just trained but *educated*! That was Edrington's passionate belief. We need "people with expansive con-sciousness enabling them to appreciate other points of view, to tolerate paradoxes, to entertain ideals, to dream," he told us before his death. Devon Edrington reached into other fields and worked hard to give us practical ways to realize a perennial dream of philosophers, an educated citizen.

3D Sound

Your ears emit sounds! Right now your ears are beaming out sounds with superlative precision over a great range. That recent discovery turned the science of hearing on its ear. "Astonishing," is how Dr. William Brownell, of the Johns Hopkins University School of Medicine, describes it. A colleague said, "It's as surprising as if your nose gave out odors."

Ear sound beams help you understand speech and also let you detect the *direction* a sound comes from. They are also on the way to enhancing people's imaginative powers. Ear beams operate like holographic radar; they act like a reference beam intersecting incoming sounds in an interference pattern.

Let's make the most of ear beams, Italian physiologist Hugo Zucarelli decided, and used them to create a new form of 3D sound recording—holophonics. If you listen to holophonics, you find yourself thrust into a new world, a world of synesthesia, the mixed senses that poets often extol. When you hear a match strike on a holophonic recording, you also smell the sulphur. When you hear the cereal snap, crackle and pop, you also taste it. Holophonic tapes can give a jolt to full-sensed imaging so important for memory, learning, and mental rehearsal of peak performance. Holophonic Superlearning Music, if someone wants to create it, might open intriguing new vistas.

Neuroacoustics

What happens when you mingle multiple sound/mind technologies together—3D sound, binaural beats, window frequencies, and more? Neuroacoustic researchers Terry Patten, Julian Isaacs, Charles Wilson, and Stuart Dubey are pursuing that idea to the cutting edge. Aware that ever since the era of the Vedic texts, mind explorers have always insisted that certain sounds influence how we think, behave, and exist, they experimented with a blend of acoustic breakthroughs in their sound labs. Results? "Extraordinary!"

Now there are many new forms of imaging, such as magnetic resonance and CAT scans, to pinpoint exactly what certain sounds do to the brain. "Clearly these sound technologies were not only compatible, they acted synergistically," the team reported. "The whole exceeded the sum of the parts." They came up with a series of "Brain/Mind Resonance" tapes and a Neuro-Acoustic Laboratories Research Kit that anyone can explore with. They created sounds designed to (a) energize productivity; (b) deepen relaxation; (c) center awareness; (d) expand consciousness. The tapes have been drawing comments from "effortless relaxation" to "evoking states of joy, oneness, bliss." (See Tools for Exploration, page 286.)

A New Octave of Potentials

Today slow Baroque is a hallmark of many accelerated systems. Now perhaps it's time to add another octave to the "sound" route to opening human capability. The inner world of music and the inner music of the world are being uncovered. Many dynamics of this inner world have been playing under the surface of Superlearning all along. If you understand them, you can use them more effectively. Just as Superlearning involves using all your abilities in concert, the next octave up has to do with how you can move in concert with the universe around you. Once aware, you can replace dissonance with a very healthy, mind-opening harmony. One route to greater harmony comes from the reclamation of ancient understanding. Another, from the dazzling work of Dr. Alfred Tomatis, member of the French Academy of Medicine and Academy of Science. His work is lofting people into higher octaves of talent and vitality and also offers proven ways to bring the learning-disabled up to speed.

Even scientists find the journey into the interior land of sound takes on mythic overtones, like searching for the lost ark. They haven't unearthed an ark yet, but seem close to a lost chord. A treasure trove of information has been unearthed about capabilities and aspects of ourselves—like your 26,400 dancing Corti cells—that most of us don't even know we have.

8
Secret Ingredients in Music

"I just can't get to sleep nights," a well-dressed visitor once complained to Johann Sebastian Bach. "I'm getting foggy. That can be disastrous in my profession, as you know. Can you think of a solution?" In short order Bach composed some special music and a harpsichordist was dispatched to play it nightly for the harried insomniac. Soon he was snoring. His insomnia was gone and his health restored. The grateful client, Russian envoy Count Kayserling, paid Bach a handsome sum for the stress-easing music. Bach named this famous music for his client's obliging harpsichordist, Johann Goldberg—*The Goldberg Variations*.

How did Bach know which chords to put into his sleep-inducing music? Did he know which chords would prove to be music for the mind, which harmonics would resonate with what Abe Lincoln called the "mystic chords of memory"?

"Did Bach and other composers know Raja Yoga?" Dr. Lozanov liked to ask. "Of course they did!" He'd answer himself emphatically. *Yoga* means "to yoke" or "to link," and composers of the Baroque era believed certain elements in music could link people to the energies of the cosmos. Composers were trained to use particular keys, ratios, and patterns for harmony, counterpoint, rhythm, and tempo. Their "mathematical" music was supposed to affect listeners by aligning and synchronizing body and mind to harmonious cosmic patterns. Music was said to be the key to worlds visible and invisible. This idea of the hidden powers of music was recognized worldwide in ancient days.

Hermetic philosophy was the glory of ancient Egypt. Its fabled founder, Hermes Trismegistus, devoted two books to the art of music, revealing how it can be used to heal a host of illnesses and evoke seemingly "supernatural feats." Hermetic philosophy holds that everything in the universe vibrates at its own unique frequency and that because of harmonic resonance there is a correspondence between all things. Ancient mathematicians noted the ratios of the different planetary cycles, counted the rhythms in nature, calculated the proportions of the human body and created a "sacred geometry"—a set of mathematical ratios. Use them in music or architecture, they taught, to resonate with basic forces of the universe and to enhance life.

These resonant prescriptions filtered through the centuries via secret societies and lodges, through guilds of musicians, architects, and masons. It's easy to see how the sacred formulas were thought to work if you imagine playing the note C on a piano in a room full of pianos. C will start sounding on all the other pianos through resonance. In the same way, if you play certain notes and harmonies, you supposedly resonate specific energies, ones that can expand the mind, others that heal, some that can harm. The ancients saw the octave, the musical scale, as pervading the cosmos and today modern science is proving the validity of their idea.

The octave principle lets you figure a mathematical ratio or correspondence between the vibrations of a musical note, a color, a chemical, or an aroma. The note A below middle C, for instance, vibrates at 213 cycles a second, relating to the color orange-yellow and the metal copper. The note B below middle C at 240 cycles a second, relates to yellow and zinc.

Ancient schools of music believed their art was the bridge to awareness and set forth a "sacred canon" of specific harmonies, intervals, and proportions to be used as *linking* sounds. As people listened to the music, cell vibrations and body rhythms would become synchronized or linked to the rhythms of the planets and plants, earth and sea. Such sounds, many wise people believed, could flood away disharmony and out-of-sync patterns. The idea that specific tones can influence you comes down also from early Semitic and Arabic sacred texts. The shamans of Central Asia, the Jajouka musicians of northern Morocco, and Indian and Oriental musicians knew musical methods for mind expansion, pain control, ability to walk on hot coals without damage, and forms of music to be followed as a path to enlightenment. Similar ideas permeated traditional music in Japan. It's not surprising that tests find that slow tempo passages of Japanese Koto music offer the same mind- and memory-boosting powers as Baroque. The koto is a Japanese harp, an oblong wooden instrument with thirteen silk strings that resonate rich high-frequency overtones.

In India performers of traditional music such as Ravi Shankar still tune their instruments to the "fundamental tone" or OM. This music is generally performed on the sitar with its seven playing strings and interestingly a dozen or more resonating strings, which vibrate harmonics. All strings must be tuned to this "primordial vibration," or "ever-sounding tone," which corresponds to C sharp (136.10 Hz) and to the color blue-green turquoise. That, however, hardly makes a note live up to the name "primordial vibration," but scientists have found something that does.

The Indian tuning tone is in precise ratio to a basic frequency of the earth itself. The sitar is tuned to the sound (if it were audible) of the earth's movement around the sun. This is called the earth year tone. When this earth-tuned music plays, supposedly instruments, musicians, and listeners reverberate to the "fundamental tone" uniting with the universe. Shankar and other sitar players say that their music embodies the principle of relaxation on the spiritual level.

Scientific proof of the ancient concepts of cosmic harmonics has emerged, some of it out of far left field. One amusing instance was born serendipitously from the woes of the Bruckman Printing firm in Munich. Bruckman had a problem. Every once in a while their presses inexplicably turned out messy work. Could it be the weather? Engineer Hans Baumer investigated; bad weather days didn't match the problem days. Then Baumer noticed something odd. The machines were acting like Aunt Heidi's rheumatism. They went awry two days *ahead* of stormy weather.

Eventually Baumer managed to preserve his scientific perspective by figuring out why. It has to do with "atmospherics," brief electromagnetic impulses the earth throws out that can change weather. The printing firm used a protein gelatin on their press cylinders. When atmospherics generated a specific sound frequency, the protein resonated in harmony, blurring the printing. Baumer made another discovery, one that brought him publication in scientific journals. He found that these electromagnetic bursts thrown out by the earth correspond to the musical scale.

"They are quite clearly in simple numerical relationship to each other, corresponding to the octave, the fifth, the fourth, the third, etc., in the field of sound," he reported. Herr Baumer overlooked a point that might amuse Americans. As Mother Earth spins about, she now and then strikes up "The Star-Spangled Banner"—at least the opening notes—"(Oh) say can you see," one of the "melodies" of atmospherics.

Proteins live and resonate in us. Two distinguished German scientists independently observed that those extraordinary information and building molecules DNA and RNA resonate to an octave tone of the earth's rotation pattern, one of many scientific examples that our flesh and blood is tuned to universal resonance.

Musical Keys That Enhance Mindbody

Of course all music contains these notes that resonate us with various elements in the universe. A recent mathematical breakthrough makes it possible to zero in on *precise* benefits of musical keys linked to *specific* helpful resonances. Swiss scientist and author Hans Cousto followed up on the mathematical calculations of ancient musicians linking sound resonances and the universe and came up with the precise calculations for the sound frequencies of the keys that resonate with each planet and their mindbody effects. He developed precision-calibrated tuning forks for each of these "planetary" keys and in the process became well known for a new and better way to tune up orchestras. For example:

- The key of G (194.71 Hz) resonates with the frequency of the earth day, the color orange-red, and has a dynamic, stimulating, and energizing effect on bodymind.

- The key of C-sharp (136.10 Hz) resonates with the earth year and the color turquoise-green. This is a calming, meditative, relaxing, and centering key.

- The key of F (172.06 Hz) resonates with the Platonic year (about 26,000 years) and the color purple-violet. It has a joyful, cheerful, and spiritual effect.

You can revitalize and enhance your whole energy system, Cousto maintains, by resonating with the tones of the planets. Through sound resonance we can sense our oneness with the universe, he believes.

To get the specific benefits of these cosmic links, select music written in these particular keys, or try out his tuning forks. You set the forks vibrating and then place them on various acupuncture points on the body in an attempt to retune and realign to universal energies. Some private Superlearning classes use these tuning forks to "tune up" mindbody before a class or to relax and clear stress (see Resources section).

Brain Energizing Sounds

"Some sounds are as good as two cups of coffee," says the eminent French ear specialist Alfred Tomatis (Toma-*teece*). It figures that we might have a musical pick-me-up. Ever since humankind began making music, music has been helping fill the needs of the day. Lullabies, war chants, sea chanties—the list is as diverse as history and culture. In our high-tech day Tomatis has opened a high-tech route to the inner power of sound that really does hold "super" powers to expand mental capability, to heal, and to energize.

"Sound can be an extraordinary source of energy," according to

Tomatis, now in his seventies, who claims to be filled to the brim with energy, needing only three or four hours of sleep a night because he plays special music in the background as he works. Tomatis didn't just stumble into his caffeine-free wake-up music.

For decades he took music's measure with complex instruments to see how different sound frequencies affect you. Which ones boost energy and which ones deplete it? And how do they do it? He came to an astounding conclusion. "The ear is made not only for hearing," Tomatis announced. "*The ear is designed to energize the brain and body!*"

You get energy through your ears? As Tomatis tracked Bach, Mozart, Gregorian chants, and the singing of OM, the readout on his scientific instruments showed him that fatigue, burnout, and the debilitating effects of stress come when the central gray nuclei cells in your brain run low on electrical potential. In other words they run out of juice. These cells act like small electrical batteries, Tomatis says. They generate your brain's electricity, powering the brainwaves that show up on your EEG. You would think these little batteries would be recharged by body metabolism. Not so, Tomatis says. And this is where a major breakthrough comes in.

Something outside of you charges up your battery cells and that something is *sound,* particularly high-frequency sound. The middlemen are your remarkable Corti cells. If you took a trip through your inner ear, after whirling around and around through the labyrinthine swirls of the snail-shaped cochlea, you'd suddenly come upon the "Corti Chorus Line," the longest line of precision dancers in the world. Arranged in rows, 24,600 long-stemmed cells dance in perfect precision to each sound, much like the Rockettes of Radio City Music Hall. The energy produced by this extraordinary dance flows to your brain and some of it also splits off through the vestibular branch of your auditory nerve and flashes to the muscles of your body. High-frequency sound energizes your brain while at the same time, it releases muscle tension and balances the body in many other ways. It even affects your posture. Some of these high-flying, power-packed sounds exist in Superlearning Music.

But you don't get the jolt of energy if you can't *hear* the high-frequency sounds. This Tomatis discovery helps explain why some

North Americans don't seem to get the tingling burst of vitality from Baroque that East Europeans did. It's a good bet that impaired hearing, caused mainly by noise pollution, is the culprit, since East Europeans don't suffer quite the same sonic assault that we do. Tomatis also discovered that you get accustomed to listening within the sound spectrum of your native language. This makes a big difference in how people pick up music. The listening spectrum for Slavic languages ranges from very low to very high frequencies. The range of American English is much narrower.

You come into this world with wide-ranging hearing, able to pick up sound as low as 16 cycles a second and as high as over 20,000 cycles. Then age, sometimes ear infections, and almost always noise pollution take their toll. The jackhammer pounding the concrete at 3,500 beats a minute, traffic, sirens, subway, booming mall music, clattering machines—all reduce our range of hearing. According to Tomatis, one of the reasons we start to feel worn out as we get older is that we can no longer hear the higher pitched sounds that could reenergize us. Dr. David Lipscomb, of the University of Tennessee noise lab, reported as long ago as 1982 that 60 percent of incoming college freshmen had significant hearing loss in the high-frequency range. Their hearing was on a par with that of elderly men. "These young people are entering their working life with retirement-age ears," said Lipscomb.

Can "elderly" ears be turned back into young ears? Dr. Tomatis to the rescue again. You can rejuvenate ears with sound itself, he determined. It seemed like a paradox—restore hearing by hearing. But as the son of a famous opera singer whose home overflowed with musicians, it was natural for Tomatis to turn to sound and music for its healing force.

Remember in high school biology learning about three well-named structures on the far side of your eardrum? The hammer, anvil, and stirrup. Now, imagine you're surfing on a sound wave in your middle ear. There they are working away, muscles tensing and releasing to position the eardrum properly, like turning a satellite dish, to respond to different incoming frequencies. Your muscles look kind of flabby, and you get the feeling they're not putting their all into the job. Suddenly there's a hissing sound. Your muscles perk up as if they'd been barked at by a drill instructor. Clench, release, pump, pump, again and again. It's a workout middle ear muscles will keep to daily until they've built themselves up to where they once again are able to set the eardrum into precise positions.

The hissing drill instructor is the Electronic Ear, a device invented and patented by Tomatis. It emits bursts of varied high/low-frequency sounds, alternating from ear to ear and forcing the middle-ear muscles to shape up. Once they do, the inner ear is "opened" and high-frequency hearing is restored. That may not seem too exciting, but you should talk with Canadian novelist Patricia Joudry, who thought the Electronic Ear might help her hearing problem. It did, but what really turned her on was "an unimaginable burst of vitality and, even better, creativity."

An "open" ear has turned out to be an Open Sesame for power learning as well as a key to turning around widespread, ever-increasing, learning disabilities.

"The ear is meant to benefit the whole person psychologically and physically," says Tomatis. You may have heard of "free energy." Tomatis' work gives that a flesh-and-blood meaning. Through the ear, he says, you can tap into the vast, natural supply of cosmic energy. There's never any shortage of cosmic energy, he observes.

Which sound frequencies do you use to light up the mind? Sounds from 5,000 hertz to 8,000 hertz recharge "brain batteries" most rapidly. The fastest recharge comes from 8,000 hertz. After checking out the music of many composers, Tomatis found that the music richest in these ultrahigh-frequency recharging sounds is Mozart's. At the same time he pinpointed frequencies that deplete mind and body: low-frequency sounds, such as noise from traffic, airports, construction sites. Some of the low pounding sounds in rock music are also "brain drain" sounds, says Tomatis.

The High Power of Frequencies

Acid rock is a draining sound for geraniums too. Since the days of Luther Burbank, it's been known that music and sound can influence vegetation. Ancient peoples, with their planting songs and rhythmic, pounding dances, probably knew it too. But in our day no one did much with this knowledge until Dan Carlson of Blaine, Minnesota, made it his life's work. After years of heavy research, Carlson pinpointed the frequency that energizes plants the way Tomatis' sounds wake up humans. It is 5,000 hertz, the low end of the range that Tomatis found influences us, a discovery that makes one marvel all the more at Mother Nature. Interestingly, the range of birdsong is also around 5,000 hertz.

Carlson embedded the pulsed 5,000 hertz sound, which resembles giant cricket sounds, in tapes of Baroque and other music. He played this "dinner music" for plants, then sprayed them with nutrients. The music helped plants absorb nutrients with 700 percent greater efficiency. They sprung up with a 99 percent growth increase. A four-and-a-half-inch purple passion plant, whose normal size is about eighteen inches, treated with Carlson's dinner music and nutrients for two and a half years grew 1,400 feet long, and right into the *Guinness Book of World Records*. Carlson's musical "fertilizer" also transformed farms having severely depleted soil. Harvests increased twenty-fivefold. Carlson's gotten five-to-one acceleration in crop production, too, and believes his sound-spray treatment could rapidly aid famine-stricken areas and ease the scourge of world hunger. In the spring of 1993 he took his expertise to Russia to help improve crops there. In 1992 Prince Charles applied Carlson's method to the Sudley Castle Gardens, garnering sixty-five roses per branch where there were five before.

Would listening to 5,000 hertz added to slow Baroque at dinner help us humans absorb nutrients better from our food? At least there may be "lite dinner music," a few recent tests show. When restaurant patrons ate to slow classical music, they munched more slowly, digested better, and did not gain weight. When people ate to rock, they ate very rapidly, didn't digest well, and gained weight. On the learning side, would a 5,000 hertz signal added to Superlearning Music help us absorb data better?

As Carlson boosted plants into the record book, biochemist Dr. Ifor Capel uncovered a sound route to lifting humans past the old records. An internationally known researcher at the Marie Curie Cancer Memorial Foundation in Surrey, England, Capel made a discovery that may enable 21st century Superlearners not only to pick up data faster but also to shift their state in a twinkling, and have real control over pain. By beaming low-frequency electrical pulses at people's brains, Dr. Capel found that different frequencies and wave-forms trigger various neurotransmitters, your brain's chemical messengers. For example a 10 hertz signal increases production of serotonin, a chemical messenger that relaxes you and eases pain.

"Each brain center generates impulses at a specific frequency, based on the predominant neurotransmitters it secretes," says Capel. "In other words the brain's internal communications system—its language—is based on frequency."

If you "speak" to the brain precisely in its frequency language, you can quickly and sharply increase the production of a desired neurotransmitter that speeds learning or pain-relieving and pleasure-producing chemicals like endorphins, the brain's home grown morphine. Scientists quickly figured out the frequencies that stimulate your major brain chemicals. Pleasure-producing beta-endorphins rise at a frequency between 90 and 111 hertz. Catecholamines, vital for memory and learning, respond at around 4 hertz. Think about it. Generate an invisible wave and influence a person's abilities, state, behavior. That's something the shadowy elements of world governments have done more than think about for some years.

On the bright side, when you know the brain's lingo, you can begin setting it adazzle with a whole new breed of learning aids—brain machines. People are beginning to connect themselves to devices that pulse hundreds of frequencies like a rich, resonating chord of inaudible music. Instruments like the Brain Tuner 5 (see page 205), for instance, generate frequencies that evoke both IQ- and memory-boosting chemicals while also proving to be powerful healers of addiction and depression.

Music tones that resonate on these same frequencies several octaves higher evidently also stimulate your mind-altering chemical messengers. Virtually everyone involved in sound therapy reports sharpened mental function and stress and pain relief. Many report euphoria. Euphoria, joy, the state that can wipe away learning blocks and bring a wonderful leap in performance. Bliss is what Dr. Deepak Chopra calls this state, and it is, to him, the healer of all wounds mental and physical.

We had to wait for technology to reveal our intimate involvement with frequencies. In the West it seems we had to wait, too, for our technology to accept something that's helped other cultures for centuries—acupuncture. Your ears are an upside-down reflection of your whole body according to ear acupuncture theory. Ear acupuncturists treat specific points on the ear to move *chi* energy along meridians to balance and heal the entire body. The major acupuncture point for whole-body anesthesia is on the lower shell of the ear (number 86 on the Heart/Lung Meridian of the ear). It's been proved that putting electrical stimulation of 111 hertz on this point stimulates pleasure-producing endorphins to the max. Stimulating the ear with specific musical sound frequencies by placing earphones directly on the number 86 point, as Tomatis Sound Therapy users do, also produces endorphins. Tomatis' treatment also seems to evoke, and when necessary repattern, some very vital sounds you heard a long time ago.

Your Most Ancient Memory

What's your most ancient memory in this life? That's the center of another discovery by Alfred Tomatis, one that reaches right down to the depths of one's being. Your most ancient memory? It's a sound. And you heard it through the dark, cozy waters of the womb. It's your mother's voice. But you probably wouldn't recognize Mom if you heard a tape Tomatis made of her speaking through fluid, something he's done thousands of times for people. What came to you through liquid inner space was an extraordinary pattern of high-pitched squeaks and whistles similar to dolphin talk or bird chatter coming through a thick jungle atmosphere. The pitch? Exactly the frequency Tomatis pinpointed as a power sound for the brain's batteries, 8,000 hertz.

Without special guidance few of us recall prebirth memories, but it's been proven they are there. Some may foment the learning blocks that hold us in a life of mediocrity. But Tomatis' sound memories relate to more than psychological limitations. These sonic patterns, he determined, are involved in the proper development of brain and body. Clinics across France use these high-frequency patterns, preferably made from the mother's voice, to work striking transformations in learning-disabled children, particularly "incurable" autistics. Part of the transformative effect of high-frequency therapy in adults, Tomatis thinks, may arise from resonating this ancient memory, the sense of mother and child as one, a feeling of wholeness that touches base with our oneness with the universe.

To help people leap ahead of disabilities and recharge, Tomatis prepared tapes of special classical music rich in very high frequencies—Baroque, Mozart, Gregorian chant. He filtered out notes in the music under 2,000 hertz. He added the inner-ear exercising sounds of the Electronic Ear, the fluctuating bursts of high/low-frequency sounds, a soft hissing noise that alternates from ear to ear and stimulates both hemispheres of the brain. He also sent more sound to the right ear than to the left, because his studies show that it improves results. At listening centers throughout France, Europe, and North Africa people plugged in to the Sound Therapy tapes on headsets, and after about one hundred hours of listening, they emerged with their hearing restored, their energies soaring. Many also noticed something very nice had happened to their minds.

France's major universities have tested the Tomatis methods extensively; scores of clinics have used his therapies for decades. A member of both the French Academy of Medicine and the French Academy of Science, he is the founder of a new scientific discipline, Audio-Psycho-Phonology (APP), which has long published its own journal. Tomatis has also written hundreds of scientific papers in scores of journals in varied fields and published several books.

Why have Tomatis' life-empowering discoveries been virtually ignored in the United States? Partly, resistance to change; partly, little government research funding; partly, little access to the data in foreign languages. It's taken fourteen years for Tomatis' autobiography, covering some five decades of landmark discoveries, *The Conscious Ear—My Life of Transformation Through Listening,* to finally be published in English.

Leaders of the American human potential movement, like Dr. Jean Houston, have begun to sound the call. Hailing Tomatis' discoveries as "virtually a Copernican revolution," she urges leading-edge explorers to look into the power of harmonics to heal our lives and reveal to us "gifts we didn't know we had."

Tomatis' breakthroughs have already improved the lives of hundreds of thousands worldwide. Thanks to a gutsy Canadian writer and some high-tech Catholic monks, they are now spreading through the grassroots of North America awakening people as never before, propelling them through the 10 percent barrier into a cascade of new talents. It would not have been the least surprising to the musician/ physicians of ancient times, nor perhaps will it be to Superlearners of the 21st century.

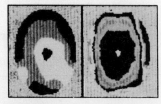

Neuroacoustic researchers use 24-channel EEG brain mapping in 3-D to chart the effects of specific elements in music—beat, high frequencies, specific tones. These before/after brain maps confirm dramatic shifts in brain wave patterns after the use of neuroacoustic tapes. Colors shift from blue/purple to red, orange, yellow, and green indicating the brain has been stimulated.

9
The Sound of
a Miracle

"The great Caruso has gone deaf!" The opera world was abuzz. The right side of Caruso's face had just been operated on in Spain, and his fellow singers were worried about the consequences. "Caruso asked me to speak to his *left* ear because he couldn't hear a thing with his right ear," said shocked singers at the Metropolitan Opera of New York.

Umberto Tomatis, Alfred's father, a well-known singer at the Paris Opera, and his colleagues had all observed Caruso's post-surgery deafness and speculated: would it damage the famous singer's career? On the contrary. Starting immediately after the surgery in 1902, Caruso was transformed from a gifted singer to the greatest vocalist in the world! It was during the years of his deafness that he achieved his greatest operatic triumphs.

Why should deafness produce such a magnificent voice? Dr. Tomatis, a veritable detective Hercule Poirot in this case, began intensive sleuthing to check out every clue. Using special instruments, he also analyzed Caruso's listening pattern from recordings.

He was on the trail of Caruso's secret. His right ear was deaf only to lower frequencies—those of speech—but he could hear extremely well the higher frequencies of music, which are rich in harmonics. Tomatis came to an astonishing conclusion: "Caruso sang so remarkably well because he could no longer hear except in the singing range!"

Further detective work on the greatest singers of Europe, like Beniamino Gigli, began to make the puzzle fit together. The greatest singers and musicians were all "right-eared." The right ear dominated their way of listening. What if he could give Caruso's listening pattern to his opera singer patients! Would it restore their lost voices? In the audio lab his sick singers put on headphones hooked up to special audio equipment. They heard themselves sing while equipment filtered out low notes and heightened high frequencies through the right ear. As they listened to their own voices this way, they felt a new well-being and sang again like angels! When they had clear right-eared, high-frequency hearing, their voices could produce full-bodied, accurate notes.

There was new hope for these professional opera singers, many of them family friends, whose livelihoods depended on their voices. Ironically some of them had become deaf in the singing range of their voices from their own high volume. The audio devices restored their voices, but how could they go out on the operatic stages of the world wearing headphones hooked up to machines? How could they hang on to this clear hearing?

Tomatis tried everything. Finally the Electronic Ear was born and patented. This apparatus conditioned the ear to hear the full sound range of music, and when it was used with his right-eared sound-filtering method, singers, actors, performers, and speakers retained the hearing improvement and could again perform sans headphones in public. They were healed. In effect the Electronic Ear gave them "Caruso's Ear"!

If you are studying singing, acting, music, public speaking, or foreign languages, when you turn on a Sound Therapy tape with the Electronic Ear, you, too, are literally benefiting from "Caruso's Ear."

It was these "Caruso" experiments that led Tomatis to his most revolutionary discovery: the link-up between hearing and speaking.

It was to make him world famous. It was recorded in 1957 as "The Tomatis Effect" in the annals of the French Academies of Science and Medicine.

"A person can only reproduce vocally what he is capable of hearing." That's the essence of his breakthrough. In other words what you *hear* is what you get. His theory holds that hearing and psyche are inextricably linked and that hearing is the key to language development, speaking, singing, learning, social communication, and consequently the balancing of the whole personality.

As Tomatis worked with the music and the Electronic Ear to restore the voice and hearing of singers and actors, both the famous and the not-so-famous, he discovered that healing sounds had even more powerful dimensions. A desperate Spanish singer came to Tomatis. After four surgeries for throat nodules he could barely talk, much less sing. Peering into his mouth, specialists recoiled with shock. So much of his nose and throat were gone, it was a cavern. After lengthy treatment with the Electronic Ear, the Spaniard achieved his dream. He became a fine opera singer. Tomatis suddenly realized something that was to have wide-reaching implications for us all. Certain sound frequencies could even overcome profound, irreversible physical damage!

The Tomatis high-frequency sound method also enhances intelligence and speeds learning. "I came to be involved in this work," says Dr. Billie Thompson, now director of the Tomatis Center in Phoenix, Arizona, "by looking for effective programs to offer others who want to improve or accelerate their learning." Her files are bulging with cases. Fourteen-year-old Chris, who had behavior problems, went from failing science to doubling his grades after the listening therapy. Eight-year-old Cindy's transformation is called "incredible," "amazing," "wonderful" by her mother. All her potentials were "covered up and just had to be uncovered."

The Tomatis tapes help accelerate learning and overcome learning problems in two ways: Sonic stimulation recharges the brain with energy, and it creates new, more efficient neural pathways. How does it work?

Our left ears have a longer, less efficient route to the language center in the brain. Tomatis tracked the "transcerebral trip" sound makes through the left ear. For stutterers lag time was 0.1 to 0.2 second—far longer than normal. Our right ears have a shorter, more efficient route to the language center in the brain. The right ear receives information more rapidly, so when it takes charge of operations, information gets processed in the correct sequence.

To make the right ear "the director" of brain circuitry, Tomatis combined the Electronic Ear with high-frequency sound, sending more filtered sound to the *right ear* than to the left. This trained the right ear to become "dominant." The electrical charge from sound applied to the right ear in turn repatterned neural circuits in the brain. No lag time, no stutter.

Dyslexia, too, vanished when the right ear became the "director" and thus repatterned brain circuitry. "We read with our *ears!*" says Tomatis. Out-of-sync neural circuitry plays a role in dyslexia, just as with stuttering, he claims. When the right ear is patterned to take charge, brain circuitry is rebalanced so that all stimuli to the language center are handled in the right sequence. His results with dyslexia have been *startling*. More than twelve thousand people have been cured with his method. So have those with learning disabilities, from Attention Deficit Disorder (ADD) to hyperactivity (see Chapter 31).

Over the past forty years thousands have made their way to the two hundred centers in fifteen different countries using Tomatis Sound Therapy. From those with disabilities to those with deafness, tinnitus (ringing in the ears), and vertigo. There have been singers, stutterers, actors, public speakers, language teachers. There have also been those with severe illnesses—epilepsy, autism, mental illness, and even stroke and coma patients.

Don Campbell, director of the Institute for Music, Health and Education in Boulder, Colorado, and author of *Music Physician for Times to Come,* asserts that over the past forty years Tomatis' method of sonic stimulation has been tested on over a million clients worldwide.

For seventy Benedictine monks at a remote monastery in France, Sound Therapy was a miracle. A new abbot had instituted reforms: long hours of work instead of chanting. Soon the monks were sluggish and exhausted despite sleeping long hours. Some just sat staring into space. Medical specialists tried countless remedies, but the monks grew worse. Seventy of the ninety were sitting in their cells withdrawn like schizoid beings. Finally, in desperation, they called for Dr. Tomatis. He reintroduced their lengthy schedule of chanting. As the monastery rang with sound again, the monks found their health restored.

The Sound of a Miracle is the title Annabel Stehli gave her book about the sound treatment that rescued her daughter, Georgie, from autism. In her moving autobiography Stehli reveals that for years, her life was a ceaseless round of heart-wrenching hospital visits as she watched her elder daughter slowly die of leukemia and her younger daughter fail to respond to treatment after treatment for autism, until finally Georgie was declared hopeless and placed in a warehouse institution.

On a business trip to Europe with her second husband, Stehli discovered the widely known Sound Therapy clinics. She *must* return with Georgie, she determined. Back in the United States at the autism institution, she had to summon every ounce of courage and confidence to battle frenzied opposition and outright threats from medical authorities and staff just to get Georgie out the door and onto the plane bound for Europe.

After several weeks of sound treatment Georgie could communicate at last. She revealed that her hearing had been so distorted that the most imperceptible sounds—even water in plumbing pipes—had caused her pain, and loud noises had brought agony and hysterical reactions. Today Georgie is fully recovered—a college graduate with a successful career as an artist.

Years later Stehli and her daughter returned to visit the autism institution. There were Georgie's fellow patients, as if caught in a time warp, in exactly the same condition they'd been in when they'd said good-bye years before. Without "the sound of a miracle" Georgie would still be one of them, thought Stehli with a sense of shock. The staff showed little interest in Georgie's recovery. The mind-restoring music could offer life-restoring hope to many thousands, she thought in addition to saving massive amounts of health care dollars, but it might take an era for the concept of healing sound to percolate through unaware officialdom. Stehli organized the Georgiana Foundation and set about spreading the news about music for the mind.

Moreover, if the amazing music could restore even severe cases of mental damage, what might it do for highly intelligent people? As Dr. Lozanov had envisaged when he first researched this music years before, could an actual evolutionary leap happen through the powers of special music?

Now some exciting new developments have made it possible for anyone to use mind-sharpening music on a do-it-yourself basis, bypassing blockage by authorities.

How the Two Superlearning Concerts Work for You

As Tomatis uncovered secret after secret about the precise way in which sound frequencies in music affect mind and muscle, his discoveries helped clarify exactly how each of the two learning concerts work for you to supercharge your mind, memory and potentials. By knowing how each concert works on the mind you can add elements tuned to your specific needs.

- The Superlearning 60-beat slow Baroque music opens a communications link to the subconscious mind, expands memory, and harmonizes right and left brain. It relaxes the body and alerts the mind. It's really Supermemory Music.

- The Superlearning "Active" Concert, which uses plenty of Mozart's up-tempo high-frequency music as a backdrop to a dramatic reading of learning material, gives a powerful energy boost to the cerebral cortex to help charge up and rebalance brain and body. Research shows that after listening to high-frequency music for a certain length of time, the brain seems to become harmonized, energized, and sharpened. It then begins to give the right signals to the rest of the system and ease begins to replace dis-ease. The whole self is revitalized.

Just as Dr. Lozanov's research has shown, by learning with these two specific kinds of music, not only can you speed learning two to ten times faster but you can also enhance health and expand creativity and potentials.

Sound Therapy Goes Mobile

Patricia Joudry, a well-known Canadian novelist, playwright, and screenwriter, emerged from a Montreal Sound Therapy clinic feeling euphoric. She'd been terrified she'd was going deaf. Now she could hear again! She was also brimming with new energy. Despite the multihour commute she made daily to the sound center, she was never tired anymore. Insomnia had vanished. A few hours' sleep was all she needed to feel totally refreshed. Her mind had new clarity. Her creativity soared. Even better, her "writer's block" was gone and her new novel came effortlessly. She felt as though she'd been "plugged into the cosmos."

Though her deafness was healed, she continued to take occasional Sound Therapy sessions. Each one yielded the wondrous mental boost, limitless vitality, serenity, and sheer joy, like a drugless high. When she had to move to the prairies, it was the marvelous mind music she regretted leaving the most. But destiny had pointed her in the right direction. After settling near Saskatoon, Saskatchewan, she discovered she was just down the road from one of the few Sound Therapy centers in Canada, one she hadn't even known existed—St. Peter's Abbey and College in the tiny town of Muenster.

Concealed behind the college's stately gardens, Joudry found rooms crammed with equipment that looked as if it were right out of a space shuttle. Decks of electronic equipment gleamed, and glistened, whirred, and blinked. The captain of this evolutionary enterprise was a bearded monk in blue jeans and sneakers, Father Lawrence De Mong, who envisioned pioneering new heights in education, health and personal transformation. He required students at St. Peter's College to put in numerous hours of listening each term. They plugged in headphones in the listening room and went to sleep on couches.

An amazing transformation was happening. Learning disabilities were vanishing. Long-term speech defects were 80 percent cured. Dyslexia, emotional disturbances, hyperactivity, and hearing problems were a thing of the past. Students felt relaxed and de-stressed. They could concentrate with ease and were loaded with creative energy. With improved hearing, foreign language learning was a breeze. Academic performance in every area had improved.

Joudry was soon a fixture in the Sound Therapy center, mesmerized, trying to decode the mystery of the music she called "ambrosia for the brain." The Sony Walkman had just arrived. "Aha," said Father Lawrence and Joudry. It had a frequency response of 16,000 hertz, high enough to capture the high-frequency sounds and overtones that are the essence of power in the special music. It takes about one hundred hours of listening to get the ear conditioned so that the brain recharging effect is retained. Now the sound treatment could go mobile! Students could listen anytime—while sleeping, commuting, or even in class. Within days the monks had prepared metal cassettes of the Sound Therapy music programs. A revolution began. St. Peter's was on Sound Therapy Walkmans—students, monks, nuns, and even the janitors. The Ursuline Convent in nearby Bruno also joined in.

They'd opened up a pipeline to a great reservoir of radiant energy. Both teachers and students listened to the Walkmans during classes. At day's end, no more frazzle.

They were discovering the secret that Suggestopedia users had delighted in years before. The music Lozanov had researched for his two concert sessions contains the special high frequencies that bring you nonstop vitality. Teachers of Bulgarian Suggestology classes amazed observers with their radiant, bubbling energy. Along with their students, they listened to high-frequency music in the active and passive Lozanov concerts, much of it the identical music used for Sound Therapy. They had not only plenty of stamina to teach all day and evening but lots of energy left over for championship volleyball.

Father Lawrence found that the Walkman Sound Therapy treatment cured his insomnia. His energy bubbled over. He drove 2,500 miles nonstop without sleep. Joudry found that going mobile with the vitalizing sound was a total stress shield and opened new talents for her.

If the marvelous mind music could go mobile, it could reach thousands of people, Joudry thought. It had to be tested. Previously a technophobe, she soon became a sophisticated sound engineer, preparing a whole series of music cassettes featuring the soaring high frequencies, filtered bass, fluctuating ear dominance, and rerecording with the Electronic Ear high-low sound-burst patterns. "The music did it!" she says of her new technical abilities.

Joudry asked a number of people to test her tapes for several weeks; finally feedback began to pour in. Young and old spoke of "new energy, mental clarity, and creativity." Some reported relief of physical ills such as tinnitus and dizziness; even severe difficulties, brain damage, and Alzheimer's were said to improve. Though not a scientific test by any means, it seemed significant that people who'd plugged in to the high-frequency sounds on their own overwhelmingly emphasized that their memory, learning ability, and vitality had taken a great leap, even if they suffered from a range of learning disabilities.

The mobile music treatment, Joudry decided, could produce results for do-it-yourselfers. They were not the same results you'd get in a clinic with monitoring and testing by specialists, but the beneficial effects of the music were there and they did not wear off. She felt the taped music might be an inexpensive, nontoxic, no-side-effect way for some people to enhance mindpower and learning as well as ease stress in this era of rapid change.

In 1984 Joudry published her book—*Sound Therapy for the Walkman,* with an introduction by Yehudi Menuhin, who'd developed a special music therapy himself. She was inundated with worldwide requests for the high-frequency music tapes. The high-tech monks of Muenster worked endlessly at copying Joudry's cassettes in "real time" to be sure the high frequencies of the Electronic Ear were captured on metal tape. High-speed cassette duplicating machines suppress some of the ultra-high frequencies, as does the compact-disc process, they say. The monks made the previously restricted and little known Sound Therapy available to the general public from St. Peter's Press. Father Lawrence's and Joudry's vision of the evolutionary powers of music to heal and rebalance began to become a reality for thousands.

"Hyperactive," "impossible," "troublesome," "stupid"—those were just a few of the comments Mrs. G. Collingwood, of Tampa, Florida, heard about her third-grader son, Freddie. He listened to the

Sound Therapy tapes even in bed. Shortly he was off of Ritalin. Instead of disrupting class, he shot to the top of it. Talents sprouted even for math, in which he'd been rated "hopeless." "It was as though his brain had simply started working and his whole nervous system had calmed down. It was nothing short of a miracle," wrote his delighted mother.

A thirty-year-old school dropout reported that after a few months of Sound Therapy his mental abilities and memory were so improved that he'd passed his high school exams and now he'd finally gotten his diploma.

"It feels as if my mind has been put through a shower," wrote another. "Like having a new head," "the sound clarifies my mind to a high sheen," "overcame inappropriate dopiness," "sheer heaven," "glowing feeling," "tuned to the joy of life." People wrote from Canada, the United States, and twenty-six countries.

For Robert Rhodes, of Seattle, Washington, the immediate impact of Sound Therapy was economic. "My choice of jobs was very limited because of my poor reading," he said. All his life he'd longed to become a chef, but because of dyslexia he could not read the recipes. After Sound Therapy he passed a two-year cooking course with flying colors, got an excellent new job, and, with dyslexia gone, could read a book in the evening. "What a great pleasure!"

Maureen Imlach, a British Columbia music teacher, revealed that after a few months on the music "I am thinking more clearly. . . . I was amazed how quickly I relearned repertoire not played for *years.*" Fingers and muscles seemed to recall repertoire on their own, and she could play well *from memory* and *without practicing*.

Fellow author Dr. Cliff Bacchus reported, "My creative doors flew open. . . . I now sleep better, think better, write better." Even individuals who'd suffered severe injuries in accidents such as skull fractures, brain concussion, and coma were reported to be on the mend. Professionals, too, began using Sound Therapy. Just like music therapist Janalea Hoffman, who'd discovered that certain music helps patients get in touch with subconscious memories, Dr. Lois Plumb, of Toronto, a psychiatrist, used it to help patients recall and deal with repressed childhood trauma. The built-in stress shield cushioned painful recollections. Prison therapists also reported good results;

and schools found the tapes helped students with learning disabilities.

Cynthia Davis, of Rhode Island, wrote that her anxiety, depression, and fatigue decreased steadily, while her creativity and fiction writing abilities soared.

Bob Doman, of the National Association for Child Development, in Farmington, Utah, made Joudry's book and tapes available to a host of parents, who've seen "dramatic results." Parents saw their children's mindpower blossom as well as recovery from dyslexia, hyperactivity, and a range of problems.

Rollin Rose, of Riverside, California, speculated excitedly that Sound Therapy can make it "literally possible to leap from brilliant to genius." That's because Sound Therapy can help unblock neural pathways, Joudry explains. That's part of why high-frequency music is so powerful when it's applied to learning, she believes.

Surveying mail she's received so far, Joudry notes that "improvement in memory, concentration, retention and ease of learning is *invariably* reported by Sound Therapy listeners." It worked equally well for old and young, she insists. "The *one main* effect that almost everyone reports from Sound Therapy, regardless of the great variety of other conditions affected, is *stress relief,*" Joudry told us. People all observed the same reaction: "I am not stressed anymore. All the little things that used to make me uptight just seem to roll off me. I can shrug them off and not let them get to me."

Of course author mail is not a documented test by any means. Whether this taped music program could work on a large scale remains to be seen. On a personal note one of us tried Joudry's four high-frequency music tapes for well over the required one hundred hours of listening. We found the hissing noise slightly abrasive but got a tremendous energy charge from the tapes, which did indeed help with stress of all kinds.

Joudry and her daughter, Rafaele, who heads Sound Therapy Australia, are currently writing a new book to update what's happened in the decade since the Sound Therapy tapes were made available to a grassroots underground.

Worldwide, do-it-yourselfers trying out this high-frequency music were confirming what Lozanov and Bulgarian scientists had researched in secret so many decades ago: certain kinds of music, with very specific frequencies, harmonics, and complex structures, have startling powers to heal and empower us. And harnessing this music to the learning process is the route to evolutionary new mindpowers. Both Superlearning concerts—the slow Baroque and the high-frequency classical—help to do this.

Recently American researchers have begun to catch up. By fall 1993 headlines appeared in *USA Today:* MOZART'S MUSIC MAY SHARPEN THE MIND. Researchers at University of California–Irvine reported in *Nature* that when college students listened just for ten minutes to Mozart's Sonata for Two Pianos in D Major (K. 448) before taking a spatial IQ test, they scored eight to nine points higher than when they listened to a relaxation tape or silence. The complex structure of Mozart's music may help different parts of the brain talk to one another, assert investigators. Such a brief recharge with Mozart's music wore off in about fifteen minutes, they noted. Both Tomatis and Lozanov found that the special music has to be listened to for a much longer time to trigger long-lasting mind benefits.

Famous American neurologist Dr. Oliver Sachs, whose achievements were chronicled in the movie *Awakenings,* testified recently before a U.S. Senate committee on aging that "the power of music is *very* amazing." The right kind of music may be of special benefit to people with neurological disorders, he believes, and may even move those who can't walk to dance, those who can't speak to sing, those who can't remember to remember.

Joudry crisscrossed North America on lecture and promotional tours to let people know about the healing, vitalizing, mind-enhancing, and rebalancing powers of this special music, so needed at a time when vast numbers of people are overflowing with anger and violence.

"What's the greatest benefit of Sound Therapy music?" we asked her.

"It's the gift of time," Joudry replied. Through the music and the sound/brain connection you can accumulate the "fundamental currency—life energy." It's a different kind of "retirement saving program," she says. Instead of having your mental powers deteriorate with age, your ear can become your antenna for life force. Stimulation has been shown to keep memory alive in the elderly.

Joudry was especially thrilled with the same phenomenon Tomatis mentioned—supersleep—concentrated, doubly efficient sleep. Very little of it is needed because the mind and body are constantly being recharged through the music. Joudry calculates that supersleep can let you lengthen your life "time" by at least one sixth, a gift of many abundant years.

Today contemporary composers like Danish-American Dyveke Spino have begun composing instrumental music featuring ultrahigh frequencies that can help recharge and rebalance mindbody. This new music can be used for power listening or for the Lozanov "active" concert as a background to a dramatic reading of lesson material or for creative visualization exercises. Dyveke has combined her new compositions with learning, to create successful new workshops called "Education for the New Millennium." Her original and inspiring music is also featured as background music on Superlearning Sports Visualization tapes.

The various components that make up music can be summoned right now to help us sail stress-free into the 21st century:

- The anxiety-easing, memory-expanding 60-beat tempo, with its easy communication with the subconscious mind
- Specific key signatures that put us in resonance with other helpful elements in the universe
- "Beat" frequencies that help concentration
- High-frequency sounds that energize mindbody and heal a spectrum of problems

All these long-sought powers of music are ready and able to assist us today. Just by listening, they can provide you with an effortless route to new opportunities.

New Age music pioneer and author Steven Halpern, whose *Anti-Frantic Alternative* music tapes are classics, asserts, "Today, more than ever, music that serves to connect us with the source of our being-ness is vitally needed." Slow Baroque music and high-frequency music appear to provide a double dividend: Not only can they help us deal with learning and the stress of rapid change but through resonance and high-frequency harmonics they provide that energizing superlink to the cosmos to help us all.

The Superlearning "Active" Concert

The second Superlearning "Active" Concert features "up-tempo" ultrahigh-frequency classical music, such as violin concertos and symphonies by Mozart—the very same music used for Sound Therapy. To Superlearn with this music, you record the *full* text of your learning material over the music and when you listen to these tapes, your data is powered into your memory by these mind-vitalizing high-frequency sounds.

This is an "active" concert. You can listen while you're up and about instead of while you rest and relax. You can actively review your text material and highlight it with markers while listening. Or this second Superlearning concert can also go mobile. You can play this music with your recorded text on a Walkman anytime while you're on the run during your day's activities—while commuting or doing chores around the house or while waiting in lines. It's a genuine time-expander. You don't have to take time to get into a special relaxed state to listen as you do with the "passive" 60-beat memory-expanding concert.

This second Superlearning concert—especially if you use the Mozart selections—has ultrahigh frequencies of 7,000 to 8,000 hertz, which have been shown by Dr. Tomatis' research to give the fastest brain recharge. The 60-beat Superlearning string music has frequencies up to around 5,000 hertz. You use the full length symphony or concerto for the active concert, not just a section of a concerto as with the slow Baroque concert. Just playing this high-frequency music all by itself, even without your learning data combined with it, can pump up mind/memory. When your material *is* recorded over this high-powered music, the sequence of the music, the melodies, and the dynamics of it—the soft and loud segments and solo passages for different instruments—all mesh with your data to help anchor material in your memory.

You read aloud the whole text of a story, play, dialogue, or dramatized material to the "active" Superlearning concert music. It's a good idea to turn even technical material into a story or dialogue to make it more interesting (see page 277). To make your recording, you read aloud from your textbook dramatically and entertainingly with plenty of feeling. You make your voice loud or soft, depending on the music. This music is rich in dynamics and contrasts, so sometimes your story is linked with a strident trumpet, sometimes with a soft cello. You read faster or slower, also depending on the music, and pause after each sentence. When you listen to your recording, words and music get linked together in your mind. As the storyline meshes with different melodies in the music, it makes recall easier. Linking words and music this way, Dr. Lozanov found, helps link right and left hemispheres of the brain, and this gives the lesson material a global imprint in your memory.

When you listen to your recording of this Superlearning "Active" Concert, if your tape player has separate controls for each ear, turn down the left-ear and turn up the right-ear volume control to give your listening session "right-ear dominance."

As we described in *Superlearning,* when Lozanov and his colleagues initially developed this active concert, it called for a very elaborate, dramatic rendition of the text, one that often required special training to perform. But now Superlearning users report that just plain reading data aloud over this special music also gives excellent results. Some Bulgarian centers have used the paced reading of four-second data chunks over this active music, too, with good results. There are many variants and they all work well. The high-frequency music itself seems to do the job of energizing mindpower and balancing mindbody. Superlearning pioneer Bruce Tickell Taylor has been logging exceptional results for years with this mobile high-frequency concert. (See Chapter 30.)

Clients of OptimaLearning in Novato, California, regularly use the dramatic "active" concert reading technique. Victor Ruiz, program manager at Hewlett-Packard, reports he found the concert reading method "extremely helpful" for preparing speeches and formal presentations for large audiences. "My experience is that when I use these techniques, I don't need any notes, because I completely trust my memory."

Many Western Superlearning teachers found this second concert too long to fit regular class schedules. But by recording the "active" concert on tape, it can go mobile on a Walkman, so students can play it anywhere without using up classroom time.

When you use the "active" concert in the classroom, the teacher reads the text dramatically over the music while students actively follow the text and make notes on it or highlight it with colored markers. Some teachers shorten this "active" concert and some have students listen outside of class. In a class session the "active" concert comes first and is then followed by the "passive" slow Baroque memory-reinforcement concert. Students lean back, relax, and get into the optimal state for learning, then listen to the data read, this time in paced, four-second "sound-bite" chunks.

Physiological research in Bulgarian and Soviet labs charted the exceptional mental and physical benefits from this classical music long before Dr. Tomatis began his groundbreaking experiments. They found in particular that Mozart's music gave high-power results in this "active" concert. It seemed to energize learning and rebalance the body. Right from the beginning, when Suggestopedia was introduced, there were headlines about the "active" concert too. "Math with Mozart" paid big learning dividends, Soviet Bloc newspapers reported.

The "active" concert is used by a number of U.S. and European Superlearning centers, particularly those offering the basic Lozanov method. If you would like to use the "active" Superlearning concert, see page 284 for more tips and a list of music selections. If you're working on your own, record yourself reading your lesson material as dramatically as possible over the music. Play it back later on a headset player as a study aid. Just playing the high-frequency music by itself while studying has also helped to amp up learning for many people. It can bring you some of the same exciting mindbody benefits that Sound Therapy users report.

10
The Business of Change

A chunk of rubble, once part of the Berlin Wall, poses a graffiti question to all who pass by: "And who will break down the walls in people's heads?" It's the right question as far as Dr. Otto Altorfer is concerned. Serving Japan Airlines as director and chief instructor of training and education for the Americas, he long ago began developing ways to boost workers over the walls of the mind to new freedom.

Well published, well regarded internationally, Otto Altorfer is a different sort of Superlearning pioneer. Rather than training people to pick up data quickly, he teaches them how to accelerate change. A warm, dark-haired man, born and educated in Switzerland, he already considered employees something other than cogs to be fine tuned; he specialized in helping them to "emotional literacy" to enhance both productivity and job satisfaction.

As a corporate trainer Altorfer was intrigued by news of Superlearning and ran an indepth study. "The proofs were compelling," he reported. "Learning can indeed be substantially accelerated." But something else was even more compelling, something Altorfer noticed when he joined executives and salespeople to experience the Superlearning core techniques: relaxation, music, imagery, rhythm, suggestion, communication to the whole mind. Accelerated learning isn't just a mechanical matter of right pacing or 60-beat music, Altorfer realized. It is a process that turns attention inward where one can reach, as he says, "reserves of energy leading to profound transformation." Just what he was looking for! Altorfer longed to make a dent in one of the most crucial, often life and death problems facing business today. How can employees and organizations overcome resistance to change?

The Bureaucracy of the Mind

Why do we so often make New Year's resolutions to lose weight, stop smoking, or spend more time with the kids, and then find ourselves making the same resolutions the next year? Why does the same thing happen in corporations? Recognizing that a more autonomous, more open structure is vital for company growth, managers spend weeks on a restructuring plan. But back on the job they behave in the same old authoritarian way. A supervisor knows full well that prejudice and favoritism are counterproductive at work. Yet he still looks down on certain people. "It's my nature." That's what many consultants say of seemingly intractable resistance to change in the workplace and establishments generally. "It's the nature of the beast." Not so, says Altorfer. We find change so difficult, we only accomplish it superficially because we need an attitude adjustment. And not the kind advertised five to seven by the local pub.

Does bureaucracy drive you up the wall? The one that may be frustrating you most is one you hardly notice, the one on twenty-four-hour duty inside your head. Every one of us is loaded with automatic operating programs. If we weren't, we'd have to keep reinventing the wheel in a host of everyday situations. How do I drive the car? What do I say to a new customer? How do I make love? Unconscious patterns, habits, automaticities, beliefs, state dependent memories patterning mind and body—there are a lot of names for these generally helpful programs playing along below awareness. Altorfer calls them *attitudes*. When your conscious decisions and unconscious attitudes are in sync, you're in business. You feel whole, capable. When they're not, you begin to feel stressed, inadequate, frustrated.

"The discrepancy between what we know and what we do is often striking," Altorfer's team noted. Experts unaccountably trip themselves up in their own specialties. Technically competent people drag down their success with swings of confidence and mood, senior employees become demotivated. And though people from top to bottom declare, "I'm all for it," there is resistance to change. That's the automated bureaucracy in people's heads at work, according to Altorfer, like any bureaucracy determined to keep to its hidebound routine.

This is why McDonald's, for one, will often advertise for new employees "no experience necessary" when it wants to institute a new procedure. It's easier to hire the untaught than change the old. It's a strong reason too for the corporate nudge to early retirement. But we're in a day where even the elder statesman of management gurus Peter Drucker is saying things like "Every organization has to abandon everything it does." Band-Aid solutions won't fuel the next leap in productivity, and to Altorfer's mind neither will intellect, technology, or technical skill. "Clearly we have now to look to the subconscious mind of people—that's where the action is."

Altorfer came up with a protocol for "self-validating," a form of self-suggestion business people use to get in touch with their unconscious attitudes and bring them into sync with their conscious goals. You don't have to be in business to have it work for you.

Self-Validating

Get into a relaxed state and perhaps play some soft, suggestive music in the background. Breathe deeply and easily as you choose something you'd like to change. Maybe you're sick and tired (literally) of finding work a struggle. You'd really like to enjoy work. Take a long sheet of paper and at the top on the left side, write "Validation"; on the right, "Response." You'll write your new affirmation over and over in the first column under Validation. For example, "I, John, experience work always as a total pleasure." (Or you might want to substitute *learning* for *work*.) You'll use three voices over and over. "I, John, find . . ." "You find . . . ," and "John finds. . . ."

If that's all you do with affirmations, you won't get far, Altorfer contends. It's crucial to listen to the comments echoing from attitudes in your unconscious. You might get thoughts like: "Work's boring." "It keeps me from doing what I want." "Dad told me work was no fun." If you're quiet, feedback is almost guaranteed, as anyone will attest to who's tried the popular affirmation "I am *very* wealthy. I am *very* wealthy." Unless you're a Ross Perot, pretty soon you hear a little voice say, "Naah, you're not!"

After you write an affirmation on the left side of the page, write any objection that rises on the right side. Take your time. Objections are normal. They open communication to the subliminal mind. Most important, they begin to pinpoint which unconscious attitudes need adjustment. You may get some surprises. Like others in the mind arena, Altorfer instructs people not to deny the contentious responses. Acknowledge them and treat them with respect. At one time these patterns came into being to serve you. Fighting is self-defeating, it only pumps energy into the old pattern. Calmly, patiently, without judgment, just affirm and affirm. You might think of yourself as Michelangelo chipping, chipping away at the block of stone, bit by bit freeing the "David" within.

Take time to imagine vividly how you'll feel, Altorfer tells clients, and what things will be like when your affirmation becomes part of your working program. Write your affirmation over and over ten to fifteen minutes twice a day for four days. That's enough to seed it, Altorfer says, adding that you should begin to experience the good effects of a new unconscious attitude, a new operating program, in about two to three weeks.

Altorfer feels so strongly about the snowballing need to equip people for change, that he retired to found the Center for Research and Education in Attitude Dimensions in South San Francisco. As walls keep tumbling down, demands for his training increase. But what about this sort of attitude adjustment? "I feel powerless toward authority" washes away with "I feel greatly honored taking orders." That's not brainwashing, Altorfer insists. It's choice. Neither the boss nor anyone else can impose attitude management on you. It's actually a move toward greater autonomy in the workplace, he contends, another ripple in the rising shift to self-reliance.

Altorfer's technique works from the inside out in corporations too. First the individual learns to manage change. Then transformation of the organization is more likely to follow. As we hurtle into the 21st century, Altorfer predicts that apart from all the business of business, companies will need to equip employees to manage their unconscious workings "in order to maintain health and sanity for the individual and prosperity for the corporations."

In other words what is good for General Motors may not be good for the country, particularly its rather stunning mismanagement of change. We may have come to a time when what is liberating for the employee is liberating for the corporation.

Don't Be a Willbe

Altorfer's validations are designed for the workplace. Outside the office you can choose more lively modes of affirming. A surprisingly powerful technique is to stand and deliver your affirmations in front of a mirror. Look yourself squarely in the eye. Speak with conviction; convince that person in the mirror that you really mean what you're saying. Let that person reflect the affirmation back to you in an authoritative, commanding way.

Remember, the creative memory that makes us who we are is a full-bodied affair. You can set up a new memory circuit a lot faster if you use all your senses. Say your affirmations aloud. Shout them out, whisper them confidentially. Or sing along. Pull up the appropriate emotions. If you enjoy learning like a kid, skip, jump, march down the street to them, do aerobics, dance. Paste Post-its, or sketch them. When you smell something heady or tasty, say them. Have fun while you saturate yourself. An expert like Louise Hay, whose books and columns have brought the healing power of self-suggestion to a huge public, often advises saying a suggestion three or four hundred times a day.

A warm surround of positive suggestion is the hallmark of Superlearning classes. Direct suggestions are usually given during relaxation or at the end of mental mini-vacations. Most suggestions have to do, of course, with the learning at hand, but there is a root suggestion that has proved its ability over and over to open the avenue to optimal performance: anything that bolsters self-esteem. If yours could use a boost, before going to specifics, work a suggestion such as "I love myself," or "I am a unique and valuable human being," or "I am totally adequate at all times," or "I am worthy of the best life has to offer." If you hear some catcalls from your unconscious, take note.

Give yourself a few good positive prompts as you prepare to learn or perform. After all, it's been written, "Ask and you shall receive." Affirming one's good is as old as history, maybe older, and it brings results. The new wrinkle today is that we know more about how mindbody works. Two things help affirmations kick in faster: First, shape and deliver affirmations correctly. Second, give them room to breathe by doing some housecleaning and getting rid of negative or obsolete "affirmations." "I don't deserve it" is as much an affirmation as "I deserve the best in life." (For housecleaning hints, see Chapter 14.)

As you probably know, affirm in the positive. Don't say, "Learning *isn't* hard." Affirm, "Learning is easier and easier for me." (Or "Learning fills me with vitality." "I feel alive when I'm learning." "Learning is safe." "I learn and remember like a sponge.")

Affirm in the present tense; it's the only time you've got. "I will remember my speech." "I will be a great tennis player." Think about it. The future never comes. Being a "willbe" is chasing that carrot on a stick. People who say, "When my ship comes in, I will . . ." wind up like the old merchants of Venice, endlessly scanning the horizon. Their treasure-laden galleons forever sink into the deeps of the unconscious reserved for "not now" events. Remember, the unconscious doesn't know what time it is. It knows only now. Engage its strength by telling it what you are now. "I am a great tennis player." "I remember my speech."

Once in a very great while suggestion can turn into almost too good a friend, as one executive found with Teri Mahaney's "Change Your Mind" suggestions. "My client said something eerie was going on," Mahaney told us. "He would be talking with his boss and suddenly blank out as if he were deaf. Occasionally the same things happened spontaneously with other people." A hearing test showed nothing wrong. Could it be the tape? The instigator turned out to be a protective line Mahaney adds to scripts: "You accept the messages that are healing and for your highest good, dissolving all else."

"That's what he was doing," Mahaney says, "providing himself instant conscious feedback on which messages were for his good and which weren't!" A little adjustment relaxed the newly aroused, protective subliminal self. It was a funny, minor kink in the business-man's changeover to a more productive life, a kink giving dramatic evidence that suggestion, particularly when combined with the Superlearning format, is a premier way to contact your deep self and get it wholeheartedly behind the business of change. "All pain is resistance to change," the Buddha taught. Why wait until you're really hurting to start navigating the changes on the way to your 21st century job?

11
Fireworks at Work

"The ideas of accelerated learning set off fireworks for me," says Helmut Huttenrauch, chief trainer for Phillips Communications Industry of Nürnberg. He first heard about it in a German seminar led by Dr. Charles Schmid, of San Francisco, another pioneering teacher who helped wake up the world to the new approach. "I was spellbound," Huttenrauch says. "I was renewed and excited by the concepts—wholistic learning that releases creativity and joy— training that takes human needs into consideration." He was inspired to set up a Superlearning center at the Phillips Training Academy that has been successfully hatching computer programmers and other high-tech workers since 1989.

Something seismic is going on in how most of us earn or will soon earn a living. The rapidly webbing, new infrastructure— digitally coded information coursing at the speed of light—is bringing what one business magazine after another calls "fundamental change," a "radical shift," and, if you're in the middle of it, a feeling that "the entire corporate world seems to be going crazy." The blue collar is going the way of the celluloid collar. There is continuing pressure to drop the old ways, learn new skills, and often to totally change careers. Phillips' Huttenrauch believes the balanced, humane, stress-easing mode of accelerated training is the best way to navigate through the chaos. It's a course that can smooth the way for more than technicians. Managers and executives are being forced to relinquish the comfort of old-shoe corporate culture, and to rethink their talents and options too. At the same time increasing battalions are working in small entrepreneurial teams or on their own. To have the mental and emotional flexibility to work and live well, people need to feel confident in their ability to develop a portfolio of skills. To be literate in the new marketplace, you need a new kind of basics, the basic equipment of a first-class, lifelong learner. You won't get it from horse-and-buggy education.

Superlearning first caught corporate eyes to answer a need that isn't new. Even before we got out of the starting gate, the CEO of the largest chemical company in Canada phoned. He'd gotten wind that we'd found a rapid, new method of learning in the Communist lands. He wouldn't have been a CEO if he didn't know that fast, stress-free training—if it really worked—could save enormous amounts of money. The stress control benefits alone mean less absenteeism from stress-generated illnesses (a cost now estimated in the billions). The bottom line: Superlearning saves time and money, and today that means *mega-savings*. Training has become the lifeblood of industry because things change so fast. Bill Fisher, manager of Education Marketing at Pioneer New Media Technologies, notes that corporate America already spends about $30 billion per year on worker training.

Technical innovations are becoming like the fabled dragon's teeth. As soon as you get hold of one, ten more pop up. What do you do if, like C. L. Hallmark, of AT&T's National Product Training Center, you have to retrain older workers who've had a long time to get used to established ways of doing and learning? "I was a little worried about some of the crusty old-timers. Many had been out of school for decades," Hallmark admitted to us after he arranged to use some Superlearning Music. He had to make employees letter perfect in handling something new and difficult: complex control boards full of alarms that light up if a phone system goes wrong. "Information must be ingrained in the workers' minds to allow prompt response to trouble," Hallmark says of these failsafe boards. Superlearning saw to the ingraining. Hallmark's team found it "well adapted to our needs and a useful technique for training in this push-button world." Built-in stress relief was a plus that employees really appreciated, Hallmark reported.

Sales and marketing people can get an accelerated boost too. Professionals at Hewlett-Packard in California and at Racal-Redac, an international computer firm in Massachusetts, for instance, grabbed hold of Ivan Barzakov's OptimaLearning to "enhance ability to communicate insights and results," "to completely trust my memory and speak without notes," "to make fast, accurate decisions in changing situations."

Accelerated learning seems almost custom-made to help the handicapped upgrade work skills, something that appealed to Dr. Carl Schleicher, of Mankind Research Foundation, Washington, D.C., who withstood a circus of negotiations to secure the rights to Lozanov Learning from the old Bulgarian government. Apart from working with industry and securing a number of U.S. government contracts, Schleicher's group teamed with business to train the blind in computer programming and other skills. The project, the first of its kind in the country, proved so successful for over a decade at providing effective, low cost, accelerated, and stress-free computer training for the disabled that it won an award from the President's Commission for the Handicapped (see page 342).

Like Hallmark at AT&T, individual trainers in many companies— Westinghouse, Bell Atlantic, NYNEX, Eastman-Kodak, Occidental Chemical, Avon, Cincinnati Bell, U.S. Postal Service, Safeway, Ryder Truck Rental (Canada), to rattle through a few—have adapted accelerated programs or at least some of the core techniques—slow Baroque and mind mapping, relaxation and guided imagery—to shift employees into a 21st century mode.

Love and marriage, education and business—they've always had a stake in each other. Now the ante has been raised by "a change in mind-set or, inevitably of paradigm," as business writer Walter Kiechel calls it, demanded by the emerging economy. You could see the change in Boston at the 1993 SALT Conference cosponsored by New England Telephone and the Minnesota Chapter of the American Society of Training and Development. Until recently SALT, a group of visionary academics and teachers, wasn't sponsored by anyone. Most of its members didn't get much support either in their home schools, staffed with tenured resistance to change. Over one hundred presenters from two dozen countries took center stage in Boston. The majority were still teachers, but many have taken their talents to an arena more friendly to innovation than school boards.

The dynamic 1993 president of SALT, Libyan Cassone, is one. Cassone began her career teaching Spanish at Harvard, MIT, and Tufts. Then she encountered Lozanov Learning, and the fireworks began. She became an entrepreneur. Now president of 21st Century Learning Systems of Minneapolis, her company provides accelerated workshops for a wide variety of businesses. She and her husband, Philip, an expert marketer, also run SpeakEasy Languages and Accelerated Learning Systems.

Save time, save money, that was the initial attractor. Now something else is beginning to happen in businesses that employ Superlearning, something that may prove even more beneficial in the way we will work in the next century. Employee efficiency goes up; motivation is increased; employee relations and the workplace climate improve; the trainee's whole self is transformed through the humanizing effects of this type of learning. "So go the trainees, so goes the corporation—the entire system is enhanced in positive ways," reports *New Horizons for Learning*.

Mainstreaming

A proven, cost-effective method, accelerated training is still far from commonplace in the United States. To see Superlearning mainstreamed in business and industry, look to the Germans. They already have the advantage of an elaborate network of training centers linked with industry throughout the country that continually turns out highly skilled workers.

"The information explosion has *forced* new ways of learning," says Helmut Huttenrauch, of Phillips training center. Here, to learn computer programming, trainees walk a roped path through a computer made of cards on the floor so that they grasp visually, physically, and psychologically the inner workings of a computer program. Later a slow Baroque concert review helps anchor the technical data deeply in memory. Workers like the relaxing concert so much, a rebellion occurred when a trainer omitted it. Employees not only learned far faster but had better social skills and teamwork as well as sheer pleasure in performance.

It's unusual to hear business trainers talking about "the greater development of humankind," but Huttenrauch does, emphasizing that beyond picking up know-how, this approach gives you "the chance of developing your own personality, creativity, openness, guts and joy of living."

Across the world in Malaysia, another trainer, Jafni Zainal, who works with engineers, state police, and the reading disabled, came to the same conclusion, contending that "Superlearning can create better people for a better world."

"Training time is money," says Dr. Dieter Jaehrling, leader of the main training centers of automobile manufacturer Audi in Ingolstadt and Neckarsulm. Here accelerated training has saved major time and Deutsche marks for many years. Savings come too from fewer sick days, the happy result, Jaehrling says, of relief of "angst and stress" built right into Superlearning.

It's humanitarian as well as cost saving to use wholistic methods that promote health, Jaehrling believes. He insists that good health is essential to on-the-job productivity, so essential that he has added autogenic training to the programs to enable workers to take control of their own well being. Autogenics could save German industry millions, he notes, just by cutting down on alcoholism.

"Discover *Fahrvergnugen*," the Volkswagen / Audi car ads urge, building a campaign around the German word for "driving pleasure." The *Vergnugen*, the "pleasure," is built right in at Audi, starting right off with how autoworkers pick up the tricks of their trade. "Fun Generates Learning," their training publications reveal, as Superlearning teaches the how-to of the latest Audi robots, lathes, electronics, welding methods, motor-vehicle mechanics, and electrical systems. Workers also learned Spanish and English. Educating the whole person led to more creative and motivated employees, trainers report.

In the former East Germany, which helped pioneer Suggestopedia, the system is still being used to help the transition. "Superlearning has a special appeal for the citizens of the old GDR because of its humanistic effect, its holistic and personal atmosphere, and the respect for the learning personality, which they experience as new and fascinating," Dr. Hartmut Wagner told us.

A Superlearning program run by Wagner's SKILL team at the IBM Training Center in Herrenberg brought typical feedback: "The most pleasant course I have attended in sixteen years with IBM."

It's not just trainees who benefit. Gail Heidenhain, a longtime force in the German Suggestopedic society (DGSL) and partner in the Delphin training company, points out, "Training of the teachers is taken very seriously in Germany. The two main emphases are the personal development of the teacher and the development of confidence in teaching suggestopedically. You teach what you are." Techniques from many fields are used, she told us, to help trainers "look at their own belief systems, overcome their own barriers to learning and teaching and discover and develop their *own* potential. Only then can they recognize barriers to learning and potential in students."

One man is responsible for over a thousand of these Superlearning trainers now populating dozens of blue chip German companies like Hewlett-Packard, Opel, Goodyear, and several powerful trade unions, Dr. Hartmut Wagner, founder of the SKILL-Training Institute of Heidelberg. For several years now Wagner's trainers have been helping many thousands of Germans work smarter, not harder, netting them better pay and longer vacations.

Wagner, after reading the German edition of *Superlearning* (and throwing the book across the room because he thought it was all hype!), tentatively tested out the method for language training at a Heidelberg private high school. A stress-control exercise! The initial reaction was giggles. Gradually students got the hang of it. "I was really flying," said one. Results were really flying too. On strict tests students who'd been weak averaged 92 percent. Students tested on multiple-choice exams got 100 percent.

"The method was so impressive and fascinating that I plan to expand its use," Wagner wrote after his initial probe a decade ago. Expand it he did, ending up with the leading Superlearning center in Germany with a staff of thirty-four. Wagner's expertise was featured in a popular German TV documentary film on Superlearning that's being shown from Nürnberg to Barcelona. (For Wagner's business training techniques and those of others, see Chapter 28.)

Helping Yourself

Most of us don't call the ultimate shots where we work, but in this do-it-yourself decade we can still equip ourselves and our children to surf the new wave. And that's the first thing to learn in your gut. It really is a new wave. Even when the ecomony bellows full bull, it won't be the same. John Naisbitt and Patricia Aburdene, the trend takers who "plead guilty of cheerfulness," recently noted an oddity: technically, for a number of years running, we haven't been in a recession. "But *psychologically* we've been in quite a recession," they say. "Now we have to talk ourselves out of it." It might help if we realized that our distress may rise from a deeper sort of worldwide recession. The old era is drawing away, like a great wave withdrawing its support, tumbling our lives like shells on the beach in its wake. The trick now is to be in a position to catch the new wave.

Stephen Barley, of Cornell's School of Industrial and Labor Relations, points out that the new knowledge workers—the technicians, specialists, and armies involved in service professions—admit they don't get much from formal education. For example, microcomputer support specialists "piece together bits and pieces from the forefront of technology and then try to integrate it with the needs of their organization. What you see them doing is scrambling to stay on top of change," says Barley. This is the new alive-at-work-and-play meaning of lifelong learning, and it's something Superlearning and its sister systems can equip you to do well. Whether your organization provides Superlearning training or not, triple-fast retraining for new opportunities can easily be a do-it-yourself project. It will stand you in good stead, too, particularly if, like so many others in the next millennium, you catch the self-employment roller coaster.

When Dr. Tatiana Radonjic-Matano took a course in entrepreneurship, she realized something was missing—the techniques to learn and change quickly. Proving herself immediately as an entrepreneur, she arranged to add her accelerated learning course to the necessary business training.

If you've never tried free-lancing, take heart. *Business Week*'s Ray Hoffman reports that a recent survey revealed that 67 percent of self-employed Americans find themselves "very satisfied" with life. Only 47 percent who called someone else boss felt "satisfied."

"Be all you can be"—some of the troops seem to be taking the slogan to heart. Top brass were intrigued with Superlearning from the beginning, in the 1970s. When we were asked to speak at the Institute for Defense Analysis, a think-tank group for the Pentagon, questions about Superlearning were a top priority. The military has used it to speed learning of weapons systems, languages, even for basic literacy skills.

Still, an entrepreneur who sells only to military bases told us that when he first began selling educational courses a decade ago, he had to give the *Superlearning* book away as a premium to the rank and file. Then bases began closing. Thousands are being thrust into the not-so-assured civilian workforce. "Now Superlearning's hot," he tells us. "Very hot."

In the same vein, when twenty-one New York City cops signed up for Dr. Radonjic-Matano's Superlearning course, she was surprised at how many were in school preparing for a second career after their twenty years in the force. The cops quickly realized that the stress-relief techniques could not only help with exams but could also be a saving grace as they worked the front lines in the Big Apple. Radonjic-Matano showed them how to incorporate learning into everyday activities—like swinging in rhythm to a learning rap, as they walk the beat.

Beyond learning data and skills and passing exams, there's another way the core techniques of accelerated learning can expand your success in the new workforce. "The system is humane," trainers say. "It develops the whole person." As you flood away hang-ups and blocks, as you value and use your senses and imagination, build self-reliance and self-esteem, you're going to become better at human relations, part of the new bottom line. Dennis Hartley, general manager of Hewlett-Packard's microwave instruments division, is a new-style leader focusing on interacting with his people. "I'm probably spending seventy-five percent of my energy on matters that could be called corporate culture. I don't think people really enjoy change, but if they can participate in it and understand it, it can become a positive for them." The people-relating-to-people approach is heading into the field too; much of the quality being built back into American products involves service.

Another rising star, Rebecca McDonald, president of Tenneco's natural gas marketing subsidiary, remarks, "You hear a lot of talk about changing the way we teach little girls because they're taught to listen and accommodate, while little boys are taught to win at all costs. I wonder if, really, we shouldn't rethink the way we're teaching boys. The rigidity that comes from expecting to win at all costs doesn't necessarily play to the new skill sets for corporate America." It may be interesting that of the many new wave execs John Huey interviewed for his *Fortune* cover story, "Managing in the Midst of Chaos," it was the female McDonald who seemed to be having the best time, enjoying, she said, "a chance to do everything over. How can that not be exciting?"

It's good to realize that the whirlwind taking us off to a new world and a new millennium, the Information Age, isn't so much about the torrent of data that slides past us. It's about a global, electronic infrastructure that is bringing a whole new organization to life. If we do it right, an expansive, liberating organization. Many will no longer be tied to a particular place to work, or punch in from nine to five. Almost anyone will be able to log into this expanding global brain, interact, add their own two cents. Seen from the coal mine or assembly line, this is playing like the gods. If we do it right, it should give you a lot more freedom, beyond the thrills of virtual reality, to smell the real red roses. A key to doing it right is keeping awake to the snowballing new routes to opening those ever-closer-at-hand resources of the human mind. We're just starting to know how to Superlearn.

Experts agree: the new world currency is knowledge. Knowledge and the ability to learn easily for a lifetime are the gold coins and venture capital of the future.

12
The Senses
of Learning

In the little town of Sixt, perched high in the French Alps, sounds of foot stomping and laughter pealed through the crisp Alpine air. The happy sounds issued from a kindergarten room in a picturesque 16th century building. Yet the students, at least in looks, were far from children. They were teachers who'd come from Finland, the United States, Italy, and South Africa to immerse themselves in the techniques of accelerated learning under the orchestration of master trainer Jenny Vanderplank. Perhaps it was the old room itself that had soaked up centuries of childish mirth that so affected the teachers—whatever... under Vanderplank's tutelage they were suddenly experiencing life with a child's fresh eyes and senses. At the moment they had burst into a spontaneous dance—the Mangrove swamp—with each teacher dancing out a different part of the swamp's complex ecosystem.

Vanderplank's students could have danced a lesson too if they'd stepped to that old routine that climaxes, "Put your whole self in and shake it all about!" The infinite variety of your senses, the colors of your emotions are part of Superlearning with your whole self. All of your senses live in a memory. The more senses you evoke while learning, the more anchors you will have to hold that learning in memory. The more routes you will have to call it back. A snatch of a melody and suddenly you're transported back to forgotten places, other faces. The Marine Band strikes up "The Star-Spangled Banner" and the words smartly march to mind. Try reciting them without the music. When golden oldies play, scores of long forgotten words drift effortlessly back into consciousness. Hearing, particularly music, hooks memory. So can smell, sometimes almost overwhelmingly.

Catch the scent of your mother's favorite perfume, or even the acrid chemical odor of a long gone toilet cleaner, and a world of memory flashes up on the instant. Superlearning pioneer Dr. Rosella Wallace speaks of an Alaskan teacher who swears by scented color markers. Her young students use lemon-scented yellow markers for spelling, cherry-scented red markers for arithmetic. When a spelling quiz arrives, they reach for a lemon-scented pen and a little extra memory. When Dr. Mary Lang, of the University of Idaho, began mini Superlearning lessons with her two-year-old son, she took care to dab him with a bit of perfume. These women aren't just running on folklore. Researchers have pegged down scientifically what most of us know by experience. At Yale, Dr. Frank Staub did it with mouth watering flair.

Staub asked his psychology students to study a string of vocabu- ✗ lary words. As they poured over the list, a heavy, sweet scent, the scrumptious, saliva-tingling aroma of chocolate, began to pervade the room. Though Staub hadn't told his students to memorize the words, two days later he checked to see how many they did recall. Once again the sweet smell of chocolate wafted in the air—for half the group. The others had to remember in plain old academic air. Staub also had a no-chocolate control group for both learning and testing. Chocoholics delight! Those who sniffed chocolate during both learning and testing remembered significantly better than either of the two chocolate-deprived groups.

Staub suggests associating different odors with different subjects you're learning. How about peaches for poetry, mothballs for math, garlic for geometry? Keep in mind, though, that for the memory boost you need the odor when you take the test or give a report.

Researchers at Bishop's University, in Quebec, also found that smell enhanced verbal memory. They treated students to Ralph Lauren perfume or jasmine incense. Memory evoking did not depend on which scent the students smelled; again the key was sniffing the same aroma when learning and remembering.

Scenting wider possibilities, Frank Staub decamped to industry. Among other things, he's working on using a sharp smell when training airplane cockpit crews in emergency procedures. The scenario: emergency strikes; the smell goes off with the warning lights, prompting the crew to react and remember in the fastest possible time. Unlike other senses, smell speeds directly to the brain. It's a quick trigger, one you can also use to summon a peak-performance state when you have to rise quickly to an occasion.

Can smells, like different kinds of music and sound, influence different parts of you? The ancients thought so. As the renaissance of mindbody-altering music blossoms, the aromatherapists are not far behind. Psychologists at Cambridge and University College of North Wales have begun some of the first clinical tests of aromatherapy. They exposed twenty-two people to chamomile oil and a placebo. Whiffs of chamomile and people's ability to summon vivid, positive imagery increased significantly. Chamomile also lightened people's moods and diminished their ability to conjure dreary, depressing scenes. Will orchestrated aromas someday swirl with Baroque symphonies in Superlearning classes?

Taste, too, can reinforce memory, as the late *New Yorker* writer A. J. Liebling knew. Reflecting on a glorious year he'd spent as a student in Paris thirty-five years earlier, Liebling wrote of a favored wine at the Restaurant des Beaux Arts. "A half bottle of Tavel superieur was 3.50 francs; I can still see the figure when I close my eyes, written in purple ink on the cheap, grayish paper of the carte. This is a mnemonic testimonial to how good the wine was."

"Tell the Juggler"

There is another sense wholeheartedly active in learning, the modus operandi of one of the three major ways people process information. Do you prefer to get needed info from a book, a report, a video screen? Then you lean toward visual processing. If you'd rather listen to a lecture, a tape, or the grapevine, you tend toward auditory processing. Maybe you like to get the feel of things or you push for hands-on experience. Then you favor kinetic/emotional processing. This relies on your sense of touch, your body motion, and emotion. No matter what your natural preference, you'll be a stronger learner if you elicit all three ways and pay particular attention to the usually ignored kinetic/emotional sense. To tap the power of this sense, sketch or paint new data and concepts. Write down as well as say a new word. Sense the beat, the rhythm of a phrase. Develop muscle memory.

Superlearning classes evoke the kinetic/emotional sense when they play games, dance, act out, or walk through problems or new experience, such as stepping through the hexagonal ring of a benzene molecule to learn chemistry. To "avoid boring computer mavens without losing the most computer craven," Peter Ginn has taken "acting out" to off-Broadway proportions.

Though Ginn's an engineer working at Dow Chemical under the big sky of Texas, his wit as well as his accent are pure products of his native Britain. If ever you have to face the difficult, often dreaded task of understanding computers from the inside out and learning assembly language, it might be worth the trip to Brazosport College in South Texas, where Ginn teaches a three credit course. The first evening you'll find the class arranged like a TV studio full of colorful posters—four sprightly Chinese jugglers and FLAGS, the dazzling performing dog, artfully created by Ann Ginn, the professor's wife. After a little relaxation, as Baroque music plays, Ginn softly reads you a text to bring the posters alive—AHLX, a juggler; IP, a Vanna White–type hostess; an illusionist named INTERRUPT. Before you know it, you find yourself a contestant in the game show "Tell the Juggler." "Anyone can play," Ginn says, "you don't even have to know how to turn on a computer."

Teams assemble, placards with arcane symbols, MVI, HLT, are passed out. Short games begin. You find yourself holding up placards at the right moment or, up on stage, going through a sequence of movements with the rest of the cast. Games are programs, and the cast acts out writing, loading, and running the programs.

"After the first class," Ginn says, "any student will be able to describe how the IBM PC's microprocessor works. In four classes forty-one concepts and fifty-plus syntactically correct assembly-language instructions are learned." Retention runs about 90 percent, enthusiasm 100 percent. Not just at Brazosport but in demos across the land, Ginn wrote us, "People are so excited to understand something as difficult as a computer in such a simple, aesthetic way that their enthusiasm is tangible!" This from a man who used to take care not to stand by the door at the end of class to avoid being stampeded to the parking lot. "The very first night of the accelerated class, forty-five minutes after dismissal, I finally had to shoo some home."

Before Ginn went accelerated, about half the students would drop the course and a couple usually failed the finals. "The first time out in the accelerated class, twenty-one registered, twenty sat the final, and no one failed." The dropout wrote Ginn a letter of apology. "That never happened before in ten years of part-time teaching," Ginn told us. Neither did being approached by students asking for an advanced assembly course.

Superlearning techniques weave through homework too. "Relax physically and mentally and go over your review sheet for ten minutes max," Ginn instructs. "Review before going to sleep the night of class, the next day, two days later, and in the twenty-four hours before the next class." (An ideal review schedule for any sort of learning.) For homework Ginn's students write their own twelve-instruction game and act it out imaginatively in their mind's eye, describing aloud what they see. After sixteen hours of game playing, confident students move into the lab to finger keyboards and learn DOS, also boosted with accelerated methods.

"Exhilarated." Even though he's put in a full day's work before, that's how Ginn feels after class. "I'm very excited about the potential. . . . The future is going to be fun." Exhilaration, maybe, but most emotions are too gushy, too unreliable, to admit into the classroom according to traditional ideas. They cloud intellect and confuse learning. That's a mistake that can knock the legs out from under your memory. Recent research reveals that emotion and memory, like eternal lovers, are impossible to disentwine. They live together in the "golden room," as ancient Taoists called it, the mid-brain, where feelings are intimately involved in encoding memory. (Some of the memory enhancing effect of Superlearning Music comes from the emotions stirred by sublime music.)

Which do you remember better—Shakespeare's *Julius Caesar* or a textbook treatise on Rome? *Gone With the Wind*'s Atlanta in flames or the notes from a history class? Part of the memory surge is the high-voltage emotional content in play and movie. Really, we learn what we feel like learning. When you amputate feeling from learning, you can wind up with cram memory: here-for-the-test-today-and-gone-tomorrow learning. Brain investigator Dr. Elaine de Beauport, founder of the successful experimental Meade School, in Connecticut, points out, "Feelings take on very pragmatic significance when we realize long term memory is based on them." Contemplating the meaning of whole-brain research, she concludes, "At the very least we will no longer be able to live with our separate distinctions of emotions and reason."

If you bumped into Dr. de Beauport, you'd find she practices what she preaches. She hooks you with a rush of emotions, even speaking at academic conferences. If you bumped into Eric Booth, as one of us did at a Christmas party, you'd find yourself picked a foot off the floor by his enthusiasm. Booth has reason, he's at the eye of a multicolored breakthrough in establishment education, one funded by the Reader's Digest Foundation, directed by Harvard's Project Zero, and assisted by the Nashville Institute for the Arts.

Learning as Art

Challenging, engaging all one's intellectual abilities, senses, emotions, drawing the whole force of the person into exploration and growth—that's Superlearning at its best. It also defines something that's been around much longer: art. Not art pinned like a butterfly to the museum wall but art as a process. Eric Booth is planning director for the experimental Eakin School Project in Nashville. At Eakin art is no longer what is politely called enrichment and popularly labeled a frill; it is the heartbeat of the school. All subjects are taught *through* art.

Walking into an Eakin classroom, you might be able to hear a pin drop as students calculate how much paint would be needed to cover a room in the castle they'd recently designed. Or you might walk into "mayhem as four groups of students rehearse a playlet in which they must debate an important issue in an invented language." Sound familiar? So do the goals of the Eakin Project: teaching to multiple intelligences and learning styles, opening the excitement of discovery and creating lifelong learners, challenging teachers to be learners and grow personally too. Another goal is to nurture understanding. Booth cites growing evidence that a preschooler's view of how the world works often persists beneath the algebra-solving, vocabulary-defining expertise of highly educated people. Art as process helps connect the links and move people from naive to mature understanding. Though they don't seem to have heard of each other, Superlearning and the Eakin Project are playing on the same stage. Let's hope they meet soon, for there are insights to compare on both sides. In the meantime, whenever possible, don't be a dry-stick learner. Open up and get the feel of things. Imagine you're an artist.

The Eyes Have It

Look at a map of the United States—the patchwork-colored states, curving rivers, slanted mountain ranges from sea to bright blue sea—and prove to yourself that a picture can be worth many more than a thousand words. Your visual sense can flash you a whole world of interrelated data in an instant. That's why Superlearners often use mind maps. Mind maps catch your eye, engage more of the brain than the traditional way of outlining, a product of the logical, A-B-C left brain. At a lecture, reading, gathering thoughts to write a paper—whenever you're working to organize a subject, try map making. Put your topic in the center like the sun and let its universe of ideas branch out, a major point here with tributaries branching underneath, another cluster there. Highlight different areas with color, blow up a key branch, add little cartoons or pictures.

    Mind mapping is also an ideal way to bring your aspirations and goals into vivid focus. The class gasped in one of Tatiana Radonjic-Matano's workshops when a premed student held up a mind map of the life he wanted to live. It was so beautifully done, with no words, just pictures. "He was a high-strung, stressed individual," Radonjic-Matano says, "and he seemed so relieved that it was okay to be visual. He'd been told at age six that he mustn't draw pictures, that he had to put his thoughts down in a linear way." Three weeks later she got a call from the suddenly visual student. He'd gotten behind prepping for a tough chemistry exam. So the week before he simply made mind maps. "I got an A!" the jubilant doctor-to-be reported as another block bit the dust.

Maps furnish a bird's-eye view that can reveal new connections, prompt new ideas. They give an extra edge when you need to recall your data. A map lights up in the mind more quickly than a list. Why? Because it's a picture. Anything you can visualize, you will learn faster and remember longer. To cite just two of hundreds of reports, David Meiers, director of the Center for Accelerated Learning in Wisconsin, and Dr. Owen Caskey, at Texas Tech University, led a year long, federally funded study of students at four colleges. Those using full-bodied imagery in learning scored 12 percent better than others on immediate recall and 26 percent better in long term retention. "We all possess, it appears, the world's finest multisensory teaching machine right in our heads," Meiers remarked.

Drs. Alan Paivo and Alain Desrocheres taught imagery and rote-memory techniques to students at the University of Western Ontario. Imagery boosted memory three times higher than repetition. That's why language learning emphasizes concrete nouns at first. A picture of *book* lights up faster in the mind than *with* or *excellence*. Many Superlearners further enhance learning during the four-second pause in the paced memory sessions by visualizing what they've just heard. When someone gives you instructions, when you learn to spell a word, when you're listening to a report, visualize. When you're reading, visualize. Good authors will help you, following the writing dictum: Show, don't tell. (If pictures don't pop easily into your mind, check out p. 143.)

About 80 percent of your brain is involved, at least to some degree, in visual processing. More than any other sense, visualizing engages the whole brain, and so can touch the whole body. Become an inner photographer, a mental movie maker, and you activate broad areas of potential. You can explore a hyrodgen atom or the

Milky Way with imagery. Like multicolored squads of helpers, you can set images to work: to expand memory, solve problems, boost performance of any sort—speech making, trombone playing, shooting par, or triumphing over disease. Images can help you break the death grip of the past and also help you seed "future memories"—goals and dreams come true.

Memory Pegs and Memory Palaces

Saint Thomas Aquinas preached the cultivation of mental imagery in perhaps his only concession to the weakness of the flesh. "Corporeal similitudes" are, he admitted, of the sinful sensory world. But they are a necessary evil, for without them a strong memory cannot exist—something needed to keep Holy Writ ever in mind. Aquinas' own memory was full blown and of a kind that doesn't exist anymore. Early on he impressed Pope Urban by creating a voluminous anthology of the writings of the church fathers. He wrote it all from memory. Like his contemporaries, Aquinas used images in a formal mnemonic system.

What we call memory pegs the ancients knew as memory palaces. Which may give you an idea of how far we've let *Mnemonics,* a fine art, older than history, slip. No laptops, no notebooks, our ancestors had to make mental notes. Educated citizens carried vast, closely peopled continents of information in their heads. Compared to the ancients, our memories are nonexistent. The stunning reach of their memory, its endurance and continuous growth, is an eye-popping example of the potential of the mind, a potential we don't need to realize. We've built the riches of memory into our books, photos, computer nets, videos.

Now and then, though, a mnemonic system comes in handy, and the classic rules still work. You can see the last pale wisps of them in late night TV infomercials. People call out twelve or thirteen different items—*dog, banana tree, Statue of Liberty*—to the memory whiz on stage. At the end the expert reels them all off from memory, to the apparent astonishment of the audience. One wonders if they would have expired had they been seated before the great Roman philosopher/statesman Seneca. His students shout out lines of poetry, dozens and dozens from different works. After about two hundred of them Seneca gets busy. He recites the lines from beginning to end, word perfect. Without skipping a beat, he reels off the 210 lines again from the last all the way back to the first. This ability to move backward and forward easily in memory came from the classic system that emphasized image and place. Pythagoras taught it; Plato, Aristotle, Aquinas used it and wrote about it.

Simply conjure a vivid image representing the first thing you want to remember, then link it, associate it, to the next thing on the list and so on. The ancients strengthened the links by stretching images out in order through familiar surroundings. In the first place they used their homes. *In the first place* is a phrase left over from classical mnemonics. Say the topic is nutrition that boosts brain power. It becomes an image: Mother Nature, the crown of her head wide open, a brilliant sun rising from her brain. This image, the topic, is set in the first place, by the door of your house. A Roman used all the rooms, halls, corners, mantels, windows, and furnishings of his home as a framework to string images, which is why he could easily remember backward and forward. You can enter the house from the front door or the back to tour your image-filled rooms.

Just as you can have different guests, you can fill the same rooms with different strings of images. As learning grew, though, most people branched out into memory palaces. Some raised whole imaginary towns. Supposedly they could go in their mind's eye to a hill above "town" and pick up interrelations, new perspectives that eluded them at ground level. During the last great flowering of mnemonics, led by the Memory Magi of the Renaissance, some scholars were reputed to have over 100,000 locations to store their images. Students of Egyptian lore, alchemy, the Kabalah, the rather fabulous Magi even built real architecture in patterns believed to resonate mental energies. They recognized a dynamic side of memory and, like Plato, thought it a cosmic connection—the royal road to cosmic power. (But that is another story; if you're interested, see *Supermemory: The Revolution*.)

You can still jog memory by linking images around your house, your school, down familiar streets. Today you can also make movies, little cartoon loops. To remember a grocery list: The Broccoli monster chases President Bush. Desperately he grabs a swath of Saran and subdues the vile veggie. A chicken hops in to peck at the Saran. Suddenly her legs shoot out from under her. She slips, falls flat in a bright yellow stream of melted butter. Overhead a great hand reaches out of a cloud holding a liter of Pepsi and pours it over the faint fowl. . . . And the 'toons reel on through your list.

We have many other ways now to enhance our memories. As Dr. Rosella Wallace points out, "Mnemonics is just a small part of Superlearning." But it's one more part that Wallace has jingled alive with happy results. To the tune "Did You Ever See a Lassie?" her kids belt out "Can you name all the oceans? There are only four: the Pacific, the Atlantic, the Indian, the Arctic." Raps and rhymes, chants and cheers, Wallace has created a bookful to help young learners install the facts of spelling, grammar, geography, math, science. *My Very Educated Mother Just Served Us Nine Pizzas.* What's the mnemonic? Wallace's students remember it's the planets moving out from the Sun: Mercury, Venus, Earth, Mars, Jupiter, Saturn, Uranus, Neptune, Pluto. Recently she added a real kinetic spark with jump rope ditties. Little kids bounce to "SmartRope, SmartRope, what's the trick, to help me learn my arithmetic? Denominator down—touch the ground, Numerator top—give a hop." Sometimes their feet trip, but weeks later their memory doesn't. (For Wallace's cheerful books, see the Resources section.)

Even if you're a bit too creaky to jump, images can keep your memory skipping along. When you conjure images for memory, make them vivid, bold, comical, bizarre, and add strange accessories—a ten-foot banana falling on a purple dog in a high silk hat. The grotesque statues scowling and leering from the niches of Gothic cathedrals are thought to have been made so weirdly to fix their lessons in memory. The ancients, however, rarely gave examples of memory images. The only useful ones, they insisted, are those you create yourself. But they did say that the most powerful memory stimulants are images related to sex and death. (Curiously, subliminal advertising today sticks almost solely to hidden images of sex and death. Curious, too, that through much of history the record shows that from statesman to church father, the elite conjured ribald parades of dirty pictures to boot memory.)

"I Can't See Anything in My Mind"

If the only picture you can turn on in your mind is a gray fog of nothingness, don't despair. Many highly intelligent folks started out with a blank screen; they had to learn to visualize. "Such people are turning images into words," says imagery therapist Sally Edwards. The images are always there, but the mind labels so quickly that the picture goes unperceived. Take a few minutes a day to turn off verbal noise, Edwards suggests. Just look around, don't name. Just see objects, lines, colors, movements. If that doesn't work, try crossing over to visuals from another sense you can easily imagine. Touch is a good one to work from; so is smell along with its mate, taste.

Imagine you are closing your hand around a long, tapering icicle. Slide your hand up and down that slippery, cold icicle. Or imagine stroking rough tree bark or rubbing your hand up against the grain of a two-day-old beard. Begin to put the touch into context, into a scene, all the while feeling, questing with your imaginary fingers. Wait for an image—even a cloudy snippet of one—to shape. With the beard it will often shape in a mirror. Maybe it's smell that piques your imagination. Pick a favorite one, such as fresh coffee brewing. As powerfully as possible, conjure the aromatic smell of coffee, the first good taste, imagine—see—your favorite mug rising to your mouth. It may take a little practice, but most people eventually cross over.

"Whatever you do, *don't* think of a pink elephant," a trainer may say. "Don't even see one little speck of pink, vibrant, shocking pink. Don't look at that pink elephant's trunk curving." That's the perverse temptation route to opening the mind's eye.

If you're still having trouble rousing a picture, try a gambit devised by Dr. Win Wenger, director of Project Renaissance in Maryland. This is guaranteed to give you an eyes-closed image to play with. Stare at a light bulb (100 watts or less) or a computer screen for thirty seconds. Close your eyes and observe the afterimage. Describe it aloud. Report color, shapes, texture, brightness, movement, everything possible in the most minute detail. Milk that afterimage for all it's worth until it fades completely. The key here is in the describing. A few sessions will almost invariably prime your picture pump and give you more intriguing things to look at. More fascinated than most with imagery, perhaps because he, too, started life with a gray screen, Wenger has developed powerful ways to accelerate learning with your mind's natural imagery.

Image Streaming

A prolific author, a ubiquitous national trainer, with degrees in economics and education, Wenger has been widening the horizons of SALT since its inception. "Image streaming" is one of his most fruitful discoveries. Many Superlearners find it can quickly extend intellectual reach, and it is also another way to take charge of change, sometimes business-saving or grade-saving change. Anyone can do image streaming. It's almost as easy as closing your eyes.

Like many Superlearning techniques, imagery streaming draws on the spectacular intelligence and speed of your subliminal mind, which is right now producing a flow of images on the edge of your consciousness, images that, like Old Man River, just keep rolling along. Close your eyes for a moment and look at what's flowing by. If you must, ask for pictures. You may get anything from a sleek Lowie locomotive nosing through a grimy railroad yard to a little girl pumping suntanned legs on a swing. The stream probably won't relate to what you've been reading. How to do that and greatly expand your grasp of material is the second step in Wenger's program. First you need practice to bring that cornucopia of images on stream at a moment's notice.

Eyes closed, for ten to twenty minutes, describe *aloud* what's streaming by. Go with it anywhere the images lead. Let yourself be surprised as you rattle out a vivid, second-by-second description. Be an inspired reporter covering a fast-breaking event to her listeners. With as much texture and sensual detail as possible, get that picture across. If you're alone, talk to your tape recorder. Practice until you've racked up at least ten sessions.

You must describe *aloud*. Without it there are no gains. Reporting your mental movies is an entertaining way to sharpen observation and language skills. But the real "magic" springs from what Wenger calls *pole-bridging*. Describing aloud prompts wider hookups between your speech centers on the far left side, or pole, of your brain and the imagery centers of the right brain. These in turn link to deeper, less conscious levels of mind—some of that potential everyone says lies waiting.

Once you're a practiced "streamer," put those resources to work to grasp a textbook or lecture, a professional article, a piece of literature—or review a business discussion. Pause and ask the stream to give you images that will clarify and keynote the topic for you. What comes up may seem totally out of left field. But keep it in mind as you go and you'll probably find it does turn up the lights and help you own the topic. Use the same technique to gain consolidating insight on many different topics. Link all the subjects you're learning in school, all the disparate topics to be presented at a board meeting.

Try streaming your problems away. To problem solve or to make a difficult concept your own, Wenger suggests you make a tape. State your problem or the concept as clearly as possible. After three minutes of silence insert a signal—clink a glass, tap a pencil. Signal again after three more minutes, and once again after three minutes to end. Then relax and play back the tape. After you hear the problem posed, ask the stream for a solution and describe it aloud. When the signal sounds, thank your unconscious and ask for a completely different stream of solution-bearing images referring to the *same* answer. And again, after the next signal. Afterward, to clarify your answer, find the common thread running through the three different sets of imagery.

Want to cut your heavy reading time by two thirds? And triple your grasp of the subject? Wenger believes he's found a way. Odd as it sounds, *before* you begin to read, Wenger says, ask for an image that "somehow will make everything in this paper come together for me and make sense." Then plow ahead. "You will discover with some amazement the first few times you achieve this effect that everything in that paper does come together and make sense—in less than a third of the time it would ordinarily take you to read through," Wenger says. "And your understanding will be many times greater than usual."

Does image streaming really expand intellect? In 1989 Dr. Charles Reinert first tested image streaming in the Department of Chemistry and Physics at Minnesota's Southwest State University and found that something more than mental hookey occurred when students turned on their inner cinema.

Twenty-five hours of image streaming resulted in a twenty point leap in IQ, Reinert's test revealed. And streaming apparently accelerated brain integration. Students who streamed could flourish in any kind of learning environment. Control groups trained in different enrichment techniques strengthened only their preferred learning style.

What about the physics final? Reinert found performance did not correlate with the amount of time students had studied. It did correlate with the amount of time they'd practiced image streaming. Those who streamed twenty hours or more aced the final.

People who have to create something often tune in to their inner image flow. Like another writer, Richard Poe, senior editor of *Success,* we find Wenger's protocol sharpens the effect. Poe wrote an article telling entrepreneurs how to stream for guidance when drastic change is called for—when it's discover a new market or perish, for instance. Poe warns, "It may take several tries before you get something you can use. But your persistence will pay off. Believe me," he says, "it works. I used the technique to write this article!"

At Project Renaissance Wenger, with his wife, Susan, is developing other ways to use pole-bridging and bring far flung areas of the brain on line at the same time. For one they are teaching young children music and math while at the same time enhancing intelligence generally.

Tidal waves of images sweep through our senses every day. Our media culture gifts us with an extraordinary ferment of pictures to associate for memory enhancement, to draw from in imaginary work. Once again, you are at the most opportune time in history to ignite powerful aspects of yourself. Perhaps the most powerful, one that often comes alive in imagery, is your imagination. After years of neglect, almost abuse in intellectual circles, the wonderfully rich, creating powers of imagination are being recognized. Learn to use it properly and you can pull off what often seem to be paranormal feats of accomplishment and change. Among other things that may be "all in your imagination" are success, health, peak performance, warm relationships. As Marcus Aurelius long ago realized, "A man's life is dyed the color of his imagination." To learn how to brighten the colors . . .

13
Imagine Yourself

Would you like to speak Russian like Gorbachev, play tennis like Monica Seles, grasp physics like Einstein? If you enjoy adventures, you can jump-start your way toward their ability with a basic Superlearning ploy: turn into somebody else. Make believe you are Seles or Gorbachev, or the golf pro, the Nobel Prize winner, or anyone who's an ace at what you want to learn. People have been stepping out in new selves since the very beginning of Superlearning, when high-ranking Communists in Moscow checked their old identities at the classroom door. Each put on a new name and memorized a new bio. For a German class one might become Gerhard, a bachelor ski instructor from Garmish, or Marlena, a chef with two children from Berlin. Cloaked completely in their new selves, these Soviets never did learn one another's true identitites. Undercover agents stayed covered. Party elite remained unembarrassed using a red-letter way to enhance learning.

Today "act as if, and you will become" is a truism regularly brought alive by Superlearners. When twelve people flew to Folkestone, England, from seven different countries for Mark Fletcher's unusually entertaining and effective "English Experience," they soon had their interest piqued as they transformed from Tamara and Klaus to Georgina Greenpeace and Dr. Martin Makeyouwell—a short, balding man who favors yellow bow ties, keeps canaries, and rides a motorbike. Switching identities is, in effect, switching into a different state, a freer one. It takes you a step away from your usual limits and fears. "I could never do that," but Georgina Greenpeace might. In character you can act with a spontaneity and boldness your usual self might shy from. For once you don't have to feel embarrassed about making mistakes, because you don't have to own them. After all, it was Dr. Makeyouwell who made that dumb error, not you. Playacting can banish a sense of struggle and engage the power of the present. It's not that you *will* learn French or astronomy but that, as the make-believe expert, you already have the knowledge, you just have to relax and let it materialize. All of us are practiced at turning into "different" people—parent, boss, child, bowling enthusiast, lover. It's not that hard to start leapfrogging ahead to proficiency by modeling yourself on the Expert.

Imagine you are Monica Seles, or simply the tennis pro, when you go out to lob balls. How would she stand, react, serve, aim? For sports, people often watch videos to help model their imagination. Learning how to invest? Read biographies of financial wizards, then assume a canny persona and ask yourself what would this Wall Street whiz look for, what strategy would he use? If you're picking up Italian, make believe you live in Roma, involve all your senses, eat Italian food, listen to Italian music, two quick routes to the rhythms and soul of a culture. You don't have to imagine you're someone famous or foreign; you can jump-start talent by taking on the persona of someone sitting next to you.

Working with disadvantaged children, Dr. Robert Hartley of the University of London was wrestling with the poor academic performance of many when he suddenly remembered something. As a boy at school Hartley was totally stuck on an important essay. Finally he wondered how a well known newscaster would handle the topic, and inspiration struck. The desperate young Hartley imagined he was the commentator, and sentences began to flow. Could make-believe, he wondered, move others off square one?

Hartley worked with children who'd done poorly on a picture-matching test. "Think of someone you know who is very clever," he told the kids. "Now, be an actor. Close your eyes and imagine you are that very clever person and do the test the way she or he would."

Open sesame! Children imagined they were clever and became clever. Scores rose significantly. The performance of the slow learners became indistinguishable from that of the high achievers, which was too much for one young man. "Aww, it wasn't me," he protested, looking at his grade. "It was the clever one that did it!" Next imaginative step, Hartley noted, was to refurbish a dingy self-image.

In a reverse example, journalist Charlayne Hunter-Gault used imagination to build a powerfully positive, healthy self-image under circumstances that would have thrown many off balance for life. In the fall of 1992 Hunter-Gault returned to the University of Georgia to hear the Reverend Jesse Jackson extol her and Hamilton Holmes for breaking the university's color barrier over 30 years before. How did a teenage girl survive the vicious racism of students and state authorities alike? "Their rocks, their bricks, their spit never touched me," she says, "because in my head I was an African queen."

Suddenly They Were Talented

Imagining you're someone else—taking on her behavior—is a shortcut to expertise. It can be as simple as Dr. Don Lofland's advice to people who want to read faster. "Look at a good reader. How does he sit? How does he hold his book? Do the same." It can be as intriguingly complex as another accelerated learning technique we encountered in the Soviet Union—a mind-blowing breakthrough to talent called "artificial reincarnation," developed by psychiatrist Dr. Vladimir Raikov. With it, science students who'd previously drawn on the stick-figure level suddenly found themselves richly talented and often turned to careers in art. Talent seemed to appear out of nowhere after Raikov shifted them into another state, a state not of pretending but of wholeheartedly believing they were Picassos, Rembrandts, Raphaels—a new form of deep but active hypnosis.

Brought to their everyday selves, students had no memory of the hours they'd lived as Rembrandt. "Don't be ridiculous! That's not mine" came many indignant retorts when they were shown their paintings. But over months expertise honed in the Rembrandt state filtered into their ordinary experience. Suddenly they were talented. There's an echo here of Masters and Houston's time-expansion ploy.

A master state shifter, Raikov reincarnated people as superb violinists like Fritz Kreisler; as inventive geniuses like Nikola Tesla; and recently as famous healers, all to fast-forward them into realized potential. They aren't Picassos or Teslas, but they do give being a quick study a new twist up the spiral. Artificial reincarnation is *not* a do-it-yourself technique. You don't want to step out of the shower one morning as Rembrandt. But it is a bravura demonstration, one still incarnating in Russia, of the reality of that old "enormous potential." A demonstration that to reach those resources, we often have to get out of our own way—even if it means becoming someone else. Why does a shift in identity evoke ability? "It's a way of giving yourself permission" is one answer. "It's a way of reaching into the vast collective unconscious" is another. Visionaries in any field seem adept at plucking know-how from the collective unconscious. That's why five people invented the telephone at the same time, or perhaps why, in his day, Edison was accused of picking other scientists' brains telepathically as well as verbally. Perhaps, too, when you imagine you are the master artist or the Turkish linguist, you tune in to Nature's memory.

Not long ago Dr. Rupert Sheldrake, Fellow of the Royal Society and a biologist with impeccable credentials, came up with a new theory. It is not immutable law that makes the world go round, he says, it's Nature's memory. In rarefied circles that idea was heretical enough to prompt the previously rational journal *Nature* to call for the burning of Sheldrake's books—which rather implies that if he's right, he's a revolutionary on the order of Galileo.

Nature's memory is built of "morphic forms." There's one for everything, for being a hippopotamus or for Japanese speaking. The more Japanese speakers there are, the fuller the memory form. Since Sheldrake's theory is a scientific one, it can be tested. For instance researchers have a Turkish poet compose a new nursery rhyme on the same pattern as an old Turkish favorite. People without a word of Turkish are then asked to memorize both the old and the new. They learn the rhyme that has been recited by generations of Turks significantly better than the newly hatched one. The same effect has been found working with other languages and codes. (And on another level, with such things as the growing of new crystals, slow at first, then faster as more exist in the world.)

It seems easier to learn something that has a robust morphic form built up by many than to learn something known to only a few. Most tests of the theory are coming down on Sheldrake's side. He points to practical applications, but no one has yet done much to connect circuits. How could you tune in to "Japanese speaking" or "physics"? Sheldrake thinks it's a matter of resonance. Just maybe, when you're in the right Superlearning state, when you truly mimic the Japanese speaker, you begin to resonate with his morphic form.

John Wade wonders whether Sheldrake's theory explains something odd that he's noted in accelerated classes. Wade separates the more fluent from the less fluent learners, into A and B classes. He teaches a well-planned lesson to class A. The next day he teaches the same, not a watered-down version, to class B. They learn it too. The reverse, teaching B before A, is a disaster. "It's an old accelerated learning trick every teacher knows, but nobody ever talks about." Morphic resonance? Sheldrake's ideas fit even better, Wade thinks, with his "percolation process." He teaches something to one student who genuinely wants to know it *now*. "Then I sit back a week or two until it percolates through the class."

Shifting your state to tune into information the way you switch stations on a radio is an old esoteric idea Sheldrake has brought into scientific terms. It could explain how genuine psychics now and then pick up large chunks of information that should be beyond their ken. Life is speeding up, so stay tuned yourself for what could be a breakthrough to a new human learning circuit. At least it's a bracing positive suggestion when you set out to learn something a lot of people know.

Most of us can't yet shift into really different states or dimensions of ourselves as smoothly as an organist shifts keys in a cantata. We need ploys, gimmicks. Hypnosis is one that prompts people to extraordinary feats. A lot of scientific data on it comes from the old USSR, where for fifty years hypnosis was mainstreamed and matter-of-factly used in a host of fields.

Like Raikov, another former Soviet, the Ukrainian accelerated learning teacher Vladimir Stefanishin pried open new reaches of the mind with hypnotic states. At the Kiev Scientific Research Institute of Psychology he explored age regression and something even more intriguing that was well delved into in the old USSR, hypnotic age *progression*. In deep trance, individuals are fast-forwarded days, months, years into the future. "What are you doing, what's going on?" Subjects are also asked in their everyday state how they foresee their future, and dreams are noted. According to Stefanishin, when eventually compared, future sight gleaned in hypnosis comes closer to reality than an individual's own predictions or his dreams. Raikov, too, reincarnated people as "inventor of the future," "physicist of the future," but details of what they "learned" were kept secret.

As Stefanishin hypnotically hatched time-travelers, passports or not, some went over a supposedly inviolable border and talked of their states before birth and after death. This sort of over-the-border journey happened in the office of Yale-trained M.D. Brian Weiss when he was chairman of psychiatry at Miami's Mount Sinai Medical Center and led to Weiss's well known (and best-selling) explorations of far memory. Stefanishin concluded that the mind can reach into five dimensions of time—which would certainly classify as an untapped potential. It was research not made public at the time; now Stefanishin would like to compare notes with interested researchers.

Like many Soviets Stefanishin tried using deep trance to accelerate learning. He led one 13-year-old boy, for instance, into a somnambulistic state, cleared his blocks against geometry, and turned him into a theorem-solving whiz. But Stefanishin, like Lozanov, came to believe that teaching individuals to shift their own states is a safer and, in the long run, more effective approach. One reason Lozanov, a superb hypnotist, developed Suggestology and Suggestopedia was to be rid of the invasive quality of deep trance to widen mental powers. Suggestion, he believes, can carry you just as far. It might be interesting to use suggestive/imaginative techniques and turn into a future self to see what comes up. Or you might want to put on another head.

Putting on a New Head

"First, you put on your heads," Dr. Rosella Wallace said to a small circle of Yupic Eskimos. She explained the technique of "becoming someone else" to quicken learning and performance. Outside, the temperature was 20 below, but in the meeting room excitement bubbled like a rich, warming broth at tiny Mountain Village, Alaska. "That method is also in our culture," exclaimed one of the fifteen Yupic teachers who'd flown by bush plane from even more remote settlements to hear about Superlearning from Wallace. "They just needed someone to give them permission to use rhythm, play, rhyme, and especially guided imagery in teaching," Wallace told us. " 'At last,' they said, 'we can teach the way our elders taught so many years ago!' "

A decade ago, home in Anchor Point, Alaska, Wallace began to intrigue third-graders with Superlearning ("It lets you do feats like Superman"). Her kids did pull off triumphs; grades rose across the board. When asked about his teacher's strange new ways, one youngster earnestly insisted, "She's not crazy. I used to get F's, now I get A's."

Once, during a lesson on Alaska, Wallace's class groaned wall-to-wall. "Oh, gross!" kids said. "Yuck!" when she mentioned that Eskimos like nothing better than a mouthful of *muktuk*—whale blubber. The next day class began as usual with students putting their imagery expertise to work. They floated on fluffy clouds, relaxing, getting into a good state to learn, until Wallace called their attention to another cloud drifting up bearing an Eskimo boy or girl. "Exchange bodies with that other child," Wallace said. "Become them. And take off on an adventure." Only soft music broke the silence as Wallace's kids roamed far-northern settlements in their mind's wide eye. Back in classs, they bent to writing stories and drawing pictures of what they'd done.

"As usual they went through the whole experience joyfully. I find this to be the best way to facilitate creative writing," Wallace says. But as the children talked, she realized they'd roused more than creativity. They'd touched empathy. They'd munched on *muktuk*. "It tasted a lot like strawberry candy," one reported. "Mine tasted like nuts," said another. All munchers agreed it was *good*. These were the kids who'd said "Yuck." "What a wonderful way to see through another's eyes and taste through another's taste buds. The possibilities," Wallace points out, "of reducing prejudice are thought provoking." As she says, "It's virtual reality without the equipment." One that could work for any age.

You don't have to borrow someone else's body to take an imaginative journey to accelerated learning. You can join "The Incredible Journey" and go rafting through your bloodstream sighting the exotic fauna and flora: machrophages, T-cells, lurking viruses. You can slog through the snowy, foot-freezing fields of Valley Forge or pop into a quartz crystal and watch it grow facets. "Being there" can sharpen your grasp and your memory of any topic.

Does it work? Perhaps because she's on the Alaskan frontier, practicality is a driving question to Rosella Wallace. Borrowing the "Head of the Careful Observer" is another imaginative shift she checked out. To improve awareness, articulation, and writing, try fitting the head of the Careful Observer over your own. To anchor your new head, vividly describe this special observer aloud: How does he act? How does he approach objects, people, events? Make him part of your imaginary world. Wallace's students loved becoming this "super version of themselves, using the observer's eyes, senses, and mind to perceive scenes as richly as the Careful Observer does." (For how the kids greatly enriched learning and memory by shifting heads, see Chapter 26.)

Wallace adapted her Careful Observer from Win Wenger's "Putting on the Head of a Genius," something he developed in part as a practical alternative to Raikov's work. Putting on heads is a time tested method you might want to experiment with, one used by Hindu and Western esoteric teachers for millennia. Today, as Superlearners turn into the Pulitzer Prize–winning author or the ski champ, you can think of it as a self-empowering form of Method acting. Which may be why so many actors have taken to Superlearning; it comes naturally. All you have to do is suspend disbelief. When Alice steps through the looking glass, you don't stop reading to argue about how flesh and blood can possibly walk through glass. You suspend disbelief and plunge into the adventure. You can do the same with your own scripts. Like Alice, stretch and shift perspective to come up with some liberating insights. You can accelerate the dissolution of learning blocks as well as pick up data. Here's one scenario, called "Remembering Who You Really Are."

What if you had just arrived on planet Earth three weeks ago? What if your talents, your personality, your memories, your whole life history had been artificially inserted into you? What if, like Arnold Schwarzenegger in *Total Recall*, you began to get little bleed-throughs of memory, little glimpses of a better you? Imagine you are beginning to remember who you really are: a special, bright, and wide-ranging, totally capable individual, a star walker. Begin to reclaim your real self. Was there something you'd come here to do? Notice your patterning, your running assumptions. Look for knee-jerk emotions. Consciously examine your beliefs. Do they reflect who you really are? Are they the stuff of a high-born spirit? Or are they low-level patterns programmed into you? Control mechanisms? Use your imagination to reclaim your heritage. Get rid of that alien programming.

Rehearsing Future Memories

As the song says, "Imagination is funny, it can make a cloudy day sunny." It can also turn your life around if you brace yourself with imaginary rehearsal. At the turn of the century the French great-granddaddy of self-help came up with his "first law." "*When the imagination and the will are in conflict, the imagination will always win,*" Émile Coué declared, and put his finger squarely on an important dynamic of the mind. He also went a long way toward explaining why all our fine resolutions to change, backed by our best willpower, often don't come true. The will chooses. The imagination carries out. It's exhausting to keep willpower running like a sleepless cowboy riding herd on a fractious group of appetites, whims, emotions, thoughts. You need to enlist imagination to keep moving smoothly in the right direction, for it's in touch with both the conscious and the unconscious aspects of you.

At the end of the century we know a lot more than Coué did at the beginning. We know that if you imagine something vividly enough and with your heart and soul bring your senses and emotions into play, your deep mind doesn't know the difference between that imagined event and an actual one. That's why mental sports training works. Your unconscious totes up your imagined stance, your reflexes, your swing, the bat solidly hitting the ball, the rush of your game-winning home run, and adds it to your bank of experience. Imaginative rehearsal works for any kind of performance, making the speech of your career or finally losing crippling exam anxiety.

Since Coué's day, and even since we first wrote of Superlearning, something else has come to light—the creative power of memory. "Use full-sense imagining," Superlearning coaches insist. The more of yourself you engage, the stronger will be the desired effect. Because you are creating memory circuits, minute shifts occur in your body as well as your mind. You need emotions, senses, the stuff that memory is made of, to build strong mindbody circuits that will play back when needed.

Get comfortable, perhaps put on some calming, 60-beat music. Using your favorite method, relax, then turn up your inner house lights and begin living a successful event in your imagination. Feel, think, see, hear, taste it if you can, as vividly as you would if you were experiencing your success.

Let's say you have to give a talk. (Forget that Gallup found that 80 percent of Americans listed public speaking as their greatest fear, and fully 50 percent of those said they fear giving a speech more than they fear death.) Imagine yourself in the auditorium. Pick up the sights, sounds, smells as the audience settles down. See and feel what you're wearing and get comfortable at the podium. Sense your eagerness to share what you know with these interested people. Feel how calm and focused you are as you begin to talk. Catch sight of an attentive person in the third or fourth row and imagine you're talking to him the way you would to a friend. Let three or four major points of your talk come to mind. Don't reach for memorized words, just feel the words coming out easily, powerfully as you need them, filled with images and even a joke or two. Don't be rooted to the spot. Imagine yourself moving about, gesturing naturally. Feel your memory flowing easily, serving up any data you need. Feel confident enough to say, "I don't know, but I'll find out" to a question you can't answer. Finally, hear the enthusiastic applause; feel the handshakes as you come down from the podium.

Plant your future memories for ten to fifteen minutes, once or twice a day. If you don't have time to do it twice, try making a little 30 second movie loop of the high points. Run it whenever your upcoming speech pops into mind. This has the added advantage of keeping you from worrying away your imaginative gains. "Plant a carrot, get a carrot, that's what life's about" is good lyrical advice from *The Fantasticks*. But neither the earth nor the mind will produce if you keep digging up the seed and fretting over it. (For more, see Section Three.)

As you become adept, remember, imagination, like the rain, waters the good and the bad. If you're a con, you can use it to enhance your next telemarketing swindle. A much more likely negative is to rehearse dire consequences unwittingly, to vividly imagine your worst fears coming true. Know you're planting those seeds, too, and swear off, or you may end up living your nightmares instead of your dreams.

Summoning your imaginative genii will accelerate ability across the full gamut of performance, from delivering your baby to scoring the big sale. Lorne Cook, who's devoted years to refining his top-grade Superlearning science classes at Toronto's Upper Canada College, used the same techniques to help one of his students leave sweaty-palmed terror behind when he played his violin in public. Cook put the boy through the familiar relaxation and mind calming routine. Then he led his student, Kristian Braun, into imaginary rehearsal. Kristian repeatedly experienced himself calm, poised, playing easily and accurately and even enjoying his performance. It worked. Kristian, who used to get so unhinged that he dropped his violin, now plays with aplomb no matter how many eyes are watching. Cook then used the same strengthening techniques to spur the school swimming team to success.

Mind is a healer. That revolutionary insight is just breaking into mainstream consciousness. A few years ago Don Schuster, the prime mover in rooting accelerated learning in the United States, faced a triple threat: cancer, pneumonia, open heart surgery. "I survived," he says, "at least in part because I always saw myself doing so." If you're imaginatively fit, you'll be ready for an unfolding human adventure as we step into a land where, sometimes, imagination can raise blood counts, shrink tumors, speed the healing of wounds, and even mimic the effect of birth control pills.

Imaginative rehearsal is a powerful way to anchor change. Use it to reinforce new behavior, particularly something you're substituting for an old negative pattern. Imagine reaching for a glass of water instead of a cigarette when the phone rings. When you do full-blown imaginary work, many specifics take care of themselves: energy, motivation, and creative ideas flow; a sense of meaning and purpose fills your life. When you plant strong future memories, goals seem to take on a life of their own. Keep imagining you're walking across the stage and clasping your hand around that diploma, that you're signing the deed to the house of your heart's desire, that you have indeed saved that rain forest, and you're more likely to live it for real. Just how powerfully mental rehearsal can work shines out in imaginative superstars like Christian Drapeau, who so honed his imaginary Tae Kwon Do moves that he became a North American champion. You can see it in imagery coach Shakti Gawain, who imagined her goal so thoroughly that she turned her first self-published book into a towering two-million-copy best seller against even more towering odds. It starts to edge toward the unbelievable with Air Force Colonel George Hall, a POW locked in the dark box of a North Vietnamese prison for seven awful years. Every day Hall played a full game of golf in his imagination. One week after release he entered the Greater New Orleans Open—and shot a 76. The story of autogenics expert Vera Fryling, M.D., is even more surprising. A part-Jewish teenager, on the run from the Gestapo, living undercover in Berlin in the eye of the Holocaust, she began to imagine she was a doctor, a psychiatrist, in a free land. Against all odds, the Nazis, the Soviet army, a supposedly terminal case of cancer, Fryling wound up on the faculty of the San Francisco Medical School. "Imagination," she says, "can help one transcend the insults life has dealt us."

All of these people used imagination to so convince and saturate every fiber of themselves with the reality of their goals that the future seemed to have no choice but to flow in and flesh out their pattern. So can you.

14
Blocks to Learning, Change, Living

What short-circuits our efforts to break through the 10 percent barrier? The answer has more to do with unlearning than with learning, with breaking free of three classical learning blocks: the logical block, the emotional block, and the ethical block. None of us is vaccinated against them. Actually we're often inoculated *with* them early on. And they don't just trip us up in our personal lives; as Otto Altorfer points out, working through us these blocks cast their immobilizing spell on efforts to change our institutions: business, education, medicine, social programs. They are the deep drummers, perhaps, that make it so inexplicably difficult to give up old fears and learn to live comfortably with our neighbors around the world. As a friend said when we were writing about memory, "The heck with remembering. How do I learn to forget?"

You'll be able to unlearn with greater finesse if instead of thinking you're confronted with some innate deficiency that trips you up, you realize you're dealing with state dependent memories. Then you understand how some strong ghosts of the past can rise to influence not just your thoughts but also your emotions, your behavior, your senses, your whole physical and nonphysical self, and cramp your abilities. Fortunately exorcising ghosts is easier than it looks in the movies.

Logical blocks can be summed up in the old adage: "If you think you can't, you can't." If you're convinced everyone has a certain wedge of intelligence identified in early school, then that's all the smarts you'll ever use. If you believe regular people can only learn so much so fast—that's why they have ten-page lessons in the textbook—that's as fast as you'll learn. A while back, if you'd known that no human could run a four-minute mile, you never could have done what Roger Bannister did and neither could the more than 1,000 people, including twenty high school students, who've run that mile since.

Logical blocks are conscious. They can be easily dissolved with information. Hundreds of thousands of people in dozens of countries have discovered they can learn faster, remember better, drop limitations, and enjoy themselves as they stretch out into new skills and talents. You don't have to take our word for it. If your logical mind balks, read some of the many papers, journals, books on the topic. If you're a teacher, you might want to look at Dr. Allyn Prichard's book *Suggestive Accelerated Learning*. Prichard and his collaborator, Jean Taylor, detail how they got so-called learning-disabled kids who couldn't read to pick up a year's worth of reading in just four months. Usual truants fought to come to class as this successful program continued for ten years.

If you think you're not too smart, look up the many experts who have concluded we use only a tiny smidgen of our innate potential. The time to worry about the size of your share is when we get to 98 percent. Or perhaps not even then, for the current consensus is that the mind is potentially unlimited. Read the stories of people like Robert Frost, Nikola Tesla, Thomas Edison, Buckminster Fuller, all of whom had trouble in school, all of whom rose to the top of their fields. (Their failure to buy into the educational establishment, some feel, was a factor in their leap to genius.)

You might also look into a most curious fact that Dr. John Lorber, a British neurologist, uncovered. It looks like you can do pretty well if you don't have any brains at all. You might even get good grades,

Lorber found, when he made a discovery that tumbled a few centuries of brain theory. For a long time scientists believed that thinking, "that all that was dear to them," as Lorber says, resided in the cortex of the brain. Lorber chanced to examine a young man with a slightly enlarged head. He turned out to be a hydrocephalic with fluid filling much of his cranium. This Sheffield University student had "virtually no brain," yet with an IQ of 126 he won honors in math and had a good social life. Lorber scanned six hundred "hidden" hydrocephalics to see how much cortex they possessed. A number had lost 95 percent to fluid. Yet half scored above the average IQ of 100. Lorber's work surely shows the brain is more redundant and adaptable than has been thought. Is it also proof that we only use a tiny percent of our capability? People with only a fraction of their "thinking brain" do as well as the rest of us.

Educate your logical mind to ensure it agrees with your goals. Let it know they are possible, particularly if you're going to follow the advice of motivational speaker Les Brown: "Do not go where the path may lead, go where there is no path and leave a trail."

Toxic Metaphors

"Foreign languages are dumb. Who wants to talk like those . . . ?" "No one in our family could ever do science." "You're so stupid. You don't deserve . . ." "Not everyone can be talented like your sister." "Only nerds play with computers." "Boy, did you look funny when you forgot your speech." "Who do you think you are, to ask questions! Don't be so smart, you won't have any friends." "Girls don't . . ." "Boys don't . . ."

These are the seeds of emotional blocks. Comments, reactions from one authority or another, usually coming when we're young, take root in our memories, unquestioned. They can keep right on playing their constricting little tunes twenty or thirty years later. No use putting yourself down for procrastinating, freezing up at exams, being afraid to ask for a raise, or making the same old mistakes over and over. Your automatic memory circuit is playing out in a perfectly natural way, just as your leg kicks if you tap the reflex point. Unlike a knee jerk, you can change your memory reflex. Instead of moaning

"What an idiot!" "I'm hopeless," put that emotional rush into chang-ing the circuit. Look for your emotional blocks. You can hear one talking when someone says, "The only thing I can draw is a small check." Or, "I couldn't learn math if my life depended on it." That's a fact, they tell you. Is it?

Write "Opinions" at the top of a sheet of paper, then list all the things you think you're not good at. Become aware that every one of them in an opinion. Often just this simple shift of perspective is enough to banish an old emotional block. You may or may not remember how an opinion got seeded. But you can at least tell yourself that apart from being dumb there could be a host of reasons why your eyes cross when someone mentions square roots, or asks how fast the man on the bike was going, if the train was . . .

When you first met arithmetic, maybe you wanted to know why it works and nobody told you. Maybe you flunked a few tests and gave up. Maybe you didn't like the teacher, she didn't like you, your parents told you math is really hard, you missed a month. Or maybe you suffered an undiagnosed problem, particularly that one Dr. Lozanov long ago labeled "didactogenic syndrome," illness caused by poor teaching methods. The point is you are not the same person you were then. And now there are a host of powerful, new learning methods. People that the music teacher once told, "*Please,* just mouth the words," are learning to sing out on key. You have options.

What's an ethical block? Early accelerated learning classes sloughed over them rather quickly—which isn't surprising. These are the most elusive blocks, precisely because they permeate our cul-ture. Ethical blocks have to do with judgments about what is right and wrong. "No pain, no gain." "Be perfect." "Nothing worth having comes easily." "Always put others first." "You have to pay for your mistakes. And pay and pay." "Suffering builds character." "It's harder for a rich man to enter heaven than . . ." It may sound surprising, but such truisms qualify as toxic metaphors. As silently and perniciously as lead in the school drinking fountain, toxic metaphors can eat away at one's ability to learn and perform.

While that "new energy" that Dr. Marian Woodman sighted rises in the human psyche, the webbing of the old society is coming into more conscious view. If you look, it's shot through with bands of fear, guilt, pain, punishment, condemnation, intolerance—enough to squeeze out the life juices, which may be why the old structure has begun to crack. At first, most people doubt they are hampered by ethical blocks. We did. But wouldn't it be surprising to grow up in such a culture and not pick up a toxic trace or two? Dr. Joan Borysenko got a jolt discovering that over half of her ailing patients thought they were being or should be punished for their sins. Borysenko wasn't in the Bible Belt; she headed The Mind/Body Clinic at Boston's New England Hospital. "I believe that the feeling of unworthiness—the wound of unworthiness—is the soul wound of Western culture," reflects Borysenko, who believes part of her healing work involves helping patients regain "spiritual optimism."

Even highly successful people often think *Whew, got away with it again* after yet another triumph. If you've taken "the rules" to heart, it's much easier to feel like the worms of the old hymns than to feel deserving. Not to debate ethics or theology, but check yourself for toxic beliefs, which are defined as anything that stultifies, demeans, binds the human spirit from healthy, joyful growth.

As Bruce Tickell Taylor early realized, Superlearning teachers are in a unique position to help people erase unconscious conditioning. Michael Lawlor, chairman of the British SEAL, and his wife, June McOstrich, in their accelerated Inner Track workshops, focus specifically on erasing limitation in order to wake potential. As blocks dissolve, English clients say new awareness of their possibilities spurs commitment to self-growth. Teachers at Moscow State University were more effusive; a number wrote, "I love you," on their assessment of the course when the Lawlors helped them dissolve their unconscious scripts of the past. "You've re-created me! I've became another person" was a common comment. "I've found inner harmony and inner beauty." All this from shedding blocks. If you want to catch hold of some of that inner harmony and beauty . . .

Dissolving Blocks

A talented watercolorist, a woman who's traveled the world, told us why she ducks speaking in public. She remembers, clear as day, the time in third grade when she got up and gave a talk on the "foh-eeb" bird. On she went until the entire class, led it seemed by her beloved teacher, collapsed into giggles. "Phoebe" was the name of the bird. The fact that our friend remembers "clear as day" is used as a bit of leverage in various NLP quick-change techniques.

To get rid of a "foh-eeb" sort of memory, you need to call it up. If it's in bright color, turn it into black and white. Dim the lights generally on the scene. Shrink whoever looms large to a tiny size. Drown out remarks or giggles with upbeat circus, Dixieland, or disco music. You'll drain the old charge from the memory. Take the measure of your memories. Check: color, brightness, height, width, breadth, perspective, sound, smell, focus—any distinctive feature. Often you'll note that strong memories are well lit and vivid. But people differ. Whatever the shape and structure of your memory, if you want to take the life out of an old bugaboo, change it, rework it the way an artist adds a swath of red or a musician transposes a chord to alter the whole.

To exorcise a ghost, you first have to recognize it's there rattling your chains. Often emotional and ethical blocks don't rise to mind "clear as day." Like Otto Altorfer's clients, you can try the affirm-and-response technique to uncover hidden blocks. Many people have experienced a real sea change simply standing before a mirror five minutes a day, saying "I love myself just as I am. I am wonderful!" If you feel your gorge rising, good. Seek out the objecting block. Or try this statement by the famous American inventor/artist Walter Russell: "Genius is self-bestowed, mediocrity is self-imposed." It annoys a lot of people. Why? What are the blocking beliefs or memories? If a particular suggestion on a self-improvement tape irritates you, trace it back. With her "Change Your Mind" tapes, Teri Mahaney finds some clients are jolted awake every night at the same offending suggestion by an ever-vigilant block.

Sometimes a block does a little sleep suggestion of its own. A New York businesswoman told us she had taken up the very salutory affirmation "I approve of me," determined to say it hundreds of times a day for two weeks. "I really did think I approved of myself in general," she told us. The third morning she awoke with a loud voice running through her head. "How could you approve of such shit!" Where did that come from? Probably from long ago. Today's need is to recognize the toxic seed of unworthiness and change it.

Whether you're using affirmation, suggestion, or imaginative scenarios to dissolve blocks, there is a key question you can ask to accelerate the process or to get moving if you're stuck. What need does this block fulfill in my life? "I'll always be just an average learner, just a regular guy." That block could be doing its best to provide a feeling of safety, to satisfy a need for a secure, defined niche, or a need to avoid added responsibility, even a need to avoid feeling guilty by surpassing one's parents or siblings. If you're having trouble shaking a block, relax and contemplate what you'll have to give up when it goes. Write down the needs it may fulfill. Needs can be quite legitimate—wanting to make others feel good, wanting to be part of a community, wanting to be loved. You're aiming to get rid of the block, not the need. Brainstorm other possible ways of satisfying the need—healthy, less limiting ways. Talk it over with "George," your unconscious. When you find one that feels right to both of you, take action and substitute it for the old ways of fulfillment. Reinforce action with self-talk, suggestion, imaginative scenarios.

To sum up, to free yourself of learning blocks:

- Be aware that a block exists.
- Ask whether it fulfills a need. If so, come up with another means of fulfillment.
- Change the limiting memory. Without judgment patiently, firmly plant a more positive pattern using affirmation, suggestion, imaginative scenarios, confirming experience.
- Expect results, but not necessarily overnight.

We've Seen the Harpy

People are waking up around the world. That's one reason Superlearning is catching on. Its energies move with the wake-up call, with the rising awareness that it's time, almost past time, to wriggle free of old, life-squeezing entanglements, personally and globally. Our ingrained negativities, more than anything, keep us from learning, from growing into self-actualized people. Too often they prompt us to look at humanity and see, with Jonathan Swift, "the most pernicious race of little vermin that ever crawled upon the face of the earth." That picture could brighten if we noted a cocoon of entanglement that all of us daily swathe around ourselves like a manic mummy: the negative bonds of self-chat.

Someone once said that if our self-chat was broadcast over a loudspeaker, we'd lynch the speaker. Easily 80 percent of most people's inner talk is negative, some aimed at others, but first and foremost at oneself and one's chances. We don't need a Big Brother manipulating media to keep us down. We've made it a do-it-yourself project. We've seen the harpy, and it is us.

If you want to strike a blow for self-liberation, take the pledge and vow you'll pay attention to your self-chat for one whole day. Bet yourself ten bucks you can keep it positive. When you catch yourself "awfulizing," to use Dr. Joan Borysenko's word, stop! Turn your chat around, come to a neutral or positive conclusion, no matter how far-fetched it seems. This exercise can help you in various ways. You'll become aware of just how negative much of your self-chat is. Your deep mind will get a break from the harpy. You'll get practice in riding the positive life current. And, if you're honest, before you can go 24 hours without awfulizing, you'll have a number of ten-dollar bills in the kitty for a treat when you test positive for a day.

Emotional Hot Wires

Just as we self-talk ourselves into straitjackets of diminished experience, we often nurture emotions that keep the classical learning blocks robust and vibrating. Very few of us have been taught to be emotionally literate, though the world's major religions have certainly tried in their way. One of our worst habits is the jagged emotional spin we give our experiences. We hot-wire them with criticism, fear, envy, anger.

Take criticism, again. "One of the craziest ideas modern society has is that criticism is good for you or that it helps you learn," remarks the prolific author and well-known Huna master teacher Serge King. You get what you reinforce. "Noticing or remembering what we haven't done right just gets in the way of learning. . . . If anyone learns under criticism, it's in spite of it, not because of it." The eclectic roots of the Superlearning systems stretch back to ancient disciplines like

Zen and yoga. Because King's discipline, Huna, the ancient Hawaiian way, flourished for centuries in isolation, it is perhaps the purest remnant left of the perennial wisdom. It's not surprising that Huna as a matter of course follows criticism-free teaching, something many hailed as a revolutionary breakthrough in accelerated learning.

Superlearning teachers sometimes have to reach into their best creative resources to avoid direct criticism. "It's interesting," one said, "how hard it is at first to resist *the temptation to make wrong*." Libyan Cassone, who works tirelessly to accelerate language learning, compares her approach to that of a coach and her athletes. "Your coach isn't going to say, 'Too bad, you didn't get to a certain mark, you can't play anymore,' " Cassone points out. "When somebody makes a mistake, instead of having a figurative alarm go off and a hook emerge to drag the student out of the classroom, we would say, 'That's okay. You made an error—that's part of life, and you'll get it better next time.' " Contrary to much expectation, in class after class, from third-graders to technical workers, students who weren't "made wrong" learned their subjects better and faster than those getting conventional correction.

It's surely been said, "Judge not, that ye be not judged." Does that mean we're to be judged in the great by and by? Or is there something going on in the here and now? Guess who might be judging us? It's axiomatic that if one marches through life in the critical mode, the person who gets made wrong the most is oneself. Then we have to learn in spite of it. And the critical mode does something else. It saps personal power, an insight Mother Teresa tried to pass on to a fervent group of antiwar protesters. Would Mother Teresa, the protesters asked, lend her renown and lead a huge antiwar demonstration? "No," said the wise old nun. "I won't march against war. If you ever hold a demonstration *for* peace, call me." When your mode is anti, you have to womp up a lot of defensive energy—emotional, intellectual, creative energy. There often isn't much left to create what you do want in life.

If you want to pluck the critical thorn out of your own hide, try affirming and living this, one day at a time, as they say in the Twelve Steps: "Today I give up criticism of everyone and everything. I give up criticizing and condemning myself. Things I used to judge as wrong I now see as simply that which is presented as wonderful opportunities for change and transformation."

It's Important to Fail

Failure! Often the mere idea closes us down and shuts us up. If you begin to experience those awful, sinking feelings of inadequacy, of being a loser when you fail at something, stop and ask yourself, what is failure anyway? Shorn of a load of learned emotions, it's an experience that's telling you to change what you're doing, you're heading the wrong way. In a sailboat, when the wind is knocked out of your sails, you correct your course. You don't sit there trying to ignore it or feeling bad about yourself. You use failure as an immediate guide. That's the perspective that let Thomas Edison sail through two hundred unsuccessful attempts to invent the light bulb, and then six hundred, eight hundred, nine hundred ninety-nine attempts. Did he feel like a failure? Of course not, he would tell you, he'd just successfully eliminated the one thousandth circuit, bringing him ever closer to the one that would light up the night.

"If you don't make a friend of failure, you'll never excel." That unexpected message came through loud and clear when we talked to a rarefied batch of corporate superstars for the book *Executive ESP*. CEOs of heavy industry with burgeoning profit margins, they spoke readily about using intuition as well as the facts to succeed. "But what if you make a mistake?" It quickly became apparent that was a naive question. They'd had loads of failures, million-dollar ones. But they didn't sit around chewing on themselves. One exec summed it up: "If you make decisions, you're going to be wrong some of the time. The trick is to learn from your failures and make more right decisions than wrong ones."

The lesson needs to be learned young. Valanne L. Henderson and Carol S. Dweck, at Brown University, took a look at how children in junior high respond to difficulty. Two basic responses emerged: a mastery response, a helpless response. The "helpless" feel anxious when challenged. Difficulty seems like a trap, pointing up their own lack of ability and even intelligence, something they think they are powerless to change. Conversely kids on the track to mastery feel excited and spurred by difficulty. They seem to feel that with effort they can become more intelligent. Flooding the "helpless" with successful experiences doesn't help, Dweck found. Sometimes it even made their problem worse. To move toward mastery, she says, these children "must learn to accept negative feedback as a source of information for future efforts rather than as a judgment about their ability."

Failure gives us information we wouldn't otherwise have. The trick is to see failure as a guide and not allow an emotional rush to swamp us. We've done a funny thing with failure, and with guilt, too, which is a form of failure. Instead of keeping them as lookouts, we've given them the helm. Failure is an innate part of the learning package. Watch very little children before they've put on our belief systems. They take one shaky step and fall down; they take another and plop. Without our emotional freight, babies know instinctively that failure is a signal to try another way. Failure is built into learning. If you fear it, you'll never learn at your best. If you know it's a guide, not an accuser, in the long run you'll probably get anywhere you want to go.

What Kind of Fire Do You Have in Your Belly?

Bets are you may really be ticked off about something. There's so much fire in the belly of humanity at the moment that it seems as if three quarters of the world has thrown open the window and started shouting, "I'm not going to take it anymore!" When we stop shouting long enough to listen, we wonder what the others are so enraged about. Answers fill volumes. Optimists can compare all the rage to a painful boil finally gathering to a head, a healthy push to throw off the poisons that have muted and kept us from being ourselves for so long. Nice but dicey. An infection can burst to drain fevers away, or it can kill you overnight. Which is why another Superlearning friend, Dr. Doe Lang, titles one of her most trenchant workshops "Anger— Fire in the Boiler Room: How to Make it Heat the House, Not Burn It

Up." Fulbright scholar, psychologist, well reviewed actress and opera singer, Lang joined her many talents to teach politicians, executives, media people—and by tape, a lot of Superlearners—how to get up in public and project themselves and their ideas. In other words how to summon that buzz we call *charisma*. Her international roster of clients learns that a pivot point on the road to charisma is knowing how to let anger lend you power, not reduce you to impotency. It's good turn-around training for learning how to change.

In these times, when change comes whether we like it or not, having the know-how to defuse anger and rage is increasingly demanded in the marketplace, in offices, and in factories. "Teaching employers and employees skills to deal with anger and resolve it could add immeasurably to the productivity of the workforce and to job satisfaction," points out Montreal lawyer and columnist Clair Bernstein. As the metal detectors go up in more and more schools, learning to defuse rage may have to come before learning much else is possible.

"Are you running anger, or is it running you?" Dr. Lang asks clients as diverse as the battered wife who refuses to acknowledge anything but a sunny marriage to the corporate giant who proudly tells her, "I don't get ulcers—I give them."

As in so much else, the trick to handling anger is to realize that no matter what anyone else has done, it's *your* anger and you have to decide what to do with it. Deny it and get sick, or blow up and cause harm to others and yourself? Through long experience Lang finds it isn't necessary to vent anger at the cause. "You can get the same satisfaction from physically and vocally discharging rage with nobody present." Then you can coolly decide what to do.

"*YOU BASTARD!*" That's the exercise Lang's clients often find helps the most. If shouting "bastard" puts you further on edge, substitute "*RAT!*" Stand, feet firmly on the floor, shoulder width apart, knees slightly bent. Begin to swing your arms in an arc, up to the left like a golf swing, then down and up to the right. Mouth closed, breathe in on the first swing up to the left. Exhale on the swing to the right. Mouth *open*, inhale as you swing left again. Now, at the top of the left, stamp your foot, shout "Youuuuuuu" as you swing right . . . at the top of the right start, "Baaaaaaaas-tard!" as you swing left, exhaling. Then begin with the three-swing warm-up and do it again—and again at least ten times. Open your throat and shout as loudly as you can.

To fully release anger, it's important to coordinate sound, breath, body, words. Surrendering to sheer rage can roil spasms of fury until you're totally drained. But *not* satisfied. Full discharge opens space for other emotions. Lang's clients quickly put their charging adrenaline to use immediately after the anger exercise to soar with the great.

WOW! Excitement, joy, anticipation, and uninhibited release fuel the rising *Wow* exercise. Crouch, hands open, palms out, and start with a whispered "*Wow.*" Let your body and voice rise while you "*Wow*" eight times, as if you've just seen the most beautiful sight in the world, the manifestation of your most spectacular dreams . . . and climax with a great *"Wow!"* Leap in the air if you can, arms flung out, head back. Doing the *"Wow"* is crucial, Lang finds, because it completes "the cycle of emotional transformation from anger to celebration."

A healthy flash of anger is as natural as an arc of summer lightning. We move into the twilight zone when forks of anger keep flashing days later, years later. To nurse a grudge is to consciously nurture a state-dependent memory, a fighting mad ghost that you can summon on the instant to set your blood boiling. It keeps you living in a time warp—body, mind, and soul in the past—and robs you of the present, the only place you can accomplish anything in this world.

Thousands have plugged into broader life in Wayne Dyer's much-applauded self-help workshops. Dyer came close to not being present. His childhood was made miserable by an abusive, deserting father, and he grew into adulthood still bound up in his anger. Until one day when Dyer went to his father's grave and finally let go and forgave him. His career blossomed. The miracles of forgiveness don't come from added luster on your heavenly crown, they spring from coming alive in the present, from taking back all the energy you've bound over to another. Yes, it can be very, very hard to forgive, yet the freedom is worth the struggle. Effective forgiveness techniques are on Teri Mahaney's CYM tapes. Affirmation and imaginative scenarios can also help and so might this: Lang's exercise helps get rid of the emotional memories that live in our muscles. One night we stumbled, or rather sloshed, into an even more practical one.

We were really mad. Like a lot of other angry people, we had reason: we'd fallen into a business and publishing mess through no fault of our own. Two years of work down the drain. We got madder. Two years of income down the drain . . . every time we thought of it . . . but that was another rub. We knew that every time we thought about it, we were feeding a hot and bothered ghost with a truly Sicilian desire for revenge. Then, too, we'd spent the past decade writing books and tapes saying, "Stay centered." "Don't give your energies away." To avoid a recall like the car companies have, there was nothing for it but to work on letting go. We did some man-overboard course correcting and gave a bookful of techniques a workout, including these two:

Relax, conjure your troubling event—and rewrite the script. Take your time. As vividly as possible, experience all going well and coming to a successful conclusion. The key word here is *conclusion*. It's a curious fact that negatives tend to linger longer in memory than positives. Few people recall the dozens of times they're told, "You're a great dancer." Almost anyone will remember, "Where'd you learn to dance, dinosaur school?" Or when a critic writes, "*As always,* he gave a terrible performance." Negatives keep vibrating like a piece of music looking for an end chord of resolution. If something's gone wrong during your day, rewrite before going to sleep. This will help you set it aside and give your subliminal mind a break from going around and around trying to fix what's past. This gambit works best if, unlike us, you do it immediately.

To get on with our lives, we had to forgive. We knew that because we'd read it in our books. To the rescue came a technique that years ago sprang from the New Thought religious movement. Relax by your favorite method and imagine you're sitting in a theater. The house-lights dim and gradually the spots focus on the person you're angry at, standing center stage. Imagine what would make her happy. Imagine little vignettes of wonderful things happening to her. See her smile with delight and relief. Do this for five minutes. Then as the curtain goes down on her, say, "I forgive you. I release you to your own good."

We thought we were over our mad, but apparently a little spark still lingered to burst alive and consume itself in the midst of household disaster. Sewage had backed up, flooding the basement of Lynn's house. It was pump and bail and pump some more until one of us sang out our grievances, each mistake, one by one, plunge, plunge down the drain. It was almost fun and lingered to give Sheila a good emotional as well as physical workout when she flew West to pump her mother's basement during the floods of '93. Not all things are accomplished eyes closed, body relaxed. To accelerate your household chores *and* dissolve blocks, keep an eye out for a likely combo.

When you talk about anger, someone usually tells you what a great motivator it is, how anger will keep you throbbing along for years. The trouble is, over the long haul it will wear out your shock absorbers. Let it go and you're more likely to prove the point: living well is the best revenge. Or in Frank Sinatra's words, "Massive success is the best revenge."

As we've said before, a major reason few of us ever reach that promised shore of realized potential is that we're not in the right state to get there. It's like anchoring on the dark side of the river. Now and then you catch a snatch of music and look with longing at the welcoming lights on the far side. But to get there, you have to weigh anchor and cut the baggage of the past that's holding you in place. From music to mind mapping, the many techniques of Superlearning can help you accelerate learning and change. But beneath them all is the invitation to let go of the grasp of yesterday and come awake in the present. More than anything, this is the route to more promising lands. Once you get under way and feel the wind in your hair, it's an exhilarating adventure.

15
Brains Are Made for Challenging

Pay attention for a moment to how you're breathing through your nose. Does the air seem to be flowing through your left or your right nostril? You may not have noticed it but your breath shifts regularly from one side to the other throughout the day. It's evidence—right under our noses—of deep brain and body cycles, evidence that nature intended us to be whole rather than one-sided creatures. As you'll see shortly, riding these cycles can also leverage learning.

The scene is a brightly lit room—props, costumes, it looks like an actor's workshop in Folkestone, England. A man sporting a golden bowler hat appears and with a quick sleight of hand plucks a walnut from the nearest student's hair. The people around him, suddenly all eyes, don't know much English, but they understand when Mark Fletcher holds up the two wrinkled halves of the walnut: a little brown model of the two hemispheres of the brain. They begin to get a taste for the rationale behind some of the goings-on as they Super-learn in Fletcher's "English Experience."

Yes, it's left brain/right brain, and you've heard it before. Super learning helped popularize the idea in the early 1980s. Like traditional education, Superlearning engages the logical, verbal, straight-line thinking, detail-attending left brain. But it also insists on pulling into play the metaphorical, imaging, synthesizing, intuitive right brain. Left/right is not a cleaver through the brain division; it's often helpful to consider them as different modes of thinking. If you want to see the hemispheric differences at work, look at America's two most popular game shows. "Jeopardy" is mainly a left brain game. "Wheel of Fortune" relies heavily on the right brain for success. Acceleration happens when you summon the strengths of the whole brain. Yet even with all the left-brain, right-brain buzz, traditional education, particularly in the upper grades, still speaks almost exclusively to the left brain—which may be why so many are dozing off in class.

"The brain is made to be challenged." That's the wake-up call coming from Dr. Jerre Levy, of the University of Chicago, a woman internationally known for her skill at uncovering the secrets of the hemispheres. Her work could help turn around a common litany: "What did you learn in school today?" "Nothing." Levy found that if you do simple tasks that involve only one brain hemisphere, you greatly reduce your attention span. Half brained is lame brained, a "half wit." Challenge, complexity, novelty—these are the things that light up both hemispheres, grab your attention, and lead to greater learning and memory. That's why conjuring vivid images (right brain) while you read a history book (left brain) leads to solid learning. That's why Superlearners studying Japanese get out of themselves and act out skits set on the Ginza. If you engage both sides of your brain, no matter what you're learning, you build up more hooks and clues, redundancy to ensure broader understanding and long term memory.

Dr. Marion Diamond is another distinguished brain scientist (and one of the few who has studied cells from Einstein's brain). Her work shattered the old negative that age freezes your ability to learn. Your brain can keep on making connections and growing throughout life because *learning breeds learning*. At the 1991 SALT convention Diamond revealed something extraordinary. Multisensory stimulation literally changes the physiology, the anatomy, of your brain, she said. It gives you more capacity. Other researchers also find that as you continue to learn, you expand the neural networks of your brain, creating ever more abundant connections. In effect you build a "bigger" brain. Which is one way to cope with snowballing information and problem solving demands. Superlearners are often of the self-reliant, do-it-yourself breed, but only recently has it occurred to anyone that self-reliance might include physically pumping up your brain, a little bit the way Arnold Schwarzenegger fleshes out his body.

Beyond exercising more areas of your brain, Superlearning techniques that may just seem "pleasant" or "fun" on the surface, relate to the very stuff of our brains. Dr. Lyelle Palmer, director of the Office of Accelerative Learning at Minnesota's Winona State University, points out that a positive learning atmosphere plays the right notes in your brain chemistry and avoids the chemical milieu aroused by fear and anger that hampers learning. "In a state of security, competence, confidence, joy, delight, and exploration, the brain hums with efficiency and absorbs massive amounts of information almost effortlessly. Time passes quickly and pleasantly, with a reaction of 'I want more, more, more of this experience.' At times learning may seem to take place incidentally."

Swimming with the dolphins—it's said to bring elation, insight verging on enlightenment. You might not take to the sea, but you can swim with the "dorphins," your brain's pleasure chemicals, that can also, it seems, lift you to new insights. Mind machine users, for instance, find that as they evoke positive, joyful states, they can ride the waves over the old horizons to learn and create with new freedom. So can Superlearners, which is why accelerated teacher Palmer dubbed the field Education's Ecstasy Explosion.

We are designed to be challenged. Our brains are set to really hum when fully engaged. What does this say about "educational advances" such as watering down the classics for children, corralling them into a small pen of approved vocabulary words? If you're just doing time in familiar country, there's nothing to entice the brain. Marva Collins teaches grammar school kids, ghetto kids in her famous Westside Preparatory School in Chicago. Books, movies, TV shows have told the story of Collins' success at turning not just some but every inner city kid that comes her way into a self-confident, self-respecting, well educated individual. "Our approach pushes students to excel, and students like to be pushed. They want to succeed. And once they have a taste of it, they will never settle for mediocrity." Marva Collins is a woman who twice turned down offers to be Secretary of Education to continue her calling: imbuing children with great expectations and prompting the wherewithal to realize them.

Almost all of us could use a Marva Collins in our lives. How often do we surrender to low expectations and let our fabulous three pounds of "wetwear," our brain, turn off? Lack of challenge isn't just boring, it's deadening—and deadly as life does go by. If you want to do more than veg out in old age, challenging your brain is more important than exercising your body. To learn how doctors are rejuvenating elderly minds by turning brain cells back on, see Chapter 20.

It's time to be a little more outrageous in the estimation of our possibilities, to aspire to goals outrageous enough to wake us up, time to reexamine and drop a raft of old truisms such as "you can only learn so much," or even "you can only concentrate on one thing at a time." Dr. Lyle Bourne, of the University of Colorado, years ago got psychology students to read while writing a composition on a different topic. With practice they could also take dictation and read at the same time and remember the content of both pieces, which should give us clues about the extent of our unused capacities.

Milton Erikson got a shocker of a clue that helped propel him into being the father of medical hypnosis and one of the seminal thinkers of our time. When he was a premed student at the University of Wisconsin, to bolster finances, he took a job as an editorial writer for a local paper. Like many creative people Erikson instructed his subconscious to work out the editorial while he slept so he could knock it out quickly in the A.M. Erikson's unconscious went one giant step farther. He awoke to find his finished editorial in the typewriter! It wasn't the elves but his unconscious wholeheartedly at work. "There was a lot more in my head than I realized," he said, a theme he kept ringing for a lifetime: We know a lot more than we think we do; we have vast, untapped reservoirs of ability.

More clues of just how much a single brain can grasp have surfaced in the recent swirl of research into multiple personalities.

We run like single-groove old gramophone records compared to the thirty-two channels some multiples operate on. One alter ego is an electronic whiz, another has a flair for art, another is a Civil War buff and an expert in hematology, another speaks Swahili, someone else teaches martial arts and has a yogi's ability to control body functions, and on and on—all in the same brain. Perhaps that shouldn't be surprising. Your brain has billions of cells. The potential connections between them is a number so far in the wild blue yonder that it exceeds the number of atoms in the known universe.

At the first International Conference on Multiple Personality and Dissociative States, in 1984, an unusual speaker, a multiple personality on her way to a graduate degree in psychology, touched on the one bright spot in her horrific experience. Sometimes she could do the work of four people. While she mentally reviewed an experiment, another self typed a manuscript, another outlined her thesis, and yet another planned dinner. An example from the far fringe, yes, but the growing edge always comes with a fringe, some strands pointing to areas where new patterns can fill in.

At the opposite pole from pathology, top talents and geniuses are rarely Johnny One Notes. Peak performers often excel in general. There is the brilliant novelist who's also the world's leading lepidopterist, or the mathematician who's a consummate cellist. On a less lofty, but no less real level, it's commonplace in accelerated learning that as you begin to engage more of yourself, ability spreads and globalizes. Athletes find their creativity sparked. Humanities majors discover they do have a feel for science. Larry Fickel, chief pilot, Pacific Southwest Airlines, found OptimaLearning increased his concentration and production at work without increasing stress. "A side benefit which I had not expected is a new appreciation for music and art. I found myself planning my last vacation around the museums of Paris."

Brain Balancing

Are you still breathing out of the same nostril? You switch sides and a different brain hemisphere becomes dominant about every ninety minutes. Centuries ago an entire branch of yoga developed to ensure devotees breathed out of the proper nostril during daily activities. Recently researchers have checked nostrils. Scientists at Dalhousie University found verbal (left brain) and spatial (right brain) ability varied markedly as breath switched and a hemisphere cycled to dominance. At the Salk Institute Dr. David Shannahoff-Khalsa, looking at similar research, pointed out that switching the breath to stimulate the left brain could give you an edge when reasoning, using language, or doing math. Alter to the right when spatial, creative, synthesizing thought is needed. Here's how.

Generally the left brain controls the right side of your body, the right brain your left side. To quickly energize your verbal left brain, press your finger against your left nostril and breathe deeply through the right. One way to switch the whole cycle is to lie down. Stay on your right side for a while and your left brain will come into dominance, or your left side for right-brain dominance. All of which can get a little unwieldy. Brian Hamilton makes more fluent use of nostril breathing in his Superlearning classes. He uses it to calm clients and bring the hemispheres into balance before learning. He follows a time tested yoga approach.

Do belly breathing for a couple of minutes. Then assume a hand position that lets you close either or both nostrils: Hold up the thumb and the last two fingers of your hand, curl the middle fingers in out of the way. Close off your right nostril and take a long, slow, gentle breath through the left. Switch the pressure and exhale through the right nostril. Do this three times. Then reverse for another cycle of three. Put your hands in your lap and take three more deep, slow breaths. Then "palm" your eyes by holding your hands over your eyes for a minute as you continue belly breathing. "Your nose," as one Dalhousie scientist put it, "can become an instrument to fine tune your brain."

The nose also knows something that we've just begun to uncover. Brainbody is one system. The shift of your breath is just part of a much deeper, all-encompassing life rhythm. Your whole brainbody system, including sympathetic and parasympathetic nervous system, cycles. It seems we are designed to focus outward for a while, then inward for a time. Inner world, outer world, in and out, a primal rhythm like breathing, but one we often override, perhaps to our detriment. Consciously riding this "ultradian rhythm" inward can, among many other things, help you solve problems, according to Dr. Ernest Rossi, a well-known Jungian who has done groundbreaking work on these primal rhythms and state dependent memory.

Rossi advises that when you're in an inward cycle, breathing through your left nostril, go with nature, relax for a few minutes. And wonder about your problem. Don't work at it. Just idly, lazily wonder and let your inner mind do its work for five or ten minutes. Often, Rossi says, your problem will resolve itself. At least you'll find yourself refreshed, occasionally, as Rossi experienced, full of joy.

Superlearning, if you use the full package, automatically engages the whole brain. Here's an exercise some learners also use to balance the hemispheres and—this is important—improve communication between them. If hemispheres are communicating as you tackle a problem, they resonate the whole brain, greatly expanding your resources.

Draw a deep relaxing breath and close your eyes. Look up to the left and imagine the letter *A*. Then look up to the right and imagine the number *1*. Look up to the left and see the letter *B*, up to the right and see the number *2*. Keep on switching back and forth until you come to *Z* on the left, *26* on the right. Now reverse the process. Look up to the left and imagine the number *1*, up to the right and see the letter *A*. Go through the alphabet. You may find one side is dragging its feet. Practice helps bring that hemisphere into balance. After a few days the process may suddenly take off on its own, flicking back and forth with great rapidity. Go with it; you're exercising your brain.

Want to stimulate your brain permanently? Dr. Win Wenger found a legal, though unlikely way. If you like fraternizing with the clams it may be just your ticket.

Hold Your Breath and Brighten
Your Brain

Win Wenger, one July day, cracked out of the shell of conventional education. He looked around at a sunny new land and wondered how he'd done it. After floating through a broad range of college courses for seven years while taking a tough summer school course, he felt as if he'd just come awake. Suddenly learning seemed as easy as rolling off a log. With the avid curiosity of a newborn, Wenger began researching academically unrecognized but, as it turned out, abundant, easy ways to expand intelligence and accelerate learning.

Though a man with a fascination for abstract ideas, Wenger made his way into a new world of high leveraged learning like a child. He built knowledge from personal experience, though it took him a few years to figure out that he'd stopped floating through academia, when he started spending time at the bottom of the pool.

Every afternoon at summer school Wenger plunged into the pool and enjoyed himself swimming underwater. It was a break that turned into a breakthrough. If you hold your breath underwater, carbon dioxide builds up in the bloodstream. This expands the carotid arteries that carry oxygen to the brain. Every med student learns about the CO_2-carotid expansion relationship, Wenger notes. No one, it seems, had thought to use it to get smart. Now Wenger's students do. For an intensive three weeks spend an hour a day underwater, holding your breath in at least two- to three-minute spans. Try it and you will *permanently* expand your carotid arteries. Here comes new life to the brain—more oxygen, more fuel, more toxins washed away. You own "a physically healthier, more intelligent brain, improving all areas of life, not just the intellectual." But you should, Wenger adds, "gain five to ten IQ points."

Play underwater tag and breath-holding games with your kids for an intensive three weeks, Wenger urges parents. Many remedial problems disappear, he says. There's also reason to think that people suffering cerebrovascular or stroke problems can be helped with easy, inexpensive underwater therapy. (Do this only under the close supervision of a doctor.)

When we first heard of Wenger's underwater route to brain enhancement, an image floated to mind. We saw a small, middle-aged Japanese man sitting crosslegged five feet down on the bottom of a pool armed with a self-invented waterproof pad and pen. His name is Yoshiro NakaMats—also self-invented. What made him a billionaire is his invention of the digital watch, the floppy computer disk, and over two thousand other patented inspirations. All of Na-kaMats' inventions have come as he sat underwater at the bottom of his pool holding his breath in four- to five-minute stretches. "The water pressure forces blood and oxygen into my brain, making it work at peak performance," he explains.

To get a genuine head start, it may be best to arrive in this world underwater. Super intelligence, superb memory, fine physical coordination—these are the traits of waterbabies. First they are deliv-ered underwater. Then, from day two, these infants are daily put into special pools to make their opening explorations of the world under-water. (They swim naturally.) Russian Dr. Igor Charkovsky, recently named honorary professor at Columbia University, is the scientific father of underwater birthing. Decades of documentation have brought him to an arresting conclusion. Entering the world and spending part of one's earliest days underwater could move human-ity off its evolutionary plateau. "Waterbabies can create new brain functions," Charkovsky declares, and will be able to solve problems impossible for the rest of us. (For the sometimes hard-to-believe story of the brilliant babies produced by underwater birthing, see *Super-memory.*)

A waterbaby may function so astonishingly well because con-necting links are established and activated globally through his whole, triune brain. We've touched mostly on the "thinking cap," the hemispheres, "the mother of invention and the father of abstract thought." But "the brain has acquired three drivers, all seated up front and all of different minds," says Dr. Paul MacLean, whose lifelong research brought the idea of the triune brain. To put it simply, you have an evolution exhibit in your head. You have three different brains that have materialized at different stages of time. Your thinking cap, the hemispheres, is the youngest, and is not as intimate with memory and learning as the older two brains.

Rising like a fist from the top of your spinal cord is the first brain, the reptilian brain, whose primal imperative is *survive*. It's a part of you that doesn't cotton much to change. With its long, long memory, this ancient of ancients favors ritual, routine, repetition, rhythm.

Excitement is welcome—actually is generated—in your mid- or old mammalian brain, a warm, lusty brain, the home of emotions and long term memory. Like a traffic controller, the old mammalian handles signals coming in from the outside and up from the inside, before they rise to verbal consciousness. Here state dependent memory knits together, making the old mammalian and its vibrant palette of emotions a power player in your ability to learn.

The ancient Taoists called this area of the brain the "golden room," a place where one could access exceptional powers. Western esoteric societies claiming descent from ancient Egypt also focused on this area of the brain, teaching, "Here one resonates memory and joy." Use these two to power reason, they said, and you will come to mastery in this world. Brain/mind science and the experience of countless Superlearners is confirming the ancient intuitions. Memory and joy—there are still mysteries to fathom in them both. But we do know that, properly ignited, they can loft you toward that happy hum of a fully engaged brain.

New and old mammalian, reptilian—such separating is a left brain mode of examining something, like focusing separately on the violins, the brass, and the timpani in an orchestra. The right brain sees the orchestra whole and hears the symphony. For Superlearning just use the core techniques, strike up the band, and ring in all the players to intensify the "music of the spheres."

16
Smart Food and Super Nutrition

"Check your vitamins and minerals," France's Dr. Monique Le Poncin tells people who are taking her famous Brain Fitness course of mental exercises. After all, she says, if you want to leap from a jalopy to a race car, horse-and-buggy learning to space-age learning, "You need higher octane fuel."

Higher octane brain fuel is exactly what you can get from substances sitting in your dinner or concentrated into supplements. Superlearning looks to your whole self. So it figures that 21st century Superlearners are involved in one of the better changes sweeping the land. People are flooding into health stores and workshops exploring the benefits of nutrition and herbs. A number of non-toxic food elements can quietly give you a healthy, helping hand up to sustained peak performance. "Befriend your body" is a Superlearning principle. An increasing number of those who've decided to open up their talents are realizing that beyond stress control and the ability to shift body states at will, ensuring that your physical self has what it needs, not just to survive but to sparkle, is part of the equation.

Food can lift your intelligence, enhance your memory, and fuel learning power. It can give you super stamina to deal with stress and overcome mind-dulling depression. It can even lift you out of pain.

It would seem self-evident that what you put in your mouth and digest to create the stuff of your body might have some influence on your functioning. But until recently establishment medicine refused to accept the well-documented idea that food, and the vitamins, minerals, and amino acids it carries, has anything to do with mental agility or disease. It's an example of enormous and, in its pain-filled consequences, pernicious resistance to change.

About fifteen years ago painstaking research at MIT began to force open the establishment mind. Dr. Richard Wurtman made the landmark discovery that our alertness, IQ, memory, mood, sleep, and even our perception of pain can be affected by what we eat. When you think, move, or try to remember something, certain brain cells release neurotransmitters—messenger chemicals your cells use to communicate with one another at lightning speed. People with high levels of specific neurotransmitters show high-level memory and learning power. Wurtman's discovery is that what you eat dictates how much and how many of these all important transmitters your brain makes.

Dr. Wurtman's team tracked the complex behavior of more than thirty messenger molecules. They tagged the specific foods you need to make them. "The brain's ability to make certain neurotransmitters depends on the amount of various nutrients circulating in the blood," he explains. The digestive tract breaks down foods into individual nutrients. Then the nutrients are off on a race up through the blood-stream at various speeds, winging toward the brain. The "winners" determine which chemical messengers get manufactured. "The brain is not above it all," says Dr. Wurtman. "It is intimately influenced by what we eat."

One superfood is lecithin. U.S. government tests showed lecithin could make people a startling 25 percent smarter. How? One of the most important neurotransmitters for learning and memory is acetylcholine. The brain makes it from a B vitamin called choline, which is found in lecithin. Dr. Wurtman tracked choline's travels on an hour-to-hour basis. He found that the amount of the all important acetylcholine in your brain depends on how much choline-rich food you eat. Choline boosts memory within ninety minutes and its brightening effect lasts four to five hours. If you need a mindpower boost for an exam or other challenge, lecithin can go right to work for you. Take it about an hour and a half before your big event. You can find lecithin and choline in egg yolks, fish, lean beef, wheat, and soybeans. (Both are also available as supplements.) Lecithin, made from soybeans, comes in easy-to-take capsules, liquid, or granules. The most potent form is called lecithin with phosphatidyl choline (PC).

"Our tests show that giving people choline increases their memory and learning ability," says Dr. Christian Gillin, of the National Institute of Mental Health (NIMH). "It makes them smarter." Calling it a breakthrough in understanding the human mind, he added, "We're very excited and encouraged by the results."

Dr. Natraj Sitaram, also of NIMH, calls lecithin a "memory pill" and reports students showed "significant" memory and learning improvements from it. He suggests about 2½ ounces (70 grams) of lecithin a day.

Dr. Wurtman, editor of the five-volume series *Nutrition and the Brain,* believes adding increased amounts of lecithin to older people's diet can be a memory age-proofer. Dr. Ronald Mervis, of the University of Ohio, has proof of the age-proofer. Seven out of eleven Alzheimer's patients given lecithin showed 50 to 200 percent improvement in long-term memory. Lecithin can help diminish the effects of normal aging on the brain from mid-life on, he reports.

Lecithin is not only a brain and nerve tonic; it also helps lower cholesterol in the arteries. It works in the bloodstream to dissolve and metabolize clogging fat, so oxygen can reach your brain more easily, keeping it sharp and efficient.

Another brainpower nutrient is found in cheese, milk, eggs, and meats. They all contain the amino acid L-phenylalanine. This amino acid is like a mother lode. Your brain uses it to manufacture an ultra important batch of chemicals. One of these key chemicals, norepinephrine, plays a major role in learning, memory, and concentration as well as in relieving depression and stress.

L-phenylalanine is the raw material from which your body makes another group of extremely important compounds—catecholamines, essential for nerve impulse transmission. These are proven to raise intellectual performance and, even better, they help you feel motivated, alert, ambitious, and optimistic. L-phenylalanine and other amino acids are not esoteric compounds. Nature built them into all protein foods. You can also pick them up in capsules at the health food store. Which is a plus for people feeling blue. This amino acid is an extremely powerful antidepressant, widely used to treat depression and amphetamine abuse. One clinical study found that 80 percent of severely depressed subjects were entirely relieved of their illness by taking 100 to 500 milligrams of L-phenylalanine a day for two weeks. Slowed-down thinking, lack of concentration, and memory loss are often the result of the depression now affecting one in four in the population.

Like siblings in a family, L-phenylalanine comes in a second form with the initials DL. DLPA, for short, has been called a miraculous, natural pain control breakthrough. Reams of glowing reports from health professionals and patients attest to its abilities to relieve pain with no toxicity or side effects. Research at the University of Chicago Medical School and Johns Hopkins University School of Medicine showed DLPA to be 85 to 90 percent effective for the control and reduction of chronic pain, equal to or exceeding morphine's effectiveness.

DLPA acts like a football lineman to bring you relief from pain. It blocks enzymes that destroy your body's own natural morphine, endorphins. They get a clear passage to the goal of relieving pain. The two forms of phenylalanine combined are a power team—they boost mental abilities, creativity, energy, and concentration; relieve pain and depression; and have a euphoric quality. They've helped many people beat cocaine, amphetamine, and other drug addictions. They can make you sparkle, with no downer afterward. Medical nutritionists suggest 1,000 milligrams of DLPA a day for chronic pain and 100 to 500 milligrams a day of L-phenylalanine. Remember, unlike drugs, nutrients take time to work.

Your body makes yet one more key learning substance from the mother lode of L-phenylalanine, another amino acid, L-tyrosine. This one's a proven "stress into success" superfood. In tough U.S. Army tests this amino acid proved far superior to drugs in helping soldiers deal with mega-stress and extreme climate changes and still be at their mental best to operate sophisticated equipment and do complex math.

"Tremendous improvement!" That's the Harvard Medical School report on L-tyrosine's effects on severe depression in patients who'd been stubbornly resistant to drug treatment. For depression, researchers suggest 100 milligrams a day.

High-Octane Mind Fuel

Skyrocket IQ by eleven to seventeen points! That's a great improvement for anyone. For the severely mentally retarded it's a life changer. In tests conducted at the Columbia College of Physicians and Surgeons, retarded children given an amino acid achieved two years in mental growth. Some recovered so remarkably well that they could lead nearly normal lives. All were treated with a genuine brain fuel, glutamic acid, another amino acid found in whole wheat and soybeans.

A recent nutritional breakthrough brought a new form of this amino acid, called L-glutamine, which can travel to the brain faster and more easily than the old molecule. L-glutamine is high-power energy for your brain. Your brain uses only two things for fuel: sugar (glucose) and glutamine. Which should give you an idea of why glutamine can wake you up. It is actual brain/mind fuel. The experiments at Columbia and other institutions that revealed glutamine's wonderfully heartening help with retardation were done over forty years ago. The results are just now beginning to be used. It's the "resistance to change" problem again. Perhaps the lag shouldn't be too surprising. When Dr. Henry Heimlich came up with his famous maneuver to save the lives of choking people, he says it took him a full twelve years to get the discovery past the establishment, including the Red Cross, and into public use.

In recent glutamine experiments Dr. Lorene Rogers, at the University of Texas Clayton Foundation, found mentally deficient children had rising IQs after getting L-glutamine. The well known Canadian Dr. Abram Hoffer, a father of orthomolecular medicine, has used L-glutamine to overcome mental retardation, schizo-phrenia, and senility. As a side benefit it eases the body's cravings for sweets and alcohol. To learn, retain, and recall with high energy and no more brain fog, 1 to 4 grams a day are recommended by nutritional experts.

Quintessential Brain Food

One revered, sometimes even worshiped old remedy has made it through medical research to be hailed as a genuine brain tonic. Ginkgo comes from the leaves of a tree with a 200-million-year pedigree, a tree that must be doing something right, because it's the oldest living species on the planet. Ginkgo extract can provide high-level brainpower, restore memory, reverse aging, and overcome harrowing mental deterioration. European researchers were so moved by test results that they slipped out of scientific parlance to call this multi-million-year-old memory tonic a "miracle." Patients with Alzheimer's and senile dementia showed "significant improvement" in eight weeks. The *Clinical Trials* journal reported Ginkgo extract "significantly reduced mental and physical signs of aging in hundreds of patients suffering cerebral vascular insufficiency."

European medical journals record the amazing ability of Ginkgo extract to improve general memory, mental efficiency, and concentration and to restore short term memory loss. It reduces stress and depression, vertigo and tinnitus. Ginkgo increases blood flow to the brain and has proven beneficial for a host of diseases that involve circulation—from hardening of the arteries to respiratory illnesses. It helps in oxygen transport, brain reaction time, and nerve signal transmission. It also clears toxins from brain and body.

In a Superlearning aside, maybe just the proximity of a regal Ginkgo tree inspired Bruce Tickell Taylor's wide ranging mental abilities. When he was a boy in Korea, a towering, ancient Ginkgo tree grew on the family property near his home. Local folks came continuously to visit the tree and leave offerings. Recently he told us the ancient Ginkgo is still putting out its delicate fan-shaped leaves, now under official government protection as a Natural National Treasure.

For a mind/memory "tune-up" to improve reaction time, awareness, clarity and vitality, Ginkgo is ideal. Used in China for over 2,800 years, it's famous as a rejuvenator. To overcome memory loss, 120 milligrams of Ginkgo per day for three months is recommended by researchers. (CAUTION: As reports flood in pinpointing the mind-enhancing effect of natural substances, bottles of brain brighteners have popped up like proverbial mushrooms. Check labels for the right milligram count.)

Overcoming Brain Damage

The central essence of wheat, the wheat germ, contains a natural substance so powerful, it can not only help the mentally retarded but even repair brain damage from accidents or illnesses such as a stroke. It's called *octacosanol*. One of America's foremost nutrition pioneers, Dr. Carleton Fredericks, did over thirty years of research on octacosanol. In hundreds of cases of people with major brain damage diagnosed "hopeless"—from coma cases to epilepsy, multiple sclerosis to cerebral palsy, encephalitis to brain poisoning, stroke to Parkinson's—octacosanol produced seemingly miraculous results. When Dr. Fredericks' own mother suffered a stroke that left her partially paralyzed with speech difficulties, four months of octacosanol brought her complete recovery. Still finding it hard to believe, her doctor tried octacosanol on twelve other stroke victims and had eleven successes.

"The basis of thinking is in part biochemical," Dr. Fredericks asserted, and he insisted that nutritional therapy including octacosanol should be tried for any case of retardation or learning disability. Dr. Andrew Ivy, the famous physiologist, revealed that octacosanol is actually able to repair damaged brain cells. Dr. Helmut Prahl, of the Dynatron Research Foundation in Madison, Wisconsin, reported that "almost all diseases of the central nervous system responded to octacosanol."

Two determined Canadian parents, Naseer and Monica Ahmad, were able to heal their "incurably autistic" child, Lee, by giving him octacosanol, and they have written a hope-filled book about their experience.

Today our environment is besieged with mind- and memory-numbing toxins in food, air and water. Lead, a severe mind damager, has been found in over 100,000 U.S. drinking fountains at countless schools. Mercury and aluminum (implicated in Alzheimer's), as well as other toxic industrial wastes shown to cause mindbody disease, are pouring into rivers and lakes and leeching into soil, where they contaminate foods. Research shows that octacosanol, along with the amino acid L-cysteine, can help protect us against this toxic invasion.

For treatment of mind and memory damage, octacosanol synthesized from wheat germ oil is recommended. Long used by athletes for stamina and endurance, the amount for brain repair is ten to one hundred times higher and takes four to six weeks to take effect. A new form, Super Octacosanol, has recently become available. Check with your health food store.

Oxygen for Mega Mental Power

You can't last more than three minutes without oxygen. Your brain needs enormous amounts of oxygen to keep going; your body's cells must have oxygen to burn food for energy. When you're oxygen deficient, it's like trying to burn damp wood—cells accumulate unmetabolized waste products that clog them up. Soon they're a breeding ground for viruses and microbes. Because of pollution, oxygen content in both water and air is down by as much as *50 percent* in some cities.

Gift boxes of oxygen canisters have become a hot-selling item, but inhaled oxygen must have its ions activated by enzymes to be really effective. In 1967, after a seventeen-year quest, the brilliant Japanese chemist Dr. Kazuhiko Asai synthesized an organic form of germanium, a substance that is a world-class oxygen bearer in brain and body. With germanium the oxygen is ready to be absorbed immediately. It renews brainpower right away.

Your brain accounts for 2 percent of your body's weight, but uses 20 to 30 percent of the body's total oxygen. Thinking—solving math problems, for instance—causes your brain to guzzle up even more of the body's precious oxygen.

In extensive tests organic germanium increased mental capacity.

It relieved symptoms of mind-numbing hypoxia (a disease caused by oxygen depletion) and relieved mental decline, memory loss, and senility. It also relieved a range of mental disorders, including psychoses, that may have been due to poor blood circulation to the brain.

Germanium "may be the most powerful immune-stimulant of all," says Dr. Betty Kamen in *Germanium, A New Approach to Immunity*. Because germanium's oxygen helps cells clear out unburned waste products, it knocks out viruses and microbes that live on toxic residues. As an oxygen catalyst and a detoxifier in the body, it powers up the immune system to fight a vast range of ills that accompany our current oxygen-deficient existence. It's a powerhouse against viral disease. It's been shown in scientific studies to help with cancer, arthritis, glandular disorders. It KOs the viruses and microbes in food poisoning (salmonella) and flu. The germanium compound does something else directly connected with the ability to learn well: It captures any toxic heavy metal in the body, discharging it completely within twenty hours. It's proven to clear up PCB poisoning and brain-damaging lead and mercury contamination from food and occasionally dental fillings. It's also a powerful endorphin producer, so it's a potent pain and stress reliever. In Japan, where germanium is widely taken as a daily supplement, it is believed not just to rejuvenate but to extend your life.

Germanium can do still more. The human body generates electricity. Organic germanium functions in the body as a semiconductor, discharging excess electricity, stimulating the flow where needed and balancing the body's electrical system. When a bone is broken or the body is injured, it emits a specific electrical pattern or "current of injury." Germanium, as a semiconductor, can help heal injuries rapidly by rebalancing electrical circuitry.

Organic germanium is found in foods—garlic, watercress, pearl barley, aloe, and ginseng. Organic germanium capsules are available outside the U.S., and 30 milligrams a day are recommended by researchers as a preventive measure. For pain relief or serious problems take 1 to 1½ grams or even more over several weeks.

Hyper-Oxygenation

Vaporize viruses and increase learning and creative abilities. Faced with the ravages of worldwide, ever mutating virus invasions, scientists and doctors are turning to a whole new range of treatments, all based on oxygen. At the same time, supercharged oxygens are a potent defense against the devastating effects on bodymind caused by constant gradual oxygen starvation in our cities. The breakthrough oxygen treatments include the use of oxygen electrolytes, food-grade hydrogen peroxide, and medical ozone, a nontoxic, superoxygen.

Research in America with "oxywater"—a few drops of *food-grade* hydrogen peroxide (H_2O_2) in a glass of water or fruit juice—has been found to overcome bacterial contaminants in water and food. "The oxywater regimen improves alertness, reflexes, memory and apparently intelligence," reports writer/publisher Waves Forest. "Alzheimer's and Parkinson's are responding to it. It may offer the elderly a new weapon against senility and related disorders." At Baylor University Medical Center, in Dallas, this hydrogen peroxide treatment cleared cholesterol from arteries, allowing more memory-boosting oxygen to reach the brain. (WARNING: Hydrogen peroxide is poisonous except in small amounts of just a few drops. There is a very narrow window of both safe and efficient use. Either try the already prepared commercial hydrogen peroxide drinks sold in health stores or get more data before dosing yourself. See Resources section.)

Clearing out toxins picked up from our polluted environment can give extra bonuses—a healthy population releases us all from bankrupting health costs. The eminent bacteriologist Dr. Edward Rosenow of the famous Mayo Clinic, who discovered the cause of rheumatic fever, pioneered early work with hydrogen peroxide. His sixty years of research convinced him that trying to chase after every single virus and microbe and hit it with a drug would be futile. Viruses and microbes are constantly mutating at high speed to ever more virulent forms—for instance, "hospital pneumonia."

While pharmaceutical companies, in the hope of hyper-profits, continue to pour research megabucks into the "superbug" chase, Dr. Rosenow's opposite approach of strengthening the whole body to resist "superbugs" is still valid. As Dr. Kurt Donsbach observes, "His contention that many of the ills of mankind were the result of microbial contamination in a defense-poor body has never been challenged." How to strengthen the whole body? Rosenow discovered that a 1.5 percent solution of H_2O_2 worked better than anything else to destroy microorganisms and toxins, because they are anaerobic—they can only exist on low oxygen. With high oxygen levels they vaporize.

Today a stream of excellent results is pouring in about superoxygen. Bethesda Naval Hospital, in Maryland, and the VA Hospital in San Francisco have shown that oxygen therapies can get rid of viruses in humans without damage to other cells. Dr. William Crook, author of *The Yeast Connection*, reveals the damage just one single microorganism can do. Running at epidemic proportions, Candida albicans causes memory loss, serious learning problems, poor concentration, allergies, hyperactivity, and massive fatigue in many people, particularly women. A number of clinics are using oxygen therapies to treat the ever-persistent candida. Patients report they can concentrate again and think more clearly.

For over thirty years in European clinics doctors have put the healing powers of oxygen to good use. They do it by infusing patients' blood with ozone. Ozone therapy has cleared up Epstein-Barr, herpes, TB, candida, hepatitis cytomegalovirus, and some claim it has even eased AIDS.

Ozone—supercharged oxygen—is now considered the best purifier for city water systems and also your pool. It provides five thousand times more rapid disinfection with no toxic residues and is widely used in Europe. Getting rid of the steadily increasing toxins in water can bring big benefits to mindbody. (For instance acid rain in water supplies has now been implicated in Alzheimer's in recent studies.)

Another new oxygen therapy—electrolytes of oxygen—offers a natural, safe form of increasing internal oxygen. You just add a few drops of electrolytes to a glass of water three times a day. Dr. Donsbach also suggests magnesium peroxide as one of the most beneficial forms of oral oxygen therapy. For more, see his book $O_2O_2O_2$. The new supercharged forms of oxygen can offer us, it seems, another route to rejuvenation of mind, memory, and body.

Smart Drugs

The race has been on for years in labs, official and unofficial, to find drugs that light up the mind. If you live in Europe, you might already be using a new class of mind-enhancing drugs—Nootropics. These are legal drugs with low toxicity known to improve learning and memory. Piracetam, for instance, boosts alertness, concentration, and learning. It is effective with the learning-disabled too. Attention Deficit Disorder sufferers, for instance, given Piracetam in experiments, showed an increase in beta ("thinking") brainwaves and a decrease in delta ("sleep") waves, improving the ability to concentrate. Hydergine, another smart drug, boosts memory, concentration, learning, and speech in both the able and the disabled. These drugs can be imported for personal use from Europe. For more, see *Smart Drugs and Nutrients* by Dr. Ward Dean. (See Resources for addresses.)

Super Vitamins and Minerals

Certain vitamins and minerals are essential for optimal brainpower. The minerals zinc, magnesium, and iron are critical. Zinc and magnesium can prevent memory burnout and senile changes in the nervous system. Because the soil in many states is totally depleted of zinc, food often contains little or no zinc, so nutrition expert Maureen Salaman recommends supplements. Dr. Don Tucker, of the University of Oregon, showed people could improve alertness, memory, and even word fluency with an oxygen-boosting iron supplement. The minerals potassium, magnesium, and calcium have also helped faulty memories and learning.

Good memory and abstract thinking can all be helped with vitamins A, B complex, and C. The well known Boston gerontologist and neurosurgeon Dr. Vernon Mark has evidence that a diet lacking in B complex can produce "dementing brain disease." Vitamin B_{15}, or, as it's also called, pangamic acid, is an oxygenator of living tissues. Soviet studies show it aids respiration of brain tissue and they have used it for years to treat learning disabilities and mental retardation with outstanding results. The nutrient RNA is vital for the brain and memory. It also protects the brain against oxidized fats that can interfere with brain metabolism. Vitamin C has been shown to raise IQ and is essential for the whole body. Two-time Nobel Prize winner biochemist Dr. Linus Pauling considers vitamin C essential for top-level mind function. Vitamin E is an important antioxidant and life extender. Like Superlearning, nutrition is synergistic—all the elements work together. To get maximum benefits from the nutrients mentioned above, a balanced regimen of vitamins and minerals is important.

Beefing up brain circuitry with nutrition has been proven to pay dividends. In a recent study of twenty-six teenagers by Dr. Stephen Schoenthaler, of California State University, in Turlock, fifteen were given vitamin and mineral supplements, the rest placebos. After three months the fifteen on supplements scored significant gains in nonverbal IQ.

The Green Solution

Recent U.S. Department of Agriculture research shows topsoil minerals are being lost now from farms at a faster rate than in the Dust Bowl of the 1930s. Herbicides and insecticides add to the depletion of minerals and essential life factors in foods. No matter how much food from these depleted soils we eat, we're still malnourished. No wonder a high percentage of the population is chronically ill.

Fortunately there's a remarkable solution—chlorophyll. Some call it synthesized sunshine. Chlorophyll is the sun nutrient that is the basis for all plant life activity on the planet. Fifty years of studies document mineral-rich chlorophyll's powers to heal everything from TB to cardiac disease, arteriosclerosis to mental depression. It fights infection and protects against viruses and microbes. In U.S. Army studies chlorophyll counteracted toxic heavy metals, lethal dosages of poisons, and even nuclear fallout (strontium 90).

You can get one of the highest natural sources of chlorophyll in tablets of Super Blue-Green Algae from Oregon or spirulina and chlorella algae grown in tanks of water. Algae also contains an unusually high concentration of vitamins, minerals, and protein. It's a complete food with all the essential elements of life.

People report feeling exceptional mental clarity lasting for hours from SBG Algae. They describe improved memory and mental focus and relief from stress, anxiety, depression, and mood swings. They report increased physical stamina. Some even feel blissed out. It has a powerful positive effect on the brain's neurotransmitters, which Japanese scientists attribute to "Controlled Growth Factor"—a group of live molecules imbued with what they call "life force" that revitalize, slow aging, and open new vistas of mindpower. Health aficionados believe that chlorophyll-rich algae will become the superfood of the 21st century. Super Blue-Green Algae can be a superroute to Superlearning.

Health and Learning

KIDS AILING MORE AND LEARNING LESS—*New York Post* . . . USA'S KIDS SCORE C—FOR HEALTH—*USA Today* . . . DEPRESSION GROWING WITH EACH GENERATION—*USA Today* . . . ONE IN FOUR WITH ANXIETY DISORDER . . . *USA Today*

"This country has a health-care crisis in the classroom," says Dr. Daniel Shea, president of the American Academy of Pediatrics, commenting on a national 1992 survey. "Poor health is leading to poor academic performance; and poor academic performance is leading to a wide array of greater social problems—school dropouts, unemployment, poverty and crime, to name but a few."

Most common were psychological and emotional difficulties, inability to concentrate, and low self-esteem. Findings reported by the *Journal of the American Medical Association* showed, "Depression is a worldwide phenomenon . . . happening at younger and younger ages," according to Dr. Myrna Weissman, of Columbia University.

Stress and anxiety levels are ultra high—a product of problems at home (abuse, malnutrition, divorce), economic problems, and environmental stresses ranging from mind-damaging pollutants to high crime. (In some places both students and teachers feel such high anxiety about crime that they come to school armed.)

Latest reports show 3 percent of the population suffer with diagnosed learning problems from dyslexia to Attention Deficit Disorder (ADD), hyperactivity to retardation. No wonder the burnout timeframe for new teachers is now down to two years. "Students come to school with so many problems, it's difficult for them to be good students," teachers lament.

Outside school systems there are the millions of retarded, autistic, and brain-damaged spending lifetimes in institutions at terrible emotional and economic cost. Now, too, there is the creeping specter of Alzheimer's engulfing 1 percent of those over sixty-five.

The gloomy news seems to keep growing. But a healthy wedge of light is beginning to widen too. The end of the twentieth century has brought a new universe of understanding of how brain, mind, and memory work. These discoveries are fostering a new sort of "tech"— mind tech, a combination of technique and technology that takes into account the biochemical and energetic aspects of optimal performance. You already hear of designer drugs and designer food. It's an easy prediction to say 21st century Superlearners will enjoy designer nutrition—a protocol set up for individual needs and aims. Bruce Tickell Taylor, for instance, finds the herbal/mineral nutrition formula Km is an excellent blend with Superlearning techniques.

Much of this breakthrough nutrition knowledge is here *now*. You don't have to wait years of lab-lag time to use these discoveries. You can inform yourself and do it yourself. Superlearning is a resonance of the ancient Socratic idea of drawing out innate genius. It's beginning to resonate now to the related goal of the Greeks and Romans: *Mens sana in corpore sano*—a sound mind in a sound body.

17
The High-Tech Mindpower Revolution

With the flip of a switch can you increase your intelligence to near genius levels? Can a machine prompt you to dazzling creativity? Can a machine give you supermemory? Can a machine replace your stress with joy? The answer is yes. This isn't science fiction. It's science fact. Mind machines that amp up IQ, restore memory loss, heal mind disabilities, repair brain damage, relieve addictions, generate optimism, even change genetic predisposition—have arrived.

"We have new technology for enhancing consciousness, rapidly, safely, right now, with no side effects," our old friend, physicist Dr. Robert Beck, told us. Author Robert Anton Wilson asserts that the fast-arriving new generation of mind machines "will mark the most important turning point in the evolution of this planet."

Dr. Beck, who, as a consultant to the U.S. Defense Department was in on part of the behind-the-scenes intrigue that led to some of these unusual devices, calls it "one of the most fascinating psycho-political stories ever to emerge." As we revealed in *Supermemory*, some machines that open new vistas of mindpower are a positive "dividend" from the Cold War. During the height of competition, as the super-powers ran roughshod over human guinea pigs in the pursuit of high-tech mind control, there were plenty of negative dividends too. Just three years ago Canadians who'd served as unknowing subjects in CIA funded hospital experiments won a multimillion-dollar class-action suit against the CIA and another against their own government because they'd had their memories completely erased.

For decades, Soviet scientists beamed pulsed electromagnetic fields at people. Which frequency made you feel depressed, stressed, anxious, even suicidal? Which ones could cripple your thinking by depleting your brain's chemical signaling system, the neurotransmitters? Which ones could wipe out your memory completely? Could someone else's memories be implanted in your mind? Which frequencies increased neurotransmitters involved with memory? Which frequency could actually knock you unconscious?

They investigated every aspect of electromagnetics as well as acupuncture and psychic force. Soon Soviets had mapped the key frequencies that influence emotions, memory, brainpower, consciousness itself. They developed electronic methods for dissolving memory. Machines for beaming toxic mindbody frequencies were focused on diplomats, spies, political prisoners, political leaders, even chess players. They even broadcast toxic frequencies long distance. It may sound like sci-fi, but it's all documented.

"Catch up!" Western defense and intelligence agencies pressured scientists. The CIA funded hundreds of ultrasecret memory experiments in hospitals and prisons.

On the plus side of the Soviet effort, researchers discovered powerful new ways of *expanding* memory and tapping in to the vast reserve of mind potentials. The Soviets had a major military problem—massive alcoholism. Quite a few generals and other top brass had developed severe short term memory loss (Korsakoff's psychosis) from drinking too much vodka. To repair memory, Soviets developed a device that beamed electrical frequencies that stimulate key brain chemicals essential to memory function. In cases of severe, long term alcoholism it generally takes *eight years* of abstinence to recover. After treatment with these devices short term memory was restored in *five days*.

Western intelligence agencies checked out smuggled devices in highly classified U.S. labs. They worked! And even better than rumored. Beaming specific frequencies at the brain stimulated it to produce essential chemicals to restore memory loss in alcoholics and drug addicts in *three to five* days. Research at the University of Wisconsin Medical School, the University of Louisiana Medical School, and the University of Texas all confirmed it too.

Dr. Ray Smith, chief of research at the D.C. government alcoholism hospital, found to his surprise that "incurable" *permanent brain damage* in alcoholics was curable in three weeks with Cranial Electro-Stimulation.

Western scientists rapidly investigated electrostimulation. Working for NASA at the Cell and Molecular Biology Lab of the Hampton, Virginia, VA Hospital, Dr. Clarence Cone made a revolutionary discovery. Damaged brain cells could actually be *regenerated* using electromagnetic stimulation at the right frequency. It meant that people with brain damage from trauma or stroke might regrow new cells through electrostimulation. NASA patented Cone's procedure.

Meanwhile a now internationally renowned scientist, Dr. Robert Becker of the Syracuse VA Hospital, discovered that electrostimulation of the body can regenerate organs and rapidly mend and regrow bones. In mapping the acupuncture bio-electric system in the body, he came to a significant conclusion. Becker found that electrostimulation, conveyed through the acupuncture meridians, stimulated the entire body's electrical field, which in turn could have profound effects on mind, body, emotions, and behavior.

Dr. Becker's explorations carried him to the study of consciousness itself. Like the Soviets he found that waking consciousness is a function of direct electrocurrents that run from negative to positive poles in the brain—a front-to-back flow in the head. If this electrical current is reversed, you are knocked unconscious. Soviets developed sleep machines that give this electrocurrent of consciousness an electrozap to cure insomnia. Strong magnetic fields can do the same: reverse the current and put you to sleep.

Becker tracked the electrocurrent of consciousness farther. When you're put under a chemical anesthetic, this current of consciousness is reversed. When you experience acupuncture anesthesia, the same thing happens, the current reverses. The same with hypnosis, magnetic fields, self-suggestion. They all alter the body's electro-potentials in the same way. Like the Soviets he confirmed that when you're hypnotized or do a relaxation exercise or visualization exercise like those in this book, you are actually altering the electro-potentials of your body. Like the Soviets he developed equipment to chart the depth of relaxation or hypnosis by monitoring the level of electrocurrents at various points on the body. If you're out cold, the negative electropotential at the front of your head drops to zero.

Are you in a rage against a boss or a spouse? Do you feel serene and calm? Dr. Leonard Ravitz, at Yale, discovered that your emotions and changes in states of consciousness radiate different energies. He could detect them precisely with an electrovoltmeter. Even *memories* of strong emotions show a marked electro-energy change. Mind, memory, emotions, he found, operate through sophisticated electro-circuitry.

Neuroscientist Dr. Aryeh Routtenberg, of Northwestern University, was among the first to discover that electrical stimulation of the brain in certain areas triggers the release of large amounts of the neurotransmitters involved with memory, learning, creativity, and above all, pleasure. The effect on the brain is similar to cocaine, which works by stimulating neurotransmitters in the very same areas. These chemicals are vital to the brain's signaling system—the keys to genius-level mind function. They relieve depression and pain *and* increase optimism and pleasure (see page 188).

As Dr. Ifor Capel, of the Marie Curie Cancer Memorial Foundation, says, "The brain's language is frequency." He too pinpointed the exact frequencies of this language. A 10 hertz signal boosts production and turnover rate of serotonin, a neurotransmitter that eases pain and depression and can make you sleepy. (This neurotransmitter is the one produced by the widely prescribed antidepression drug Prozac.) Beta-endorphins were stimulated at 90 to 111 hertz; catecholamines, important for the consolidation of memory and learning, at around 4 hertz.

When people take drugs like amphetamines and cocaine, these

same brain chemicals are released, giving one a "high"—a heightened sense of brilliance, creativity, and optimism. These drugs force the sparkle by preventing neurotransmitters from returning to their home bases. They're all out "transmitting." But once the basic supply is used up, the crash comes. The drugs stop working. When drugs like cocaine flood the body, the "little factories" in the brain stop manufacturing their own natural painkillers. This makes drug withdrawal total agony.

In Hong Kong neurosurgeon Dr. H. L. Wen was using electroacupuncture as anesthesia for brain surgery when he suddenly discovered that patients who were heroin addicts recovered completely from drug addiction with no withdrawal symptoms. He went to work with addicts, stimulating the acupuncture anesthesia point number 86 (Heart-Lung) on the shell of the ear, with an electrocurrent of 111 hertz, the frequency that makes the brain produce endorphins. Within forty minutes of applying the voltage, the brain's ability to produce its own painkillers started up and within three to five days was back to normal. Addiction and withdrawal symptoms were gone. Electrical stimulation of the brain at the proper frequency and waveform could quickly and sharply increase the levels of specific pain-relieving, pleasure-producing, and mindpower-producing neurotransmitters in the brain.

By 1973 Dr. Wen had cured 140 heroin addicts. Scottish surgeon Dr. Margaret Patterson studied Wen's methods in Hong Kong. Back in England she developed highly sophisticated machines that produced neurotransmitters by electrostimulation of the brain. Then she set up her own treatment center in California. Famous clients were flown in, some on stretchers—rock superstar Peter Townshend for one, guitarist and composer for The Who and creator of the hit rock musical *Tommy*. A drug addict for years, Townshend had spent a fortune trying to kick his habit. Within forty minutes of applying the device, the heroin was counteracted. Ten days of treatments later he was over his addiction to heroin, alcohol, and cocaine, with no withdrawal symptoms.

"There was a sense of inner joy," says Townshend. He'd fallen into addiction after a series of catastrophic career crises. "You learn something about your human potential, the powers you have to deal with whatever crises come your way."

"The implications of this work are stunning," said physicist Bob Beck, the expert on electromagnetic fields, long employed as a consultant to the Department of Defense. Beck, a close friend of Meg Patterson, was soon swept into an adventure of discovery. He studied all her research and everything he could uncover in the Defense Department. Working with spectrum analyzers and sophisticated equipment, he came up with a device: the Brain Tuner 5+, which broadcasts the frequencies of the three "magic" ranges of neurotransmitters—enkephalins, catecholamines, and beta-endorphins. He set up the frequencies in bundles. Instead of sounding one for each neurotransmitter separately, he put 256 frequencies together like a resonating chord of music. His device, smaller than a Walkman, runs on a 9-volt battery and is safe. The Brain Tuner has electrodes on a stethoscope-like headset that fit in the hollows behind the ears. Acupuncture points behind the ear effectively circulate electrostimulation on the "Triple Warmer" Meridian. You wear the device just twenty minutes a day.

Double-blind studies were done at the University of Wisconsin on the BT 5+'s capabilities to overcome drug-withdrawal symptoms and it did the job. Studies at both Wisconsin and the University of Louisiana showed it could boost IQ from twenty to thirty points. BT 5+ stimulation appears to enhance neural efficiency, researchers stated.

Users report the BT 5+ reduces stress, improves short and long term memory, helps learning, increases energy, improves concentration and reduces pain, anxiety, depression, and sleep requirements.

Dr. Donald Kubitz, of San Francisco, one of the first American doctors to study Dr. Wen's work with electroacupuncture on addicts, believed electrostimulation could be enormously beneficial for autistic and other mentally handicapped children. Both the BT 5+ and electro-acupuncture could prove powerful new ways to open fabulous new dimensions of mind as well as overcome disabilities and addictions. Now the latest model, the BT 6, has just made its debut.

Couch Potato to Couch Potential

Can a curiously revolving couch vastly expand mental agility as well as mend retardation, autism, and brain damage? This chaise longue really does have reams of documentation to prove it can sharpen mental efficiency, release stress, and open new possibilities. The Graham Potentializer, a couch that revolves horizontally counterclockwise about ten and a half times a minute, was developed twenty years ago by David Graham, a Canadian electronics engineer.

Robert Anton Wilson, an expert in new mindpower technologies, calls it "the most exhilarating of all the brain boosters around."

Megabrain author Michael Hutchison reports that "for several days after each use I felt refreshed and seemed to work better, think more effectively, and felt surprisingly energetic and calm." Others call it a mind "defogger" and "focuser." It seemed couch potential could turn even a couch potato into a dynamo.

Independent tests showed the revolving couch could sharpen anyone's mind. For the brain damaged and learning disabled it had life-changing powers. An ambitious test program began in the 1970s in Toronto for fifteen hundred brain-damaged and profoundly mentally disabled children. Over a period of months they rode the special rotating couch. Tests measured brain functions, IQ, and brainwave activity.

The average change in each subject's neuro-efficiency quotient was an enormous 25 percent improvement. Subjects showed increased alpha waves, balanced brain hemispheres, and changes in EEG parameters of great magnitude that were consistent and highly significant. The machine "definitely does something beneficial to the brainwaves," reported Dr. J. P. Ertl, a well-respected Canadian psychologist.

What that means in everyday life can be seen in a two-year-old with Down syndrome, who suddenly, in one month of treatments, developed all the fine motor responses of a normal two-year-old.

Five-year-old Bruce suffered with severe brain damage and was so hyperactive, he had to wear a helmet. He slept barely three hours a night and went on raging, house-destroying rampages. After forty sessions he slept normally all night, his mental functioning improved, and he had better motor coordination.

Twelve-year-old Pat suffered brain damage at three and was spastic and autistic. She couldn't walk and barely spoke. Totally withdrawn, she slept fourteen hours a day. After forty sessions she began talking meaningfully. Her stamina, endurance, and energy increased and she could walk and handle utensils. She slept less and her attention span increased. She was reclassified as trainable. We interviewed parents of some of the test subjects and heard that improvements lasted and even continued.

The secret of the couch? The rhythmic circular motion, according to Graham. It affects all the body fluids, especially in the inner ear. Motion causes electrical signals from the inner ear and the fluids of the semicircular canals to travel to parts of the brain that regulate balance and motor activity. These link with the mid-brain limbic system and the higher brain. The motion triggers electricity and chemicals that increase activity in all parts of the brain, lighting up neural networks and forging new connections. "This brings a dramatic increase in motor and learning capabilities," says Graham. "Movement is like a nutrient."

And Dr. Tomatis insists that "sound is a nutrient." It seems specific sounds and motions work like electrostimulation and set off a shimmering range of helpful activity throughout brain and body.

Ocean waves and human cerebral spinal fluid both average 10 to 12 cycles a minute, and Graham's couch operates at 10.5 cycles per minute. Combining this primal rhythm and motion helps produce the profoundly soothing, stress-relieving effect. A device at one end of the couch produces a mild 125 hertz electromagnetic field, which interacts with the body's own fields as the couch moves. By externally changing the electrical activity, chemical changes are produced in brain and body similar to an energy transfusion. It's like a brain exercise that improves neural responses. Graham has evidence that this vestibular-stimulation treatment can help regenerate brain cells. Certainly the damaged children seemed to have recovered lost brain functions. Graham's rotating couch in a weak electromagnetic field mimics the "earth experience."

We live on a rotating earth that moves us through its electromagnetic fields.

Dr. Sung Choi, of the Medical College of Virginia, showed that "kinetic therapy"—gentle, continuous motion or rocking of critically ill patients—significantly reduced the time they spent in intensive care units.

In the U.S. tests subjects who rode the couch showed a definite acceleration in learning of math, reading, and spelling. Math abilities in particular improved. Other tests confirmed that Graham's apparatus increases neuro-efficiency. The couch produced clear-cut physical, neurological, and consciousness-raising benefits.

Graham no longer manufactures the couch. But three new motion systems have been developed, each producing impressive results. Integrated Motion System (IMS), invented by Dr. Larry Schultz, is a couch that tilts and rocks like a raft in a gentle sea. One M.D., after a session on the IMS, got up and did a back flip—his first since college. His muscular coordination had been fine-tuned by the device. A coma patient in a San Jose, California, hospital who was placed on the IMS got dramatic relief from lung congestion, suddenly opened his eyes, and was able to focus and watch people. A young girl, suffering brain damage from birth, was blind, unable to move and racked with dozens of brain seizures a day. After several sessions on the IMS, seizures declined substantially and the child was able to move on her own.

IQ Symmetron, another Schultz invention, is a contour chair with an orbital platform that revolves through a multiphase wave experience. The chair effect creates profound relaxation within minutes— a kind of "tidal weightlessness."

The SAMS (Sensory and Mind Stimulation) Potentializer was designed by biomedical inventor Marvin Sams after years of testing the Graham device. SAMS is a recliner chair that rotates imperceptibly at three RPMs. The vestibular stimulation is combined with an inaudible tone. Brain tests show it greatly improves the neuroefficiency quotient.

Information on motion machines can be obtained from: *Megabrain Report* and Tools for Exploration. (See pages 414–415.)

"Memory Pollution" Busters

Mind and memory fog can be caused by common things all around us—heaters, TVs, hairdryers, waterbeds, computers. Electromagnetic pollution in our everyday environment has been shown to cause confusion, depression, and poor mental function. At the U.S. Navy's Pensacola labs, scientists tested people's short term memory while a mild magnetic field common to appliances was beamed at them. Memory declined.

Soviet tests of Extremely Low Frequency (ELF) magnetic or electric fields showed they could produce hyperactivity and disturbed sleep patterns. Switching fields on and off desynchronized the brain and interfered with the brain's hypothalamus, which is important for logical and associational thought. Soviets found the specific ELF electric fields that can harm acetylcholine, a neurotransmitter extremely important for memory. Microwave bombardment at certain frequencies reduced two more neurotransmitters essential for memory—norepinephrine and dopamine.

Dr. Robert Becker, author of *Cross Currents: The Perils of Electropollution—The Promise of Electromedicine,* discovered that the jumbled barrage of electromagnetic fields in the average big city could have very negative effects on mind, memory, and body. Powerful transmissions from TV and radio towers, high-tension electrical wires, airport and military radar installations, and radiation from household electrical appliances—all created a kind of electronic smog. Electronic smog can affect memory, cause learning disabilities and depress the immune system. It can cause a variety of mental and behavioral disorders including depression. Magnetic fields at the homes of suicide victims were 22 percent higher than at houses of controls. In addition the World Health Organization warns that exposure to ELF electric fields can affect you physically right down to your cells, leaving you feeling fatigued and burned out. Becker also documented birth defects, cancer, and Alzheimer's.

Some years ago, the Soviets began using ELF fields as memory weapons and began beaming them at the U.S. Embassy in Moscow and other diplomatic targets. Scientists began a crash investigation to develop ways of protecting diplomats and others from these unhealthy, confusing electromagnetic waves. They developed devices that we can use as shields to protect ourselves from harmful electronic smog.

The earth has its own magnetic field, which pulses at about 8 cycles per second. Humans are oriented to live in the earth's natural field, and it acts as a biological clock for us. Confronted with both a confusing field and the 8-cycle field, the body responds to the 8-cycle field and rejects the unhealthy one. Scientists have developed devices that pulse at the natural earth cycle of 8 per second and have tested them extensively. Dr. Sheldon Deal, of the Swan Clinic in Tucson, Arizona, showed that if people had an 8-cycle earth resonance generator near them and were bombarded with unhealthy electromagnetic pollution, they remained unaffected.

Stewardesses report these devices help them overcome jet lag. When the first astronauts returned to earth with certain health disturbances, NASA discovered they could be overcome with the 8-cycle earth pulse. NASA builds the pulsing magnetic field of the earth into all manned spacecraft now.

Danish-born Toronto inventor Niels Primdahl developed Relaxit—an earth-field generator. Testimonials in his files show it not only overcame electronic smog, it also helped insomnia, motion sickness, migraines, cramps, and stress. Tests at Laurentian University showed the generator induced a relaxed state.

Dr. Andrei Puharich developed a tiny 8-cycle generator that's built into an attractive wristwatch that has been subjected to exacting U.S. Navy tests. They showed that "the shielding instrument appears to block signals that may be harmful to the body."

Bio-Battery—Mind/Body Rejuvenator

"Found to aid the body in *every* direction." "Necessary for anyone who uses the brain a great deal." These are the words of America's most famous psychic, Edgar Cayce, still known around the world for the many unusual remedies he dictated for those who appealed to him with all manner of ills. He recommended using a "bio-battery" in over 25 percent of his health-counseling cases. Cayce dictated the plans for the device more than sixty years ago, and we may be just becoming aware of the rich legacy he left.

Everyone should use the bio-battery, according to Cayce, because it keeps the body and mind completely tuned up. Unlike other devices mentioned, Cayce's supposedly works on the body's subtle energy, the chi energy of acupuncture—which doesn't sound as outlandish now as it did in the 1930s. The Association for Research and Enlightenment (A.R.E.), in Virginia Beach, has six decades of records on the battery's achievements. Case histories report the device has helped alleviate dozens of ailments, from scleroderma to cerebral palsy, arthritis to neurasthenia.

Cayce prescribed the bio-energy battery most often for cases involving mind and memory. "It can almost build a new brain," Cayce said. Whether the condition was amnesia, senility, brain damage, or retardation, the device could help, he said. "Memory is never lost!" Cayce claimed. Like the yogis who could demonstrate supermemory, he said memories are stored safely outside the physical body. The bio-energy battery could restore our communications network with our memories, he maintained. This could make learning superrapid and easy.

We are constantly repairing and replacing the cells in brain and body. By using the bio-energy battery, he said, these replacement cells are attuned back to their correct pattern. Thus whether brainpower loss was due to deterioration from age, disease, or accident, the bio-battery could help restore it. The device could give stability and strength to the system and rebalance it. In addition it relieves stress.

The world began to wake up to the promising new field of energy medicine in the 1980s. Discoveries in biomagnetics, bioelectricity, acupuncture, subtle energies, and vibrational medicine opened up new horizons for healing and rejuvenation. The Fetzer Energy Medicine Research Institute launched rigorous, double-blind tests of the Cayce devices. They discovered the Cayce device stimulated the brain's production of dopamine. This neurotransmitter in turn produces two more powerful brain messengers, key to high-level mental function and relief of stress and depression. The device also helps the endocrine system.

Despite years of harassment by authorities eager to stamp out the battery, clinical testing went on quietly, first with Dr. William McGarey and then with Harvey Grady, research director at the A.R.E. Clinic in Phoenix, Arizona. Grady, who has used the battery himself for years, finds it an excellent stress reducer and calls it an "unclaimed inheritance." In addition to positive results for a variety of conditions, battery users singled out stress relief in particular, describing the device as "a harmony generator" and "an energy booster." We've used the battery ourselves and can confirm its stress-shedding effect.

U.S. Psychotronics Association researcher Phil Thomas reports good progress with several of his battery test subjects. For instance a twenty-seven-year-old quadriplegic man, brain damaged right after birth, was able to speak sentences and showed improved memory and concentration.

Bruce Baar, of Downingtown, Pennsylvania, a battery researcher for twenty-nine years, told us he had personally witnessed a case of mongolism achieve complete recovery after several years of treatment. Baar designed and manufactured the modern, easy-to-use bio-batteries tested in the Fetzer experiments.

Like acupuncture the bio-battery evidently helps redistribute and equalize energies to give mindbody a complete tune-up. Used in a special way, with gold solutions, it's claimed to be a rejuvenator, an energetic fountain of youth perhaps. For more on the little known secrets of the bio-battery, see *Supermemory*.

Alpha-Stim

The Alpha-Stim is one of the most popular mind machines used by more than a million people since 1981. This tiny five-ounce device heightens mental functioning, relieves pain, and accelerates learning. It is endorsed by the U.S. Olympic Committee Athletes Advisory Council and recommended in medical and dental textbooks as well as by *The American Chiropractor*. It works by Cranial-Electro-Stimulation (CES) to accelerate learning and improve memory. In addition it has a built-in TENS unit, which blocks pain by electrical stimulation through the skin.

Insiders in the mind-tech field consider the Alpha-Stim the most reliably effective device around. The idea of the CES machines is to induce a "following response" from the brain. By influencing the tides of brainwave activity, the CES lets you shift mental gears into more powerful states without the "driving" effect of some of the very intense light and sound machines.

This CES machine stimulates the brain to produce endorphins, the pleasure chemicals involved in accelerated learning. Pleasure chemicals are involved in memory consolidation. They bring a state of well-being where one can reach greater creativity, concentration, and high-level mental functions. They relieve the down feelings that can sabotage your creative and mental powers.

Mike Hercules is one of the top U.S. researchers of CES and how it can enhance your creativity, mental functioning, and even evoke superpotentials. An aerospace specialist at NASA, Hercules was one of the first to delve into Russian Electro-Sleep Machines and decode which electrical frequencies open specific states of consciousness relating to everything from accelerated language retention to psychic perceptions.

Mind Man

Mind Man, developed in Germany, is a unique addition to the mind-tech field. This device offers the widest range of cranial-electro-stimulation available—0.5 hertz up to 510 hertz. The German Federal Health Administration has given Mind Man its blessing, authorizing its use by physicians and therapists. Studies show it can produce specific effects ranging from energy boosting, to creativity and intuition enhancement, to memory improvement and sleep induction.

Virtual Reality

Paul Schuytema is one of the few Americans who has gone to a planet on the Inner Sphere, a planet of arid plains and purple twilight filtering from two low-slung crescent moons. Equipped with thirtieth-millennium tech, Schuytema won a shoot-out on that lonely planet against the enemy, Marasaki, and only as he depressurized back into 1993 Chicago did he remember to stop holding his breath.

A writer, he'd signed on at the BattleTech Center, created by Virtual World Entertainment, which owns two other intergalactic command posts home in Japan. Virtual reality—using headsets, eyebands, gloves, and soon whole-body suits—grabs hold of your senses and gives you a full-blown experience of being there— anywhere technoimagination can envision.

"Virtual World Entertainment has stumbled into what could be the next drug: a virtual experience so real that I felt the primitive, puny technology of our twentieth century as soon as I stepped back into reality," Schuytema reports. Traveling in virtual reality raises your pulse, "excites the sweat glands, pumps the adrenaline and washes euphoria through the veins." Euphoria born on a far purple planet or lakefront Chicago? "I can't be sure," says Schuytema.

Like early TV, the fast-looming world of virtual reality is bursting with promise for entertainment and learning. With a little luck we may get a meld. Today's Superlearners tomorrow may accelerate finesse of all kinds, from driving a car to piloting an SST, from practicing a slalom run to giving a speech and quieting hecklers— all through experience gained in virtual reality. It's an amped-up version of Superlearning techniques such as imaginative rehearsal and visualization. Just as people who shift their brain states with beat frequencies or control their blood pressure with musical biofeed-back learn, with experience, to produce the desired effect without the equipment, virtual reality may give people the practice nudge they need to become elegant imaginers—and learners—on their own. Virtual reality is the most generalized, flexible technology in this chapter. Don't be surprised if other mind machines gravitate into this world-generating approach, opening novel, almost firsthand adventures in outer and inner reality.

One Hundred Percent Better with Mindscope

Interactive TV is gliding down the information highway right toward your living room. Pretty soon you may be using it to give a 100 percent lift to your concentration and learning. Mindscope, the brainchild of Barry Bittman, M.D., director of the Headache Center Neurology

Institute of Western Pennsylvania, in Meadville, has already been giving people that bonus.

Bittman considered how you usually do biofeedback. Hooked to monitoring machines, you sit in the lab while an assistant quietly gives you relaxation suggestions. Feedback on how well you're doing at lowering your blood pressure, for instance, may be shown as a computer bar graph or be heard as a fluctuating tone. Bittman got a bright idea. Make the feedback not just more user-friendly but part of the process. And engage people in a way that allows them quickly to summon a blood-pressure-lowering state anywhere, without lab support.

Few people develop the skill to evoke the image of a bar graph sufficient to bring on a conditioned relaxation response. Bittman turned to the latest tech, the Pioneer LD-V8000, an advanced laser-disk player that can search for and grab a video frame at lightning speed. If you were reclining in an easy chair in Bittman's lab today, you might be treated to a serene picture of a Hawaiian waterfall on a thirty-five-inch TV. Instead of a technician's suggestions, you'd hear the water rushing, leaves rustling, birds calling, and see a white swan winging through the sky. Signals monitoring your muscle tension flash through the equipment. The more you relax, the clearer the scene becomes. As you relax more and more, the scene grows closer and closer, until you begin to feel you're really there. That's interacting. Your physiology is controlling the TV picture.

Erasing physical ills and phobias, sports training—Mindscope has a host of potential uses. Help for learners is one that Bittman's team quickly developed.

"Constant and rapid change has become paramount to success in modern day America," they point out. Yet "the evolution of learning skills has not kept pace with the emergence of information."

Two sets of volunteers—actives and passives—looked at a list of twenty words and read a story for ninety seconds. Bittman tested their memory and comprehension. Then all enjoyed ten minutes of watching a colorful Hawaiian sunset on Mindscope. As the "actives" released muscle tension, the scene grew clearer and the sun slowly dipped toward the horizon. The "passives" simply looked at the calming scene with no control over what happened.

Relaxation counts. Tested again for retention and comprehension, "passives" scored 48 percent higher than before. But something else counts too. The interactive group did a whopping 135 percent better. Bittman neatly proved a Superlearning point. The right state for learning is body relaxed *and* mind alert. Interactive multimedia underlines another Superlearning premise: Engage more senses and the whole brain to pump up learning. This new, suggestive TV training shows promise, too, for the learning disabled—ADD sufferers, for instance.

You can't barrel around connected to Mindscope. But one of Bittman's headache clients discovered that training can click in even while driving through a snowstorm. As the roads got more slippery and the snow blew more fiercely, the woman felt her neck tighten and a nasty headache begin to rise. She "did not reach for a pill nor attempt a relaxation exercise," Bittman reports. "Rather, inadvertently, she blinked her eyes for a second and recalled the image of a white bird peacefully flying across the Mindscope waterfall scene. To her astonishment the neck pain and headache suddenly disappeared." With a little training you could probably flash in to one of your best states for accomplishment in the exam room, office, basketball court or anyplace.

Mindpower Fitness Machines

"One day mind machines may be the brain-training counterpart to Nautilus or cross-country ski contraptions," says author Michael Hutchison. He foresees people pumping neurotransmitters and brain boosters on their home mind machines the same way they now exercise on NordicTrack.

The machines described above are only a handful of the hundreds of new mind machines available. Every day, worldwide, high-caliber new ones are developed and manufactured. There are many more designed to be used on your home computer. (For more, see *Supermemory, Megabrain, Megabrain Power*, and *Megabrain Report*.)

Mind-tech machines could be the solution to widespread learning problems. Brain studies of many Attention Deficit Disorder people show that they have extremely slow brainwave activity, the kind associated with sleep. Drs. John Carter and Harold Russell showed that stimulating ADD children with light/sound or biofeedback stimulation at beta frequencies (18–21 Hz) greatly improved their functioning. They documented IQ gains of twelve to twenty points. One subject climbed an amazing thirty-three points. Dr. Alan Childs, of the Healthcare Rehab Center, of the University of Texas, successfully used cranial-electro-stimulation for people with memory problems—amnesia and memory loss from head injuries. The Lumatron, a device that provides colored light stimulation of the eyes, was used by Carol Rustigan, of California State University, to treat the learning disabled. She documents major gains.

There are lots more questions. What happens if you combine several modalities together—brainpower nutrients, high-frequency sound, mind machines, and Superlearning? Float-tank sessions are already combined with Superlearning for happy results. Mind machines and self-hypnosis have proved a dynamite combination.

Though they may only be well known in certain high-flying circles right now, the potential of the mind machines already available is spectacular. Could they soon prompt any of us to genius level? Could these mindpower machines save a graying population from a forgetful old age? Could they rehabilitate crack babies and drug addicts? Could they rapidly help us overcome massive illiteracy? Could they restore the brain damaged to normal lives? Can they enhance scholastic performance on a wide scale? Could they help the economy and unemployment by helping us overcome the skills gap? On the other hand will these machines fall into the hands of "cyberpunks" and be used to sabotage society?

At the beginning of the twentieth century human ingenuity brought forth extraordinary machines—cars, radios, planes—that soon powered the wealthiest society in history. Knowledge is the currency of the 21st century. Is human ingenuity once again rising to the occasion and starting to bring forth a different kind of technology that will lift us to a new kind of wealth?

18
A Language in a Month?

"How do you feel about learning?" That question topped the initial questionnaires handed out to fifteen Siemens employees embarking on an English course at the University of Munich. Siemens, the global electrical giant, famous for innovations such as the retractable roof of Toronto's Skydome, was one of many businesses to put the practical promise of Superlearning to work. Siemens employees had agreed to go directly from a long day's work to the university for a four-hour English language class every evening. They'd be videotaped, interviewed, examined, and scrutinized in ultra-thorough fashion by *three* different university departments—languages, empirical pedagogy, and educational psychology.

Pioneer Gail Heidenhain, longtime president of the German accelerated learning society (DGSL) and head of her own training firm, who created and taught the course, checked the questionnaire responses. "Depends what you have to learn," most said.

Soon the business people felt the day's stress melt away as they relaxed and visualized themselves on vacation. They imagined being in London's Covent Garden. They listened to English vocabulary over soothing slow Baroque music. Instead of boring drills, they played "The Price Is Hot!"—an original Heidenhain game.

After 70 academic hours the Siemens employees faced a challenging English test usually given after 230 hours of study. All but two passed the exam, and even they were borderline. That's acceleration—better than a three-to-one speedup.

Questionnaires showed the employees had also changed their minds. Now they said their feelings about learning depended on *how* they were learning and how a subject would be taught. A large number also confided they'd come to a new awareness: *They could learn anything.* They had discovered their hidden potential for learning. University statistics backed up their comments, showing significant improvement in students' innate motivation to learn.

Videos offered proof the new facility with English wasn't just book learning. When English-speaking guests joined a party the last night of class, videotape caught the Siemens employees confidently chatting in English with them for the whole evening.

Like many other forward-looking international firms, Siemens was aware that to compete and win in the global economy, some familiarity with other languages has become a necessity. And Superlearning, they discovered, could cut the time and cost by one third or more.

The economic unification of Europe, the North American Free Trade Agreement, the globalization of world economies, the crumbling of the Soviet Bloc and vast shifts of workers and refugees from country to country—all these factors have boosted exponentially the need for rapid foreign language training worldwide. Across North America, enrollment in language courses has soared as students realize a language can give them an extra edge in the fiercely competitive job market. Language skills also open up the information highway in other countries by bringing access to life-enhancing new discoveries in fields like medicine and science.

The Times of London asserts, "Company and marketing executives will find after 1992 that it is a handicap not to be fairly conversant with at least one other major European language—and preferably two or three." And *The Wall Street Journal* headlined, AMERICAN MANAGERS WITH LANGUAGE SKILLS OPEN MORE DOORS.

Not only managers are polishing up their languages. Even assembly-line workers at firms like Audi in Germany are speeding through Superlearning English to make travel more fun and enjoyable. The new Chunnel, for the first time in history, opens a land link between Europe and Britain, bringing greatly expanded travel, trade, and cultural exchanges.

From the moment Suggestopedia surfaced, it mated with language learning. Early tests of the method itself were done with languages, to ensure that students didn't have prior knowledge of a subject. But once word got out, need fueled the rapid spread of accelerated language learning around the world. The Soviets particularly snatched up the new and better way. They had reason. Not only did the USSR have over 160 official languages but foreign language training was considered essential for science, technology, medicine, trade, defense, and the worldwide Soviet spy network. For years the elite of the Soviet political world, undercover world, even hosts and hostesses for the Moscow Olympics, trained rapidly in foreign languages with the Suggestopedic method.

The prestigious Maurice Thorez Moscow Foreign Languages Pedagogical Institute became one of the foremost centers in the world for Suggestopedic language teacher training. Soon from the Frunze Military Academy in the Kirgiz Republic near the Chinese border, to the University of Norilsk in the Arctic Circle, Soviets were learning to speak up quickly and without stress in foreign tongues. *Pravda* was just one of many Communist media that began to trumpet, YOU CAN LEARN A LANGUAGE IN A MONTH!

East Germany drove to particularly spectacular success. At the Mnemology Center, University of Leipzig, Drs. Klaus Janicke and Dieter Lehmann reported that in a *typical* foreign language experiment students learned 3,182 lexical units and idiomatic phrases in thirty days with 94 percent retention. A medical doctor, a regular member of the language team, monitored the profuse health benefits daily. They decided to use the slow Baroque music for *both* the dramatic and the rhythmically paced presentations. Their startling results streamed out regularly in their journal, *Wissenschaftliche Berichte*.

The distinguished Dr. Galina Kitaigorodskaya, director of the

Center for Accelerative Teaching and Learning Foreign Languages, University of Moscow, has been bringing new languages alive in people the accelerated way, longer than anyone except the original Bulgarian researchers. Initially she taught a group of engineers and scientists English and French with the method. Results were so conclusive—they learned faster, spoke better, made fewer grammatical mistakes than with old methods—that Kitaigorodskaya never looked back. "I have personally trained about one thousand teachers," she recently told Michael Lawlor of SEAL. Her trainees taught others, and she estimates there are now about ten thousand teachers in about 150 institutes across what used to be Soviet lands.

"What do you consider the essential elements of the method?" Lawlor asked Kitaigorodskaya. "Joy of learning, relaxation, use of the subconscious, development of the students' belief in themselves, communication in the true sense of the word." The joy seemed to have spilled over into the professor's life, Lawlor noted. Walking in the woods with Kitaigorodskaya near her dacha outside Moscow, they came across a playground. Lawlor was amused to see Galina immediately get on the big wooden swing and chuckle with pleasure as she swung higher and higher. "This quality of joyful playfulness, not exactly common in a university department head, is the key to her success in introducing Suggestopedia to adult learners," says Lawlor.

The crumbling of the Soviet Empire has generated urgent demands for Kitaigorodskaya's teachers. Many, she says, are helping newly hatched businessmen learn the languages of international trade. But that's only one problem in the newly formed republics. To give a single example, in Estonia, with a population of just 1.5 million, Russians suddenly find themselves a minority greatly pressured to speak and write Estonian. Suggestopedia is used to teach Estonian to Russians, Russian to Estonians, and the now necessary English, German, and Swedish to both. Since the walls have fallen, Western teachers have come to help in this language-salad world. Today they are bringing in fresh techniques that have been constantly evolving in the West.

When Superlearning reached the West, reports like *Pravda*'s began showing up here. "Canadian Pacific, which tested the system for two years, found its executives learned French two to four times faster than through other methods," said the New York *Daily News*. The Canadian *Financial Post* said, "It will cut the time devoted to training." CAN STUDENTS LEARN A YEAR'S WORK IN GERMAN IN 10 WEEKS? YES, INSIDE PEGASUS SCHOOL, said the *Vashon-Maury Island Beachcomber*, of Washington State, reporting on an extraordinary private school using Superlearning from top to bottom. SUPERLEARNING—A NEW TEACHING SYSTEM MAY REVOLUTIONIZE EDUCATION, chimed in *Saturday Night*. *Newsweek* called it one of the few promising methods for teaching English.

Professional journals, too, began reporting attention-catching results. The Washington State Department of Health and Social Services reported that by using Superlearning techniques, Indochinese refugees learned English five times faster. At Iowa State University students learned Spanish seven times faster. And from Australia's Woden TAFE College, John Wade revealed, "I have used the Superlearning methodology with adult migrants learning English. The results from a controlled experiment in 1984 show that *long term memory retention increased sixfold*." The famous U.S. Foreign Service Institute in Arlington, Virginia, also began to take it up.

A class is one thing, but what about do-it-yourself language learning? As there were few courses, a grassroots movement took hold, and determined learners began using Superlearning Music to make their own tapes and help themselves learn languages. "I have cut my learning time for Greek vocabulary by about 60 percent using your tapes," wrote Phyllis Prince from Mesa, Arizona. Others tried Superlearning taped language courses. For one, George Jacobson, president of Jacobson Printing Company, found that a brushup of Spanish with Superlearning brought back his almost-forgotten college Spanish in time for a trip to Mexico. Other travelers reported that just listening to Baroque-backed phrases on overnight flights to Europe summoned back long-forgotten intonations and vocabulary so vividly that they were ready to use them when they landed in Paris or Munich.

Accelerated language learning reached North America largely due to the efforts of Dr. Jane Bancroft, associate professor of French at the University of Toronto. A language specialist with degrees from

Harvard, the Sorbonne, and the University of Manitoba, plus training in music and music theory, Dr. Bancroft visited Suggestopedic classes in all of the Soviet bloc countries at the height of the Cold War. It was a time when education secrets constituted spy territory, but along with her surreptitiously concealed tape recorder, she got into demonstration classes intended for Soviets as well as those for Westerners. The Bulgarians, holding back for political reasons, sometimes put on phony demos for foreigners.

The Secret of Acceleration

Many Westerners who rushed to see the new "miracle system" had little or no knowledge of language methods. Many mistook standard language training methods for the secrets of memory-expansion and acceleration. "The secret must be in the chairs!" insisted a few really naive observers.

Bancroft figured the tape she had of the demos for Soviets must contain the secret. What made these courses more effective? How were they achieving acceleration, academic excellence, and stress reduction all combined? Persistently sleuthing for clues, she plowed through our files, Lozanov's original unpublished thesis which we had, videotapes, previously classified sleep-learning research brought out of Hungary, mental yoga, even the accidentally revealing accounts of Communist ideological attacks on the method. She invited Dr. Lozanov to lecture at Scarborough College, and got investigated by the Mounties.

At last Bancroft's stopwatch uncovered some subtle differences. The demo for Westerners featured 74-beat music with conversational text reading. The demo for Soviets started off with 74-beat music and then slowed down to steady *60-beat* music with precision data-pacing on an eight-second cycle. This must be part of the neuro-acoustic breakthrough that mobilizes the subconscious and expands memory, she calculated. She revealed all in 1975 in the booklet *The Lozanov Language Class*. Certain elements in the Bulgarian government immediately placed her on the "Enemies of Bulgaria" list. It was at a time when Bulgarian spies went around poking people with poison-tipped umbrellas.

Undeterred, she kept testing. Communist authorities used the traditional tactic of mounting a disinformation campaign. Another episode in the Balkan Intrigues began swirling around a language method! Garbled instructions for worthless slow-learning programs showed up simultaneously at various centers and were published in journals. Capitalizing on our account in *Psychic Discoveries,* Bulgarians sold flawed programs to enthusiastic North Americans, who shelled out healthy amounts of hard currency.

Scientific research on music and yoga for mind-sharpening was still scarce in the West. The system was so interdisciplinary, few were expert in all aspects. People followed false instructions ritualistically, not having a clue about neuro-acoustics. They substituted wrong music, which deflected memory. Some tried party animal antics as language practice. One eager Canadian TV network produced an *entirely inaudible* French course, appropriately called "French in Bed." Alleged Suggestopedia vanished behind thunderous music and dashing waves. Even the Canadian government, after complex negotiations with the Bulgarians, bought a definitely *de*celerated, disastrous failure of a French program for their civil service employees.

Just when it seemed that rapid learning was stuck in its tracks with a train about to roar over it, a small band of dedicated people familiar with leading-edge mind-tech got it untied and back on its express course. Bancroft and colleagues worldwide began achieving four- to sevenfold acceleration in language training, coupled with academic excellence and stress release. Based at the University of Toronto, Bancroft became the first to publish papers on the method in mainline, academic journals such as *The Modern Language Review*. She unveiled her around-the-globe explorations of brainmind technologies, including those of Dr. Tomatis and Dr. Caycedo, in the *SALT Journal*. The fast track to fast language learning began to spread.

As the Cold War warmed, the Bulgarian government negotiated with Mankind Research Unlimited of Washington, D.C., to set up franchised Lozanov Learning. Language learning classes first gave the public a taste of this spectacular new way to learn. Bulgarian authorities for a while also allowed Dr. Lozanov the rare privilege of traveling internationally. Suggestopedic centers concentrating on language learning started up in many European cities.

The Baltics seemed to have a special affinity for the new way. Some years ago the government of Finland, for instance, asked permission to include part of *Superlearning* in an official English program designed for their public school system. Now the Finns have soared into the stratosphere with accelerated methods not just for languages but for their entire state school curriculum. Startling advances revealed at the 1992 International Suggestopedia Conference in Finland left professionals stunned and inspired. "A testimony to the extraordinary strength and creativity of this tiny nation!" enthused the British Journal *SEAL*.

The Danish government, too, recently funded accelerated language learning projects in schools, while the Swedes are using it to cope, quickly, with an enormous influx of refugees from the Middle East and the Horn of Africa. Many of these immigrants don't know the Latin alphabet; some are successful businessmen who can't write at all. Using supertechniques and Total Physical Response methods, David Kettlewell and Karin Skoglund had such motley groups spouting Swedish in just weeks.

Front-runners in the early race to anchor accelerated language learning in France were Fanny Saferis and Jean Cureau, of Paris. Saferis, at the École Française de Suggestopédie, has been quickening English with the traditional Lozanov method for many years now. At the Lycée Voltaire, Cureau combined Superlearning with Sophrology to get a startling ten-to-one speedup in English learning.

Now there's another language that may soon demand Superlearning from a host of people. It's Esperanto, the one-hundred-year-old universal language. Australian teacher Vera Payne made accelerating Esperanto her specialty. She told us, "Esperanto has a very special role to play in bringing about greater understanding between people of all nationalities." It enables people to get to know one another so easily, and it's the ideal language for travel and corresponding, she explains. "When you're with other Esperantists, no matter whether they're German or Swedish, everyone can communicate."

A very simple, universal language always sounded like a good idea, and it's known that people who first learn Esperanto find picking up other languages much easier. Yet somehow it's never really caught on. It had to wait for the computer age. Esperanto is now the official language of the International Cybernetics Association. Recently the European Economic Council selected Esperanto as the most cost-effective bridge language for computer translation. At least in Europe it's a decision with boom-time ramifications for Esperanto. If machines communicate via Esperanto, some humans have to know it too. Happily, using Superlearning, Payne finds that just twenty-five hours of training can have you making new friends by speaking Esperanto. It can also help you open up new business opportunities as well.

Fellow Australian John Wade was literally precipitated into new language methods when he started out on his first assignment thirty years ago. Crossing a steep ravine on a rope bridge deep in the rain forests of New Guinea, Wade's baggage carrier tripped on the bridge and Wade's box of teaching materials fell into the ravine, never to be seen again. No supplies could come in for four months, and Wade had to rethink how to teach from scratch.

Ten years later Wade showed, through stringently controlled tests, that Superlearning methods could help immigrants to Australia learn English *six* times faster. Soon, at Woden TAFE College in Canberra, they had Australia's largest accelerative learning unit. In 1986 the first Australian videos for teaching accelerative English were produced at the college and are now used widely in Australia for training new immigrants. Student enthusiasm levels have been sky high. Not only has Superlearning English allowed these newcomers to plug in to the workforce and begin earning six times faster, but it's also been a boon to the Australian economy. In 1990 Wade received the Achievement Award from the government of the Australian Capital Territory.

Another of Wade's successful accelerative works is *Quick 'N' Easy QWERTY,* which lets newcomers (or anyone) learn the computer keyboard so they can begin word processing in English within eight hours. That's EIGHT HOURS!

Today Wade, perhaps the best known accelerative teacher in Australia, has received a clutch of prestigious awards. His popular books and workshops meld the latest mind-tech developments with basic Superlearning techniques for a megapower mix. Ex-Soviets, apparently impressed by Wade's modifications of Suggestopedia, recently invited him to teach a stint at the Moscow Military Academy and at the International Space Center in Krasnoyarsk in Central Siberia. He was one of the first Westerners to see this previously off-limits facility. "I wonder how they heard of me?" he wrote us in his latest letter.

Maybe it was the "Druzhba Link" (Friendship Link)! British language experts Michael Lawlor and June McOstrich, who helped found SEAL, the British accelerated learning organization, have determinedly set up a support network between SEAL members and Suggestopedic teachers in the former Soviet bloc. SEAL members have adventured across former USSR lands and Russian experts have toured England exchanging ideas. The Lawlors, directors of Forge House in England, a language and inner-development center, have crisscrossed Russia with their highly acclaimed workshops to demonstrate how Suggestopedia blends naturally with Western mind techniques like kinesiology, psychosynthesis, and the Alexander Technique.

On their lengthy travels they recently discovered how necessary cross-cultural ties can be. Dr. Alexander Bolakhanov invited them to his university in Perm, an old industrial city that was completely shut to outsiders until 1990. The Lawlors realized just how great an Anglophile their host was when they stepped into his living room, an exact replica of one described by Conan Doyle in *The Adventures of Sherlock Holmes*. Though Bolakhanov was vice-chairman of the college language department and had taught English for twenty-five years, the Lawlors were the first native English speakers he had ever met.

Superlearning ultra-fast languages can help us across a wide spectrum of activities—from global business and trade to immigration, to plugging into foreign information highways, to making international travel more profitable and enjoyable. For Superlearning language how-to and tips from Superlearning language users worldwide, see Chapter 25.

19
World Class and Weekend Sports

Today pro teams, college teams, daily joggers, and weekend duffers are leaning back and conjuring victorious moves in their mind's eye. That's been part of Superlearning since the beginning, so it's not surprising that academics like Toronto's Lorne Cook often find themselves doing double duty shuttling between the science department and the athletic department to hatch high achievers with Superlearning.

Powell Blankenship teaches tennis in San Diego. "Following the Superlearning suggestions," he reports, "I made a tape for one of my students, Brian Teacher." Teacher came alive and won one of the four major pro tournaments in the world. It wasn't a sure thing. After he arrived in Australia to compete in the national championships, the young tennis player decided he wasn't up to it and turned around to catch the next plane home.

"At the airport Teacher found that his feet would not take him to a ticket vendor," Blankenship says. "It was as if a posthypnotic suggestion to win the tournament prevented him from leaving Australia. So he went back, played the tournament, and won. Teacher followed this with an incredible run of good tennis and moved his ranking from the twenties up to number seven in the world. This remarkable achievement," the coach declares, "followed on the heels of his use of the Superlearning tape."

Guidelines for sports are easy. Particularly if you're a Superlearner, for the core techniques you've picked up can help you tremendously in athletics—or any other kind of performance. To begin, relax. Autogenics is a good route because it will also shorten recovery time if you're working out mentally after physical practice. Play Superlearning Music to heighten the learning mode, as judo instructor Dr. Lloyd Migita does, for instance, in Hawaii. Then begin to work out mentally, using, of course, all your senses as if you were really there.

Say you are a high diver. Begin a mental movie review of the day's dives. Immediately correct any mistakes you made. Stop and rerun the scene, over and over, until your actions unfold perfectly. To root the training, use two perspectives: first watch yourself, second experience really being there. In a bright, focused scene, see yourself making a great dive, a perfect 10. Next jump into the scene and, with full-sensed imagination, feel yourself soaring off the platform, your body in perfect balance. Feel the cool water as you knife through the surface. . . .

You have a delicious freedom in mental training. If you ski, you can freeze your slalom run on an instant, check out your position, back up, ski in slow motion, zoom to a closeup of your knees. Sometimes the slow motion mental training carries over into the real event. Athletes in hair-trigger sports like skeet shooting report experiencing time expansion. Subjectively it seems as if they have all the time in the world to track, aim, and fire. We've also heard tennis aces speak of seeing a return shot slowly float up to them big as a basketball, impossible to miss. If you've ever been in a car rocketing toward a collision, you know the mind can throw the world into slow motion. Time manipulation is another potential that needs to be researched.

To make a tape, use the Superlearning Music and start with relaxation and mind calming. Cultivate a feeling of joy. (When you learn to communicate with your brain using feeling and imagery, you may find you don't need outside stimulants or even painkillers, for your brain has a treasure chest of chemicals greater than any pharmacy.) If you're having trouble keeping to workouts, try this. With all your senses, imagine, experience, something you really love to do, such as kicking back and listening to your favorite music or reading a great mystery. Squeeze your left knee. Then imagine working out, and squeeze your right knee. You've set triggers. Imagine what you love to do again and squeeze both knees, both triggers, crossing over delight in what you love to your training. (Before crossing triggers, be *sure* the strength of your pleasurable feeling outweighs your negative feeling for training.) Then embed some powerful, positive, motivating suggestions in yourself. Leave ample time, with nothing but the music playing, to train mentally. Wind up with another strong flourish of power suggestions.

No matter how you're training, set a trigger for yourself—press two fingers together, pull your ear, whatever. Trigger your supremely confident success state. Use this trigger particularly after you've made a mistake in the heat of play. If you focus on the golf shot that went in the sand trap, the bad line call, the bowling ball that missed picking off a spare, you'll defeat yourself. The immediacy of sports highlights the necessity of dropping the deadwood of the past, on the instant, and acting in the unencumbered present. It's the mark of the champion in any area of life.

Dyveke Spino is a champion, a unique one in two fields. Trained as a classical concert pianist, she composes well-regarded New Age music under her Danish first name, Dyveke. She's also been known as "the mother of the New Age fitness movement" ever since she and her former husband, champion runner Mike Spino, founded the Esalen Sports Center in California. Dyveke took to Superlearning like a marathon swimmer—which she is—takes to water. Underprivileged kids, boardroom execs, all manner of people have attended Dyveke's Superlearning Sports workshops to transform both their technique and their approach to athletics. The killer instinct, she points out, the dominating, aggressive approach to sports, has filtered down to us from ancient days when sports and military training were often one. It's time to shift, Dyveke says. She sets clients on the road to experiencing sports and lifelong fitness generally as "a way to awaken higher aspirations of the human spirit." They also learn to play tennis better, to jog or marathon with more ease, speed, endurance.

Dyveke coaches with a full complement of techniques: imaginative rehearsal, energy and "right state" exercises, actual practice—all buoyed by special tones and music. As a tennis player, during a twenty-minute mental set you might breathe in light through the crown of your head, swirl brilliance in energizing patterns through your body, use color to flush away old errors. You might imagine standing lightly at the baseline, watching the tennis ball float to you in very slow motion, feeling complete confidence, feeling your spine rippling like a mountain stream as you rise to your stroke.

If running is your love, Dyveke might coach you in concentration and visualization to release cramps and circumvent injuries. Then as you stride rhythmically along your imaginary running path, your neck begins to feel like a flexible stalk of bamboo gently connecting your head and shoulders, your knees begin to feel like springs. You summon your own inner coach: deep cellular wisdom connected with all of life. You experience the power, energy, courage, dignity of the panther, the leopard, the cheetah. You begin to become pure energy. . . .

Even if you're an armchair athlete, the evocation of energy, the sense of connection to all life, and the powerful mingling of music and imagery in Dyveke's work can be an expansive experience. In the best Superlearning tradition she lifts training away from the purely mechanical and repetitive. She leads you to the sheer joy of performance. You won't turn into a killer, but you've got a good chance of becoming a winner.

Sophrology and Supersports

Alfonso Caycedo felt he was living his destiny. The Dalai Lama himself had ordered Tibetan texts at the monastery in Lhasa to be opened to him, a rare privilege for a Westerner. It was a culminating, three-year stop for Caycedo in his quest for routes to nurture abundantly healthy people, healthy in body, mind, and spirit. For the past three decades Sophrology, the system created by this medical man with an unshakable vision, has taken hold in Europe as a way of curing the sick—and of hatching high-flying athletes.

Raymond Abrezol, a tall, athletic-looking Swiss Sophrologist who loved to climb mountains, ski, scuba dive, and swim with dolphins, quite naturally spearheaded its move into sports. Caycedo's special "dynamic exercises"—part autogenics, part meditative moving exercises similar to Eastern subtle energy and balancing routines—are at the heart of all applied Sophrology. Dynamic exercises are a book in themselves. But here are some tips drawn from Sophrology coaching that has proved enormously successful with competitive, world-class athletes, both pro and amateur. Dr. Abrezol lists eight major training steps:

1. Learn to become mentally relaxed at will.
2. Learn to become physically relaxed at will and become conscious of your body image. Through visualization and inner perception strengthen your sense of your body image. (This worked wonders for a member of the Swiss national ski team who came to Abrezol complaining of a lack of coordination and strength. As he developed a conscious picture of his whole body schema, something clicked. His strength increased dramatically. He became a medaled member of the team at the Albertsville Olympics.)
3. Consciously develop a confident optimism. Dissolve negative, critical memories and replace them with joyful ones in the present.
4. Learn to concentrate in the here and now so that you are totally present, body and mind, during competition.
5. Use Caycedian exercises to become filled to the brim with energy, great joy, and dynamism.
6. Sharpen perceptions, your sensing of competitors and teammates.
7. Practice self-mastery by projecting into the future. With imagination carefully prepare your body consciousness and know that what you project will take place.
8. Develop detachment.

"Coaching for a professional hockey team differs from training a sprinter of course," Abrezol says, "and different aspects are emphasized preparing people for a regatta, say, than for an around the world sailing competition." And for boxing. A 27-year-old middleweight hoped Sophrology could help him overcome his debilitating "deep emotional anguish" before bouts. He feared both the outcome of the fight and the eyes of the spectators watching him. Abrezol coached him in the Sophrological repertoire, from gaining a clear body image to substituting joyful present memories for past negatives. He learned to clench the toes of his left foot to trigger relaxation at any moment; between rounds he practiced deep breathing routines and neck moves to bring oxygen and clarity to the brain. This once-shrinking boxer won five out of six of his next fights, three by KO, and in March 1991 became the European middleweight champion. He wrote, "Sophrology also quickly began to serve me in everyday life. I discovered other values, came to know myself, and can now face difficult problems."

Ensuring athletes are coached for life beyond sports is a strong point with Abrezol. "After a few years of adulation they are forced to retire at a young age. Sophrology carries them to success in living." You often hear that sports builds character, creates leaders. Like Superlearning, the Sophrological approach, particularly when coaching children and teenagers, would seem to build people better equipped to succeed in this millennium or the next than the still prevalent bullying, walk over their face, win at all costs approach.

Using the same Sophrological basics, Abrezol rescued the daughter of a skier he'd coached to a medal in the Grenoble Olympics. This overweight 15-year-old had hurt her knee; now she shied away from speed, a definite block in competitive Alpine skiing. Mindbody training, with extra emphasis on mental pain control, gave the teenager a buoyant sense of self-mastery. Pounds dropped away as she moved to the top of the Swiss Junior National Team, then won first in the Junior World Championships.

Weeks before a competitive event Abrezol's clients begin building success circuits into their body consciousness. Over and over, in exquisite detail, they imagine the whole day that will be from the moment they toss back their covers in the morning. In their mind's eye, and body senses too, they experience the day step by step: from eating an energy-packed breakfast, driving to the stadium, pausing to trigger a success state before taking the field, through the entire competition, to the sound of the cheers and the weighty feel of gold going around their necks. It's "make my day" Sophrology style, and it works.

If you trained with Abrezol, you'd notice he has an unusually melodious, sensuous voice that seems to draw you irresistibly into bright mental images. This is a staple of Sophrology, called *Terpnos Logos,* a term taken from Plato. It comes from an old idea that certain voice tones, like music, can subtly affect the listener. Abrezol also uses music, Turning Sound especially, to help athletes control pain (see Chapter 7).

In a 1993 issue of the French edition of the *Caycedian Sophrology Review,* Louis Fernandez surveyed Sophrology's glittering success in high-level sports, noting that 80% of the coaches of European national teams now have an approach based on Caycedo's vision. Fernandez counted dozens and dozens of Olympic medals and world championships: Alpine skier C. Quittet won the World Cup in his sport; D. Bouvet won the World Cup in Nordic skiing. The French national fencing team twice won silver in the world championships; boxer Richard Sylla ten times successfully defended the French title, was European champ, WKA title holder, and retired undefeated. Holder of the 400-meter world record, runner A. Canti trained with Sophrology, as did Thierry Vingeron, 400-meter Olympic silver medalist. Cyclists P. Da Rocha and Phillip Boyer caused a scandal when they copped second in the world championships. At 29, they were considered over the hill. It must have been drugs, people said, but tests revealed it was Sophrology that gave them a winning jolt. As it did the Beziers' pro rugby team, nine times champions of France, and the 1992 French University champion rugby team. Olympic medals in table tennis and world titles in rowing and volleyball are just part, Fernandez said, of an embarrassment of riches.

Sophrology also brought success in another kind of Olympics, Fernandez reports, the World Olympiad of Trades, where professionals from 37 different trades compete. From 1950 to the 1980s, France's team rarely even won honorable mention. In the mid-1980s toolmakers, industrial designers, mechanics, stonecutters, chefs, and hairdressers turned to Sophrology. In 1987 they won five medals. In the 1989 competitions at Birmingham, England, France bore off eleven and won first in overall team standing.

Like Abrezol, Fernandez follows Caycedo's vision and sees Sophrology extending far beyond competition. Practiced on a high level, he says, "it becomes an existential quest, opening you to maximum freedom, responsibility and transcendent personal expansion." Sports images pepper the talk of American leaders. Maybe it's time to add a few sprung from the science of harmonious consciousness, Sophrology.

20
Old Brains and
New Tricks

"Picture an old candle," says Dr. Monique Le Poncin. There may be only a stub of wax left, yet the flame stands as tall and bright as when it was new. The candle is the body as we age, the flame can be the mind. As a little girl in Brittany, Le Poncin spent happy hours with people whose wax was running low. "They pampered me and told me good stories. Those old people of rural Brittany were often real forces of nature and had prodigious memories." Her enchantment with the wise old folks of her childhood led Le Poncin, after a many-pronged scientific career, to create and lead France's National Institute for Research on the Prevention of Cerebral Aging at Bicêtre. She knew you do not have to go downhill mentally as you age. She has her own groundbreaking brain research to prove it.

Trained in neuropharmacology and physiology, specializing in memory, Le Poncin was one of the first in France to use imaging technologies like tomography to chart the bustle of activity that lights up in animal and human brains. If you're worried you're beginning to lose it because you're getting older, Le Poncin will tell you flat out:

There isn't enough bustle in your brain. You are using only a minute part of your resources. You have too many quiescent, unstimulated brain cells or neurons, a case, scientifically speaking, of "hypoefficiency." In plain words again, it's use it or lose it.

In our hyper times, elders often feel they've been shoved on the shelf when they retire or start to slow physically. They begin to disengage from life. As their focus narrows, more and more areas of the brain lack stimulation, causing focus to narrow even more in a downward, vicious cycle. Overspecialization at any age can bring on the same deadening effect, Le Poncin finds. And so, increasingly it seems, can middle age if people let their neurons go with their waistlines. When something out of the ordinary rut occurs, they lack the brain flexibility to respond efficiently. They don't have the cerebral wherewithal to change. These are the people who turn up at the institute's Brain Fitness centers across France, complaining, "My boss wants me on a computer. I can't seem to keep up with it." "My promotion involves speaking German. I'm too old to learn a language." (Le Poncin notes that not long ago it was 60-year-olds who worried about their memories; now it's a common plaint of 40-year-olds. U.S. doctors also remarked on this unhappy trend when we were researching memory.)

Signing up for Brain Fitness is like preparing for physical workouts. You undergo a quick assessment of your mental and physical state. Are you depressed? Do you need glasses? Much muddleheadedness ascribed to age comes from blurred senses. Sometimes memory returns like magic with a new pair of specs or a hearing aid. Next you have a "brain print" taken, pictures of the bustle or lack of it in your head. To dissolve anxiety and get you in the right state to exercise, there's a scientific pep talk. The body declines with age, the brain doesn't have to. Yes, we lose brain cells daily, about two billion by old age, but that leaves 13 billion, which is more than enough. In the last decade researchers around the world have found that both old dogs and the cells of old brains can learn new tricks. They keep right on growing dendrites, making connections, learning—if they have something to entice them. That's the key to lighting up your life again—enticement, motivation.

The importance of motivation stands out starkly in one of Le

Poncin's most important discoveries, for once a rat experiment with genuine significance for all of us. When she set up conditions to kill motivation in rats, they fell into inertia. Their brains began to turn off the lights, hordes of cells became quiescent. Shortly—and this is the breakthrough point—quiescence turned into actual physical degeneration of the neurons. Brain damage occurred. Cells went downhill, even though she had done nothing physically to the animals. All she did was erase motivation. Le Poncin and her many colleagues have years of evidence that people can fall into the same pit.

The "joyful" gerontologist Alex Comfort insisted, "Old people become crazy for three reasons. Because they were crazy when they were young. Because they have an illness. Or because we drive them crazy." To drive a sinking old person in the right direction, entice him into motivation, and if you're following Le Poncin, give him a month of Brain Fitness exercises. Similar to the puzzles in "mind teaser" books, these mental workouts exercise various kinds of thinking: perceptual, logical, and visuospatial among others. "Mental agility returns at a spectacular rate in most people," Le Poncin reports, supporting her comment with reams of highly significant statistics, not to mention hundreds of reawakened clients.

When a finely tuned athlete is hurt, she usually recovers faster than a couch potato. Similarly a widely awake brain is insurance. You can draw on it. "It gives you strategic mobility," Le Poncin says, if you're rocked by seemingly overwhelming change in the outer world, or if you're felled by a stroke or head injury. You will have fit battalions of neurons ready to step into the breech and be trained. New American research at Columbia University and U.C. San Diego backs up Le Poncin's assertion. Highly intelligent or well educated people with more neural networks and more abundant connections between them are much better able to withstand brain scarring without noticeable effect than those whose brains are less developed. They are also slower to show the ravages of Alzheimer's if it comes. That's something else Le Poncin is willing to put money on, even though it will take years to collect proof. If you keep exercising your whole brain, if you don't let too many cells become quiescent, you can prevent or at least stave off for a long while any sort of brain degeneration, including Alzheimer's. "Brain Fitness," Monique Le Poncin says from experience, "is a bet on the future." A future full of life like that embodied by the wonderful old people of her childhood who, with their contemporary William Butler Yeats, knew that old age can be a meager time "unless soul clap its hands and sing, and louder sing for every tatter in its mortal dress."

Retire—or Refire?

"I'm Superlearning French to keep my mind young," Ben Eizig, an 86-year-old San Francisco lawyer, wrote us. Ben was "having so much fun," he went on to Spanish. A seventy-five-year-old Californian called to say he was putting together Superlearning vocabulary tapes for crossword puzzlers. A woman in Florida reported she'd organized a Superlearning art history group in her retirement community. These are just a few of the old people who call up full of vinegar to tell us what they're doing with Superlearning. "The hardest years in life are those between ten and seventy," remarked Helen Hayes, who went on to enjoy twenty-two easy, active years. Because Superlearning exercises the senses, evokes different modes of thinking, and is designed to drain anxiety and build self-esteem, it would seem to be custom-made for older learners. It is a different, full-bodied approach to Le Poncin's Brain Fitness. The American brain scientist Marion Diamond told a SALT conference about her research that also shows lifelong learning can keep our brains healthy—and growing. An idea that, according to reporter Karolynn Flynn, led one SALT participant to a happy insight: "We do not age, we grow chronologically gifted." Used in a game-filled, noncritical group, Superlearning can give *meaningful* social interaction often so lacking for the elderly. Nobody is made wrong, everybody is made right. For the first time in their lives people may find learning is a heady experience, something wonderful that they can do too. As they say, "It's never too late to have a happy childhood." Superlearning could help turn around the meaning of "second childhood" and make it a second chance at adventure and growth.

Can Superlearning help people damaged by strokes? We used to say, "Can't hurt, but . . ." That was before we met Commander Charles Croucher, who had retired from the Canadian navy and moved to

Spain, not to build castles but to indulge a lifelong passion for linguistics, a passion shared with his wife, Alma, who also had degrees in linguistics. Retirement dreams turned into a nightmare. A truck knocked Croucher off his bike, causing a severe concussion quickly followed by a stroke. When he was fit enough to walk in his garden again, Croucher wondered why bother? Much of his language was gone; he couldn't remember nouns in French, Spanish, German—and even worse, in English. "I thought my life was effectively over," he wrote.

After a year of little improvement Croucher visited his brother-in-law in New York, a learning innovator who had read *Superlearning*. With the connivance of a Japanese graduate student and Alma, he set up an experiment. The Commander would try to pick up Japanese, a language he'd never studied. But before the Baroque played, the team had Croucher work on a Tokyo University homestudy course for three weeks. Worse than nothing; the frustrated Commander said he couldn't remember a thing, he was a goner as far as learning went. That's when they introduced the conservative Commander to a "better way," putting him through the fullest Superlearning regimen, right down to a suggestive atmosphere of sushi and green tea.

Croucher got a shock on his first quiz; he remembered most of the vocabulary. Soon his efforts turned into a controlled educational experiment. Results, duly documented and published in the international journal *Incorporated Linguist,* showed Croucher learned 94 percent of what he studied. His wife, who served as control in the experiment, learned 95 percent of the material. "We were able to absorb a minimum of twenty to twenty-five simple Japanese phrases a day without stress," they reported. "This means that studying half an hour every weekday, one could gain the basics of Japanese or any language in two months. . . . Unlike other methods known for quick learning and as quick forgetting, tests proved a high level of retention."

Croucher's lost languages began to fill in; best of all, he knew he could still learn. Or maybe the best, as he said, was being able to go out by himself again. Lost ability often spontaneously returns to stroke patients. We can only speculate about Superlearning's role. Maybe the high-frequency music helped, or the confidence building imagery, or maybe the holistic approach hastened the training of fit but untutored brain cells. As far as helping stroke patients goes, we still have to say, "No promises." But it just might help, particularly if you add daily doses of octacosonal and perhaps Ginkgo, which has been brightening up millions of damaged or old brains in Europe and Asia for years (see Chapter 16). As we finish this book, a letter arrives from Rosella Wallace. A friend, she says, has just begun a little Superlearning with a man who suffered brain damage falling off a roof and has memory loss similar to Croucher's. "And," Wallace writes, "it's definitely helping!"

There's another way to keep your mind young it seems—be a Superlearning teacher. Instead of retiring, as one gent put it, they "refire." Many are working harder than ever, free to make bigger waves as they push to help others find better ways to learn and teach. Retired Al Boothby not only takes on the "worst" classes in his old school district but he also engages younger teachers—or, as he wrote recently, "time to retread a new batch of teachers with Superlearning and bring them up to speed." That's something that surprised us at first. It was the older teachers, not the Young Turks, who swept up the ideas of Superlearning and adapted them to their own circumstances. It made sense when Bruce Tickell Taylor pointed out that "after decades of teaching, one becomes painfully aware there has to be a better way." The older teacher can draw on a life of experience to set the Superlearning techniques humming.

In retirement Taylor set up the Accelerative Tutoring and Transformations Institute, where he's built an invaluable worldwide network of interested teachers and learners. He's made tapes to be tested in a dozen Third World countries, and he put his Superlearning expertise to work when he took up ballroom dancing and when he decided to brush up his French—even though his teacher would have none of it in the classroom. Taylor's also fashioned a simplified tape method of Superlearning, good for old or young (see Chapter 30).

Italian director Federico Fellini evoked the dreamlike mysteries of life on film for decades. Still dreaming in his seventies, Fellini said, "If you do what you were born to do, I think you will never grow old." When the family leaves home, when retirement arrives, for many the curtain is just going up on Act Three—a third of their lives lies open before them. For some it may be a first chance to explore what they were born to do. The well known, and older, psychoanalyst Rollo May thinks creativity is the answer to aging: "By creativity I mean listening to one's own inner voice, to one's own aspirations." One can take up almost anything, says May, "but it must be something fresh, some new idea that takes fire. . . . *Fresh* is the word I use, not *young*. The older we get, the fresher we ought to get." As you're the scriptwriter, you can get as fresh as you dare and create something unique.

When ninety-year-olds were set to pumping iron in nursing homes, their muscle strength increased dramatically. Even more so, at sixty-five or seventy the core techniques of Superlearning can help muscle you up to take the plunge into new territory. It may be new territory that desperately needs you, says Karen Sands, a former Fortune 500 executive who fled the crumbling corporate pyramid to begin her own business, Future Works, to help women in particular find new fulfillment and achievement in aging. "By 2000 about a third of our population will be over fifty," Sands points out. Rather than their being a drag on the economy, Sands see a reservoir of talent and experience needed to help build a more humane society in the new millennium, a particularly necessary resource in light of the educational disasters attending the younger generations. Like every other structure, our concept of aging is beginning to crack wide open. It's a good time to be growing old; you can help shape the new face of age.

As you head into new territory, you may have to go back to school. If you find your mind doesn't work quite as quickly as a nineteen-year-old's, don't lose heart. Remember this paraphrase of a comment the eminent British brain scientist Sir John Eccles made to a quick-witted graduate student: "When you're trying to put something together, you only have one mental file drawer to search. I have whole cases full." A number of recent studies find that people over sixty, often way over, have as great a capacity for learning as young people. In theory at least, seniors should learn better than the young. They have so many more associations, so much more context to link learning with. The young can be book smart. The old, with a little effort, can end up being wise. And make the third act what it's supposed to be—a dramatic, satisfying climax.

21
Creativity

Maya Angelou is a poet and professor, an author of award-winning books, a playwright, historian, actress, civil rights activist, and singer. That's among other things. Asked to what she attributed her remarkable creativity, Angelou replied, "I do not think of myself as unusually creative. I think we all come from the Creator, each human being streaming with the glory. So each one of us is creative."

So we are, deep down somewhere. Angelou went on to say that being challenged was her blessing; it sparked her to exercise her God-given gifts. Challenging yourself to engage, to set humming the whole world of yourself, will take you a long way toward widening the creative stream. Robina Salter got onto that idea right away.

A well known science writer featured in topflight Canadian publications, Robina Salter has more recently become a well regarded novelist. In the early 1980s, covering a New York conference as a staff science writer for the University of Toronto, she came across *Superlearning*.

"There seemed to be something familiar about it, as though it made sense of something already at hand. Little wonder. We can fuel body and brain with oxygen through deep breathing. We can visualize a scene, recall a good memory, tune the body's internal rhythms to the slow, steady beat of Baroque music. Superlearning, it seemed, would put the components together in a physiological sequence. Superlearning would be like coming home to one's Self, like being totally present at a family reunion of the mind and the body, like being a constant and consistent player on that same family team instead of being a spectator, a bencher waiting for an occasional chance to play. With Superlearning, I pictured home runs in life would become the norm, without stress and strain."

Good reporter that she is, Salter checked out Dr. Jane Bancroft's Superlearning French classes at the University of Toronto's Scarborough College. "I saw students retaining and readily recalling French vocabulary and phrases. But something else was also happening. Dr. Bancroft said the students reported improved health, better relationships, and generally more effective ways of moving through life."

Then Salter dropped in on the prep school classes Lorne Cook teaches at Upper Canada College. "I observed the students lying on their gym mats learning and recalling science and math tables. They were also learning how to overcome preexam and presports competition jitters."

Convinced she was indeed seeing people at a reunion of mind and body, Salter got a Superlearning Music and Relaxation tape and began using the method every morning. Things began to happen. "An assignment I wrote on how we may influence mind/brain activities by the thoughts we choose won recognition from the University of Maryland as the best article of the year to appear in any North American university magazine." And something else began to happen to Salter. "Gradually I began to move from the strongly left brain science writing to the more creative right brain thinking. I began to write my first novel." It was *Hannah*, later published by a major Canadian firm McClelland & Stewart.

"Every morning I would lie down, follow the steps of the Superlearning tape [relaxation, mind calming, positive suggestion], and then begin to write. Ideas flowed freely, unhampered by resistance from the analytical left brain. The method began to add to my creative thinking by lessening self-doubt, fear of failing, and by quieting the inner critic.

"I continue to be helped by Superlearning as I write a novel called *Ten Hours in an Afternoon.*" As she kept to her Superlearning writing routine, Salter noted that the effect spread. "In a work on nonfiction, *An Island in Question, A Personal Pathway,* I saw how Superlearning clears the mind before sleep, possibly enhancing the two-way traffic between the conscious and the unconscious, making dreams more memorable and vivid. The material for the whole work came to me in three nights of dreaming."

Salter is in demand as a speaker throughout North America. Recently she told us, "I have been using Superlearning to prepare my material for workshops. In keeping with Superlearning teaching, I record my material, carefully spacing each unit of information. I also visualize an audience, a lectern, words going forth clearly, steadily— to receptive ears. The method frees a speaker from the need of notes, the recall being in a reliable sequence."

Like Bancroft's students, Salter notices a spillover effect. "After some years of applying Superlearning techniques, it has become a way of life. For example, when my mind is being barraged with the anapestic beat of rock music in the shopping mall, I can 'turn on' Bach or Vivaldi and tune out the destructive assault. It's also helpful when facing a painful dilemma in life, steadying the body and mind, opening the door to receive helpful insights into solutions, answers.

"And so my acquaintance with Superlearning created a paradigm shift in my life."

The creative self is part of that larger Self that Ralph Waldo Emerson saw looming over us. You don't have to create creativity, you just have to allow it. The routine Robina Salter follows relaxes the set structures of the mind, hushes the inner critic, bolsters the adventuring self, and reunites mind and body.

Take off in your imaginative body and soar through the window of the mind's eye into universes of adventure. Superlearning teachers find that a few minutes of imaginative travel sets students' creative writing and painting abilities flowing naturally. So do other imaginative prompts. Start image streaming, for instance, to find a unifying symbol or image to weave your art around. Or a symbol to unfold new emotional significance in your work or when performing other people's compositions. Ride inward on the ultradian rhythms and wonder. Go to your favorite spot in nature and conjure up your muse, your guide. Put on the head of—almost anyone. A famous artist, a careful observer, a character in your play—or how about a Pleiadian for a new perspective?

If your creativity emerges on stage, accelerated learning can get you in the spotlight in double time. Just ask Anne Galceran, who uses the method in secondary school in Sabadell, Spain. One afternoon Galceran was surprised by a phone call. "Help!" pleaded the director of the town's theatrical troupe. A play was opening that night, the star had fallen sick, but he hated to cancel. Critics from Barcelona were coming! Could she teach another actress the lines?

At six that evening Galceran met with Rosa, the substitute actress. Galceran relaxed her, told her not to strain to get the words but instead let her mind make pictures of what was being said. As soft Baroque played, they began breathing exercises, then Galceran read the script, a dramatization of witchcraft in long-ago Sabadell. One hour and fifty minutes after they'd begun, a surprised director heard the women chorus, "Ready!" The show went on, Rosa was a hit, and the other actors began buzzing about a new way to be a quick study. Accelerated learning "is making its way in Sabadell," Galceran wrote in the *SALT Newsletter*, "a way that will help us to discover the infinite dimensions of mankind."

Sound and Creativity

You might want to use high-frequency sound to break through to creativity. Patricia Joudry first discovered Sound Therapy's effect on talent. Already a well-published novelist when she first underwent Tomatis' clinical treatment for her hearing disorder, Joudry was also suffering from another debilitating problem—severe writer's block. A few weeks after therapy began, "the dam burst, as it were, the block collapsed, and now—more than a dozen years later—I can say that it has never returned." Joudry keeps inspiration flowing at a high level by listening daily to high-frequency music on her Walkman.

Vancouver artist Marian Bainsworth tells an arresting story of talent ignited by the higher octaves of sound: "I worked for fifteen years in a drafting office following graduation from art school, as I felt sure I would never make the grade as an artist. My work was rejected everywhere. I put the lid on the talent I once felt I had and went about earning a living at a job which was sheer drudgery. I had no other choice. But my inner discontent grew so acute that I finally began casting about in desperation for some way to ease my stress. I began listening to the Sound Therapy tapes most of the day while at work.

"After about six months I experienced a sort of inner release, a new sense of courage—even bravado—and I up and quit my job and decided to use my small savings to set myself up as an artist, come what may. Friends and family thought I'd taken leave of my senses. But I felt an inner core of strength, a faith that my buried talent was pushing up through the surface of my mind and was ready to flower. And so it proved to be.

"There were many struggles before I began to find a market for my art, but find it I did. I am now working full-time as an independent artist. I keep up my Sound Therapy religiously, feeling sure that it caused the opening within me. Or perhaps it just removed the block that was preventing my talent from developing."

Another person with what she termed terminal writer's block, Tulsa, Oklahoma, teacher Marilyn Hughes, used OptimaLearning to hurdle ahead on a creative course. For an article in *Focus* magazine, journalist H. Delehanty checked out Ivan Barzakov and Pamela Rand's clients: "Almost every OptimaLearning graduate I interviewed talked at length about experiencing a quantum leap of creativity. One woman who hadn't written more than a paragraph in years suddenly started creating magazine articles in her head and jotting them down feverishly during lunch breaks. A man who had been an occasional painter found himself coming home from work and painting abstract canvases until the wee hours of the morning."

Mastering the Mechanics Quickly

If your attention isn't occupied with the mechanics of artistic performance, your creativity has a greater chance to flow through. You can use Superlearning techniques to get your role down, as Anne

Galceran did in her "star is born" story in Spain. You can use imaginative rehearsal to banish jitters, as Lorne Cook helped young Christian Braun do before his violin recital. Win Wenger used accelerated means to transform a friend who could barely stumble through a joke into a snappy stand-up comic. At the University of Missouri Drs. George Petrie and Linda Rose set out to teach poor, culturally disadvantaged children to play the piano using accelerated techniques. The course finale was a recital joined by children taught traditionally. Independent music judges ranked the now-advantaged children significantly higher than the others as they remembered and played their music with greater proficiency. If you want to strengthen musical memory, a number of people find the high-frequency sound tapes help them summon back, note perfect, pieces they haven't played in years.

George Guthridge considers himself a writer first, a teacher of Reverse Instruction second. He's published dozens of short stories and in 1992 his novel *Child of the Light*, written with Janet Gluckman, was published. Guthridge's talent is double strength, his degrees are in writing, and he's taught "all kinds of writing" for years. His undergraduates at the University of Alaska Fairbanks–Bristol Bay discover how to design, research, and write a report in two days flat. As with the Reverse Instruction that he teaches graduate students at the university, Guthridge has laid out steps "specific as ties on a railroad track" for writing. They seem to liberate talent. One of his high schoolers was runner-up in the National Fiction Contest, while a junior high student came first in the International Fiction Competition. Their success, Guthridge says, comes from knowing how to find an uncommon topic and set limits for their piece. If this sounds like your route to accelerating talent, contact him (see page 347).

Creativity isn't confined of course to artistic work. You can find it flashing out anywhere, in a legal brief, a teaching technique, a cooking class, a new gadget, or that most exhilarating creation, a fully realized life. You can use Superlearning techniques specifically to enhance creativity. But if you're occupied learning other things, you may still begin to feel new creative pulses. As so many people have found, as you engage yourself, the effect begins to globalize, spreading like morning light across the land.

22
On the Edge

"May you live in interesting times," an old Chinese saying goes, laying it on you as a blessing—or a curse. We seem to be living in the ultimate of interesting times, as though the roll of the millennium had turned up the volume and spotlighted our world, leaving no place to hide. People are on edge, and all in all it doesn't seem wise to keep waiting for the rescue party. To find the blessing, we need to grab hold of new possibilities in ourselves and in the world. Upbeat possibilities. Evolutionary possibilities. An urgency of possibilities in our era of chaos within and chaos without.

Superlearning systems are surely not the only route to what Win Wenger sights as "our high human heritage." But they are a potent starting point and then some. And unlike many other good ideas, right at this moment accelerated learning offers clearly proven ways to begin to solve some of our knottiest dilemmas, problems that are both public and very personal. How will we learn? How will we earn?

"This is a wake-up call!" (sound familiar?) declared Secretary of Education Richard Riley in September 1993, revealing the results of a government study just as the kids headed back to school. Back to . . . ?

"Forty-seven percent of Americans are illiterate," Riley reported. "They lack the basic reading, writing and arithmetic skills to compete in our increasingly complex economy."

That's ninety million of your fellow citizens caught in what David Toolan, an editor of *Commonweal,* called "the most frightening thing I've heard on the news in years." And the disaster is gathering speed; a decade ago "only" 33 percent of our people were functionally illiterate. Some kids of course are learning well. But why does what was routine in the 1930s, 40s, and 50s so often wind up now as *news* on TV magazine shows? What's going on? Is this the land of the free and the home of the stupid? From Uzi-toting violence to absence of values, drugs, poverty, pollution, parental delinquency—everyone has her bit of a reason for the mess and probably a bit of the truth. But what's deep down out of whack may be more basic, a root dissonance jumbling efforts to hold the system together. That's what turned up when Don Schuster and his artist wife, Loki, rather than trying to fix education, focused on learning. They did it large scale, in a way no one has done before.

In a history-embracing, multicultural study the Schusters sought out the kind of learning that has accompanied each stage of a civilization as it cycles through time. Looking through their wide-angle lens, it is no surprise that many of us choke at the thought of learning and change or that literacy nosedives and kids in masses drop out of school. We're frozen in a frame of reference that suited the last stage of our growth, and it's strangling new growth. Historically, learning compatible with our stage of civilization—which is potentially a flowering, culminating stage—is open to spontaneity and emotion as well as to reason. It's learning that engages imagination and the riches of the arts. A stage when self-directed freedom overshadows regimentation and interest flows toward exploring a whole human self, the subliminal and the sublime.

Perhaps that's why accelerated learning just feels right to so many diverse people. It's in sync with where we're at. Or where we hope to be in 2001. That's why Dr. Mayumi Mori for instance thinks that though her country's educational system has been a triumph for a century, it's more vital than ever for people to learn how to learn to ensure that "Japanese will become participants instead of spectators in the 21st century." As Mori intuited, cracks are beginning to multiply in Japanese institutions just as they are everywhere. No matter how well an institution served in the past, if it doesn't go on its own version of the "infinity walk" and come into harmony with the extraordinary changes reshaping life, it's on a slippery slope.

Right from the start there was a dramatic tip-off that superstyle learning supplied something missing elsewhere. You could see it particularly with the bad-news kids. About-to-be dropouts, exposed by pioneering teachers to that "better way," overwhelmingly dropped back in. The learner-centered approach struck a resuscitating chord in high achievers, too, freeing them to sail over boredom and frustration into wider reaches.

Almost half the out-of-school population can't read, write, or figure well enough to assure anything close to a good job, maybe not even a job at all. Superlearning has proved ideal in country after country for picking up basics in a hurry. Half a dozen professors have created full-blown and tested accelerated reading programs. Why is all this know-how still just kicking around the edges of society?

One quarter of our ninety million illiterates are immigrants, more than tongue-tied with language difficulties. As John Wade so strikingly showed the Australian Immigration Department, accelerated learning can quickly ease newcomers of diverse background and age into becoming fluent members of society without undue trauma. It's a match, too, for those who don't emigrate but try to better themselves against long odds where they are. You can do Superlearning anywhere for almost no money; a boom box and maybe a speaker in the middle of the village will suffice. Some of the most moving letters we've gotten came from young Bantu men in South Africa striving to become nurses who'd gotten Superlearning Music and techniques from a visiting Englishwoman. They wrote of their now-materializing dreams. For the first time, they said, they believed they could have a future.

Attention deficit disorder, dyslexia, dysgraphia, autism—learning disabilities are so epidemic, you could think they were catching. Superlearning can help some; so can a host of other not-that-new breakthroughs, particularly the work of Alfred Tomatis, which has been tested, published, accepted by the French Academies of Sciences and Medicine, and used to help tens of thousands for four decades.

If you look around, we're hip deep in solutions. Can we really afford to keep on "keeping on," staying brain dead to the possibilities? The enemy—it's us? That's the cry of a bygone decade. What we need is something like "damn the guilt, drop the victim role" and full speed ahead with the rallying cry of a teacher who experienced Superlearning with Rosella Wallace and wrote, "Every teacher, school board, student, principal, anyone who has anything to do with education should take this class and begin to use her principles and practices in the classroom now, now, now!"

"America's Edge Will Come from People"

" 'The haves and have-nots' is coming to mean those who can learn and those who can't, and they're getting further apart," one manufacturer remarked hearing Secretary Riley's statistics. People who hire don't need government data to know that the deadweight of the nonworkable force has us teetering on an edge. But there are a lot of edges today.

State-of-the-art keeps streaking by. That's because we're in the Information Age, right? "Forget it," says Tom Peters, one of America's top management experts. "The information age is just about behind us. Now we're headed for a new era of 'creation intensification.' From San Jose to Beijing, 'value-added' is coming from the application of what's above the shoulders, period."

As the familiar fast-forwards into multiplying new scenarios, just about anyone is in danger of becoming illiterate in his field. Or at least feeling it's impossible to stay on top of things. Superlearning can give a high-octane kick to training and retraining. It raises skills and lowers stress, saves time, money, and resources. Wrapped in Baroque from Ohio to Heidelberg, older workers find it easier to slip the grasp of habit and to change over to new techniques. No small accomplishment, one New York garment maker will tell you. "The hardest part of my job," Fred Levine said on *The MacNeil/Lehrer NewsHour*, "is getting my workers to change when necessary. *That's* hard." Talk to that overseas prospect in his own language, fix your pharmaceutical line firmly in mind, learn to operate, retool . . . the accelerated way can open up almost any learning situation. Productivity blossoms, as Dieter Jarhling of Audi emphasizes, with healthier people in a humane environment. As American Secretary of Labor Robert Reich says, "America's edge will come from people."

But the greatest cachet of the Superlearning approach is more deep-seated, basic, like the blueprints of our genes, something you can carry with you anywhere.

"We're in an environment where education—for life, for everyone—is the game," Peters states. Lifelong learning, uh-huh. Business psychologist Marsha Sinetar looked at predictions that 70 percent of us will do entrepreneurial work in the 2000s and realized we need a fresh approach. "Personal reinvention or personal entrepreneurship," she calls it and lays the groundwork in her best-selling *Developing a 21st Century Mind*—that's a mind "creatively adaptive," flush with "learning resourcefulness." Uh-huh. Business experts of various stripes reiterate: Learn how to continually "reinvent" and "recreate" yourself for success in the 21st century. Exhausting, even as an idea, looked at from the old assembly line thinking. Yet easily in the natural order of things if you commit to the new human state of the art—being a super learner.

Plainly we have to abandon our old, glum feelings about lifelong learning, fostered by the sausage stuffing of horse-and-buggy education. It's time to take a fresh look at the landscape. Most any tree you've known keeps branching up, out, widening its circumference, bringing forth new seasons of leaves and fruit. But, as writer Tam Mossman notes, "People vegetate mentally and physically in a way that any healthy vegetable would find appalling!"

It's natural to keep learning and growing for a lifetime. "When learning is an adventure, every moment of life holds new opportunity. Your birthright is to be a scout, not a pack mule," insists MIT honors graduate Pete Saunders, Jr., head of Inner Human Potential.

Imagine an adventure, calm or raucous as you want, in sensing, imagining, thinking, discovering for a lifetime. Or just relax and flow with William Blake's "life delights in life."

Like *Star Trek,* the next generations of Superlearners are already pushing the edges out. Some worlds they'll claim are in view: the use of sound, scent, energy fields; the use of interactive global information webs and virtual reality to escape the classroom box. Twenty-first century learners will be state shifters, some with tech, others using only themselves as the instrument. Mindbody—we've just begun to plumb the single system. As insights deepen, so will our capacity to handle the transformative energy of the arts, the awesome creating power of imagination and memory. And how about finally integrating our so-called paranormal powers as new generations push to go where only superstars have gone before?

Learning breeds learning, imagination blithely leapfrogs upon itself. "The world is not only stranger than we imagine. It's stranger than we *can* imagine," said the British biologist J.B.S. Haldane early in the century. As life has switched to supersonic, probably most of us will be around to be surprised at what does come true.

In part the future will be what we envision ourselves to be. And we can only do that in the present. As far as Superlearning goes, this is what's available at present to help embody your vision:

- The means to learn faster, expand memory, and develop a more integrated self
- A perspective and some necessary personal equipment to help you ride the chaos and take charge of change
- The know-how to become a "state of the art" human being and keep learning, pushing out your edges for a lifetime
- And . . .

There's something else, less noticeable, that has been spreading in all the accelerated systems, quietly as fingers of light stretching across the lawn. The business mavens talk of constantly re-creating yourself. Catch the echo . . . re-creating . . . *recreation.* Our present is offering us the opportunity to pick up on the politics of joy.

Endorphin-Powered Learning

That's the physical part, the pleasurable brain chemistry of something new, something powerful and hopeful you can grab hold of in the chaotic. A new worldview, a new world, is coming in and, to put it simply, when the game changes, so do the rules. Prodded by duty, worry, fear, we've slogged away and made the most of that 10 percent of ourselves. The new game seems to demand a different sort of energy to carry us across the limits into our high human legacy. Listen to voices from very different perspectives:

"The ground of a healthy, whole life is this form of consciousness called bliss," insists physician Deepak Chopra. "Bliss is the closest thing to a life force that nature has provided." Across the spectrum, professor of education Lyelle Palmer, after long experience with accelerated learning, strikes a new academic note, writing of "Education's Ecstasy Explosion," an echo of Georgi Lozanov's "Life should be a ceaseless flow of joy." Taking the pulse of the times, former Peace Corps exec Chris Griscom rings the theme in her powerful book *Ecstasy Is a New Frequency*. To put it succinctly, as Joseph Campbell years ago advised, to make the most of yourself, "Follow your bliss." It's hard to ask for a more attractive motivator—but how do you catch hold of the energies of joy?

"I've been thinking about the opposite of joy," stress expert Lisa Curtis remarked recently over dinner. "I don't think it's sorrow. The opposite of joy is *fear*."

It's an insight that can pick you up. You can think of joy as the froth on the wave. Or you can experience it as the wave that can carry you to a multitude of accomplishments, a wave as natural as the waves of the sea. It's an ancient idea. Both Scripture and the wisdom schools held that order, harmony, and abundance are born of joy, not the other way around. Why don't we feel it more often? Probably because we block the innate joy of life with guilt, anger, *shoulds*, criticism, worry, feelings of unworthiness, and all our other negativities, which, traced to their root, are simply fear. As Tatiana Redonjik-Matano finds with her high achiever clients, "the key to further accelerating ability is getting rid of the blocks." Just as corporate structures are being dismantled to allow new flexibility and growth, we need to dismantle the old blocks in ourselves. After all, everybody knows you have to drop your baggage before you can ride the waves.

Here, too, it's an opportune time to make a move. The garbage is coming up outside and inside. If you're aware of something, you can begin to deal with it. Accelerated learning with a humane, nonjudgmental approach, the use of sublime music, relaxation of body and mind, engagement of your senses, emotions and imagination, harmonizing of conscious and subliminal minds, offer one route to dropping the blocks of the past to release the joyful energies. Use it or any other approach, the point is: do yourself the greatest favor you can right now. Find your way to let go of the past and come alive in the present. You can always keep your balance *if* you live in the right now, in the present. It's one of the secrets of Maslow's "self-actualized" people. As the song says, "I haven't got time for the pain . . ." And the clock is ticking.

"The Times Are Too Dangerous"

One Saturday morning, not long from now, you're going to open your eyes on the 21st century. And? Maybe it will be a golden age. "Humanity has just entered what is probably the greatest transformation it has ever known. . . . Something is happening in the structure of human consciousness. It is another species of life that is just beginning." So said the towering Pierre Teilhard de Chardin around the middle of this century. Since then ever more "best thinkers," from physicists to philosophers, are chorusing that we are in the gathering midst of something else again. To British scientist Peter Russell, author of *The Global Brain,* it may be an evolutionary "leap such as occurs only once in a billion years." To an elder statesman of Canadian journalism, Stanley Burke, it's "the ultimate renaissance." To Swiss Sophrologist Raymond Abrezol "it's not a revolution, it's literally re-evolution." The consensus: we're poised at a breakpoint where evolution is no longer automatic but depends on consciousness, on us. Interesting times.

It's tough not to rear apocalyptic images about the turning of this millennium. It is the time of the breaking up of nations. . . . Centuries of prediction, spelled out in hundreds of texts, sacred and secular, or carefully handed down as oral history seem to be emerging right on schedule. Even the schedule portends. In our terms it's a millennium, in Plato's it's the turn of a Golden Year almost 26,000 years long, in the mathematics of the ancient Mayas it's the end of the last Katun or cycle of time. As though to confirm the schedule, a curious phenomenon is happening worldwide. Secrets are pouring out. From the Maori to the Hermetic wisdom schools, to the Hopi and even the Freemasons, knowledge once kept only for the tribe or the initiate is going public. The Tyrana of Central America are the only pre-Columbian people still in existence, a feat they managed by never even speaking to outsiders throughout the centuries. Recently they decided—just once, never again, to speak out, via the BBC! Their purpose: to alert "younger brother," us, to the dangers of the changes at hand. It's beginning to feel like a third act closer, when the whole cast and all the plot lines stand revealed as the curtain rings down. "The world is now too dangerous for anything less than Utopia," was Buckminster Fuller's answer to "What next?" Consciousness researcher Trish Pfeiffer points out that at the end of the Kali Yuga—the darkest of the ages that Hindu scripture sees cycling time—it is said that, after the stage is cleared, a golden age unfolds to begin the cycle again. "For us perhaps the Cosmic Age." Maybe.

IF YOU WANT TO FLY, THAT COCOON HAS TO GO! is a T-shirt quip we quoted introducing Superlearning. Butterflying seems a little precarious in the hammering upheavals today. And yet . . . in chaos theory, which has recently captured more than scientific imagination, it is the butterfly you read about. The flight of a single butterfly, it is said, can invisibly, unpredictably influence the mighty weathers of the world.

Each of us has a unique flight pattern, a flutter of influence, greater perhaps than we imagine, both now and in the world that will be. Somewhere, deep down, we all have the right stuff, the promise of our high human heritage. The surety that it's there and the keys to begin to unlock it are more powerful than ever before. What is not sure is our answer to the question forced by the cycling millennium. Will we sleep or will we wake? We've tossed through a violent, feverish night in the 20th century into that surreal edge between sleeping and waking where bright snatches of awareness mingle with the urge to just roll over.

It's now, or maybe never, time to say with our renaissance poet Maya Angelou, all together—"*Good Morning!*"

Section Two

HOW-TO HANDBOOK OF SUPERLEARNING

23
How to Reach the Optimal Superlearning State

Superlearning, in general, is any system of *accelerated* learning that: releases stress, maximizes memory and potentials, works on both conscious and unconscious levels, enhances the whole personality globally, improves health and creativity, and is enjoyable.

Our specific form of Superlearning uses the following techniques to do this: psychological relaxation and visualization routines to dissolve stress and help you reach the optimal mindbody state to Superlearn; 60-beat Baroque music that releases stress and anchors memory; course data broken up into brief "sound-bites" presented with rhythmic pacing and intonations over the slow Baroque music. We also recommend the high-frequency music concert and dramatic reading of text—a brainmind energizer and rebalancer.

To speed up your learning, the first step is slowing down your body rhythms while keeping your mind alert—getting into the optimal state for Superlearning. Our form of do-it-yourself Superlearning brings you into this best state in four easy steps:

1. Release all stress and tension in your body.
2. Calm and refresh your mind, releasing worries and anxieties.
3. Reexperience a success point in your life and let the positive emotions of joy and accomplishment flow through you and into your current learning situation.
4. Breathe in patterns that increase oxygen flow to the brain and help synchronize hemispheres.

A great many people have achieved excellent results following this basic protocol. Most spend a full twenty minutes on the routine, doing the four steps in sequence for the first few weeks. The full routine is also available on tape, prepared by stress management expert Eli Bay, of Toronto's Relaxation Response Ltd. Once it's second nature, you can move into your best state in three or four minutes. You can of course do any of these steps independently before learning or performing. Important tip: Many find that playing Superlearning Music in the background while doing this mini-stress-control program facilitates communicating with the subconscious and increases the program's effectiveness.

Step 1 Dissolving Stress

Wave of Relaxation

Stand or sit. Tense your muscles gently and briefly, starting with your toes and legs, upper legs, lower back and abdomen, upper torso, shoulders, chest, arms, and face. Feel your whole body tense from toes to head. Hold the tension for a couple of seconds. Then let a wave of warm relaxation flow down through your body starting with your head. Let it roll over your neck, arms, shoulders, back, abdomen, legs, and feet. Let the wave roll away strain and fatigue. Note where you're carrying or storing tension in your body or where muscles are tight or knotted. Let the wave of relaxation roll over them. Feel the tension in your muscles wash away with each wave. Now tense and relax your whole body with a wave of relaxation. Do this two or three times.

Add a few neck rolls to improve circulation to your head. Feel completely relaxed as you sit or lie down and move into the following exercise.

Visualization for Stress Control

You can either tape this exercise for yourself or read it through and do it from memory.

Make yourself as comfortable as possible. Loosen any tight clothing. Feel very, very relaxed. Take several slow, deep breaths. As you breathe easily and deeply, say to yourself:

"As I breathe easily and deeply and feel deeply relaxed, I visualize myself on the seventh floor of a building. The walls I see are painted a vivid, warm, red color. I walk down this red hallway to the end, where I arrive at the top of an escalator marked 'Down.' It's a special silver-colored escalator. It is smooth, noiseless, completely safe and dependable. I step on the escalator and feel myself beginning to glide down. I hold the rails with my hands and feel completely safe. I am descending without any sound, very slowly, very safely, very securely. I am descending on a very relaxing journey to my main inner level, a level where I know I can make connections to my inner self. I continue to ride down, feeling myself relaxing and unwinding . . . relaxing and unwinding.

"I take a deep breath. As I exhale, I repeat '7' several times. I picture a large number 7 standing out against the vivid red walls of this seventh floor. Red color seems to float past me as I continue my relaxing ride downward.

"I get off the escalator. I have now reached the sixth floor. As I walk along the hall to the next Down escalator, I see a giant number 6 printed on the bright *orange* walls of this sixth floor. Surrounded by this bright orange color, I step onto the top step of the Down escalator. Once again I slowly and effortlessly glide downward. I take a deep breath, and as I exhale, I repeat 'six' several times and clearly see the pleasant orange walls all around.

"I feel myself unwinding and relaxing as I smoothly ride down to a still more restful and pleasant area. I am now on the fifth floor. I see the fifth-floor sign and notice the walls are a very bright golden-yellow color. I get off the escalator and walk through this corridor of yellow to the next Down escalator. I take a deep breath and, while exhaling, I visualize the number 5. I mentally repeat 'five' several times while enjoying this beautiful, joyful golden-yellow color. I get on the next escalator and continue to float downward. I feel very comfortable. I let myself go and simply enjoy the colors.

"I see the fourth floor sign and notice the walls are a restful, lush grassy green. I get off the escalator on the fourth floor and walk through this clear, emerald-green color to the next escalator.

"I take a deep breath and, while exhaling, I visualize the number 4. I mentally repeat 'four' several times. I enjoy the clear, rich green all around me as I step on the next escalator and glide calmly downward through the wonderful green to a still more pleasant and relaxing area.

"I reach the third-floor sign and see the walls of this floor are a brilliant, clear blue color. I feel myself filled with this peaceful, calm blue. I am surrounded by blue. I pause for several moments on the third floor and I visualize a quiet scene from nature—a favorite place where I've always felt that I could be the most relaxed—a blue lake, or a calm blue ocean, or fields, or mountains spanned by a broad blue sky. I feel again the same sense of harmony, of deep relaxation I felt then. I enjoy the flowing blue color all around me and feel a very pleasant, very restful, very relaxing sensation.

"I take a deep breath and, while exhaling, I visualize the number 3. I mentally repeat 'three' several times.

"I step on the next Down escalator and begin once more to glide downward smoothly and easily to a still more pleasant, more relaxing area of soft and restful color.

"I see the second floor sign and I see that the walls on this floor are a rich, vibrant purple color. I get off the escalator. I take a deep breath and, while exhaling, I visualize the number 2. I mentally repeat 'two' several times. I sense this rich purple all around me and I feel extraordinarily comfortable and relaxed. I move through this purple and feel the color move through me as I walk down the hall to the next 'Down' escalator.

"As I descend through the deep purple to a still more pleasant and relaxing area of color, I see the sign FIRST FLOOR. I notice that this main floor is a luminous ultraviolet color. The escalator glides softly downward and I get off on the first floor.

"I take a deep breath and, while exhaling, I visualize the number 1 and repeat 'one' several times. I enjoy the luminous ultraviolet color all around me and feel myself bathed in its glow. I have now reached a very, very relaxed state. I feel very rested, healthy, and relaxed. I am now at my main inner level. At this level I can easily connect with other areas of awareness in my mind. I continue to rest and enjoy complete relaxation. I breathe deeply and evenly. I enjoy this complete relaxation. (Pause)

"I affirm that I am a unique person.

"I am achieving my goals.

"Learning and remembering are easy and fun.

"I am supremely calm."

Add affirmations that will direct your inner mind to your current goal. (See below.)

"To leave this main inner level, I count down from 3, 2, 1. On the count of 1, I open my eyes. I feel alert, serene, centered, refreshed, and free from all tension."

If you are doing this four step program straight through, use this countdown to return to your day's activities *after* the fourth routine. (Note: If desired, you can substitute flights of stairs for the escalator. For alternate stress releasers and relaxation techniques, see Section Three.)

Affirmations

Affirmations can help anytime, but they are especially helpful when you are in a relaxed state of awareness. Customize your own, keeping them short, rhythmic and positive. Repeat each affirmation four or five times.

Affirmations for Learning

I release myself from my past performance.

I can do it.

Learning is easy for me.

Remembering is easy for me.

Learning _____ is easy.

I am uncovering new abilities.

My mind works rapidly and effectively.

I am successful.

Before a Test, Exam, Interview, or Audition

I am supremely calm and confident.

I remember everything I need to know.

I recognize the right answers at the right time.

My memory works perfectly.

I have all the time I need to complete the test.

I concentrate easily from beginning to end.

Step 2 Visualizations for Mind Calming

Getting rid of worry, anxiety and fear of failure gives your abilities a chance to shine. Imagining yourself in a beautiful spot in nature is a proven way of soothing the mind and releasing worries and pressure.

You can imagine yourself taking a walk in a favorite park or a woods, or across hills or mountains like those in *The Sound of Music*, or just sitting by a lake in a summer or winter countryside. Or you may want to go to the beach. Choose anyplace in nature that brings you serenity. After you've ridden the rainbow to the bottom of the escalator and affirmed your abilities:

Go to a beautiful beach at a favorite vacation spot.

Feel the warmth of the sun. Smell the delicious, fresh sea air.

Walk along the beach, right to the edge of the water.

Feel the warmth of the sand under your feet and trickling between your toes as you walk.

Absorb the intense, sunny blue of the sky and the turquoise blue of the water.

As you walk along the edge of the water, feel the waves gently lapping up around your ankles. The waves feel so refreshing.

Feel a light breeze blowing softly against your skin. Cares and worries and troubles gently drift away on the wind. Now they are far, far away.

In the distance you hear seagulls calling to each other.

Watch the sparkling pattern of the sun dancing on the water. Enjoy this scene as much as possible.

If you're doing the mind calming exercise on its own, you might enjoy heightening the effect with background music like Steve Halpern's "anti-frantic" music, or environmental "sounds of nature" CDs. The mind calming mini-vacation can be varied from day to day. (For more visualization exercises, see Section Three.)

Step 3 *Excel*ebration! Joy of Learning Recall

Celebrate your abilities and accomplishments! Your additional potentials are all there just waiting to surface. What summons them? Emotion—specifically the emotions of joy, pleasure, gratitude. Joy is a powerful emotional messenger that communicates with your inner mind so that it can work with you, not against you. The "no pain, no gain" philosophy got us to the 5 percent level of our potentials. Now with endorphin-powered Superlearning, it's *through exhilaration to acceleration*. Joy may be the key to opening the remaining 95 percent of our potentials.

Joy has even proved its muscle in the lab. Neuroscientist Dr.

Aryeh Routtenberg, of Northwestern University, was the first to discover that the same pathways in the brain that generate pleasure-producing endorphins are also the centers of *memory* consolidation. Even rats who got the "joy treatment" (endorphins triggered by electro-stimulation) became "superlearning rats." Dr. James Olds charted these rats' high marks on IQ, memory, and maze tests. They doubled their learning speed. Joy and its by-product, neurotransmitters, enhance learning and memory. People who "love what they do" produce brain messengers that enhance their abilities to do what they love. Mind machines improve learning and memory by triggering these intelligence-boosting endorphins. You can do it at no cost with your own innate equipment. Reexperiencing a joyful moment or a celebration and letting that positive feeling suffuse the present moment or challenge is a key to excellence.

Summoning a Best Memory

Return to a time in your life when you really felt good about a success or an accomplishment. It can either be a recent time or when you were very young. It can be a success linked with learning or a time when your memory worked at its peak. It can even be getting the key word that solved a tough crossword puzzle, or when you enjoyed something fascinating in a book, movie, or TV program. It can be when you made a discovery of something intriguing or prepared a marvelous dinner. It can be in sport event like the time you hit the baseball home run. It can be a childhood experience, like the day you first rode a bike. It can be in school or college, the time you received recognition or an award. It might be the day you passed the driving exam and got your driver's license. It can be the day you had a triumphant performance on the stage, or the time you won a prize in a contest. It can be anytime you felt pleased and excited and accomplished.

Recapture the winning feeling of that successful experience. Feel the details of that pleasant experience as completely as possible. Imagine yourself in that situation again. See exactly where you were. Were other people there? Was it indoors or outdoors? How did your body feel? Scan your head, hands, stomach. Try to relive your thoughts and the thrill and fun of achievement. Remember the eagerness and excitement you had about this joyful experience. Feel the pleasure of sensing your mind, memory, and body functioning together with ease. Hold on to that special "kick." Let it flow through you when you relax and listen to a Superlearning lesson tape. *Excel*ebrate!

Step 4 Breathing in Rhythm

Breathing deeply and rhythmically brings oxygen to your brain, and oxygen fuels learning and memory. Rhythmic breathing also synchronizes brain hemispheres and synchronizing fuels creativity. In addition slow, rhythmic breathing helps slow mindbody rhythms to the optimal state for learning.

Sit comfortably in a chair or lie down on a couch or bed. Relax by your preferred method. Close your eyes and take a slow, deep breath through your nose. Inhale as much air as you can hold comfortably. Try for just a little bit more air. Now exhale very slowly. Feel a deep sense of relaxation as you exhale. Try to force out just a little bit more air.

Practice these deep breaths for a few moments. Inhale as much air as possible with a real "belly breath." Slowly exhale and pull in your abdomen at the same time. Take another deep breath, as much air as possible. This time hold it for a count of 3 and exhale very slowly. Relax. Try to inhale air in an even, continuous breath.

Now begin to make your breathing rhythmic. Inhale to a count of 4. Hold to a count of 4. Exhale to a count of 4. Pause to a count of 4:

Inhale—2, 3, 4

Hold—2, 3, 4

Exhale—2, 3, 4

Pause—2, 3, 4

Repeat four or five times. Relax and try to slow down your breathing even more, this time to a count of 6.

Inhale—2, 3, 4, 5, 6
Hold—2, 3, 4, 5, 6
Exhale—2, 4, 5, 6
Pause—2, 3, 4, 5, 6

Repeat four or five times. Relax and try for an even slower breathing pattern—a count of 8.

Inhale—2, 3, 4, 5, 6, 7, 8
Hold—2, 3, 4, 5, 6, 7, 8
Exhale—2, 3, 4, 5, 6, 7, 8
Pause—2, 3, 4, 5, 6, 7, 8

Repeat several times. If possible, try to do some rhythmic breathing before a Superlearning session.

If you have done the set of four Superlearning exercises in sequence, use this simple countdown to return to your day's activities: "Now, on the countdown of three, two, one, I open my eyes and feel alert and refreshed, free of all tension. Three, two, one—eyes open. I feel alert, serene and centered." Shake your hands at your sides and stretch.

During the actual Baroque memory expansion session you will breathe to a different, shorter pattern, holding your breath during the four seconds data is given, breathing in and out in the four-second pause. At first you might want to practice this a little bit before learning.

Superlearning Memory Concert

Before a Superlearning session it's helpful to look over the material you want to learn and review. Try to do it as vividly as possible. Make crazy, exaggerated images to help anchor technical data. Try games, puzzles, or even write info on posterboards, spreading them out on the floor in a pattern and walking through them so that you remember kinetically as you walk. Use all your senses. Underline material with different colored markers or markers that have different scents in them, or dab different aromas (e.g., chocolate or peppermint) or perfumes on pages of specific course data you must ingest. Make up catchy rhymes from learning data and tie the words to pop songs. For more tips from experienced Superlearning users, check the next sections.

You might find it helpful to do a five minute review before you go to sleep at night, a week later, and then a month later to really anchor material in your long term memory.

For a Superlearning memory expansion session, all you need is a tape recorder and/or someone to read the material aloud to you.

1. Follow the four-step relaxation routine to get into the optimal state for learning.

2. Turn on your Superlearning course. If there are eighty to one hundred data bits, the tape will run around fifteen minutes. It may be one you've prepared yourself or one you've obtained from a Superlearning center. The voice will read the material rhythmically—four seconds of data, then a four-second pause. Varied intonations will keep the material interesting.

3. Silently read your course data following along with the recited material. Try to hold your breath when you hear the data. Breathe out and in during the pauses. If you find this breathing pattern difficult, omit it for the time being and just let your breathing flow along with the rhythm of the music, and it will pace itself naturally. If possible, try to form images of the data during the pauses.

4. Once you've gone through the whole lesson, you'll hear the slow, 60-beat music begin. Lean back, relax, close your eyes, and listen to the same material again. Don't strain, just let your mind float between music and data. The concert will last about twelve to fifteen minutes.

After the memory expansion session you may want to quiz yourself to see just how much you've absorbed. It's important to try to use the material you've listened to. If it's a new language, try some games or puzzles to practice new vocabulary, or have a friend ask you questions. If it's science data, review it again and see how much you recall. For specific suggestions, see the rest of this section.

In the next day or so even more of the data will pop into your mind. Superlearning has a snowballing effect. The more you do it, the faster and easier it gets. At first you may want to repeat the same lesson several times to get it 100 percent. Like any skill, it gets easier. You'll be able to learn more by the tenth lesson than the first, and you won't need as many repetitions.

Over and above speeding learning, all by itself, this global Superlearning process benefits your health, memory, and creativity and helps open up new abilities.

24
How to Prepare Your Own Superlearning Program

You can use Superlearning for just about anything. People have adapted it for real estate law, sports rules, Morse Code, science data, medicine, spelling, math, grammar rules, computer programs, typing, foreign languages, even sanitation regulations. It's helped salesmen remember products, price lists, customer's names. Stockbrokers have used it to remember stock names and ticker codes. You can use it for phone numbers, astrology, Bible verses, nutrition data, menu terms, wine lists. If you're heading to Atlantic City or Reno, you can even use it for memorizing cards and gambling odds. If you're a traveler, you can use it to memorize foreign exchange rates for your currency. It's a big help for hobbies, from bird watching to collectibles. Some people even used it to win contests.

The memory reinforcement session is most easily done on tape. It consists of two parts: paced reading of data *without* music; paced reading of the same data *with* Superlearning music.

Here's how to make a tape: Get your data together. Put it into note form and try to reduce each note to a small chunk of about seven to nine words. Research has shown that small data bits are readily absorbed by your memory. (That's why phone numbers have seven digits.)

For instance if your topic is:

Inventors: "Edison: Thomas Edison invented the light bulb."

Arithmetic: "Four times four is sixteen."

Geography: "New York State capital—Albany."

Languages—French vocabulary: "Good day!—*Bonjour!*"

Computers: "MS-DOS is a computer *D*isk *O*perating *S*ystem."

Rhythmic Pacing of Data

Now you're ready to record your data. Superlearning uses an eight-second pacing cycle. You say your data during the first four seconds, remain silent during the next four seconds; say your data in four seconds; pause four seconds; and so on.

Scientific research shows the four-second pause allows time for brain cells and memory to absorb and register the data better so that it's easier to retrieve.

Suppose you're preparing the arithmetic multiplication table:

1 2 3 4	**1 2 3 4**
"One times one is one."	Pause
"Two times two is four."	Pause
"Three times three is nine."	Pause
"Four times four is sixteen."	Pause

How to count out four seconds? The old way of counting seconds —"One potato, two potatoes, three potatoes, four potatoes"—gives a rough idea, but to make pacing precise, there are several easy ways. Use a prepared pacing tape (available from Superlearning Inc.), or use a metronome or stopwatch, or make your own pacing tape.

To make your own pacing tape, put a blank sixty-minute tape into your tape recorder. You'll need a stick or spoon and a watch or clock with a second hand. Turn on "Record" and tap the stick or spoon every four seconds as you time yourself with the clock or watch.

To record your material on the eight-second cycle, think of it as divided into two units of four seconds each: Talk Unit—Pause Unit, Talk Unit—Pause Unit, Talk Unit—Pause Unit. State your material in the first four-second Talk Unit. Be silent during the next four-second Pause Unit. And so on. You don't have to fill up the entire four seconds of the Talk Unit if your data are very brief. The Pause Unit just becomes longer. If you have a lot of material to cram into the Talk Unit, speak quickly. Think of it as an answering machine where you have to get your message in before the beep. If the data runs over into the Pause Unit, the pause can be shortened to two seconds. If your data is really long, just break it up and spread it out over several Talk Units. Once you practice with eight-second pacing, you'll find it easily becomes almost automatic.

Intonations

To keep interest high in cycle after cycle of what you have to learn, research showed that varied intonations are a big help. They erase boredom. Superlearning uses three different voice tones: (a) normal; (b) soft, whispering, conspiratorial; and (c) loud, commanding. These three intonations repeat over and over.

Here's how it sounds on the multiplication table:

"One times one is one."	normal
"Two times two is four."	soft, whispering, conspiratorial
"Three times three is nine."	loud, commanding
"Four times four is sixteen."	normal
"Five times five is twenty-five."	soft, whispering

Some people have done Superlearning successfully without the intonations. So if you have problems with them, or omit them, Superlearning will still work for you. However, the more components of the system that you use, the more successful it is. For foreign language vocabulary, intonations are used only for the foreign words, not for the English translation.

Amount of Data Per Session

Once you've become accustomed to the method, you can absorb 50 to 150 new bits of information per session. The more you practice with the method, the more you'll be able to absorb. Results snowball, and it gets easier and easier to do. The do-it-yourselfer, who is aware of the possibilities, may soar up to record amounts of material. As you open up more potentials, you probably won't have to listen to a data tape more than a few times.

With the eight-second cycle, you cover seven and a half data units per minute. One hundred data units will take around thirteen minutes. Fifty vocabulary words will take about six and one half minutes. Eighty words, around ten minutes.

Twelve-Second Cycle

What to do it if your data consist of long, unwieldy, lengthy sentences? There are two solutions. Use two seconds of the Pause Unit frame time for the data and add it on to the four-second Talk Unit giving you six Talk Unit seconds for data. Or move to the twelve-second pacing cycle.

The twelve-second cycle is good for learning rules, principles in math, long definitions, regulations, and so on. Research showed that people remembered a long definition or rule better when the complete thought was given. This long material can be spoken over three four-second segments or, if necessary, read out in its entirety.

Here's how spelling can be done on a twelve-second cycle: Say the word; spell the word; define the word or use the word in a sentence.

1 2 3 4	**1 2 3 4**	**1 2 3 4**
exhilarating	e-x-h-i-l-a-r-a-t-i-n-g	It's exhilarating to learn fast.
endorphin	e-n-d-o-r-p-h-i-n	Brain messenger chemical that eases pain.

The breathing pattern for the twelve-second cycle is: Inhale 4 counts; hold 4 counts; exhale 4 counts.

Taping Your Program

Put your material on tape so you can listen to it anytime. Start off with short batches of data, and as you become skilled, make longer tapes. If you're using a click tape to time your paced reading, you'll need two tape recorders, one to play the click tape and one to record you reading to the pacing of the clicks. If you're using a metronome or a watch to time your paced reading, then you'll just need one tape recorder to record your material.

The fastest and easiest way to set up your Superlearning concert session is simply to record your paced reading on tape *without* music. When you're ready to add the music to the listening session, use two tape recorders. Play your 60-beat music on one tape recorder. Play your data tape on the other tape recorder.

If you want to make a complete Superlearning lesson tape with the two readings of your data, one without music and one with music, you will need three tape recorders. Play the click tape on one tape recorder and the music tape on another. Keep the music volume low. On the third tape recorder, record yourself reading over the music to the pacing of the clicks. Keep the music volume low and be sure you're clearly audible over the music. Both the eight-second pacing and the twelve-second pacing cycles are recorded the same way, once without music and once with music.

When you're ready to listen to your Superlearning tape, first take a few minutes to relax and get into the stress-free, optimal learning state.

If you're learning with another person or you're coaching someone, you don't have to tape the lesson. You'll need one tape recorder to play the Superlearning Music. You simply read the data aloud with pacing. Then read it again while the music is playing. During the first read-through your listener follows the text. During the read-through with music, your listener relaxes and listens with eyes closed.

Dramatic Presentation

In addition to the paced reading with intonations, some Superlearning users have found that the Superlearning "active" concert session along with a dramatic reading of the text or material can be very effective. This classical concert features plenty of high-frequency music proven to revitalize mind and memory.

A secret of one of the most successful Superlearning reading programs in the United States was using this dramatic presentation of an entire story over music. In this case they used the slow Baroque music for both the dramatic presentation and the paced reading. The East Germans have used this slow Baroque for both the dramatic and the paced readings for thirty years with enormous success.

Record the material you have to learn—a story or dialogue or set of data—and read it aloud with real oomph. The advantage of this active concert is that you can play it back anytime, while you're working around the house or doing chores. You don't have to be in a relaxed state to listen to it. You can record yourself as the music plays in the background, or use two tape recorders for playback—one with the music and one with your taped material.

Dr. Ivan Barzakov's years of experimentation show that just reading aloud with music (whether you record it or not) appears to enable the brain to assimilate large amounts of information of any kind on any subject with ease and high retention. He's been training students, teachers, trainers, and managers in the technique of Reading Aloud with Music with good results for many years. He has distilled some key insights.

Read aloud over music for five to twenty-five minutes each time. Schedule this reading just before going to bed and right after you get up in the morning, he suggests. Highlight the information you need to read, or select a full length story or language dialogue. Pause after each sentence. Divide long passages into short phrases and pause after each one. As you listen to the music and begin to read, try to follow the mood of the music. Listen to the music and vary your voice according to the tempo and mood. If you start to feel bored or tired, take a break. Students report the technique is easy and gives a lift to general well being.

Bruce Tickell Taylor's successful method of using the Superlearning "Active" Concert is in Chapter 30.

Exploring Components

As you work with the whole Superlearning system, you may find some elements help you even more than others. Some people found that playing the music again after the lesson while they did a quiz on the material really gave them "total recall."

Many have found that playing Superlearning Music while they do the relaxation exercises and affirmations also made the stress-control program powerfully effective.

Some researchers found that synchronizing breathing with the paced data gave exceptional results.

The elements all interact. Early research showed that affirmations for better learning used all by themselves gave a 60 percent improvement. Synchronizing breathing to the paced data read over music gave a 78 percent improvement. All of these elements together gave a 141 percent improvement in tests conducted by Dr. Don Schuster. For more on the "why" of these different elements, see *Superlearning*.

Superlearning Music—How-to

You can obtain Superlearning slow Baroque music from Superlearning Inc. and many of the accelerated learning centers in the United States and Europe. In addition you can obtain freshly minted, new 60-beat music by contemporary composers from the locations listed in the Resources section.

If you would like to make your own Superlearning Music tape, a list of slow Baroque selections is included. Each selection is usually very brief—two to four minutes, so you will need to record several of them from several different tapes, CDs, or records to make a twenty-minute tape. Most libraries have a music section that includes Baroque music. Add a couple of minutes of fast tempo music to the end of your tape as a wake-up signal to aid the transition back from the relaxing concert.

The slow section in a Baroque concerto is usually the Largo or Andante movement. When you get a recording of a concerto, you will have to check with a metronome or stopwatch to see that the music is actually played at or around the 60-beat tempo. The conductor of the orchestra may set a tempo that's much faster than 60 beats a minute, according to how he or she wishes to interpret the music.

If you play an instrument, you can record music yourself at the 60-beat tempo to use for Superlearning.

Superlearning "Active" Concert

The music for this classical concert is used in its entirety, so you just have to obtain a tape or CD of the full symphony or concerto.

Getting Started with
Superlearning Music

The elements that make up music—tempo, beat, keys, high frequencies—can all bring us remarkable benefits if they're put together with the right formula for the right purpose. All you have to do is turn on the tape and listen. If you have reason to believe your hearing is not 100 percent or if you have learning disabilities, check Sound Therapy (page 350) and hearing boosters (page 354).

If you're a friend, parent, or teacher planning to introduce 60-beat Superlearning Music to others, it helps to play it cool. If it's played quietly in the background while data is read aloud, students, especially youngsters, are frequently not aware of the music. If it's necessary to introduce the music, just say it's specially formulated and metered music designed with a specific purpose of speeding learning and bringing supermemory and that it's been successful worldwide for thirty years. The music is not a personal choice for entertainment listening.

If your target listeners have such strong ethnic, cultural, or other prejudices that they refuse to listen to the European Superlearning Music, use the freshly composed music listed below. Clarify that all ancient cultures developed specific music to induce relaxation and altered states. Don't use non-60-beat music to get acceptance. Every kind of music has been tested, from country western to rock to pop to jazz. Sixty-beat produced the best results. If it is impossible to use

Physiological Changes During Supermemory Sessions Compared to TM

	Supermemory Concert of Slow Baroque Music (60 b.p.m.) During Intense Mental Activity (learning 100 foreign words)	*Transcendental Meditation* (Reciting a mantra)
Electroencephalo-gram (Alpha brain waves: 7 - 13 cycles per sec. Beta brain waves: over 13 cycles per sec. Theta brain waves: 4 - 7 cycles per sec.)	Alpha brain waves increase by an average of 6%. Beta brain waves decrease by an average of 6%. Theta waves unchanged.	Alpha brain waves increase. Some increase in Theta waves.
Pulse	Pulse slows by an average of 5 beats per minute.	Decreases significantly with a mean decrease of 5 beats per minute.
Blood Pressure	Blood pressure drops slightly (4 divisions of the mercury column on an average).	Tendency to decrease with intermediate fluctuations.
Body Motility	Sitting comfortably. Body relaxed.	Sitting comfortably. Body relaxed.
Awareness	Relaxed concentration	"Restful alertness"

60-beat music, a metronome beating 60 beats to the minute can be substituted.

Conducting a comparison test, studying so many days to rock versus the same amount of time with 60-beat music, has proven very convincing for many, as demonstrated by Dr. Bancroft and Leo Wood. Some people apparently crave rock to get energy and brain stimulation. It's now known that high-frequency sounds like some found in Superlearning Music can also energize the brain. Once a potential Superlearner experiences this brain recharge, it can make it easier to convince him or her to try Baroque for learning.

When researchers told us they planned to use Superlearning for profoundly deaf students, we didn't hold much hope that an audio system would work. Yet the deaf were able to "sense" the slow music beat through bone conduction and they benefited from the slow, rhythmic pacing. Using sign language, researchers trained deaf students in relaxation and stress control. They signed the learning data in rhythmic, dancelike pacing to the music. Superlearning, the so-called musical-memory system, accelerated deaf people's learning.

You can also benefit from sound by using special tuning forks. Each fork in a set resonates at a specific frequency and can be placed on specific acupuncture points on the body to help rebalance the body and energize the mind.

If your target listeners are music students, tests at the University of Toronto's Scarborough College, conducted by Dr. Bagriana Belanger, showed that they have a tendency to listen to music with the analytical left brain, criticizing performance or recording instead of allowing the music to induce the optimal learning state. Music students can benefit from additional relaxation training, which will also help them in their performing careers.

Superlearning Music Selections

Some Slow Baroque Music Selections for Superlearning

Vivaldi
> Largo from "Winter" from *The Four Seasons*
> Largo from Concerto in D Major for Guitar and Strings
> Largo from Concerto in C Major for Mandolin, Strings, and Harpsichord

Telemann—Largo from Double Fantasia in G Major for Harpsichord

Bach, J. S.
> Largo from Harpsichord Concerto in F Minor, BWV 1056
> Air for the G String
> Largo from Harpsichord Concerto in C Major BWV 975

Corelli—Largo from Concerto No. 10 in F Major from Twelve Concerti Grossi, Op. 5

Albinioni—Adagio in G for Strings

Caudioso—Largo from Concerto for Mandolin and Strings

Pachelbel—Canon in D

Some 60-Beat Music Selections by Contemporary Composers

Janalea Hoffman
> *Mind Body Tempo.* Piano and orchestra.
> *Deep Daydreams.* Instrumental music. Side 1 is at 60 beats; side 2 is at 50.
> *Music for Mellow Minds.* Piano and strings.
> *Music to Facilitate Imagery.* Piano and strings.
> *Children's Meditation Tape.* Features "The Dolphin Song," relaxation games, and guided imagery for ages two to eleven.
> *Rhythmic Medicine.* Video of 60-beat and 50-beat instrumental music synchronized with visual images.

William Duncan—*Exultate—Music to Expand Learning.* 60-beat guitar music.

André Gagnon—*Lullaby for My Mother.* From his album *The St. Lawrence* (Columbia Records). Slow-tempo music in the Baroque style for piano and orchestra by this famous French-Canadian composer and performer.

Music for the Superlearning "Active" Classical Concert

Mozart
  "Haffner" Symphony
  "Prague" Symphony
  Concerto for Violin and Orchestra No. 5 in A Major
  Concerto for Violin and Orchestra No. 4 in D Major
  Concerto for Piano and Orchestra No. 18 in B Flat Major
  Concerto for Piano and Orchestra No. 23 in A Major
Beethoven—Concerto for Violin and Orchestra in D Major, Op. 61
Brahms—Concerto for Violin and Orchestra No. 1 in G Minor, Op. 26
Tchaikovsky—Concerto No. 1 for Piano and Orchestra in B Flat Minor, Op. 23; Violin Concerto in D Major, Op. 35
Chopin—Waltzes
Haydn—Symphonies No. 67 in F Major and No. 68 in C Major

High-Frequency Music for Brain Recharging and Vitality

Music selections with very high frequencies able to give mind-body the most rapid recharge: Mozart: Violin Concertos 1, 2, 3, 4, 5. Mozart: Symphonies Nos. 29, 32, 39, 40. Mozart: String Quartets. Mozart: Sinfonia Concertante. Contradances. (A British audiologist is investigating benefits of high-frequency music without the Electronic Ear and filtering of low frequencies.)

For Sound Therapy applied to languages and learning disabilities, see Chapters 25 and 31.

Lozanov's Suggestopedic Active Concert, which uses plenty of Mozart's music as a background to a dramatic rendition of lesson data, not only meshes right and left brain but, according to Tomatis, would also provide an energy boost and balance to brain and body at the same time.

Dr. Tomatis also suggests Gregorian Chant for "charging the brain," calling it "sublime brain food." There are several excellent tapes of Gregorian Chant performed by the Monks of Solesmes in

France and by the Benedictine nuns of Saint Cecilia's Abbey on the Isle of Wight. Choral music, however, is not suitable for the Superlearning "Active" Concert reading.

Where to Find the Music

Superlearning Inc., 450 Seventh Avenue, Suite 500, New York, NY 10123.

Ostrander & Associates, 1290 West Eleventh Avenue, #105-SL, Vancouver, BC V6H 1K5.

Ostrander & Associates, 4325 Steeles Avenue West, #410, Downsview, Ont., Canada M3N 1V7. For 60-beat music tapes by Baroque and contemporary composers; high-frequency music by Mozart and contemporary composers; Sophrology music tapes (Turning Sound) and programs; 60-beat Superlearning Music with subliminal suggestions for transformation.

Mellow Minds, P.O. Box 6431, Shawnee Mission, KA 66206, and Rhythmic Medicine, 4557 Walnut, Kansas City, MO 64111. For information and contemporary 60-beat music tapes and CDs by Janalea Hoffman.

Expanded Learning, 125 West Second Avenue, Denver, CO 80223. For 60-beat guitar music by William Duncan.

Sound Therapy, Steele & Steele, P.O. Box 105, Lund, B.C., VON 2GO, Canada; and Sound Therapy Australia, P.O. Box A2237, Sydney, South, New South Wales 2000, Australia. For catalog of Joudry's Sound Therapy tapes; book, *Sound Therapy for the Walkman;* information.

Sound Listening and Learning Center, 2701 East Camelback Rd., Suite 205, Phoenix, AZ 85016. For information on Dr. Tomatis' research and his books, *The Conscious Ear; Education and Dyslexia; About the Tomatis Method* (ed. T. Gilmor).

Centre Tomatis, 68 Blvd. de Courcelles, 75017 Paris, France; Tomatis

International, 2, rue de Phalsbourg, 75017, Paris, France. For treatment of hearing problems, learning disabilities, and other illnesses.

Institute for Music, Health and Education, P.O. Box 1244, Boulder, CO 80306, and the Listening Centre, 5 Sultan St., 2nd Fl., Toronto, Ontario, Canada M5S 1L6. For information on music and Tomatis.

The Lind Lists, P.O. Box 14487, San Francisco, CA 94104-0487 for music sources for accelerated learning.

Scientific Enterprises, Inc., 708 119th Lane, Blaine, MN 55435. For Carlson's high-frequency sound and music tapes for accelerated plant growth.

Life Rhythm, P.O. Box 806, Mendocino, CA 95460. For tuning forks developed by Hans Cousto and his book, *The Cosmic Octave—The Origin of Harmony.*

Tools for Exploration, Inc., 4460 Redwood Highway, Suite 2, San Rafael, CA 94903. For neuro-acoustics research, tapes, and machines including the Edrington Binaural Signal Generator.

The Monroe Institute, Route 1, P.O. Box 175, Faber, VA 22938; and Interstate Industries, Inc., Box P.O. 130, Nellysford, VA 22958. For Hemi-Synch "beat frequency" tapes for enhanced learning.

For information on sonic breakthroughs, signature sound, and high-frequency music tapes by Dyveke Spino, contact Superlearning Inc.

National Association for Music Therapy, 1133 Fifteenth Street, N.W., Washington, DC 20005. Publishes *Journal of Music Therapy.*

Helen Bonny, Music RX, ICM West, P.O. Box 173, Port Townsend, WA 98368.

Halpern Sounds, 1775 Old Country Rd., #9, Belmont, CA 94002.

Sound Healers Association, P.O. Box 2240, Boulder, CO 80306.

25
Superlearning Languages—How-to

How to Organize Your Language Material to Make a Tape

Here's how a sequence of several foreign language phrases would be set up to be paced on the eight-second cycle. The material is set up with the native language on the left, target language on the right. That's so you can form a mental image to link to the new foreign words.

On average, nine short words fit the four-second time frame. A long phrase or sentence can be split up over several eight-second frames. It's better to present vocabulary in a phrase than as individual words.

Intonations (normal {N}, soft/confidential {S}, loud/commanding {L}) are only used with the target-language phrase, not the native language translation. The material is set up in sets of three on the page, to match the intonation cycle. Intonations help make long batches of phrases and vocabulary easier to remember and help reduce boredom. However, they can be optional if you have any problem with them.

Here's a sample from the Indonesian language:

1 2 3 4	1	2	3	4	Intonation
silence	Thanks.		*Terima kasih.*		(N)
silence	Many thanks.		*Terima kasih banyak.*		(S)
silence	Please.		*Tolong. (Silahkan.)*		(L)
silence	Yes/No/Maybe.		*Ya/Tidak/Barangkali.*		(N)
silence	Excuse me.		*Maaf.*		(S)
silence	That's all right.		*Tidak apa-apa.*		(L)
silence	Good morning.		*Selamat pagi.*		(N)
silence	Good afternoon.		*Selamat siang.*		(S)
silence	Good evening.		*Selamat malam.*		(L)
silence	How are you?		*Apa kabar?*		(N)
silence	Fine thanks.		*Kabar baik.*		(S)
silence	And you?		*Dan anda?*		(L)

Unit Eight

Eating Out

Good day.	*Buenos días.*
A table for two . . .	*Una mesa para dos . . .*
. . . please.	*. . . por favor.*
The menu please.	*El menú, por favor.*
The waiter./The waitress.	*El camarero./La camarera.*
An ashtray, please.	*Un cenicero, por favor.*
A knife/A fork	*Un cuchillo/Un tenedor*
A spoon	*Una cuchara*
A plate	*Un plato*
A glass/A cup	*Un vaso/Una taza*
A napkin	*Una servilleta*
A chair	*Una silla*
Pepper and salt	*Pimienta y sal*
Sugar	*Azúcar*
Water	*Agua*
More butter.	*Más mantequilla*
Nothing more, thanks.	*Nada más, gracias.*
Enjoy your meal!	*¡Que aproveche!*
To your health!	*¡A su salud!*
Where are the restrooms?	*¿Dónde está el lavabo?*
The check, please.	*La cuenta, por favor.*

Sample page from *Superlearning Spanish*® showing how to set up language phrases on the eight-second cycle.

How to Use Your Superlearning Language Tapes

**LEARN TO RELAX –
RELAX TO LEARN**
Stress-control program
lets you dissolve tension
and learning blocks.

BREATHE & READ
Read the text & breathe
to the beat of
rhythmically timed
language phrases — a
proven memory booster.

**RELAX TO
SUPERLEARNING MUSIC**
Relax as you hear
language phrases over
60-beats-a-minute
music that eases
stress; unlocks
mind potentials.

If you have ultralong material, use the twelve-second cycle explained on page 276, or simply read the whole thing over several eight-second frames.

Because a lot of material is presented at once, the printed text should be set up with lots of space surrounding it on the page so that it doesn't look formidable. A text with tiny print crammed to the brim on the page suggests that the job of learning it will be tedious. For the first few sessions start with twenty-one new vocabulary phrases. As you gain skill, sessions can lengthen to fifty or even one hundred.

Up-to-date language phrase books for tourists can easily be adapted to the Superlearning format, and they tend to deal with concrete everyday situations you'll encounter on a visit to the target country—going to a restaurant, bank or post office, or touring famous attractions.

Note: Many commercial outfits have rushed out language courses claiming to use this accelerated method. Many use old, outdated language courses because their copyrights expired and they could be exploited. Many of these old courses aren't as suitable for the accelerated method as courses designed specifically for it. These new courses feature up-to-date multimodal presentations and concrete imagery for visualizations. (See some of the courses listed.)

Once you've organized your language phrases, you're ready to record. You'll need two tape recorders. Play a four-second click tape on one tape recorder and record yourself reading your vocabulary phrases on the eight-second cycle on the second tape recorder.

When you're ready to listen to your tape, first get into the optimal state for learning with the exercises in Chapter 23. Play your vocabulary tape through once and follow the text as you listen. If possible, try to hold your breath while you hear the foreign words. Breathe out and in during the silent pauses. (If the breathing cycle is a problem, skip it till you're an old hand at doing these tapes.) Next play the tape again, this time with your second tape recorder playing the special Superlearning Music in the background at the same time. Lean back, relax, and listen as the 60-beat music anchors the phrases and pronunciation in your memory.

If you're a total beginner with a language, it's best to listen to one of the tapes available recorded by a native speaker to get the pronunciation correct before you embark on recording your own vocabulary tapes. Even if you're taking an actual accelerated course, many instructors have documented improved language skills and greater acceleration when students listen to Superlearning tapes at home. (Note: if you're teaching a foreign language and your class time is limited, let students use the visualization tapes for optimal state learning or vocabulary tapes at home to supplement the course so that class time can be focused on new material and language activities and games using multimodal senses.)

To make a Superlearning "Active" Concert language tape, you'll need two tape recorders. Select some dramatic, interesting material in the target language—maybe a dialogue, or a story, or an article from a magazine or newspaper. Turn on a tape of the mind-sharpening "active" concert music and read the whole story or article over the music as dramatically as possible. Tape yourself reading over the music. Play this "active" concert tape when you're commuting or doing chores or whenever. It will not only help enhance your grasp of the new language, but the special music will increase your overall mindpower.

If you're working on your own, make liberal use of the visualization routines in *Superlearning* as well as Section Three of this book, especially the exercise in which you see yourself in the future. See yourself in the near future enjoying talking fluently in your new language to native speakers. Picture yourself in that particular country enjoying a special event, a party, a business discussion or a shopping adventure and communicating with ease and pleasure.

If you're working on your own, take advantage of every opportunity to try out your new language skills. Go to restaurants specializing in food from that country. You'll have a good chance of meeting native speakers. Many cities have cultural clubs too. One really enterprising Superlearner came up with one of the most novel and effective ways to practice we've heard of. She practiced her language skills with dogs that understood the target language, playing games, giving them commands, and chatting them up.

To try out a Superlearning language course for travelers, contact Superlearning Inc., 450 Seventh Avenue, Suite 500, New York, NY 10123. Languages available: French, Spanish, German, Italian, Indonesian. Each course has been recorded by a native speaker and covers four hundred phrases (approximately one thousand words, with some repetition). Each course includes three cassette tapes and course text and comes complete with a Visualization Program for Stress Control and Optimal Learning State.

Language-Teaching Program— How-to

As political currents in the Soviet bloc ebbed and flowed, so did aspects of Lozanov's method. When yoga was "in," language courses started with several days of Raja Yoga training—breathing and concentration exercises to expand abilities. In 1971, when Communist authorities suddenly declared yoga "hostile to our country" not to mention "bad for health," out went yoga from Suggestopedia. Music alone could effect the relaxation training, they asserted. In Western countries, where stress levels are sky high, the most successful users have restored some form of stress control or concentration training drawn from various brainmind disciplines.

The Original Suggestopedic Language-in-a-Month Program

Ideal class size—twelve. Very comfortable chairs arranged in a circle. Room decor as attractive as possible. Posters featuring language material embedded in the pictures.

The student begins the class by changing his or her identity. Each person is given a new name, biography, and prestige profession in the new language country—ambassador, doctor, architect, filmmaker, company president, and so on. If students are strangers to one another, real identity is never revealed. The new identity frees learning abilities from past performance. Students don't need to fear making mistakes and looking foolish. Under the protection of the new identity, people also feel free to express desires and aspirations or to get over shyness or inhibitions.

Language course organization: thirty days, four hours per day. The oral course has four thematic dialogues with six hundred lexical units, four to five times the normal course content. The full course includes at least two thousand vocabulary words covering the core basic working vocabulary of a language. Each dialogue contains 120 to 200 phrases. The written text is arranged in sets of three on the page. The first eight days are entirely oral. The course material is built around everyday, concrete events that would be encountered during a trip to the target-language country—a trip to a city, restaurant, sports competition, shopping mall, bank, or a visit with a family in their home.

The first reading of the text is done by the teacher with lots of gestures and mimelike charades to get the meaning over with as little translation as possible. Body language and nonverbal cues must be organized to enhance communication and learning. The teacher's mental attitude must include affirmations of success and *never* an attitude like "Why am *I* stuck with these duds?"

The course material is read a second time, this time with the class repeating the phrases after the teacher. They may sing songs containing vocabulary words or act out a segment of dialogue in a brief sketch.

"Active" Concert

Music: classical music by Mozart or some other composer on the list on page 284. The teacher reads the text in as dramatic and animated a way as possible and follows the dynamics of the music by varying voice level to the music. The native language is read first so that students can form an image of an object or visualize a situation. Then the teacher reads the phrase in the new language, pausing briefly after each one. Students try to mentally pronounce the phrase while following the text.

After this reading is completed, students stand up and stretch. They may do some neck rolls or other physical exercise and some deep, rhythmic breathing.

Memory-Reinforcement Session

Part 1 (Outer Concentration): The students breathe deeply and rhythmically and relax completely. Students follow the text and repeat to themselves as the teacher reads the language phrases in four-second bits followed by a four-second pause. Each phrase is read in a different intonation following the cycle: loud-commanding, soft-confidential, regular-declarative.

Part 2 (Inner Concentration): Same material repeated with slow Baroque music in the background. Students close texts and relax to soothing 60-beats-a-minute music with their eyes closed. Teacher gives the phrases a second rhythmic reading over the music played at low volume. The passive concert session ends with a few minutes of upbeat, bright music.

Following the two concert sessions the teacher uses a cluster of methods to activate the language material being absorbed. Students can divide into conversation groups of twos or threes. They can play games, sing songs, do riddles and jokes, solve problems, have contests, use mime, answer questions. Sometimes the teacher throws a ball to students, while asking questions, and each must be ready to catch it and answer. Or students divide into twos. As they toss a beach ball back and forth, they must say a number in the new language. Next they must add a color to the number—"Pink Six," "Blue Four," and so on.

A second review: Students read and translate supplementary texts with the same vocabulary but in different combinations. Linguistics and grammar may be explained. To correct mistakes, the teacher gives correct examples in a nonhumiliating way. Students may also act out sketches of the material or create stories and playlets.

There are frequent quizzes. They provide feedback and proof to students that they really have learned the language many times faster than normal.

For more on this original form of Suggestopedia, see Dr. Lozanov's book *Suggestology and Outlines of Suggestopedy* and *Creating Wholeness Through Art,* by Lozanov's colleague Dr. Evelyna Gateva. (Available from SALT.)

Contact: Centre of Suggestology and Development of the Personality (directors, Dr. Georgi Lozanov and Dr. Evelyna Gateva), c/o Sofia University "St. Kliment Ohridski," 15 Ruski Boulevard, Sofia 1000, Bulgaria.

Superlearning and Some Western Variations

"Appropriate in the Middle Ages!" That's what Dr. Bancroft calls current college teaching methods. "Today's students are operating under a great deal of stress, including everything from complex family problems to the distractions of rock music and TV," she says. Her stress list also includes windowless classrooms with poor air circulation and lighting. She battled "sick building syndrome" long before government studies confirmed that sealed buildings with air lacking negative ions can cause health problems. Bancroft cites as further stresses junk food and "back-unfriendly" chairs, which encourage poor posture.

To help her organize her language program, Bancroft called on Eli Bay, of Toronto's Relaxation Response Center, whose clients include a "Who's Who" of Canadian corporations. Bay shaped a stress control program to go with her college French courses. (For a tape version of his outstanding programs, see below.) Bancroft emphasizes that Westerners need relaxation training to reach the optimal learning state and that because of high stress levels, playing the music alone may not be enough to induce this key learning state.

In her version of the method Bancroft dropped the "active" music concert and focused on the slow Baroque concert because of its memory-enhancing powers. Because most Western students had Walkmans and cassette recorders, extra memory reinforcement could be done at home with tapes instead of during precious class time. She put her entire course on tape. At Superlearning Inc., Sheila, who also has a background in language teaching and music, prepared basic taped language courses with the Superlearning format and music. Bancroft found the taped French course greatly helped students retain vocabulary and has used it for corporate training as well. She noted an interesting effect when Toronto business people, reluctant to learn French, listened to the tapes for two weeks before beginning her course. The music and the format seemed to help anchor the sounds of French in the unconscious.

Bancroft's results have been exceptional. Not only did students learn French faster and with ease, as mentioned earlier, they were almost more delighted by the disappearance of various health problems after taking the French program. Aside from learning a language, they acquired wellness skills for life that enabled them to sail confidently through learning situations as well as deal with relationship problems. Bancroft began to train employees of numerous corporations with her Superlearning French program, and she has given workshops for thousands of people throughout North America on Superlearning. (See the list of her published materials.)

Contact: Dr. W. Jane Bancroft, University of Toronto, Scarborough College, West Hill, Ontario, Canada M1C 1A4. Relaxation Response Inc., (Director, Eli Bay), 858 Eglinton Avenue, West, Suite 108, Toronto, Ontario, Canada M6C 2B6. (Stress Control Programs). For Bay's recording of the visualization program for stress control and optimal-state learning, order Tape #101 from Superlearning Inc., 450 Seventh Avenue, Suite 500, New York, NY 10123.

Sound Therapy for Languages

"Repeat after me, *headache*." — "Hee-adakka."
 "Ho*tel*." — "*Hot*er."
 "*Time*table." — "Tim-*id*abul."
 "*Voilà*." (Vwa-*la*) — "*Voy*la."
Most language teachers can recall an instance of similar outcomes after hours of patient coaching. Thanks to the discoveries of Dr. Alfred Tomatis, practical, effective remedies are available.

"We speak and read with our *ears*!" Dr. Tomatis asserts. Every language is its own "sound universe," he explains. To speak it, you first have to be able to *hear* it correctly. People differ in their range of hearing according to the languages they learned in childhood. They get used to listening to those frequencies that are part of the mother tongue. French people, who are used to listening in a narrow range 800–1,800 Hz., have more difficulty learning English from British instructors than from Americans. That's because British people speak English in the 2,000–12,000 Hz. range, while Americans speak in the 750–3,000 Hz. range. (Even some Americans can have trouble understanding English spoken with certain British accents!)

The Italian ear can "hear" frequencies between 2,000 and 4,000 Hz. The Russian ear is tuned to a frequency range from the lowest to the highest frequencies that the human ear can normally perceive.

"It has always been said that the Slavs 'have an ear' for languages," observes Dr. Bancroft, "and Tomatis' research proves this statistically." You have to hear first in order to be able to reproduce the sounds. "His work shows," says Bancroft, "that a native English speaker could be 'deaf' to the subtleties of French vowels, all packed into a narrow frequency range."

If you can't hear the sounds, hours in language labs and accent clinics are wasted, says Tomatis. As hearing impairment is widespread in North America (one study showed that over 60 percent of college entrants had hearing loss), it may be a factor in the low achievement in language studies.

Tomatis has created his own language method, combining an audio-visual system with his Electronic Ear Sound Therapy, which opens up the inner ear to a wider hearing range. His method has much in common with Superlearning using high-frequency music and yoga concentration. Superlearning Music with high frequencies also helps expand your listening range.

Listening to Sound Therapy music tapes, however, can be combined with any language system and will be especially helpful for students trying to learn a language whose frequency range is very different from their own or for anyone having difficulty understanding and pronouncing the new tongue. Ear acupuncture, too, has proven highly effective for restoring impaired hearing and can be a boon to language learners. (For more, see *Supermemory* and Tomatis' books, *The Conscious Ear* and *L'Oreille et Le Langage*.)

Tomatis Language Programs are available from: Language Skills International, 2975 Treat Boulevard, Suite C5, Concord, CA 94518.

"Superstudy"

John Wade, nicknamed "the Australian guru of accelerative learning" by Aussie media, first crisscrossed his own country and then the rest of the globe giving his acclaimed "Superstudy" workshops. His *Superstudy* book and cassette—do-it-yourself ways to "switch into" a state of enhanced learning—have become best-sellers down under.

Wade's Accelerated English courses, which give a six-to-one speedup in language learning for immigrants, were produced on video at Woden TAFE College in Canberra and are widely used. His success garnered him the Achievement Award from the Australian Government. His latest book, *Teaching Without Textbooks—Accelerative Learning in the Language Classroom*, reveals a treasure trove of proven ideas for English as a Second Language. He has added techniques from yoga, t'ai chi, shiatsu, and kinesiology to boost energy and concentration in classes. Another big hit among his accelerative works is *Quick 'N' Easy QWERTY*, which enables users to master the computer keyboard in under eight hours. Designed for children, it's fun for anyone (see page 324).

What to do if you find yourself having to teach in less than ideal conditions? Here's a Wade solution drawn from some of his teaching adventures in outposts from New Guinea to Timor.

Not all of Wade's language triumphs have come in the plummy circumstances of a modern classroom in the Australian capital. With visions of a relaxing four months in a tropical paradise, he contracted to teach English to university instructors on the tiny Indonesian island of Timor. The University of Nusa Cendana in the capital, Kupang, turned out to be made of Quonset huts. Rain drummed so loudly on the tin roofs, he could scarcely be heard. Horn-tooting minivans blared pop songs through sixteen hi-fi speakers as they passed beneath class windows, wide open in the oppressive heat; a massed choir practiced down the hall. Wade discovered the teaching method used in Timor was quite simple. The person with THE BOOK was the teacher and read it to the others, who were the students. The usual dropout rate was 100 percent. And administrators frowned on innovation.

Wade summoned his best *Superstudy* magic. He put his students through hoops of imagination. They came to feel the iron frames and straight plywood seats of their chairs as marvelously comfy. They learned to blank out noise, their attention focused on the music that became softer and softer. As they followed mind calming instructions in English, they might find themselves as red corpuscles flowing happily through the bloodstream—reinforcing the previous day's English science lesson. Wade made particular use of the new make-believe identities people took on for the class. What had that other person been up to? What was he doing last night? Students described imaginative exploits in English, which then became the material for the day's lesson. This is a particularly effective technique that anyone can use. It saves the teacher some effort. More importantly as students provide their own content, they become engaged, interested. Results were outstanding.

Wade's video, *Accelerative Learning*, is available from: Community Education, Australian Capital Territory, TAFE, P.O. Box 826, Canberra, A.C.T. 2601, Australia. *Teaching Without Textbooks*, CIS Educational, 247 Cardigan Street, Carlton, Victoria 3053, Australia. *Quick 'N' Easy QUERTY*, Tonal Typing—Publisher, P.O. Box 363, Civic Square, A.C.T. 2608, Australia. *Superstudy* kit: P.O. Box 20, Lyons, A.C.T. 2606, Australia.

Accelerated Esperanto

Vera Payne has pioneered teaching the "world language" Esperanto with accelerated methods. She teaches at the Australian Esperanto Association Summer School in Adelaide, South Australia, as well as at the Accelerated Language Centre in Perth. Students gain a handle on Esperanto in twenty-five hours, able to converse, sing, play games, and enjoy themselves making contact with other Esperantists worldwide. She has dropped the "Active" Concert, substituting more activities. Payne has prepared a ninety-minute Esperanto cassette, which students take away for follow-up. For more, contact: Vera Payne, 36 Donegal Road, Floreat Park, Western Australia 6014.

New Dimensions for Languages

In San Francisco accelerated learning pioneer Dr. Charles Schmid, a gifted, theatrical teacher, was among the first to found a center— Languages in New Dimensions. Schmid, with degrees in music, psychology, and foreign language teaching, added the latest developments from Neuro-linguistic Programming and James Asher's Total Physical Response—methods that teach all the senses—visual, auditory, tactile, kinesthetic—by presenting material in different modes—games, puzzles, skits. He also used lots of visualization, relaxation, and mental imagery training like that in *Superlearning* with the music of Halpern and Kobialka as well as programmatic music by classical composers. A visualization session of a visit to a famous location in a foreign country would start off in the mother tongue, and by the second half of the course you would hear it in the target language. Anxiety about understanding is by-passed. Students also got cassettes of the courses backed with slow Baroque music to take home for added listening practice. Schmid also devised highly creative and interesting course materials.

Schmid, a past president of SALT, traveled the world turning on trainers, teachers, and consultants to a better way right up until his death in 1992. He helped the spread of Superlearning through German industries.

He also produced an excellent line of Baroque music tapes. For a list of tapes and courses, contact The LIND Institute, P.O. Box 14487, San Francisco, CA 94114. Also using Schmid's approach and texts is SpeakEasy Language Center (founded by Libyan Cassone), Calhoun Square, 3001 Hennepin Avenue South, Suite 301-A, Minneapolis, MN 55408.

"Total Physical Response"

Like Schmid, Alaskan teachers Tam Gisler and Ann Arruda added Asher's Total Physical Response method to Superlearning to create full-length taped language courses, backed with Superlearning Music. Their *Teachables-N-Touchables: TPR Programs* teach through physical involvement and action. Dynamic games, drawings, songs, and other action-based activities integrating all five senses make language learning fun and boost retention. These courses in Spanish and French are available from Gessler Publishing Co., 55 West 13th Street, New York, NY 10011.

Bypassing "Ted's Tears"

The NLP/Superlearning combo is a dynamic one that's favored by many experimenters worldwide. In Japan we visited Dr. Charles Adamson's outstanding Suggestopedia Center in Nagoya at Trident College. Adamson was teaching English to young women to prepare them for entering the business world—still a tricky proposition for females in Japan. As documented in many papers, his enthusiastic students made extraordinary progress in English without the usual anxiety and hesitancy about speaking. Some of Adamson's innovations were featured on a Superlearning video when he joined us for a Superlearning presentation at Tokyo's famous Kaidanren Hall.

Adamson, now at Shizuoka Institute of Science and Technology in Fukuroi, labels his job "TED'S TEARS"—"Teaching English to Disinterested Students" and "Teaching English as a Required Subject." Adamson, too, has thrown out the usual textbooks. Instead he concocts tales on the order of the comic-strip-like adventure stories that are endlessly popular with young Japanese. Apart from sidestepping texts that students find boring and irrelevant, this technique removes the suggestion that one can only learn an officially sanctioned segment at a time. Adding to his accelerated skills, Adamson recently become a certified NLP practitioner, because, he says, "I am finding that NLP offers the most prospects for improvement." Contact: Dr. Charles Adamson, Shizuoka Institute of Science and Technology, 2200-2 Toyosawa, Fukuroi 437, Japan.

British Acceleration

If you found yourself in England in one of Geoff Pullen's highly successful accelerated language classes, you would be handed paper and colored pencils and asked to draw colored pictures of the images that popped up in your mind after a guided visualization. Pullen, of the University of Brighton, has added techniques from transpersonal and Jungian psychology. "These drawings can be very revealing from a Jungian perspective," he says, and "can be used to give personal insights to students and to promote self-esteem."

In addition to teacher training at the university he also has twenty-hour weekend accelerated French intensives for business people. With a battery of objective tests, he has tracked the before-and-after anxiety levels in students and found "remarkable changes" in lowering anxiety. Students have emerged so refreshed, energized and enthusiastic that a group banded together to rent a château in France and run more accelerated French courses there. Contact: the Language Centre (Geoff Pullen), Brighton Polytechnic, Falmer, Brighton BN1 9PH, England.

At Lyminge, Kent, near Folkstone, you're greeted by a "Party Bag" of imaginative surprises at "The English Experience." You'll find yourself surrounded by props, costumes, wigs, and hats to dramatize playlets at this center founded in 1987 by Superlearning pioneers

Mark Fletcher and Richard Munns. They offer two-week intensive language courses and teacher training. You go on imaginary trips across England to intriguing spots. One of their teaching techniques is a "Souvenir Diary" that each person fills with pictures, notes, mementos as if they were on a once-in-a-lifetime trip—which, as they come to understand the real breadth of their capabilities, perhaps they are. Contact: The English Experience, Brambletye, Woodland Road, Lyminge, nr. Folkestone, Kent CT18 8EP, England.

Beautiful Forge House, a substantial country estate at Kemble, on the edge of the Cotswolds, is a major center for language and life skills in Britain. Directors Michael Lawlor and June McOstrich explain: "Forge House exists to foster personal growth through the learning of foreign languages and other communicative skills." It's the outcome of their combined twenty-six years' experience with Western Language Centre and ten years with Inner Track Learning. Lawlor and McOstrich also helped to found SEAL, the very international British accelerated learning organization. They've also set up Druzhba-Link, an exchange program with Suggestopedia teachers throughout the former Soviet bloc.

Accelerated language courses are available in French, German, Spanish, Russian, and English as a Second Language. They also provide home-study courses and cassettes. Inner Track Learning dispenses transformative study skills and teacher training courses. It blends innovative methods from Accelerated Learning and Suggestopedia with yoga, educational kinesiology (Brain Gym), autogenic training, the Alexander Technique, and psychosynthesis. Inner Track focuses on bringing teachers alive to their own expanded potentials before they begin accelerating students. Yoga techniques help teachers liberate body/mind and get in sync with goals. Teachers' reactions to Inner Track training have bordered on the ecstatic.

For a brochure, contact directors Michael Lawlor and June McOstrich, Forge House Centre for Language and Life Skills, Kemble, Gloucester GL7 6AD, England.

Natural Order for Language Material

At Sixt, in the French Alps, Jenny Vanderplank, who hails from South Africa, runs an outstanding accelerated language center. She was a yoga teacher in Paris when she attended one of Lozanov's seminars. She immediately saw speed learning's roots in yoga. She has written two texts and a book of games for accelerated learning and, in addition to her language classes, does presentations throughout Europe. She has added the ideas of Stephen Krashen about the predictable "natural order" of how we learn grammatical structures. The average analytical, graded textbook goes against this natural order, she says. If language course material is global, rich, and roughly tuned, language structure and grammar will be learned faster. Contact: Chalet de Sixt (Jenny Vanderplank), No. 14 Maison Neuve, 74740, Sixt France. Also in France: Trajectoires Associées, (director, Lonny Gold), 149 rue St. Honoré, Paris 75001, France.

Learning Expansion

Back in America, Expanded Learning, a veritable 21st century center, was founded in 1978 in Denver, Colorado, by Dr. Diane Davalos, who now has a staff of seven accelerative learning teachers. They have taught languages and the methodology to over two thousand people in thirty U.S. cities, Canada, Costa Rica, Nicaragua, Brazil, Paraguay, Argentina, Venezuela, Mexico, Liechtenstein, Switzerland, France, and Spain. Davalos distilled her fourteen years of experience into a handbook, *Activities to Expand Learning,* helpful not only for languages but for anyone from business trainer to facilitator. "I learned more Spanish in six days than I did at the Defense Language Institute in three weeks," enthused Julian Harris of Camarillo, California, about Davalos' courses. Expanded Learning features "Leave 'n' Learn" trips to fascinating Spanish locations and even courses in medical Spanish. Their catalog features additional taped courses, such as the *Accelerated Learning* courses by Colin Rose. For catalog and course schedule, contact: Expanded Learning (director, Dr. Diane Davalos), 125 West Second Avenue, Denver, CO 80223.

Humor and Languages

The language division of OptimaLearning has flourished with the special linguistic talents of Pamela Rand and her husband, Dr. Ivan Barzakov. Rand, a native San Franciscan, is a graduate of the University of Grenoble and the renowned Movement, Mime, and Theater School of Jacques Lecoq in Paris. She combines her talents as a gifted comedienne and actress with her abilities as a professional educator and linguist to bring an extremely welcome added dimension to accelerated language learning—*humor*. Rand has pioneered a delightful program, "The Clown Within," which probes the zestful inner springs of humor, and has added many of these creativity releasing techniques to her superaccelerated language programs. Trained by both Dr. Lozanov and Dr. Barzakov, she has conducted French and English programs worldwide. Barzakov holds degrees in linguistics and speaks eight languages.

The two have collaborated on taped foreign language courses for *very* young youngsters—starting at age two-and-a-half and up to fifteen. And they've built into these accelerated courses some of the ideas of Dr. Tomatis and James Asher's Total Physical Response. In *Language for Kids—Learn Along with Your Child* you'll find fresh and original songs for kids, an illustrated workbook, and lessons backed by 60-beat Baroque. Full length accelerated learning courses for adults are also available. Contact: Barzak Educational Institute, 885 Olive Avenue, Suite A, Novato, CA 94945.

Professional Training

Superlearning can also help professionals to loft over exams in record time in order to get needed credentials or certificates. Rocklin, California, teacher Ruth James, for one, wanted to be credentialed as a Language Development Specialist. She put together her own tapes to prepare for the state exam. On side one of her tape she recorded over Baroque music essential points from educational experts—i.e., principles of Dr. Stephen Krashen's theories of language learning. On side two she used the eight-second cycle over

Baroque to record specific definitions from the texts—i.e., "*halo effect*"—*favorable bias toward the person being tested*.

James was so pleased with her own results and high score that she's arranged to use our Superlearning Music and now markets a "Stress-Free Success for the LDS" cassette to help other teachers. "The exam is, to say the least, a very hard test," James explains. "Many teachers fail repeatedly, and some never pass at all."

"Very positive feedback!" is the verdict from teachers who've tried her tape. "Our most dramatic was from a teacher who resented that he *had* to take the exam. He had no intention of putting in time or effort and didn't care if he passed." This reluctant dragon did go to class and listen to James' tape, but never turned a page of the required reading. "He told us that, to his amazement, he did pass the exam."

"Another trainer told us of teachers taking the exam and not remembering the answer needed—but they wrote correct answers anyway. "From 'brain to hand' as he said." To get a tape, contact: Ruben James Enterprises, 5607 Miners Circle, Rocklin, CA 95765.

Open Sesame for Languages

Worldwide there are literally tens of thousands of teachers and trainers using Superlearning methods for languages, each adding their own unique spin to the core techniques. There are far more than we could ever list. To track down a teacher near you, contact SEAL or SALT or the accelerated learning society in your area:

SEAL
17 Crabbe Crescent
Chesham, Bucks., HP5 3DD England

SALT
3028 Emerson Avenue South
Minneapolis, MN 55408

German Accelerated Learning Society (DGSL) (director, Gail Heidenhain)
Kampenwandstrasse, 6
W-8011 Baldham (nr. Munich), Germany

(The results and video of the Siemens English training experiment are available from DGSL.)

Groupe de Recherche sur le Yoga dans L'Education (R.Y.E.), director, Micheline Flak c/o College Condorcet 61, rue d'Amsterdam Paris, France

26
Coaching Your Child—
Preschool Through
High School

Preschoolers

In Moscow, Idaho, Dr. Mary Lang overheard her two-year-old son keeping track of things while he played—he would say numbers, loud, soft, numbers in intonations. It sounded like her very special Superlearning program was working. Though she was good at what she did—a doctor of education who'd taught at Auburn University, a speech pathologist for preschoolers, and now a postgrad student of computer graphics and video production at the University of Idaho—traditional education no longer inspired Lang, and she planned to start a graphics business. But there was one bit of education she couldn't put aside. She was determined to give her little son some good learning experiences early on to avoid some of the pitfalls of classrooms to come. Very quickly she realized that early learning methods for reading and math required far too much repetition for her active, into-everything, two-year-old. Then she came across the Superlearning book.

At a quiet time of day Lang put her son in a La-Z-Boy recliner in front of the TV and dabbed him with a touch of perfume to wake up an extra sense. A puppet introduced the lesson on quantities. Then a color video filled the screen with red balls demonstrating a quantity—two, six, and so on. During the four-second frame the number is spoken four times in intonations. Next comes a four-second pause as the picture wipes away. Then the next quantity lights up. This toddlers' Superlearning session takes only forty-eight seconds and presents three numbers. Like adult programs, the lesson first runs without music, then repeats with the special Baroque. Later in the day Lang dabbed her little boy with memory reinforcing perfume, and they played addition and subtraction games for about five minutes.

Not every parent can make videos, but they can easily take advantage of another technique Lang used. She taped her son saying his own positive affirmations. "I like to do math. I like to read words. I am well." After he'd been on medication for an ear infection for three months, she had him say, "My ears are well." "For the last six months," Lang reports, "since he's been listening to the tapes, he hasn't been ill once." The little boy hears his own upbeat suggestions as he sleeps and in the morning. His success at learning worked as a big positive suggestion to his mother. Sighting a new professional horizon, she's staying in education to develop early learning tools.

"To take advantage of toddlers' unique ability to utilize photographic memory," Lang is testing a program aimed at children younger than thirty months. She's switched away from perfume as a link to memory; to hook baby memories, she suggests food smells. Her new math program includes a video, two interactive games, and two cassettes. One features simple math principles backed by Baroque. The other is a rappin' and rhymin' tape to boost memory à la Rosella Wallace's games that lure Alaskan kids to learning.

Opposed to much traditional theory, Lang, along with some other Superlearning teachers—Wallace for one—and writers like us, believes toddlers can have a ball learning. (Which is not to say, bedevil your infant with academia, firing up "Little League learning" pressure for you both.) "Almost all of our greatest achievers in philosophy, science and literature were deliberately taught to read long before school age," points out Dr. Ragan Callaway, of the Ontario Institute for Studies in Education. Callaway set up successful reading programs for three- and four-year-old junior kindergartners at the Kingslake Public School in North York, Ontario. The key for the Ontario toddlers—who, teachers said, sought out reading—proved to be short periods of one-on-one instruction.

One Alaskan preschool teacher invited George Guthridge to try Reverse Instruction with her toddlers. Soon the teacher reported she was flooded with calls from parents asking, "How is my child learning so much?" Guthridge's program (see Chapter 30), which builds a strong foundation of basics with Superlearning, can save teachers a great deal of time. Parents, too, if you're going to follow Pat Joudry's route. Eyes brimming with tears, Joudry's young daughter asked, "Mummy, does kids *have* to go to school?" After reflecting for a long moment on her often stated belief that "the only way to stop kids from learning is to send them to school," Joudry said, "No," and embarked on an adventure in home schooling. American parents teaching their own find that all or at least key parts of Superlearning fit with any home schooling philosophy.

No matter where they're learning, if you make sure your child is equipped with the basics, you'll go a long way toward ensuring her future. Psychologist David Geary, of the University of Missouri, gave two groups of first-graders, one Chinese, one American, a batch of math problems. The Chinese came up with three times more correct solutions than the U.S. kids. Chinese aren't inherently smarter, Geary says, but they know their basics. Practice has made them automatic, so the conscious mind can spend its energies on thinking and problem solving while the Americans fumble along counting on their fingers. Practice, practice, practice, is Geary's answer. That's where Superlearning can be a boon; it can embed the basics securely without endless, boring rote practice. Start early; the extra edge keeps widening. By third grade, Geary found, the young Americans were dismally behind their Chinese counterparts.

If you'd ever followed the learning accomplishments of one-year-old waterbabies in Russia, you'd know that even infants can blossom in multifaceted, healthy ways. (We're leaving out just how accomplished some are because without a lot of background data, it's frankly unbelievable.) Waterbabies aren't nerds. Fifteen years later they are well balanced, sociable, and often wonderfully talented human beings. From his studies Callaway, too, found that early learning is a plus, increasing the flexibility and complexity of one's central nervous system.

As Mary Lang experiments with ways to open the world to preschoolers, her learning tools are taking a leap into the 21st century. She's pushing out the edge of another new field, mating virtual reality and learning. You can see this sort of education in Newcastle upon Tyne, where ballpoints and calculators have been replaced by the tracker ball-controls of snap-paced video games. English teenagers are designing factories, taking a turn on lathes, driving forklifts, all on their computer screens in the first European school experiment with virtual reality. Pulling images from a computer library, a student builds a new factory, or, as one did, creates a whole Renaissance city from original drawings. Then they're off adventuring inside their creation. They "experience the excitement that comes with being able to control and explore the world they design," says project director Trevor Pemberton. His students have already been hired by a local firm to design a 3D model of a new building complex. That's a big first step; we'll be interested to see where Mary Lang is in the next millennium.

With full scale virtual reality you break through the computer screen into a simulated three-dimensional world. Sensory data comes through headsets, data gloves, and body suits, so you experience tactile sensations, sights, and motion as if you were there. It's a high-tech tool that will power any kind of 21st century training, but no matter what age you are, its possibilities for Superlearning are spine-tingling. Be there when you stretch out near the surf on a mental vacation, or feel the kick as you wind up a contract winning sales presentation in imaginative rehearsal, really experience the senses of an expert like the Careful Observer, float into new realms with Baroque. . . .

Many parents write us about doing ad hoc Superlearning with their children. Most preschoolers seem to respond well to music, suggestion, and imaginative play. Not surprisingly, they often shine at language learning. You've heard of toddlers living abroad who pick up another language as easily as they breathe foreign air, while parents struggle to blurt out a grocery order. One of Rosella Wallace's teacher trainees opted to use Superlearning for his class project to get his preschoolers speaking their grandfather's language, Norwegian. He considered his experiment a success. (For language courses for two-and-a-half-year-olds, see Chapter 25.)

Learning in the Womb?

Is it ever too early to give the apple of your eye a head start? Should you buy a "pregnancy phone" and talk to a fetus through a tube pressed to the mother's abdomen? Or rhythmically rub her belly until the fetus kicks back to "improve the child's intellectual capacity for life." California obstetrician Dr. F. Rene Van de Carr and a few others say so. Time will tell on that one. What is known is that the scientific view of a baby's abilities has flipflopped. Gone is the old *tabula rasa,* the idea that your baby arrives blank as a sheet of paper.

"Infants are much more than we thought," says San Diego psychologist Dr. David Chamberlain, who is battling to save "21st century babies from being regarded with 19th century prejudice." To back up his contentions, Chamberlain cited over 160 scientific studies in a talk at the 10th World Congress of Prenatal and Perinatal Psychology. News is coming in fast that memory is alive in the womb; so are dreams and the senses, especially hearing. Newborns can learn and remember, it's been shown, and even add. But word is not spreading fast enough, Chamberlain feels, pointing to circumcision and medical procedures still routinely done without anesthesia based on the discredited idea that babies are just creatures of reflex who feel no pain. They do. Most parents have always known their baby was more like a responsive bundle of joy than a bundle of mechanical reflexes. In the next century, Chamberlain predicts, science, too, will focus on a newborn's sense of self, emotions, communication, and learning abilities.

We don't anticipate Superlearning in the womb—but you might want to serenade your unborn with a little of the music. Thomas Verny, M.D., of Toronto, is one doctor who has gathered a stack of arresting evidence that memories formed in the womb can be long-term and can influence life on the outside. Verny's detective work is fascinating; if you want some happy-memories insurance for your baby, check his book, *Nurturing the Unborn Child*. Verny and colleagues tested the effects of music on babies in the womb. Perhaps because of the high-frequency sound, Mozart has a good effect. But mainly Verny recommends Baroque, which is why some mothers-to-be are playing Superlearning Music. A couple have told us that playing the same music after birth does wonders soothing a fretful infant, reminding them perhaps of cozy days in the womb.

Coaching School-Age Children

Dr. Rosella Wallace's raps, rhymes, and jump rope jingles are a great way to lure children into learning and to embed basics. Home schoolers give them a workout. "I've had the good fortune of working with third-graders who haven't had their imaginations completely impaired by the educational system," says Wallace, who's now a consultant and teacher trainer for the University of Alaska. "Their world is filled with fantasy, and I've found that they are very willing to use it to make positive changes in learning habits or behavior." If your school isn't filling the bill, you can train your child's imaginative skills before, as Wordsworth says, that splendid vision fades into the light of common day. For instance, you can make a game of techniques like the Careful Observer (see page 155) and, as Wallace showed, greatly enrich learning.

Facing a museum trip with thirty-five kinetic kids, Wallace decided to try something a lot of parents would love to do: put new heads on their youngsters. Days before, each student donned her observer head and took a trip into the future, to the museum. "Slow down," Wallace advised as in their mind's eye they walked into the museum. "Instead of pushing ahead, let others go first as you roam the halls, with a friendly, cheerful attitude." As Careful Observers the class noted colors, textures, smells, and what was beautiful and interesting in the things they'd already studied: Arctic birds, tools, fossils. After some minutes of silent adventure, Wallace's kids described in ringing detail what they'd "seen" at the museum.

On the day of the class trip kids wondered what song their "Rappin' and Rhymin' Teacher" had concocted for this lesson. Soon, to the lilt of "Puff the Magic Dragon," they were singing "I am a Careful Observer / I talk about what I see / I see the colors, I smell the smells / Superlearning for you and me."

It took hardly a moment for the museum guide to realize she had a different sort of class on her hands. At the door a few pretended to put something over their heads, then all began walking slowly, purposefully. They sized up exhibits intently, a number softly recounting to themselves what they were seeing. The guide began fielding "the most interesting questions I've heard from such a young group." Soon she whispered to Wallace, "They're noticing things I haven't even noticed before!" Weeks later each kid could flash back in her mind's eye to check the color of a feather, the white shape of a bone; like the memory palace of old, the museum became incorporated in their imagination.

Like Wallace's Observers, almost any technique in this book can be adapted for children. As George Guthridge does, you might even encourage your child to research a subject and create his own Superlearning tapes (see Chapter 30).

With his wealth of accelerated experience, it took Don Schuster just two hours to turn around his nine-year-old grandson, Jim, who was barely scraping through arithmetic with the lowest marks. For the first hour he taught the little boy to create an imaginary playroom in his mind, a place where he could relax. Jim was to go there whenever he even thought of arithmetic. "Can my kitten, Mickey, be in the playroom too?" Jim asked. "Sure," Schuster agreed, "but in the playroom Mickey is a very special cat. He knows all the answers to any question you may have about arithmetic or whatever." All Jim had to do was relax, pet the magic cat, and listen for his answer.

The second hour grandfather and grandson stretched out on a bed. Schuster went through the "six times" multiplication table. As he spoke, Jim visualized. Then, while slow Baroque played, Schuster rhythmically repeated the numbers. Finally he gave Jim a short quiz. Months later the boy proffered his report card. "There was an A-minus in arithmetic!" Schuster says, adding that the reason the accelerated approach worked so well with Jim is that all six necessary elements were there: suggestion, relaxation, fun, imagery, rhythmic review, and a quiz.

Homework

"Homework or home schooling should be part of the whole relationship between parent and child, not just a demand on the parent's part that comes around eight o'clock," remarks Brian Hamilton, who had long experience in family counselling before teaching Superlearning. Among other things, Hamilton suggests that his clients stay in the room while their kids do homework. "When they're done, have them stretch out on the couch or get into bed if it's time. Play the Superlearning music and just read your child's homework—spelling, geography, or whatever." This not only reinforces learning, it also reinforces the connection between parent and child. "It's a very nurturing experience at bedtime," Hamilton says.

Walter Deehring, from Peoria, Illinois, a top man in direct marketing, has run companies, bought, sold, and created them. After reading *Superlearning* he decided to build up something closer to his heart, his twelve-year-old daughter. She didn't seem to be absorbing anything in school; worse, she loathed reading, a problem reflected in her F/D-grade average.

"I began by adopting the Superlearning relaxation theory. A rested mind is much more willing to absorb information," Deehring contends. Next he led his daughter through a good dose of guided imagery, building self-esteem, prompting her to believe she was more than capable of racking up A's and B's. In her mind's eye she experienced what it would be like to go through a whole school day fully prepared in each class, how she would feel if family and friends considered her a great learner.

"This was the teaser, once it was established, I reinforced it every thirty minutes or so during our sessions, which, the first two weeks, ran three hours a day. I adopted the Superlearning techniques of speaking data in a low, medium, and loud voice, repeated at least once in these early studies." Deehring took care to eliminate his girl's preconceived ideas—that topic's really boring, this subject's tough. "What's interesting?" he asked himself about each topic, and together they found an answer. He made sure reading assignments ended on a cliff-hanger.

Deehring's daughter saw her imagined success materialize. "I still reinforce success at the beginning and end of our sessions, which are now shorter." Starting with ten minutes of relaxation, father and daughter study two subjects for fifteen minutes each, take a break, then learn two more and wind up with bolstering imagery. "At midterm my daughter was a D/F student; by the end of the term she had straight C's. In other words she began turning in A and B work. This term [1993] she is getting B's or better.

"Now she is hungry to learn!" Deehring says proudly of the daughter who used to loathe reading. "Superlearning is what helped me structure my daughter's learning curve and open her potential." Deehring was so encouraged by his daughter's success that he began to turn a chary eye on the learning methods foisted on his other children, like those in his son's Spanish class. He knew firsthand there was a better way. Now he plans to put together courses other parents can use with their kids. Someone has to do it. "If our children are going to flourish in a global economy, they need to know the techniques of global learning," businessman Deehring insists.

"We must, in the educational process, teach the value of global understanding. We must educate young people to exercise global awareness, ambition, and joy. The world is their arena," says international writer and metaphysical teacher Chris Griscom. Equipping kids to give and take in that arena is what this former Peace Corps leader is doing in Santa Fe, at the Nizhoni School—which means "beauty way" in Navaho. Teenagers from Europe, Asia, and America live and learn together about global economics and entrepreneurship in a wide-ranging curriculum that leads them to delve into their inner worlds as adventurously as they explore the outer world, as they move toward Griscom's vision of "a sound mind, body, and soul in a sound Humanity."

Helping kids learn how to flourish in the next century is a top priority for Atlanta's Dr. Mary Harris. An experimenting education professor at Georgia Tech, she sent Superlearning vocabulary tapes home with teenagers. "They worked very well," she says, "if they used them." Often all that's needed is a parental assist like the father who determinedly played the tapes as his kids went to sleep and while they were eating breakfast. (This is reminiscent of a simplified accelerated learning routine Bruce Tickell Taylor created and uses with good success himself. See Chapter 30.) Now with her own company, Harris' government funded Millar Harris Project is helping teens in Junior ROTC with SAT basics. "Many show real promise," she says, but just as they're opening their wings, they bump up against SATs and scholarship tests and crash. "Really it's the schools that have failed them," Harris remarks, saying they lack the knowledge of more advantaged kids. Once her "troops" are secure in the basics, Harris plans to have them take their know-how back to friends in their home schools—a good idea, common to many cultures where learning is a co-op, community affair.

When Superlearning with children—or anyone else, for that matter—remember, we learn in spite of criticism, not because of it. When working with your own kids, it's both hard and important to avoid "the temptation to make wrong." Instead of shouting "Wrong!" you can often correct indirectly by devising songs, games, and drawing projects in which the right answer becomes apparent. At least be neutral, nonjudgmental in corrections, clearly discussing the work, not your child's ability or personality. As the Brown University researchers found, one's response to failure—feeling either helpless or masterful—develops young. It's important to nurture the masterful approach and to see failure as a guide to try a different way, a clue toward solving a puzzle.

You can spot potential entrepreneurs when they're three feet tall, says UCLA economist Marilyn Kourilsky. "They detach failure from themselves and just go on to another idea." According to Kourilsky, almost 25 percent of kindergartners do this naturally, but only about 5 percent retain the ability by high school. "Many of my colleagues believe that the nature of the school experience wipes out tenacity," Kourilsky explains, "you take a test once, and if you mess up, you've failed." Quizzes at the end of Superlearning sessions are often open-book tests, whether computer programming or learning sums. Learners compare notes; they work together to come to the right answer. You can do the same with your own child, so that instead of rote memory she develops the ability to seek and learn.

Remember, You're a Voter

In a perfect world all of us would first learn how to learn before we set out on our adventure through life. Kids in many classrooms are still breathing nineteenth-century air. What can you do about it? "If enough parents get mad at the mess that educators have wrought, maybe we can get the schools back to some worthwhile teaching instead of just baby-sitting," Bruce Tickell Taylor suggests. Become involved in your school, spread information, and, Dr. Allyn Prichard advises, "Remember, you're a voter."

An early traveler to Bulgaria, Prichard, a former Peace Corps volunteer who pioneered Superlearning successfully from grammar school through university, knows about voting. He served as a representative in the Georgia State Legislature. But that didn't save the exceptional reading program he and Jean Taylor created, a groundbreaking model that, via their book, has spread around the country and overseas. A new principal appeared who didn't cotton to anything out of the ordinary; the accelerated course was terminated, and Taylor took early retirement. Prichard, on to other educational projects, decided he needed a break from establishment opposition to change and is finishing up a two-year turn at the University of Shanghai, with an eye to politicking again when he's back. Prichard has been around the globe and the ever-widening world of accelerated learning. The next millennium is ticking closer. Maybe politics is a necessary route to shaping the changes that will get our kids ready and short-circuit the sort of boneheaded resistance that shoves them back into a no-exit box.

Until the repercussions of the great revolution in brainmind understanding tumble the old educational structures, you may have to help today's child accelerate on his own. As Alvin Toffler, author of *Future Shock,* observed, "Parenthood remains the greatest single preserve of the amateur." The root meaning of amateur is one who pursues something out of love. Open up the exhilaration of learning for your child, give him the tools to make the most of his ability, and you'll have a gifted child in more ways than one.

27
How to Superlearn Science, Computers, High-Tech

"Air conditioner: Carrier," says Lorne Cook. His mellow voice intones, "Mr. Carrier invented the air conditioner. Electric light: Edison. The electric light was invented by Edison."

Ten children lying on a carpeted floor, with closed eyes, look as if they're sleeping, as quiet music plays in the background. This is Upper Canada College prep school in Toronto, where Superlearning has been used for science classes for over a decade. In carefully controlled comparison tests with traditional methods for science, the control groups tested out at 70 to 75 percent. The Superlearning groups repeatedly averaged *95 percent or more* on science exams.

Not only did youngsters excel at science and speed up learning but many reported they really benefited from the stress control. "Superlearning is really fun, and it helped me get a lot accomplished," said one.

Cook has pioneered with Superlearning for ten years in the

courses he gives at York University too. "There's such a huge gap between what we know about the brain and the way we teach," says Cook. "There's a sort of conspiracy against success throughout our school systems. People get very suspicious if you use techniques that have the class average in the nineties. We're happy with mediocrity instead of success."

Being "happy with mediocrity" in science training can be a direct route to mediocrity in the economy and to unemployment. Rapid high-tech training is one of the essentials for success, prosperity, even survival, in the new global economy. An undereducated, unskilled workforce is being blamed in part for Britain's spiral into massive unemployment and economic disaster. North America, with a 30 percent school dropout/failure rate, is on the way to becoming a Third World unskilled workforce in the Information Age, experts fear.

Superlearning is particularly suited for science and high-tech because it eases stress and relieves the boredom and phobias often associated with technical training—the idea that math, statistics, and technology are deadly dull. Superlearning is even easier to set up for science and high-tech than it is for languages because conversational practice is not required. Also, it's easy to do on tape.

Superlearning's acceleration is a money saver for high-tech training. With accelerating changes in high-tech itself, by the time you've been trained with horse-and-buggy methods in space-age technology, the field has already changed and you have to start all over again.

One of the first to report a ten-to-one acceleration in science learning was Dr. Donald Vannan, of Bloomsburg State College, in Pennsylvania. Dr. Vannan taught elementary science methods. Beginning in the mid-1970s Vannan prepared his Superlearning science course on tape complete with Baroque music. He trained his students in relaxation techniques, then had them listen to the tapes. Control groups got the usual science lecture. Science tests graded by computer showed a startling difference. In the 220-student control group 11 percent got an A grade. Of the 200 Superlearning science students 78 percent scored A. As semesters and years passed, Vannan's Superlearning science students kept on soaring. Soon 82.9 percent got A's in science, and then 84.6 percent.

Science material is generally very easy to reduce to simple note form, and the small chunks of data required for Superlearning (e.g., "Brass—an alloy made of copper and zinc"). The International Learning Center, in Garland, Texas, put together a whole tape like this on alloys for science students. "Phenomenal . . . perfect or near-perfect results," they reported to us.

At the Woodrow Wilson Junior High School, in Des Moines, Iowa, a similar scenario had been unfolding for years. Superlearning pioneer Charles Gritton spoke in varied intonations: "Iron. Symbol Fe. Strong as Iron. Mercury. Symbol Hg. As the days get warmer, the mercury rises." Fifty to one hundred new science terms were introduced each day. The class listened to Baroque music, relaxed at their desks, and breathed in time to the music. On tests all 115 of Gritton's eighth-grade science students reached a 97 percent average—and stayed there. The students' elation was contagious. Gritton uses skits to make science data exciting. For example, students take on identities of famous scientists and explore a Pacific island for phosphates. He adds environment records to mind-calming sessions. For more, see Gritton's book, *SALT: Suggestive Accelerative Learning Techniques: Theory and Applications*.

Leo Wood, of Tempe, Arizona, was burned out and ready to quit after twenty-four years of teaching high school chemistry to bored, discouraged, failing, and *disappearing* students. After hearing about accelerated techniques from Ivan Barzakov, he gave them a go. In 1991 87 percent of his students were in the A-to-C range. (Previously the failure rate was 52 percent.) They'd learned five times faster, and enrollment in chemistry went up.

In addition to relaxation and slow Baroque music, Wood added storytelling, games, skits, and demos to chem class. He's created twenty-five chem songs including one about ions to the tune of "Rudolph, the Red-Nosed Reindeer."

As news of success with Superlearning spreads through a community, it helps create a psychological environment that reinforces the effectiveness of this mind technology—"de-suggesting barriers," as Dr. Lozanov says. Wood's student Jennifer Morrow discovered this at the local pizza parlor. Studying her chemistry homework while eating lunch, she hummed Wood's song "Polyatomic Ions" to herself.

Suddenly, to her surprise, everyone in the whole pizza parlor chorused along with her. They were former, successful Wood students who still remembered "Polyatomic Ions." At local football games these former chemistry students would burst into the "Ide—ate—ite" song about suffixes of chemical compounds.

Wood has earned the Distinguished Teaching Award in Tempe, Arizona, and in 1990 was selected to demonstrate accelerated chemistry to the U.S. Energy Commission in Washington, D.C. Wood's work is featured in a new book on "brain-based" teaching, *Making Connections: Teaching and the Human Brain,* by R. and G. Caine.

"Close your eyes, relax and prepare to take an exciting fantasy voyage through outer space. Pretend you are an astronaut about to enter a spacecraft for a journey in space." This guided imagery "tour of the universe" was developed by Nancy Ellis of the Guggenheim School in Chicago, an elementary school which uses accelerated methods for the entire curriculum. As students relax on lawn chairs, they hear quiet music as the story continues. "See yourself entering the ship. As you look around you see many new instruments you will be using during your trip. You see a large spectroscope, an instrument that will analyze the composition of the sun and the stars."

The visualization experience always puts the learner in the center of the action. Ellis explains, "You remember things better when you are a part of them."

For the dramatic "Active" concert with brain-boosting music, Ellis has created dramatic scripts like "The Verdict" about astronomy for young star searchers. *Judge:* "Order in the court! Our case today is a complaint by Ms. Milkyway. Ms. Milkyway, please come forth."

Ellis uses the method not only for factual learning but for concepts too. "One of my most difficult tasks was teaching outlining," says Ellis. "Only 60 percent to 70 percent of the kids would get it the first time through." With accelerated techniques 100 percent master it in a week, she reports. Because Superlearning methods mobilize the vast resources of the unconscious for learning, they can help not only memory but abstract thinking, creativity and problem solving.

Guggenheim principal Michael Alexander, who was on a quest to rejuvenate a "semi burned out faculty," had all the teachers at the school take accelerated training with Lozanov Learning of Washington, D.C., becoming the first school in the nation to have its entire faculty go through the course. Thanks to accelerated techniques, the Guggenheim School, which had previously been 17th out of 17 in the district (with teacher burnout at a similar level), soared to *first place* within a single year.

"I've been revitalized," said Nancy Ellis and other staff members. Students gained new self-esteem and self-confidence as potentials opened up. "At first they thought we were dumb," said a seventh grader, "but then we come back smiling, telling them all we learned." Nearby, Glenbrook North High School set up a Human Potential Center where parents could send their children for a bit of this whole-brain learning. Enthused the *Chicago Sun-Times* in headlines, *It's 'Superlearning' Era Here*.

Turning dull data into attention grabbing imagery and dramatic scenarios isn't new (one of the authors still remembers a high school organic chemistry course presented as "Carbon Jones"—a takeoff on the musical *Carmen Jones*). But combining dramatic material with the other elements of rhythmic pacing and mindpower music gives a synergistic effect that vastly accelerates learning.

Physics professor Dr. Don Lofland was so impressed with the results he got using Superlearning for physics—that he quit! He left his job as Chairman of the Physics Department at West Valley College in Saratoga, California. He set up Powerlearning Systems of Santa Cruz and went on the road to spread the word and a trail of *Super-learning* and *Powerlearning* books.

Computer language—that's the language more and more people have to be conversant with today. See Chapter 12 for the brilliantly innovative methods developed by Peter Ginn to quicken training in computer programming. High-tech training doesn't have to mean high cost either. Ginn's "Game Show" winners learned computer assembly language with 90 percent recall. Game-show participants bearing posters with computer assembly language symbols—AHLX, IP, ALU, and BUS—walked through a simulated computer, figured out how to operate it, spotted a "continuous loop" and learned how to shut it down. Said a colleague, "You bastard! You did more with two hundred dollars' worth of posterboard than I did with eight thousand dollar computers and a two thousand dollar interactive video course!"

One absolutely basic computer skill is learning the keyboard. For youngsters or oldsters (if they didn't learn to type) it's an essential. "Bees queue for an hour to see the Queen." "Flying fish with fleas." They're part of *Quick 'N' Easy QWERTY,* a phenomenally accelerated program that teaches the computer keyboard in *less than eight hours*. Developed by Australian John Wade, it's an audiocassette package that's been speeding thousands of kids to computer and typing skills. The techniques are so much fun, any adult would get a kick out of learning with the program too.

"*Quick 'N' Easy QWERTY* is a masterpiece of accelerative-learning strategies," says Dawn Griggs, president of the Accelerative Learning Society of Australia. "By incorporating NLP principles, students learn with their visual, auditory and kinesthetic channels simultaneously. Through the unique cross lateral patterning of the keyboard exercise, students make use of the whole brain learning system that is kinesiology. And the special music that glues the positions of the keys into the memory is a skillful application of Superlearning."

Another excellent computer keyboard program has been developed by Gote Berqvist, of Sweden, and it's used in the Finnish state-school system, which has been a hub of acceleration for ten years. The Finns have a treasure trove of materials. Berqvist's unique program incorporates Bach's music, exercise instructions in English, and such memory-stimulating devices as a ring containing a candy that you unwrap and eat. It tastes of lemon: *L* for the *L* finger! You learn the computer keyboard or touch typing in fifteen hours with this system. *The SEAL Journal* calls it "sheer enchantment."

Dr. Hideo Seki, of Tokyo, was a professor of computer sciences before his retirement. His students can be found worldwide at computer firms. Seki realized Superlearning could be adapted to large lecture halls with classes of four hundred or more instead of the ideal small group of twelve to fifteen (see page 16).

This course was on electricity and magnetism, based on Seki's own textbook. Working at Tokai University, he came up with helpful adaptations that anyone can use for technical subjects for any size group.

Seki used suggestions only on the first day of the academic term, giving students affirmations for success and excellence. The regular lesson program was set up like this:

- Ten minutes of mood-setting music while class files in. (He used Japanese koto music or Mozart's "Eine Kleine Nacht Musik" for this introductory phase.)
- Presentation of new material—an oral lecture with overhead projection of diagrams, equations, and so on.
- Active Session—paced data presentation with synchronized breathing.
- Display Session—visual data displayed on the screen with overhead projector.
- Passive Session—rhythmically paced data presented over slow Baroque music.
- Conclusion—several minutes of fast-tempo, allegro music.

During the Active Session Seki instructed his engineering students to breathe rythmically in unison as he read the course data with rhythmic pacing and intonations. Breathing was timed by a very appealing sound signal derived from the sounds of nature—a running brook. Rhythmic breathing is a classic technique for synchronizing brain hemispheres, unifying mindbody, and increasing IQ through improved oxygen supply to the brain.

The Display Session is Seki's innovation. It's a kind of visual concert session. Using an overhead projector with transparencies, he silently projected colored diagrams of data, such as Maxwell's Equations, on the classroom screen while meditative music played in the background. Diagrams of electric currents and circuits were done in bright red. Diagrams of magnetic fields and lines of force were done in bright blue. He interspersed pictures of famous scientists, instruments, landscapes, and models of phenomena. The background meditation music played a role in helping students relax and concentrate and contributed to the effectiveness of the memory recap session.

The class concluded with rhythmically paced data backed by slow Baroque music for memory reinforcement. Here again the class synchronized breathing rhythms to the "brook" signal sound embedded in the music.

Students attended a sixty- to ninety-minute class just once a week. On term exams the number of students who scored over 80 percent soared up almost three times higher. This form of accelerated technical training for large classes can readily be used in large university lecture halls, says Dr. Seki. It's an ideal format for learning scientific data that's essentially visual.

28
Superlearning for Business and Professional Training

Accelerated training saves time and money on a large scale and that—the bottom line—was the initial motivator that drew hundreds of businesses and corporations worldwide to implement Superlearning core techniques. The information explosion and ultra-rapid high-tech changes have forced many companies to move to accelerated methods that can keep up with the torrent of changes leading to the new markets and new business structures of the 21st century. These companies are now reaping rich residual rewards from this global learning method. Not only do trainees learn new skills at high speed, but also health improves as a result of the stress-dissolving strategies that are built right into Superlearning. Absenteeism decreases. Employee efficiency and motivation increase. The entire climate of the workplace can improve as a side effect of this humanizing, transformative training method (see Chapter 11).

"This nation must make a deep commitment to learning for a

lifetime," says Nell Eurich, author of *Corporate Classrooms*. Responding to the needs of all workers will determine America's productivity and position in an increasingly competitive and interdependent world, she asserts.

The time-saving, balanced, cost-effective components of Superlearning can make lifelong learning something to look forward to instead of a chore. Whether you're part of the "learning industry" and corporate America, a small business employing just a handful of people, or an entrepreneur looking to upgrade your own skills, elements of accelerated learning can give you a lift.

In this country Superlearning has come to be employed in the workplace in a variety of ways. Many trainers follow the do-it-yourself route, familiarizing themselves with the system, then experimenting on the job to adapt it to their company's needs, as H. L. Hallmark did at AT&T.

An increasing number of firms hire outside consultants. David Meiers, director of the Center for Accelerated Learning, in Lake Geneva, Wisconsin, began pioneering this route over a decade ago using a nice mix of left brain explanation and right brain icebreakers, games, and hands-on experience. After completing a large government funded research project that proved the clear power imagery has to anchor learning, he patented a right-brain learning machine to give people images with their tapes and music.

More and more SALT members are following Meier's path into industry to train trainers. Minneapolis based Libyan and Phillip Cassone's System 2000 Accelerative Training and Development Program, for instance, is presented entirely in the accelerated format. Trainers practice adapting their existing courses to the new approach, discover how to increase effectiveness by addressing individual learning styles, and learn how to incorporate memory management techniques into training.

The familiar business workshops and seminars have created hundreds of enthusiasts who carry word—and the bonus of their own enhanced performance—back to every conceivable sort of company. A lot of them have been ignited by Dr. Don Lofland, head of PowerLearning, in Santa Cruz. A tall, slim gent with a tidy beard and a beret, Lofland looks like he might be an artist. A physics professor, he has perfected the art of waking people to their own possibilities. "My God, I'm speaking Portuguese!" clients exclaim after Lofland's rut-shaking opening demo. Then they're ready to consider opening up the throttle at work as they experience ways to use music, enhance memory, mind map, speed-read, and manage time. Enthusiasm rides high even months later as many participants discover they still remember 85 to 90 percent of their quick-study Portuguese. In his book, *PowerLearning,* drawn from training over fourteen thousand individuals, Lofland focuses on making people aware of learning styles. This way they can make the most of their own inclinations and are helped in targeting more potent ways to communicate with colleagues and customers.

Superlearning methods are also edging into business as companies move to ease the cost of stress-related health problems. Corporate stress-buster Eli Bay, of Toronto's Relaxation Response (the voice on the Superlearning Relaxation Tape), has taken his stress control programs to hundreds of North American blue chip companies as well as to professional organizations. In Europe Sophrology's health-enhancing programs that teach imagery rehearsal, build concentration, and confidence are used for training in a wide array of trades and professions (see Chapter 19).

The founders of California's LIND Institute, the late Dr. Charles Schmid and Dr. Lynn Dhority, presented workshops worldwide on the application of accelerated techniques in business, industry, and professions. Dhority is an all-round teacher's teacher who captured a lot of attention at the University of Massachusetts when his students picked up two years of German in a single quarter. They learned it well enough to stage a drama in German, something that eluded language majors with years more study. His book, *Acquisition Through Creative Teaching: ACT,* has been a boon to many teachers and trainers.

The technologies of the future that can help build prosperity will require training in even more ever-changing, high-tech skills. "I discovered there's no such thing as boring material," reports Helmut Huttenrauch, the busy chief trainer for Phillips Communications Industry of Nürnberg. As he plunged into accelerated training, his own creativity blossomed, too, as he transformed dull manuals into excitement. Workers imbibed technical data through puzzles, posters, and games. His trainees, for instance, divided into teams and set out to win a new Monopoly game Huttenrauch invented. While they were having fun rolling the dice and moving around the board, they also quickly and easily learned MS-DOS (the computer operating system). In another gambit trainees walk a roped path through a computer made of cards on the floor so that they grasp visually, physically, and psychologically the inner workings of a computer program.

Across Germany Superlearning is accelerating skills in fields from stenography to electronics, languages to computer sciences at training centers linked to Siemens, Opel, Goodyear, IBM, Rank, Xerox, Olivetti, Unilever, Hewlett-Packard, Metal Industry Union of Baden-Württemberg, Hannover Academy of Industry and Trade, Industry Language Center of Stuttgart, to name some.

The trainers at Hartmut Wagner's SKILL-Training Institute in Heidelberg are in the midst of the accelerating buzz of industrial activity. They work with trainers from each industry to create a Superlearning pilot course for specific high-tech specialties, like automobile robot technology. The pilot plan is complete right down to graphics prepared by an artist and decorating tips for the training room. To train trainers following Wagner's protocol:

- Start off with guided goal visualizations for *self-motivation;* prepare visualizations to do with trainees in which they picture how they and others will profit by the new knowledge and skills they're learning
- Help them prepare guided visualizations in which trainees will see themselves in the *future* operating the new machine or program correctly
- Show them how to do NLP and relaxation training
- Show them how to use more "entry channels" for getting the information to the trainee more effectively and how to use visual, auditory, and kinesthetic modes of training
- Show them how to set up simulators of the machines
- Give them practice in reading data aloud with 60-beat music

- Show them how to set up the concerts that anchor the material in memory
- Show them how to transform dull data into mind-catching visual, auditory, interactive, and kinesthetic learning materials—puzzles, games, walk-throughs and models, posters, flipcharts, transparencies, beamers
- Show them energy exercises to use if the work is physically demanding
- Show them how to use new techniques that help their workers open up their potentials and their whole personalities

Frequent questionnaires track the impact on trainees and fine-tune the program to their needs. For instance at the IBM Training Center in Herrenberg, trainees responded, "I found it really super." "There was no sagging of energy around midday." "Even more material could have been presented." When asked if they'd gained anything on the personality level, thirty-nine out of forty-nine responded, "Very much."

Unification with the former East Germany has put extra strain on individuals, companies, and the whole economy in Germany, and these stress-easing Superlearning methods have been helping to ease the transition. The former East Germany, which helped innovate Suggestopedia techniques and used them for years for medical training and languages, still has a number of Didactica Centers using accelerated training systems.

Back in America another firm, OptimaLearning of California, takes its broad spectrum courses into businesses here and overseas. "Super Productivity with Better Health" is one seminar Barzakov took to Poland and back to Bulgaria to help his former countrymen and women keep their balance in the riptides of transition to a free economy. He gave technical-engineering people and health professionals the know-how to relax at will, keep confidence high, and sustain concentration and memory. Dr. Ivan Sojanov, a Bulgarian psychologist, tracked the newly accelerated class members for two years. Personality stabilized, he found, and says that rather than fading away, "benefits are cumulative: concentration, memory, creativity continue to improve."

Ultra-fast professional training not only opens up new opportunities but makes career switching easier and less expensive, as Brian Hamilton, of New York, discovered. After a decade-long active practice as a psychotherapist, Hamilton decided to change careers and enrolled in premedical study at Columbia University. That's when he tried Superlearning. It worked so well for him, he soon found himself in yet another career switch, that of entrepreneur. He founded Hamilton Accelerated Learning Systems, and hundreds of professionals in medicine, nursing, law, education, engineering, even air traffic control have been speeding up with his "Study Mate" program. "I've explored dozens of learning methods," he told us, "but again and again I go back to the basic Superlearning techniques. There's something profound there. They really work." Recently five physicians showed up for his workshop at Brown University's Learning Community; Hamilton arranged to track one through postgrad studies to get data for his goal: a Superlearning program circulating through the American Medical Students' Association.

An eminently practical idea, say med students who've written us. One dropped off a crumpled note at our office. "IOU $20,000," read the scrawl. "That's how much Superlearning saved me, getting through med school in quick time." (If the doctor is reading this, we'll settle for ten!)

29
How-to Roundup: Superlearning for Reading, Grammar, Math, the Blind, TV Game Shows

Superlearning Reading Program

A Superlearning reading program that gives students a four-to-one speedup (a year in twelve weeks)—and leaves them happy and self-confident was developed at the Huntley Hills Elementary School in Atlanta, Georgia, by Dr. Allyn Prichard and Jean Taylor. It has a long track record. For well over a decade it's turned students labeled "as intractable as could be imagined" into good readers. Many, despite seven years of instruction and two years of remedial training, still could not read until they took this program. The following easy-to-do procedure has resulted in comprehension improvement even for the most severely disadvantaged readers. In just a few weeks with Super-learning, students on average leaped ahead eight months in reading ability. For grades four through seven there was almost a five-to-one speedup.

One of the secrets of their successful program is a variant of Lozanov's "active" concert. In addition to the usual paced reading of text over music, they added a *dramatic* reading of a story over music but used slow Baroque Superlearning Music instead of Mozart. It's a procedure the East Germans have also used for many years with great success. Here's how they did it:

> Text: Barnell Loft series *Getting the Facts,* booklets A through F.
> They chose this text because it contained everyday situations that could readily be dramatized.
>
> Time frame: an alternating two-day cycle of forty-five minutes each.

Day One

1. Warm-up activity: Phonics games. (Commercially produced phonics games are available at teachers' stores.)

2. New vocabulary presentation: They used context and kinesthetics to introduce words. Each word comes with a fill-in-the-blank sentence (e.g., "*Trick*—"What _____ is the dog doing?") Students trace the word, write it in the blank, and take turns reading their sentences.

3. Relaxation review with music: Students lie down on rugs, close their eyes, and relax while teacher gives three to four minutes of visualization suggestions. They may take a fantasy trip or imagine they're relaxed with picture patterns the students thought up themselves, for example, "My head feels like a marshmallow . . . my eyes are like Nerf balls . . . my arms are like spaghetti." (For more children's visualization techniques, see *Superlearning*.) The teacher gives suggestions emphasizing the worthiness and uniqueness of each student. They're asked to picture a mental screen where they'll see images tied in with the vocabulary words. The teacher reads the vocabulary words over Superlearning Music in the rhythmic format

with intonations. She pronounces the word, spells the word, uses the word in a sentence. After a pause to let the lesson sink in, the teacher gives suggestions for general health and academic excellence and brings students back to alertness.

4. Students act out a play involving the words introduced. Afterward the new words are again read aloud before they leave class.

Day Two

1. Phonics games.

2. Review of previous vocabulary.

3. Present story material with Superlearning Music background: Students lie down, relax, synchronize breathing with the music, and do mind-calming exercises. Teacher reads a page directly from the text over the musical background, this time giving an emotional, dramatic, theatrical rendition. Students relax and open up to the visual imagery suggested by the story.

4. Pause. Return to wide-awake state.

5. Oral reading of story material: Students read aloud from story booklet and teacher corrects any errors.

6. Comprehension check: Students answer questions provided in the text.

For more on their method, see Prichard and Taylor's book *Accelerating Learning*.

This reading system can give literacy a four-year leap in one. It can be used for home schooling, coaching, or regular or remedial school settings and could be especially powerful in the hands of literacy volunteers.

Photo Reading

"A few days' training in rapid reading, as long as it's very easy, is a strong help before beginning accelerated learning," says Dr. Hideo Seki. The ever investigating Seki was the first member of SALT to publish data on a new form of speed reading; photo reading is its name in the United States and Europe. Instead of letting your eyes do the plodding, on this reading route you allow your unconscious to do the processing and at lightning speed connect data with what you already know. Information processing is Seki's field; he's had hands-on experience of Lozanov's theory of teaching on the double plane (to conscious and unconscious), and he was a natural to quickly test this rapid reading system brought forth in Japan in the 1980s by Akihiro Kawamura.

Photo reading is literally eye-opening. In a class held by Seki's group you'd learn to widen your angle of vision, picking up peripheral data as sentences scroll by on a PC. The goal: Let your unconscious take a snapshot, imbibing a whole page in a glimpse. As in the United States, equipped with fast page-turning techniques, you're then put to speeding through books. In a published report, Seki said that his own and his students' reading became at least ten times faster.

Photo reading may be an idea whose time is now. Independently of the Japanese, Americans too began claiming supersonic reading speeds launched by the same principles. NLP trainers in many cities teach photo reading, as do some accelerated learning teachers. In a sense photo reading is a specialized case of Superlearning. The same core techniques—being in the right state of body and mind, feeding data to and accessing it from the unconscious, dissolving learning blocks—are evoked but applied to reading instead of, say, language learning. This system, too, involves a fresh shift in perspective. It "is about busting old paradigms that limit our choices in learning and reading. It is about being open to the greater possibilities of the other-than-conscious mind," says its leading U.S. proponent, Paul Scheele, of Learning Strategies Corporation, in Wayzata, Minnesota. Once you're connected to your brilliant second self, your unconscious, Scheele and others maintain you can photo read hundreds of pages in a very short time—just a few minutes—then be able to zero in on the key nuggets to win a court case, clinch a sale, ace a thesis. This belief echoes the time-expansion work of Erickson, Raikov, and Houston and Masters, where people are prompted to get out of their own way and let their unconscious do the work in a fraction of the usual time.

Speed reading has been around and working for over half a century, yet it's still rarely used in business or education. Photo reading is a much more organic system, which flows with the nature of our expanding view of ourselves. It may well be standard equipment for 21st century Superlearners.

Superlearning for English Composition and Grammar

Within three weeks of using Superlearning to learn English grammar and punctuation, students "conversed" in grammar as "fluently" as most people discuss the weather, says Chemeketa Community College professor Dr. Stephan Cooter of Salem, Oregon. After ten weeks, objective tests showed students had mastered spoken and written English grammar. One day an expert grammarian dropped in on this Superlearning English class. To Cooter's delight his students were faster and more accurate than the expert—the man who'd actually invented the class. And this from students who previously couldn't remember what an apostrophe was.

In fact Cooter had endured fifteen frustrating years of students' grammar amnesia. He had to find a better way. That's how he came to create "Grammatica Unexpurgated," a global learning grammar text. He put the rules and formulas of grammar and sentence structure into imaginative story form with lots of rhyme and rhythm, short phrases, image-generating elements, and exciting plot. Even the "why" behind grammar rules formed part of the story.

In class, students were given new identities—names drawn from parts of speech—"Professor Participle," "Mrs. Predicate," "Mr. Article," "Geritol Gerund"—while they put the newly learned rules into action. He taped the grammar and punctuation principles in rhythmic format over music using the two concert sessions, classical and Baroque. Relaxing along with the students as they listened in class, he felt more energized than he had in sixteen years. He needed only four hours' sleep and used the extra time to read five hundred books. The extraordinary results were so energizing that this grammar program's been running for many years now.

At Niagara County Community College, Margaret Saunders Laurie also discovered that Superlearning could tune up grammar for students. She prepared several tapes covering grammar rules and usages in the Superlearning format, each one accompanied by image-triggering comments. At the beginning of the term she gave her classes relaxation training and played the grammar tapes. "Students effortlessly absorbed correct English," she told Lynn when she lectured at the college, "and it stayed with them throughout the college year. They made very few grammatical mistakes on written term papers," she said.

Jean Culwell, a teacher from Oakridge, Oregon, used Superlearning techniques for eleventh-grade composition classes and reported, "My students seem much more self-disciplined and attentive all the time, and I believe this results from the relaxation and concentration instruction." We need "to educate the whole person, not just left brain and right arm," she wrote us.

Superlearning has been a boon for spelling and vocabulary learning, too, and Dr. Allyn Prichard's excellent SAT vocabulary course is available on tape.

For youngsters learning grammar Rosella Wallace has developed raps, rhymes, and songs, now available on tapes accompanied by workbooks. Country crooner Tom Bodette, of the "Motel Six" commercials, is the tape MC for some of these Anchor Point, Alaska, elementary class singers. Wallace's classes consistently reached the 91 percent level on national SRA tests thanks to Superlearning and her appealing and memorable songs.

Superlearning Math

STUDENTS' MATH SKILLS FAIL GRADE was once again the front-page headline in *USA Today*, April 1993. Once again the "Nation's Report Card," prepared by a government board, the National Assessment of Educational Progress, painted a dismal picture. Out of the quarter-million students assessed, a meager 25 percent of public school students were proficient in math at grade level.

Superlearning has been helping many students break out of the math tailspin and progress right from arithmetic to advanced math, including algebra and trigonometry.

Skill with numbers is essential for a wide range of professions from engineering to accountancy. Innovator Nancy Marresh applied

LESSON THREE

1.	ALLEVIATE	to moderate
2.	APPRAISE	to estimate generally
3.	ARGOT	jargon
4.	CLAMOR	noise
5.	CONCUR	to be of the same opinion, to agree
6.	CONDONE	to forgive
7.	DITHER	state of trembling excitement or fear
8.	ELUCIDATE	to explain, to make clear
9.	EXPEDIENT	suitable for the purpose, proper under the circumstances
10.	EXTOL	to praise
11.	GULLIBLE	easily deceived or cheated
12.	INDOLENT	tending to avoid exertion or effort
13.	INDUBITABLE	certain, cannot be doubted
14.	INTUITION	direct knowledge of truth without use of reason
15.	MAGNANIMOUS	generous in forgiving insult or injury
16.	MALIGN	to injure [verbally]
17.	MALLEABLE	adaptable, capable of being shaped
18.	NON SEQUITUR	conclusion that does not logically follow
19.	OBSOLETE	discarded, no longer in use
20.	OSTENSIBLY	apparently
21.	PATHETIC	causing pity or sympathetic sadness

Sample page from *Superlearning Vocabulary* by Dr. Allyn Prichard.

acceleration to accountancy and came up with "The Accounting Game," a full-scale accounting program you cover in just two days. Donna MacNeil, managing director of our mail-order firm, Superlearning Inc., flew to Toronto to take this numbers workshop and found it turned a formidable learning task into a pleasurable experience.

Math expert Dr. Allyn Prichard has created prototype courses on tape that can transform even mathophobes into mathophiles. Prichard begins every math course with visualizations that help reduce anxiety and fear of failure in math. Math tests are visualized in advance, like an athlete visualizing a successful ski run at the Olympics.

Here's how you set up basic arithmetic for use with the Superlearning system:

THE RECTANGLE

1. A rectangle is a 4 sided figure with the opposite sides equal

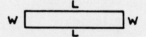

2. The sum of the lengths of the side of a rectangle is its perimeter

   (P = Perimeter)

3. Formula for the perimeter of a rectangle
   P = 2L + 2W

4. Area equals the number of square units contained in a rectangle

   (A = Area)

5. Formula for the Area of a
   rectangle   A = L × W

Sample page from *Superlearning Basic Mathematics* by Dr. Allyn Prichard.

27. MAJOR ARC OF A CIRCLE

Part of the circle lying outside the rays forming a central angle

(*Major Arc: $\overparen{AXB}$*)

28. SEMI-CIRCLE

all points of a circle lying on one side of a diameter

(*Semi-circle*)

29. THE MEASURE OF MINOR ARC EQUALS THE MEASURE OF ITS CENTRAL ANGLE

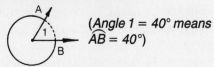

(*Angle 1 = 40° means $\overparen{AB}$ = 40°*)

30. THE MEASURE OF A SEMI-CIRCLE EQUALS 180°

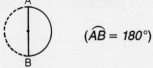

(*$\overparen{AB}$ = 180°*)

31. A DIAMETER THAT IS PERPENDICULAR TO A CHORD BISECTS A CHORD AND ITS 2 ARCS

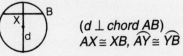

(*d ⊥ chord AB*)
$AX \cong XB$, $\overparen{AY} \cong \overparen{YB}$

Sample page from *Superlearning Geometry and Trigonometry Review* by Dr. Allyn Prichard.

Superlearning for the Blind and Physically Challenged

Mark Rew, twenty-four, who'd been blind since birth, read *Superlearning* in braille and realized that this audio system that enhances memory could be a boon to the blind. He contacted Dr. Carl Schleicher at the Lozanov Learning Center in Silver Spring, Maryland, in order to learn additional techniques. As of 1984 Rew's career took a big leap forward. He was a computer programmer. Suddenly he had expanded skills for troubleshooting. His supervisors were so impressed, they asked him to check out programming problems.

Using his new skills in relaxation training and visualization plus the slow Baroque music that facilitates a connection to the subconscious mind, he found it easy to mentally picture an entire computer program. He could remember it and see it in his mind. "I can mentally find bugs because I can see what's happening with the program," he says. He didn't even have to go through the braille printouts. He developed a talent for visualization like the great Nikola Tesla, who could run entire experiments in his mind.

Schleicher, director of the Mankind Research Foundation, realized that other blind people could benefit the way Rew had. "Mark was an inspiration," says Schleicher. With a grant from the U.S. Department of Health and Human Services, he helped the Lozanov Learning Center set up a course with the American Technical Institute for Rew and a sighted consultant to teach other blind computer programmers. In class, blind students along with their Seeing Eye dogs, practiced relaxation training. The course covered automated industry terminology, how to remove blocks and barriers to learning, how to improve memory and focus the mind, creativity and problem solving, plus a "Success, Self-Esteem, and Prosperity" program. Students also got tapes of high-tech training materials to use at home. Dr. Schleicher was convinced the program could produce blind data processors and computer programmers who were as skilled as sighted ones. Results of the first controlled tests showed the two top persons, who were totally blind, scored substantially higher than most of the control group of sighted persons.

The project, the first of its kind in the country, got under way ten years ago and is still going strong. Training for blind and other physically handicapped individuals at the foundation has produced skilled operators of automated equipment, computers, and word processors. "It's a method that helps remove barriers that hinder or prevent the employment of blind or handicapped persons," Schleicher told us. The technique helped to open a whole new range of high-paying job opportunities for blind persons in the rapidly expanding computer and information processing industries. This Superlearning program for the blind proved so successful, it won an award from the President's Commission for the Handicapped.

Individuals, corporations, organizations for the blind, or vocational rehabilitation groups who are interested in the program can obtain a kit of materials and a videotape from Mankind Research Foundation.

How to Use Superlearning to Win TV Game Shows

One of the longest-running Canadian winners in the 1980s of the Hollywood TV show "Jeopardy" revealed to us that one of her secrets had been adding Superlearning to overall game preparation. Barbara Hansen, of Vancouver, explained that Superlearning had given her an extra edge in competition with other game players, enabling her to walk away with tens of thousands of dollars in prizes.

Whether you want to play for high stakes or just for fun with friends, Superlearning can give you a multifold boost—super recollection and fast response. If "Jeopardy" is your goal, get the book by Alex Trebek, which gives examples of questions in each category of the game. Make notes and put the data into the Superlearning format. Record it with the Superlearning background music. When you're ready, relax and listen to the material in order to make it your own. You can also review topics while simply playing Superlearning Music in the background.

Other TV game shows where you have to recall word definitions or similar data can also get a helping hand from Superlearning. If you want to amaze your friends at party games like Trivial Pursuit, just do a little preparation ahead of time with the Superlearning system.

If you are actually going to be a contestant on a TV game show, it's a good idea to practice one of the relaxation techniques included in Section Three so that you can bypass stress, nervousness, or distractions during the contest. Under the spotlights and in front of a live audience, it can sometimes be more of a challenge to get the right answer than it was in your living room.

30
Accelerative Introductory Method and Reverse Instruction

Scenting a better way, Bruce Tickell Taylor first tackled the worst of four fifth-grade spelling classes in his Windsor School District in California. After a term of Superlearning, standard tests revealed the "slow" children had leaped a year ahead of the "best" class in spelling ability. Kids' self-esteem rose with their grades. Since then Taylor has worked with learners of all ages and in many countries. As his experience percolated, he came up with the Accelerative Introductory Method, or AIM. Schools in California and Australia found good success with the approach and Taylor adapted it "for immediate self-study use." This simplified introductory approach has four steps:

1. Prepare equipment: Put a blank tape on your tape recorder. Put a music cassette on your tape player. In the first go-round you

will be hearing the music of the Active Concert, dramatic music, often high-frequency music, such as Mozart. (For suggested selections, see Chapter 24.) Also, have a slow Baroque music tape on hand and at least one set of earphones and, if possible, two single earplugs.

2. Prepare yourself: Breathe slowly and deeply, think *Calm* as you inhale, then exhale with a real smile. Inhale calmly, exhale smilingly ten times. Close your eyes and look up toward your brow. Count down from ten to one. Imagine you're floating on a cloud to a glorious tropical island. Stretch out on the beach in the warm sun and experience all the sights, sounds, gentle breezes. Lying there, wholly relaxed, think of *a word known to you alone,* which will trigger this state whenever you want to learn. Know learning is now easy and enjoyable. Drift back to your chair, where you will learn with ease and speed. Count from one to five and open your eyes, refreshed and alert.

3. Plug your earphones into your player. You'll be listening to the dramatic "active" music as you tape the material you want to learn. The point is to hear the music but not to let it record on your data tape. As Mozart plays, record your data. Just speak clearly and slowly.

4. Data recorded, rewind the tape. Put the slow Baroque on the player. Get comfortable; lie down if you can. Play your material along with the slow, memory enhancing Baroque. Taylor suggests using two single earphones Attach one to listen to the Baroque, one to hear your data. Or just use your speakers.

Use AIM tapes at odd moments. Music and data when you're home, data tape alone when you're driving, on the bus, and so on. Taylor encourages listening to the AIM tapes as you drift to sleep and as you wake up. He concocted a do-it-yourself pillow speaker. Put the two single earphones, connected to music and data, in a soft plastic cassette case with a hole punched in the side. Listen to data with Baroque at night, data with stirring dramatic music to get yourself stirring in the morning. A year or so ago Taylor used this handy approach to become a superstar in learning French.

Reverse Instruction

"There's Daniel Boone style learning and there's the Ben Franklin style," says George Guthridge, who based his remarkable Reverse Instruction on the Daniel Boone approach. Guthridge's success in lifting often highly disadvantaged kids to academic excellence would strain the bounds of fiction. His method is "reverse" because it literally reverses the usual educational approach of the last thirty years. This is Franklin style—learn by trial and error, move from the general to the particular. The basic facts, the essentials to carry into life, come at the end—the wrong end, according to Guthridge. "It's like trying to build a house without a foundation." It collapses, just the way learning dissolves soon after finals.

Daniel Boone style learning, on the other hand, builds from the bottom up. "Be sure you're right, then go ahead" is a bit of advice that Boone actually wrote down, according to Guthridge. As a frontier analogy he points to how a young Eskimo learns to hunt. First he memorizes what his father does. Next he familiarizes himself with the tools, guns, snares. Then he begins to conceptualize about the weather, the movement of ice floes. Finally, with his acquired experience, he can become innovative and creative.

Whether teaching high school math, sixth-grade history, or third-grade science, Guthridge uses the same steps. First he builds a strong foundation of quality elements, or kernels, as he calls them: the key facts or concepts of a subject. He uses Superlearning, "the most powerful method in the world for memorization." Next students become familiar with various aspects of the topic. Here, too, Superlearning helps. Each student looks up a different bit of data, then the whole class makes a Superlearning tape. Eventually one student makes a tape for the class each day. At the same time kids soak up a subject from three angles: academic experience, personal experience, and emotional (artistic) experience.

Education is part of the life cycle in Eskimo cultures, Guthridge remarks, and he works to create a "community of learners," something common to many societies. Little kids, for instance, brainstorm ways to bring more reading into the home and then act on them. High-schoolers take reverse education to lower grades; the cheerleading squad, for example, shows up to help fifth-graders learn the causes of World War I.

Guthridge's third step is conceptualization, mastery. Students begin to think about what they know, identifying problems and possibilities that don't have known answers. Finally comes the innovative stage. Students create a project of lasting value. It might be materials for next year's class, for example, or publishable articles, or short stories.

Reverse Instruction has tremendously accelerated learning and brought exceptional performance to Alaskans of all kinds and ages. It "bumps them to excellence," as Guthridge says. Both he and his kids have won a clutch of awards as documentation accumulates that he's materializing Devon Edrington's vision: citizens who know the facts and have learned how to think, create, and dream with them.

Guthridge has laid out very specific steps for learning that can help you stay on a fast track with interest high. Now at the University of Alaska, Fairbanks–Bristol Bay, he's geared to long distance communication, teaching many classes by satellite audio conference. Material is available to use on your own, including teaching methodology. "It takes teachers thirty-seven hours to master the system. After that they will save *enormous* amounts of time," Guthridge insists. "I hardly ever have to take even one piece of paper home." Contact: International Institute of Reverse Instruction, University of Alaska, Fairbanks–Bristol Bay, P.O. Box 1070, Dillingham, AK 99576.

31
Breakthroughs for the Learning-Disabled

"Listening is the road to learning," says Dr. Alfred Tomatis, the Paris ear, nose, and throat specialist whose discoveries about the ear/psyche link have had worldwide impact over the past forty-five years. The function of listening, he found, has very far reaching effects on development, learning, and social abilities. (See Chapters 6, 7, 8, 9.)

Recent research shows that listening to high-frequency music has even greater power than previously thought. It has been documented in many thousands of cases to help overcome a wide range of learning disorders and associated behavior problems aside from hearing and speech difficulties. It has helped people who have dyslexia, attention deficit disorder, hyperactivity, autism, and Down's syndrome.

Sound Therapy doesn't just alleviate symptoms. It goes right to the fundamental cause of the difficulty. In a great majority of cases this begins with impaired functioning of the ear. Sound Therapy works to restore the full physical response of the ear as well as a person's emotional receptivity to sound. The undermining of a child's self-esteem by learning difficulties can result in severe, disruptive behavior problems in school and at home.

Hearing can be damaged by ear infections, illnesses, drugs, noise pollution, accidents, prenatal damage, or emotional trauma. Inner ear muscles can stop functioning as a defense mechanism to protect a child from disturbing input.

Acoustic scientists at the Virginia Merrill Bloedel Hearing Research Center, in Seattle, report that the Corti cells responsible for hearing can be regrown. "Hearing aids will soon be a thing of the past," say scientists. Both Sound Therapy and ear acupuncture have been documented to help restore these Corti cells.

Sound Therapy for Dyslexia

Language is processed in the left hemisphere of the brain. The right ear communicates most directly with the left hemisphere. For speech sounds to reach the brain efficiently, the right ear must take a leading role in listening. Dr. Tomatis asserts that people with dyslexia don't have right-ear dominance, so the order in which they hear sounds becomes jumbled. Sounds reach the brain at different speeds, so letters get reversed—and *pat* becomes *tap*.

The balance between the two hemispheres of the brain has to be restored to overcome dyslexia, says Tomatis. In dyslexia the route for phonic analysis—assigning sounds to visual symbols—has been damaged. Sound Therapy restores the functioning of this route and eliminates the origin of the problem. The Electronic Ear exercises incorporated into Sound Therapy give the inner-ear muscles a fitness workout so that the ears become the pathway to language assimilation. Music is a highly organized series of sounds, which the ear has to analyze. Sound Therapy has built-in right-ear dominance to educate the right ear to become the directing ear. When right-ear dominance is achieved, the problem of reversal disappears, says Tomatis. More than twelve thousand dyslexics have recovered as a result of treatment at his clinics.

People with dyslexia often develop a sense of inferiority after failing repeatedly. Many furtively develop elaborate ways to conceal this disability. Sound Therapy has an emotional bonus too. It requires no extra effort, no struggle or painful reminder of any inadequacy. Once a person can interpret sounds accurately and easily, concentration and motivation to learn and communicate increase and self-esteem soars.

Dyslexic people should listen to Sound Therapy tapes thirty to sixty minutes a day or more. Listening can be done during sleep, play, homework, or commuting. The tiny earphones that fit into the ear can be used and taped in place during sleep if desired. Sound Therapy specialists recommend a special exercise for dyslexics—reading aloud while holding an imaginary microphone in the right hand.

"We read with our *ears,*" Dr. Tomatis asserts. He's proven that if our hearing is out of whack, it can affect neural circuitry and reading ability. Might America's massive illiteracy problems be related in part to widespread hearing impairment caused by noise pollution and infection?

When the Westerhof family, of Winnipeg, tried Patricia Joudry's Sound Therapy tapes on their son, John, the first thing they noticed was "terrific improvement in reading." His dyslexia cleared up in two months of listening and he no longer had to take Ritalin, prescribed for his learning disabilities. "It is like a miracle," wrote his mother. It was typical of hundreds of letters Joudry has received about the power of harmonics to heal dyslexia and improve reading.

Attention Deficit Disorder

ADD is a congenital disorder that affects 20 percent of boys and 8 percent of girls. It is believed to be caused by a deficiency in the brain's transmission system. Ear and brain don't work efficiently. Indiscriminate auditory reception leads to concentration problems. Often children with ADD also have behavioral problems and poor social skills. Sound Therapy retrains the auditory reception process and opens the ear to certain sound frequencies. This rehabilitation for the ear reorganizes the auditory transmission to the brain. Sounds can be selected instead of being a distraction. Stress and tension are reduced.

Thirty to sixty minutes a day of listening to Sound Therapy is recommended. If an ADD child is hyperactive, he or she can listen during sleep.

Very dramatic results have been achieved for children with ADD, reports Rafaele Joudry, director of Sound Therapy Australia. Overactive children show decreased activity and less aggression; underactive children are energized. As listening discrimination is retrained, memory and concentration improve as well as motivation and learning.

Autism

"The storm doesn't sound like a machine gun anymore," Annabel Stehli's daughter told her. Georgiana, after auditory therapy, had rebalanced her hearing and could now hear without terrifying, grotesque distortions. During her years in an institution for autistics, she recalled that ocean waves had seemed like thundering tidal waves; water in plumbing pipes, like the crash of Niagara Falls; rain, like earthquakes and floods. "I thought everybody heard that way," she told her mother, "and coped with it better than me." In *The Sound of a Miracle* Stehli recounts her long journey through a kind of medical system hell, till she finally discovered in Europe that hyperacute, distorted hearing can be a factor in some forms of autism. Today Georgie is a college graduate with an art career and marriage plans.

Recent neurobiological data published in medical journals confirms that autism is caused by brain damage. Tomatis believes that because of this damage, autistic children find certain sounds excruciatingly painful, and they relax the muscles of the inner ear as a defense. Soon the muscles lose their tonicity. They then hear all sounds very imprecisely and close themselves off from oral communication. Sound Therapy, by rebalancing the brain's sound filtering mechanism, has been able to help many autistic people overcome hyperacute hearing and restore normal verbal communication.

Tomatis discovered that the earliest memory we all have is the sound of our mother's voice coming to us through our liquid world as preborns. These first sounds are all high-frequency sounds—above 8,000 hertz. At his clinics for the autistic, Dr. Tomatis has created a "sonic rebirthing" program. By reawakening the child's ability to hear high frequencies, it recalls this earliest auditory experience and enables emotional contact to be made with the mother and then with others. Therapy includes listening to his or her own mother's voice filtered through the Electronic Ear to 8,000 hertz.

The Walkman form of Sound Therapy with high-frequency music has produced benefits similar to listening to the mother's voice. It can also be done long term. Reports indicate that after hearing improved, autistic children showed better interaction and communication with family members and emerged from their emotional isolation. Sound Therapy could be done in conjunction with a nutrition program including octacosanol, which has helped repair brain damage in hundreds of cases.

Down Syndrome

Studies show that 75 percent of children with Down syndrome have hearing impairment, often due to recurrent middle-ear infections that cause adhesions, which further damage hearing. Early treatment with Sound Therapy has greatly aided language development. As a full range of hearing is restored, it becomes easier for these children to produce intelligible speech.

Sound Therapy Australia reports that long term listening to high-frequency sound tapes has produced significant results for all areas of development for children with Down syndrome.

Other Conditions

Sound Therapy can be applied for stuttering; hearing problems— hearing loss, vertigo, and tinnitus; insomnia; motor-control integration; even for prenatal listening for a happier baby. Some centers have obtained Sound Therapy tapes for a group of children, so they can take turns listening. Joudry's reader mail indicates a wide range of severe difficulties that have responded to some degree to high-frequency sound. Parents of Carla Gaunt, a brain-damaged, mentally handicapped Saskatoon teenager, stated that Carla's speech and memory improved with three months' listening treatment. The Bentley family, of Edmonton, reported that their daughter, a musician, who'd suffered two skull fractures, brain concussion, and coma from a traffic accident, had been diagnosed "incurable." After five weeks of listening she was able to the play the piano and read music again.

The National Association for Child Development, in Utah, has recommended Sound Therapy tapes to many parents, and director Bob Doman reports that they've seen dramatic results with dyslexia, hyperactivity, and many other things.

For more about Dr. Tomatis' research, see *Supermemory; Sound Therapy for the Walkman* by Pat Joudry; and *The Conscious Ear* by Alfred Tomatis.

Ear Acupuncture

The recent discovery that our ears emit sounds (see Chapter 7) has made possible highly sophisticated new ways to diagnose hearing impairment, even in tiny infants. If your ears stop broadcasting, it can mean hearing problems.

Fortunately yet another new way to restore fading hearing has been gaining advocates. It's ear acupuncture. Specific points on the shell of the ear, stimulated by various forms of acupuncture treatment, have led to full recovery from deafness. The Chinese report that 90 percent of even profoundly deaf people treated with acupuncture regained hearing. Dr. Mario Wexu, director of the Quebec Institute of Acupuncture, conducted extensive tests at the Montreal Institute for the Deaf and Dumb. He reports "outstanding success." Even after a few treatments most children improved by 15 percent and some by as much as 40 percent. For more details, see *Ear Acupuncture: Gateway to Rebalancing the Body* by Mario Wexu.

Ear acupuncture theory holds that our ears are an upside-down reflection of the entire body. Stimulating specific points on the ear with needles or electrical or sound frequencies has been shown to provide effective treatment to the entire body. Stimulating point #86 on the Heart-Lung Meridian on the lower shell of the ear produces endorphins—the body's own natural pain relievers and pleasure-producers. This is the major point used for anesthesia. Sonic stimulation of acupuncture points with devices such as the Sonafon, which emits mixed sound frequencies in the 10,000 hertz range, produces results similar to electro-acupuncture. Sound Therapy music, with sound frequencies up to 8,000 hertz, played through earphones covering the entire ear, obviously stimulates ear acupuncture points which convey energy to the whole body. This may be a factor in Sound Therapy's effectiveness.

Signature Sound

Sound researcher Sherry Edwards has developed a new computerized system for analyzing the frequencies in a person's voice which form a unique "signature sound." If specific frequencies are lacking in the sound pattern, it can indicate certain illnesses. Restoration of these frequencies by treatment with sound can aid in the recovery from a host of maladies, she reports. Her sound treatments have helped many with learning disabilities including retardation and autism.

Superlearning for Learning Disabilities

"The most rewarding and productive classes of my professional career as a reading specialist." That's how Jean Taylor of Atlanta, Georgia, described her experience as the first teacher in North America to use Superlearning for the learning disabled in 1974 at the Huntley Hills School. The results? A four-to-one speed-up in learning. Working with Dr. Allyn Prichard, the two set up remedial reading programs for severely retarded students as well. Students' self-esteem soared as they found themselves easily catching up. Students themselves helped create new "Relaxation Games." They'd quickly discovered that the visualization adventures took the pain and anxiety out of learning. For more than a decade these same astonishing 4-to-1 results continued. Their methods and experiences are detailed in Prichard and Taylor's remarkable book, *Accelerating Learning: The Use of Suggestion in the Classroom*. Some form of relaxation training should be part of every child's training, they believe. It's a health and learning skill for life. While all their students made good gains, some retarded twelve-year-olds soared to college level reading abilities.

Prichard and Taylor's research pinpoints students likely to gain spectacular benefits from their Superlearning program: they should be age ten or older; and be capable of developing skill at relaxation training and visualization.

Anxiety and fear of failure are virtually universal with learning-disabled students, observed educator Wally Nelson of Kansas City. He felt that Superlearning techniques such as relaxation training, soothing music, and subconscious processing could be enormously helpful for these students. In 1978, at the University of Kansas Medical Center in Kansas City, Nelson set up a controlled test of Superlearning for learning-disabled children ages six to eight. They had four 40-minute sessions on word retention. Test scores showed a whopping 75 percent improvement, which was significantly higher than the control group. The learning-disabled children with the best relaxation response scored the highest, he noted in his report in the *SALT Journal.*

Just relaxation training alone produced exceptional results in a 1983 test of 801 learning-disabled and emotionally disabled children in twenty-four different schools in four states. All used a taped relaxation and handwriting improvement program by John Carter. IQs climbed, and students made one-quarter- to one-half-year gains in reading, spelling, and arithmetic. Carter noted that once these highly significant gains were made, they continued to accrue.

Alaskan special-ed. teacher Debbie Evensen reports that Superlearning techniques have brought great success with students suffering with Fetal Alcohol/Drug Effects. Together she and Superlearning pioneer Rosella Wallace tailored a curriculum to fit students' needs. Relaxation training helped them avoid becoming overstimulated and frustrated, and "shutting down." Learning materials in rhyme presented over the music were not only enjoyable but helped facilitate both memory and retrieval of information. Kinesthetic activities (jumping rope to math facts), plays, and videotaped activities all helped them with their neurological handicap. Reports Rosella Wallace, "Their teachers were astounded! They improved dramatically."

Recent breakthroughs with mind machines may hold new hope for people with Fetal Alcohol Syndrome, or those born with crack addiction. (See Chapter 17.)

Iowa teacher Charles Gritton used Superlearning to tutor two learning-disabled students in math and spelling. After relaxation training and their first Superlearning session covering fifty tough spelling words, they took a quiz. Both scored 90 percent. Pretest scores were 20 and 30 percent. Both were stunned. After more Superlearning sessions scores in spelling and math rose to 90 to 100 percent. The kids excitedly told Gritton, "It's fun to learn, it's easy."

Dr. Don Schuster used Superlearning to teach math and reading to learning-disabled ninth-graders for one-tenth of the school year. Math scores went up by a 1.4-year gain and reading a 2.2-year gain.

Dr. Cecilia Pollack of New York used special imagery, music, and relaxation to teach learning-disabled children spelling. With a "magic" pencil they were to imagine themselves tracing the letters on beach sand. Scores were eighteen correct out of twenty. "Boy, that felt good!" one said.

Today there's more and more medical evidence that music like that used in Superlearning and Sound Therapy can be especially helpful for people with mental, emotional, and physical handicaps. At the Ivymount School, in Rockville, Maryland, music therapist Ruthlee Adler reports that, "While the seriously handicapped may ignore other kinds of stimulation, they respond to music." Famed neurologist Dr. Oliver Sacks, whose work was the basis of the movie *Awakenings,* found that patients with neurological disorders, who were unable to talk or move, were often able to sing to music. Both hemispheres of the brain are involved in processing music. "The neurological basis of musical responses is robust and may even survive damage to both hemispheres."

Many children get a weak start in life as low-birth-weight or premature babies. Clinical researchers at the UCLA School of Nursing, in Los Angeles, and at Georgia Baptist Medical Center, in Atlanta, tried soothing music mixed with heartbeat sounds. Premature babies gained weight faster and were able to use oxygen more efficiently. At Tallahassee Memorial Regional Medical Center low-birth-weight and premature infants who listened to soothing music for one and one-half hours a day only spent an average of eleven days in the Newborn Intensive Care Unit, while the control group averaged sixteen days.

Other studies suggest that music may not only increase production of endorphins but has also been documented to change an element in saliva, salivary immunoglobulin A, which helps speed healing, reduces infection, and helps control heart rate.

The discoveries of Dr. Lozanov and Dr. Tomatis about specific elements in music, such as the power of high-frequency sound and the stress-reducing 60-beat tempo, can make it possible to use music with precise effectiveness.

Dr. John Knowles, former president of the Rockefeller Foundation, observed that, "The next great leap in the health care of the American people will be when the people learn to take care of themselves." Contemporary composer Steven Halpern, whose *Spectrum Suite* has been scientifically documented to produce relaxation, says, "It is possible that humans can learn to follow a healthy diet of sound to *keep* themselves in tip-top shape and in radiant health."

Sophrology for Learning Disorders

Sophrology has a long track record for producing exceptional results with retarded and learning-disabled children. Pediatrician Dr. Mariano Espinosa, of Madrid, has used Dr. Caycedo's Sophrology training methods on problem children from Spain and South America for years. At his institute retarded children with severe motor-coordination problems perform Sophrology physical exercises with extraordinary skill. After several months of coordinated body/mind training, tests showed their IQs had risen substantially. In 1974 Dr. Espinosa received the international gold medal in pediatrics for his achievements with the learning disabled.

For more recent breakthroughs that can help with learning disabilities and mental handicaps, see Chapters 16 and 17.

Resources—Breakthroughs for
Learning Disabilities

• Sound Therapy, Steele & Steele, P.O. Box 105, Lund, B.C., Canada VON 2GO, and Sound Therapy Australia, P.O. Box A2237, Sydney South, New South Wales 2000. Catalog of Sound Therapy tapes; *Sound Therapy for the Walkman*, by Pat Joudry; and information.

• National Association for Child Development (director, Bob Doman), 814 West Southampton Court, Farmington, UT 84025. Information on Sound Therapy tapes for learning disabilities.

• Sound Listening and Learning Center, 2701 East Camelback Road, Suite 205, Phoenix, AZ 85016, and the Listening Center, 5 Sultan Street, 2nd Floor, Toronto, Ontario M5S 1L6, Canada. Information on Tomatis Sound Therapy.

• Centre Tomatis, 68 Boulevard de Courcelles, Paris 75017, France. Sound treatment for learning disabilities.

• The Georgiana Foundation (director, Annabel Stehli), P.O. Box 2607, Westport, CT 06881, and Autism Research Institute (director, Dr. Bernard Rimland), 4182 Adams Avenue, San Diego, CA 92116. Information on auditory training and autism.

• Acupuncture International Association, 2330 South Brentwood Boulevard, St. Louis, MO 63144, and Acupuncture Foundation for Canada, 10 St. Mary Street, Toronto, Ontario M4Y 1P9, Canada. Information.

• Sherry Edwards, P.O. Box 12184, Denver, CO 80212-0184. Leading-edge research in the use of sound for full-spectrum healing of disabilities and other illnesses.

• Collège International de Sophrologie Médicale, 50 avenue de la Gare, CH-1003, Lausanne, Switzerland; l'Université de Sophrology Caycédienne, Xalet Flor de Neu—PAL (LA MASSANA), Principality of Andorra. Information on Sophrology. See also Resources for Chapters 16 and 17.

Section Three

EXERCISES

Stress Control

"Thanks for putting the sunshine back into my life!" a Swiss woman wrote to Pierre Schwaar, a successful "pillar of the community" businessman in Lausanne. Schwaar has an unusual avocation. Working in collaboration with Dr. Raymond Abrezol, he heads up the Swiss Sophrology Association's stress-prevention efforts. He's received hundreds of other heartening notes telling of people's delight in overcoming ills, from depression and insomnia to back pain, respiratory, and intestinal disorders. All of these happily liberated people had learned how to shift their body-mind states using routines developed by Dr. Alphonso Caycedo.

Helping people to a new lease on life is the association's goal, but businessman Schwaar was also struck by another big plus. So were Swiss health insurance companies, who could hardly believe their cold, hard statistics. Health claims by people trained in Sophrology *decreased by 40 percent*! A major Swiss insurance company was so impressed by Sophrology's effectiveness at improving physical and mental health and thus cutting costs, particularly for such things as ongoing prescriptions, that in 1991 it began issuing a special health policy *paying* in part for individuals to take Sophrology stress control training and also covering payments to medical Sophrologists as an alternative treatment should the policyholder become ill.

By 1992 more than sixty thousand Swiss had taken the Sophrology courses. The common report is that it helps in all areas of life— jobs, education, relationships, sports. Money managers to the world, the good Swiss burghers seem to have found a new way of managing both their finances—and themselves.

Meanwhile, across the Atlantic, STRESSED OUT AND SICK OF IT made front-page headlines in Canada's national newspaper *The Globe and Mail*. A 1992 national study revealed a staggering 47 percent of Canadians surveyed felt "really stressed," and "burned out," and 33 percent reported being depressed. The cost of stress-generated ill-nesses to the Canadian economy? One billion dollars a year.

Big bucks, but a drop in the bucket compared to the price of stress-related illness in the United States with our juggernaut costs. As the debate rages about how to provide health care, why not question the idea of just piling the same old approach to health higher and deeper for more and more people? One can jump to fresh perspectives on our school problems by shifting focus from educating to learning. Along with good medical care, why not explore people's abilities to help themselves, and show them how, without pills or prescriptions? Considering the continuing Swiss experience of 40 percent fewer insurance claims, new ways to wellness could be a tax-free route to solving health insurance costs.

Getting the stress out of learning from kindergarten to job retrain-ing is fundamental to Superlearning and its sister systems. To give you a wide choice of routines, here are some powerful, proven, classical programs that can give you the liberating ability to shift your body and mind to healthier states.

If you like to be guided by tapes, there are many out there. Superlearning Inc. has worked with some of the experts we think are outstanding. There are tapes by Swiss Sophrologist Raymond Abrezol; two classics, autogenics and progressive relaxation, often recommended by doctors, are now recorded by Eli Bay, one of the top corporate stress control trainers in Canada. Dr. Vera Fryling, one of the foremost autogenics experts in America, has prepared tapes combining autogenics and Superlearning. But of course you can do it yourself. Just give the following instructions a workout. If you wish, you can record them to play back anytime when you're ready to do the program. (For additional stress control programs, see *Superlearning*, which also includes a program specially developed for children.)

Breathing for Mindpower

There's a documented, cost-free mind-enhancer that requires no special equipment or tapes. It's versatile and portable, so it can go anywhere. It's invisible, so it can go right into an exam room, business meeting, or in fact any location. It's fast and easy to do at any time, and it brings results within minutes. It's rhythmic breathing.

Speech professor Dr. Robert Rivera, of Valley College, in Van Nuys, California, tested students after they'd done a simple breathing exercise for several minutes. On average, IQ jumped 10 to 20 points. There was better blood flow and oxygen circulation to the brain. Better oxygen supply to the brain improves thinking ability. The brain needs energy to run, and it uses oxygen to burn its fuel—glucose. The less oxygen in the brain, the more likely you are to make faulty judgments or feel emotionally down, says Rivera. He believes geniuses get that way from having good oxygen supply to the brain. Aside from enhancing intelligence, *rhythmic* breathing helps synchronize the two hemispheres of the brain leading to increased creativity and originality.

These basic breathing exercises can be done regularly and are especially helpful if done immediately before any situation where you face a challenge, for example, a critical meeting, exam or speech.

Inhale for 8 counts. Hold your breath for 12 counts. Slowly exhale for 10 counts. Repeat 10 times.

Gold-Blue Energy Breathing

This color breathing exercise is a "worry buster." It can charge up your energies when you feel tired and depleted and it aids concentration and visualization.

Lie down in a comfortable spot with your head pointing north, feet south. Put your hands, palms up, at your sides. Take a slow, deep breath through your nose and visualize sunshine-yellow energy pouring through the top of your head and traveling through your body and out the soles of your feet. As you slowly and evenly breathe out, picture cool blue energy coming up through the soles of your feet, slowly moving through your body and going out through the top of your head. Continue to breathe *in* yellow; *out* blue for ten to fifteen minutes. You'll start to feel a tingling energy current pulsing through your body with each in-and-out breath. The gold-blue energy recharge will help you focus attention and concentration more easily.

Sound Bath

This exercise helps you clear away brain-drain noise and sounds that have bombarded you during your day.

Select a tape or disc of your favorite relaxation music. Lie down in a comfortable position and turn on the music. Take several deep breaths and let go of all tension. Allow the music to flow through you and over you, washing away all the junk noise and sounds that have pounded you all day. Let the music rinse away any sound pollution. Let yourself get immersed in the music. Notice how it resonates different areas of the body. Picture different cells in your body dancing and moving to the nourishing sound vibrations. Let the music energize and relax you. Take several more slow, deep breaths as the music ends, and let go of all tension.

Shower of Power—for Cleansing and Conditioning

This visualization exercise is a great way to start your day.

When taking a shower, imagine you are standing under a golden waterfall of pure, tingling energy.

Breathe deeply and regularly absorbing the healthful negative ions from the splashing water.

Feel the golden energy flowing through the top of your head, down your spine, and through your arms and legs, soaking into every cell.

Feel your entire body filled with pure, vibrant energy.

Visualize the day ahead. Imagine that you are achieving something that you want very much. Affirm that you have unlimited power and energy to do it. Get emotionally enthusiastic about doing it and the benefits of doing it. Consciously and strongly intend that it shall be done.

As the water cascades over you, feel any tension, worry, and anxiety you may be holding wash away down the drain leaving you refreshed, recharged, and ready to greet your day with enthusiasm and confidence.

Progressive Relaxation

This relaxation exercise helps relieve muscular tension and stress accumulated throughout your body. Tense muscles gently. It's not like a strenuous physical exercise. If you get a muscle cramp, ease up. The point is to get rid of tension stored in muscles.

Get comfortable in a quiet place. Do a few neck rolls to improve circulation to your head. Drop your chin to your chest and roll your head in a full circle to the right and to the left.

Sit on a chair or, if you prefer, lie down on a couch or on the floor. Loosen any tight clothing. Make yourself very comfortable. Scan your bones and muscles and let the weight of them sink into the chair or floor.

Close your eyes. Take a slow, deep breath. Exhale. As you exhale, feel tension beginning to float away. Say to yourself, "Relax." Take a second slow, deep breath and, on exhaling, feel tension being carried away as your breath flows away. Relax. Take a third slow, even, deep breath. Exhale. Imagine tension leaving your muscles. Say to yourself, "Relax."

Now tense up your toes as tightly as possible. Curl your toes tightly, tightly. Hold that taut, tense feeling in the toes as you count from 1 to 5. Now relax your toes. Let that tension float away. Relax your toes completely and feel the difference.

Now tense up your toes, feet, and muscles in the lower part of your legs. Make those muscles very, very tense, but keep the rest of your body very relaxed. Hold that feeling of tension to a slow count of 1 to 5. Study that tension. Now relax. Enjoy that feeling of total release from tension.

Now tense up the muscles in the upper part of your legs as well as the muscles in the toes, feet, and lower legs. Make those muscles as tense as possible. A little bit tenser. Feel that tension. Study that tension. Hold that tension as you slowly count from 1 to 5. Now relax. Feel every bit of tension floating away. Feel those muscles unwinding and letting go; unwinding and letting go. Tell those muscles to relax a little bit more.

Now tense up the buttocks. Hold that tension as you slowly count from 1 to 5. Now relax that tension. Let it float away.

Now tense up the muscles in your lower back and abdomen. Note how it feels to have your body all tied up with tension. Scan the locations where you're holding tension. Tense those muscles even more tightly as you count from 1 to 5. Now let it go. Let it all go. Relax, unwind, and let go. Let the tension drain out of every muscle. Let go of all your weight. Tell your body to relax those muscles just a little bit more. Note how good it feels to let tension go from your muscles.

Now tense up the muscles in the upper part of your torso. Hunch up both shoulders. Tense up the muscles in your chest and back. Make those muscles even tenser. Feel that tension to a slow count of 1 to 5. Now relax. Exhale and feel all those muscles in your chest and back relaxing. Feel the tension between your shoulder blades floating away. Feel all those muscles relaxing, unwinding, letting go. Feel all the tightness and tension leaving and flowing away. Let those muscles relax still more.

Now tense up your arms and clench both fists. Really feel that tension in your hands as you slowly count from 1 to 5. Now relax. Let your arms feel like wet noodles. Enjoy the release from tension. Feel how good it is to be relaxed.

Now squinch up all the muscles in your face. Tense your jaws. Clench your teeth. Tighten your scalp. Squint your eyes. Tense every muscle that you can. Hold that tension as you count from 1 to 5. Then relax. Smooth out all the muscles of the forehead. Release the muscles you frown with. Relax your scalp. Relax your eyes. Relax your mouth. Relax your jaws. Remove all the strain and tension. Relax all the muscles in your face and head. Notice how good it feels to get the tension out.

Now tense up every muscle in your entire body. Start with your toes, legs, abdomen, back, chest, shoulders, arms, fists, neck, and face. Be as tense as you possibly can. Clench every muscle in your entire body. Hold that tension. Count from 1 to 5. Now relax. Now let go. Let tension flow out from every muscle in your body. Relax. Unwind. Let go.

Feel a pleasant relaxing feeling spreading over your entire body. It's a comfortable, pleasant sensation. Note how good it feels to be completely relaxed. Mentally scan your entire body from head to toe. Is there any area still not relaxed? Tense it, hold it, relax it. Your body is now completely relaxed.

Enjoy the pleasant feeling of relaxation flowing through you from head to toes and back up again. Notice how good it feels to completely relax all your muscles. Let waves of relaxation flow freely from head to toe and back up again. Enjoy this feeling. While you relax, you can do some of the affirmations on page 266.

Now, as you count from 1 to 5, you begin to open your eyes. As you do, you feel alert, refreshed, energized, and free of tension. 1, 2, 3, 4, 5—eyes open.

Each time you practice, it gets easier and easier to release tension on command. You'll be able to shift quickly into a relaxed state in which muscle tension vanishes. A few minutes of relaxation relieves tension, fatigue, and stress. It helps concentration and lets your mind stay alert and active.

Scan and Relax

An excellent variation on this Progressive Relaxation exercise is the Scan-and-Relax Routine, a technique that's highly recommended by Eli Bay, of Relaxation Response, in Toronto. You do the above exercise in exactly the same sequence, but instead of tensing up your muscles, scan them for tension and then release that tension. This scanning strategy avoids any problems with overtensing or cramping up of muscles.

Start with your toes. Scan them for tension and then release it. Check your legs for muscle knots or tense areas. Then let that tension go. Scan your buttocks, lower back, and abdomen for tense, tight muscles. Let the tension go. Check your upper torso, shoulders, chest, and back. Release that tension and tightness. Scan your arms, neck, jaws, face, and head for tension. Relax that tension. Let it go. Notice how good it feels. Scan. Relax. Unwind. Let go.

Autogenics

An almost automatic stress-releaser is how Russian doctor A. G. Odessky describes autogenics. Once you've learned these simple exercises, when stress appears, so will release, moving the whole bodymind back into harmony. Dr. Odessky developed this program to help dancers, athletes, teachers, actors, cosmonauts, even chess masters soar to success. It is the program Christian Drapeau used to "make a great work upon myself."

Just seven to ten minutes a day practicing these basic techniques will sooner or later produce the desired effect. It's ideal for busy people, says Odessky. It's like psychological gymnastics for psychological fitness. It's helpful in every area, from business to sports. In addition autogenics has a long history of rebalancing serious physical illnesses. Once you've learned these basics, you have a skill for life; you'll be able to reach this powerful state in seconds, anywhere, and in any circumstances.

Choose a quiet place to practice where you won't be disturbed.

Assume one of the following comfortable positions:

Sitting back—Relax in a recliner or an easy chair with your head resting against the back. Put your arms and hands on the armrests or on your thighs. Legs and feet should not be crossed but be comfortably positioned with feet turned slightly outward. Keep your eyes closed.

Lying down—Lie down on your back on a couch, bed, or soft rug. Put a pillow under your head. Your arms, slightly bent at the elbows, should rest palms down beside your body. Legs should be relaxed, apart, and feet pointing slightly to the sides, not straight up. Eyes closed.

Sitting up—Sit on a chair or stool and let your head hang slightly forward. Let your arms and hands rest loosely on your thighs. Position your legs comfortably, feet pointed slightly outward. Eyes closed.

Warm-up

Imagine you are putting a "relaxation mask" over your face. This soothing mask smooths your frowns, tension, and wrinkles. All the muscles of your face relax and let go, relax and let go. Your eyelids close and rest gently. You focus your eyes on the tip of your nose. Your jaw hangs loose with your mouth slightly open so your teeth don't touch. Put your tongue on the inner gumline of your upper teeth as if you were silently pronouncing a *d* or a *t*.

Begin very gentle belly breathing, that is, breathing in deeply without straining in any way. As the air flows in, feel your abdomen fill with air and puff up. As you breathe out, feel it sink in and empty out. Breathe slowly. Exhale twice as long as you inhale. With each breath increase the count. Inhale, 2, 3; exhale, 2, 3, 4, 5, 6. Inhale, 2, 3, 4. Exhale, 2, 3, 4, 5, 6, 7, 8. Start inhaling on a 1 or 2 count, then increase to 6 or 7. Don't strain.

Now cycle backward down to where you started. Breathe in 6, out 12. Breathe in 5, out 10. Breathe in 4, out 8. Right back to 1 again.

Do this for two or three minutes.

Step One—Heaviness

You begin by developing a pleasant feeling of heaviness in your body. Begin with your right arm. Say to yourself:

My right arm is getting limp and heavy.	(6–8 times)
My right arm is getting heavier and heavier.	(6–8 times)
My right arm is completely heavy.	(6–8 times)
I feel supremely calm.	(1 time)

Open your eyes. Get rid of that heaviness in your arm. Bend your arm back and forth several times. Take a few deep breaths. Relax again. Scan your relaxation mask. Do the cycle again. Do Step One, the Heaviness exercise, for about seven to ten minutes, two or three times a day.

If you have trouble imagining your arm is heavy, hold a heavy object with your right arm and say aloud, "My right arm is getting heavier and heavier."

Do the Heaviness exercise with your right arm for three days.

Then continue with the same formula for your left arm, both arms, right leg, left leg, both legs, and arms and legs—for three days each.

My left arm is getting limp and heavy, etc.	(3 days)
Both my arms are getting limp and heavy, etc.	(3 days)
My right leg is getting limp and heavy, etc.	(3 days)
My left leg is getting limp and heavy, etc.	(3 days)
Both my legs are getting limp and heavy, etc.	(3 days)
My arms and legs are getting limp and heavy, etc.	(3 days)

Step One—the Heaviness exercise, takes three weeks. If you experience a genuine sensation of heaviness in arms and legs, you're ready for Step Two. If not, practice a little longer until you get the desired effect. Some people have done it quickly in once-a-day practice, but it's better to have a firm foundation to build on.

Step Two—Warmth

Begin with your warm-up for about two minutes. Do one cycle of the Heaviness exercise for arms and legs for one minute. Once you feel a sense of heaviness, begin to learn how to arouse a feeling of warmth on command:

My right arm is getting limp and warm.   (6–8 times)

My right arm is getting warmer and warmer.   (6–8 times)

My right arm is completely warm.   (6–8 times)

I feel supremely calm.   (1 time)

As you repeat the formula for warmth, try to imagine that your arm is very, very warm. Some people imagine putting their arm in a pail of warm water, or they imagine a hot arm under a hot sun.

Follow the same pattern as for the Heaviness exercise. Do the right arm for three days; the left arm for three days; both arms, right leg, left leg, both legs, both arms and legs—all for three days each. You'll have mastered it in three weeks. Then do this final formula summing up the first two exercises:

My arms and legs are getting limp and heavy and warm.   (6–8 times)

My arms and legs are getting heavier and warmer. (6–8 times)

My arms and legs are completely heavy and warm. (6–8 times)

I feel supremely calm.   (1 time)

Between cycles of the warmth formula open your eyes, move your arms and legs, and throw off the feeling of heaviness and warmth. Then invoke it again. As you mentally say the formula, visualize your arms and legs getting heavier and warmer.

If you have any problems visualizing warmth, actually run warm water on your arms or legs and say to yourself, "My arm is getting warmer and warmer." Wait for your arm or leg to feel heavy before doing the warmth formula. If it doesn't feel heavy, repeat the heaviness exercise until it does.

Step Three—Calm Heart

Start with the warm-up. Repeat in short form the heavy/warm formula. Say each phrase three or four times. In the beginning do this exercise lying on your back. Mentally sense your heartbeat. Sense it in your chest, throat, or wherever. If you're subject to headaches, don't feel for it in your head. You may prefer to rest your right hand on the pulse point of your left wrist or even on your chest. Usually, in a relaxed state, you can feel the beat. Then repeat silently to yourself:

My chest feels warm and pleasant.	(6–8 times)
My heartbeat is calm and steady.	(6–8 times)
I feel supremely calm.	(6–8 times)

Do this exercise two or three times a day for seven to ten minutes for two weeks. If you're unable to do this exercise after practicing, go on to the next one.

Step Four—Breathing

Do the warm-up. Repeat the following:

My arms and legs are getting limp and heavy and warm.	(1–2 times)
My arms and legs are getting heavier and warmer.	(1–2 times)
My arms and legs are completely heavy and warm.	(1–2 times)
My heartbeat is calm and steady.	(1–2 times)
I feel supremely calm.	(1 time)
My breathing is supremely calm.	(6–8 times)
I feel supremely calm.	(1 time)

Do this exercise to gain control over your breathing seven to ten minutes, two or three times a day for two weeks. You'll know you've mastered it if you can climb stairs or jog and still breathe calmly and rhythmically at your own command. Instead of "supremely calm" an alternative final sentence for this exercise is:

It breathes me.	(1 time)

Step Five—Stomach

This exercise is to help you arouse a pleasant feeling of warmth in your solar plexus—the area above the waist, below the ribs.

Do the warm-up. Repeat in short form the heavy/warm formula and the heart and breathing formula. Then add:

My stomach is getting soft and warm. (6–8 times)

I feel supremely calm. (1 time)

To help generate the sensation of warmth in the solar plexus, you can rest your right palm on your solar plexus while you do this exercise. Gradually you will feel your solar plexus radiating warmth. Some people prefer the formula "My solar plexus radiates warmth."

Do this formula for seven to ten minutes, two or three times a day for two weeks. The exercise is completed when you can rouse definite warmth on command.

Step Six—Cool Forehead

This exercise lets you learn to experience a feeling of coolness on your forehead. Do the warm-up. Repeat in short form the formulas for heaviness, warmth, heart, breathing, and stomach. Then say to yourself:

My forehead is pleasantly cool. (6–8 times)
I feel supremely calm. (1 time)

Imagine a fresh breeze blowing on your forehead and face. If you don't feel coolness right away, stand in front of an air conditioner or a fan and say aloud to yourself, "My forehead is cool." Do this exercise two or three times a day for seven to ten minutes for two weeks. When you definitely experience a sensation of coolness in your forehead, you've completed Step Six.

Step Seven—Recap

You are now ready for the final roundup formula, which is in effect graduation from Level-One Autogenics. Do the warm-up. Repeat in short form the formulas for heaviness, warmth, heart, breathing, stomach, and forehead. Then say:

My arms and legs are heavy and warm.

My heartbeat and breathing are calm and steady.

My stomach is soft and warm, my forehead is cool.

I feel supremely calm.

Repeat the final formula several times. If you've mastered the full series, you'll be able to say this once or twice and immediately achieve the pleasant, calm, stress-free autogenic state. You are in control. The ability to reach this state strengthens with regular practice. Maintenance practice is five minutes, twice a day. Whenever you need to summon this special state—whether it's facing some competition, test, audition, or challenge—you simply say to yourself, "Arms and legs heavy, warm; heart and breathing calm, steady; stomach warm, forehead cool, calm." You'll be immune to any stress, whether it's public speaking, negotiating a business contract, or taking an exam.

Tips on Doing Autogenics

Repeat the formulas verbatim, but with imagination and careful visualization and sensing of the suggestion. The sensation of heaviness and warmth may make you sleepy. If you tend to fall asleep, try doing the exercise in the sitting-up position. Don't leap out of a session. Come back gradually. Open your eyes and move around. Stretch. Flex your muscles. Throw off the heaviness and warmth. Many people experience relief from various stress-related problems well before they complete the cycle. As you come into inner equilibrium, you feel a decrease in fears and worries and a big gain in self-confidence. When you are in the autogenic state, you may want to do some affirmations.

Second Level Autogenics

Classical second level autogenics involves six visualization and imaginative exercises. These can be found in *Superlearning*.

How to Add the Power of Gravity to Visualizations

The ancient Oriental discipline of Qi Gong (Chinese) or Ki Gong (Japanese) enables you to unify mindbody and gravity and tap into universal chi energy. Chi energy opens abilities, enhances sports prowess, heals, balances, energizes, and protects. It is said to be the secret of longevity and a way to open the reserves of the mind. Unified mindbody in harmony with nature is the basis of the Japanese martial art of ai*ki*do.

The Chinese government has set up military Qi Gong clinics across China that not only treat military personnel but train soldiers in the method to help civilians. The Beijing center, headed by Dr. Wan Sujian, has even treated Chinese leader Deng Xiaoping's son.

In Hawaii the Department of Education began *ki* training on a voluntary basis in elementary schools with the hope of improving students' learning, self-confidence, and self-discipline.

To reach the powerful unified Ki Gong state that opens up new capabilities and powers, you begin by rooting yourself into the earth's gravity.

Step One—Sense Your Gravity Point

Sit on a chair or cross-legged on the floor with your back straight. Face forward with your nose in alignment with your navel. Mentally focus on an imaginary point one inch below your navel, the center of gravity of your body. To get a full-sensed awareness of this gravity point, imagine for a moment that you are riding a bicycle, about to stop and still keep your balance. Sense the center in your body that you must keep aligned to keep your balance. Bring your awareness back to sitting in your chair again and focus on this point one inch below the navel for several moments. If need be, place a finger on the point an inch below your navel to focus attention.

Now sense yourself at the center of the universe. Begin reducing the sphere of the universe by half, by half, by half, bringing it down into your center point. Keep focusing on it, reducing by half, infinitely. Let your consciousness drop into this point. Hold this sense of centeredness and oneness with the universe for several moments. Wherever you are, your gravity point is always the center of the infinite sphere of the universe.

Step Two—Relax Totally

Use your favorite method to relax completely, or do this one:

Sit in a chair and let both arms hang naturally at your sides. Shake your hands as fast as possible so that your whole body shakes. Do this while continuing to focus your concentration on your gravity point—a point one inch below your navel. Then stop and remain quiet. Relaxation combined with concentration on the gravity point puts you into a state of power relaxation.

Step Three—Let Your Weight Fall, Let Gravity Support You

Let the full weight of every single part of your body fall into your chair or to the floor. When an object is dropped, it falls. Now just let the earth's gravity relax your body. Sense the weight of your arms, legs, shoulders, back, and hips being totally supported comfortably on your chair or on the floor. Feel the chair and floor fully supporting your weight so that you don't have to. Gravity is taking care of all the weight you've been carrying around. You feel lighter, rooted, totally relaxed and calm.

Step Four—Radiate Ki Energy from Your Hands

Sense *ki* energy flowing through your body and extending from your hands. Allow this vital energy to flow down your arms and out of your hands and fingertips into infinite space. Fresh *ki* energy pours in from the universe, recharging your body and mind, healing, rebalancing, and energizing. If there's any area of your body that is sore or aching, place your charged-up hands on it. Hold this unified state for several minutes. Then take several deep breaths. Stretch and feel energized and refreshed.

Practice this procedure for reaching this powerful, focused state that unifies mindbody, cosmos, gravity, and *ki* energy. Once you are able to move into this unified state with speed and ease, you can perform this exercise anywhere, enabling you to mobilize extra energies for any challenge of any kind whether physical or mental.

A simple test shows if you are truly in this unified state. It can be performed by a friend. When you are rooted in your gravity point, ask a friend to try to push you over by pushing on your chest or shoulder. If you are knocked over by a push, you need more practice.

Oriental martial arts such as aikido are based on the concept of coordinating and unifying mindbody to let *ki* energy from the universe flow through. *Aikido* originally meant "the way to harmony with the energy of the universe." When you function on the basis of coordinated mindbody, it gives you an extra edge for any challenge—job interview, exam, business negotiation, sport.

If you have to study or memorize material, breathe deeply, focus on the gravity point, and extend *ki* from your hands. It will boost concentration, memory, and learning. You may also find it gives you extra circuitry to use, because this technique is the secret behind extraordinary feats performed by Qi Gong masters.

Guided Visualizations

Creating Past, Present, and Future Memories

Every minute of every day you're creating memories. The point of power over memories is right now. Memories are *real* energy. Recollecting memories can change the electrocurrents in your body, and these changes can be detected on instruments. Remembering something that made you angry or unhappy actually has a physical effect on the body. Remembering something joyous has a positive effect on mindbody, memory, and learning abilities.

With the following memory programs you are actually changing the energy charge on these memories from negative to positive. Many people report feeling energized, invigorated, and immensely healthier after clearing away negatively charged memory patterns. They've also been released from repeating the same mistake or taking the same wrong track again. This skill is very important for performance and sports training. You can clear away a "blast from the past" and create exciting future memories of the "future you" with new skills and abilities. You can create "memories" of meeting yourself in the future and seeing yourself experiencing exactly the successful life-style you desire.

Tips for Doing the Exercises

- Avoid logical questioning and speculation. Simply concentrate on your topic and tune out any distractions.

- When doing visualizations or imagining, engage every sense. Visualize in as much detail as possible—colors, forms, shapes, textures, tastes, scents, and sounds.

- For maximum effect and to conserve energy, it is recommended that whenever possible you do these exercises in a seated position, facing forward with your spine straight. Proper alignment is important so as not to block the flow of energy along the spine. Keep your hands resting on each other (palms up on your lap).

- Do a full-bodied visualization. Until you've trained your sub-conscious, it might mistake your visualizations for day-dreams. A physical stimulus, however, impresses your subconscious with a greater sense of reality. Some light physical exercise such as a few "jumping jacks" or briefly running on the spot just before you start your visualization helps tell your subconscious that you mean business. After a number of repetitions of this combination, you should be able to drop the physical stimulus and accumulate your supercharge by breathing and visualization alone, under any circumstances and in any location.

- Right timing is important. It's especially good to do creative visualization at night just before sleeping or in the morning just after waking. These are the times when the mind and body are often deeply relaxed and receptive. A brief relax-ation and visualization done at midday will relax and renew you and help your day to flow more smoothly.

- Adding Superlearning Music, or 60-beat music, to visualiza-tion sessions has produced fully documented, exceptional results, especially in reaching deep levels of memory (see Chapter 7). Other music designed for visualization can also be used. For best results play the music softly in the background.

Dial Direct 1-800-SUB: How to Get Directly in Touch with Your Subconscious Mind

If you are consciously aware of the beliefs held by your subconscious and the motivations that keep them operative, then you can use logic and alternative-motivation strategies to make changes. Beliefs and memories may be hidden or suppressed in the subconscious. Fear of the consequences of changing can keep them suppressed. Many are accepted as facts instead of beliefs or opinions. In order to develop fully and freely, you must get to know your subconscious. Once you've identified some of your beliefs, you can begin to consciously program changes in your subconscious mind. If you remain unaware of your subconscious beliefs, you tend to operate on "old tapes" instead of being the director of your destiny.

With contemporary technology you can actually fax a prayer to the Western Wall in Jerusalem.

In your imagination you can now dial direct "toll-free" to your subconscious mind using the latest phone technology. If you wish, you can name your subconscious. Since ancient times people have given personal names to concepts and energies in order to establish personal rapport. You may want to call your subconscious by your middle name. Dr. Don Schuster suggests calling it "George," as in the phrase "Let George do it." Be careful that the name doesn't establish a sense of separateness. Naming the subconscious can be useful in directing the subconscious to provide information and make changes, as well as in teaching it how to carry out instructions.

You can get better acquainted with your subconscious right now. You can identify and eliminate belief blocks, tap the resources of inner mind to get information, solve problems creatively, receive answers to questions. You might want to explore your relationship with money—why you have feelings of financial insecurity or why you may have blocks to having mega-prosperity. You might want to explore problems with self-esteem or ask about relationships—dealings with a problem boss or relative. You might want to explore health—why you have certain allergies or a weak back. You might want to explore fears—why you fear going against authority or fear taking responsibility for certain things that happen in your life. You can select a different topic each time you "dial direct."

> Take a comfortable position. Close your eyes and raise them slightly upward. Breathe slowly and deeply through your nose. Now take a deep breath and, while slowly exhaling, feel a wave of warm relaxation flowing gradually over your entire body from your toes to your head.
>
> Follow your preferred technique for relaxation.
>
> When you feel completely relaxed, imagine you are in front of a modern telephone with a viewing screen on it. Dial "1-800-SUB." Hear the phone ring. Wait for it to be answered and for the screen to light up.
>
> The first step toward a clear two-way conversation is to make sure you and your subconscious are on the same wavelength by choosing a dialogue that will make subconscious beliefs stand out more clearly. Start with the following four statements, slowly repeating them several times each and leaving space between them to receive your inner answer:
>
> 1. I have the ability to . . .
> 2. I deserve to . . .
> 3. I have the desire to . . .
> 4. I have the determination to . . .

Repeat these statements over "the phone" on your dial-direct call, filling in the topic. For example, "I have the ability to be prosperous, I deserve to be prosperous, I have the desire to be prosperous, I have the determination to be prosperous." Other topics might include health, self-esteem, relationships, and so on. You can select a different topic each time you dial direct.

The responses may come in the form of words, but sometimes

there will be physical responses or images along with the words or alone. Positive responses (encouraging words, good feelings, or positive images) mean that there is good subconscious support for what you want to do. Negative responses (criticism, argument, bad feelings, muscle tension, negative images, or no response of any kind) means you have blocks to work through. If the response is in words, you will have a better understanding of the specific beliefs involved.

Your response may come in the form of a dialogue. The subconscious often also communicates very well by symbols, often better than in words. Ask your subconscious for an image or a symbol for the thing you're asking about. The first image that comes to mind on the screen, no matter how bizarre or seemingly unrelated, is a symbolic message of how your subconscious relates to the situation. It's up to you to interpret the symbols. Ask your subconscious to give another image if the first symbol is not clear. Pause and consider the wisdom your subconscious brings forth.

Once you have a clear rapport with your subconscious, you can use this dial-direct exercise to contact a more complete source of information about yourself, information that can be used to ask questions and solve problems. Describe your problem or ask your question. In describing the situation, give as much detail as possible. Be as objective as possible. This is an objective action—the creation of a scenario in which you are not subjectively involved so that you can remain nonattached and thus acutely perceptive. Distance yourself emotionally to avoid re-creating old anxieties and negative feelings. Remember, this is a "long-distance" help line. Think about the problem or area of your life you want to know more about.

If there's no answer on the dial-direct call, wait for the answering machine and leave your message. Believe that your subconscious will get back to you with an appropriate answer as soon as possible. The answer may come in the form of a dream during sleep or as a sudden inspiration or idea during the course of the day.

When you are ready, hang up. Let this scene fade from your imagination. Slowly return to your normal surroundings and to a more aware self. Open your eyes. Take several deep breaths. Stretch and feel energized and rested.

Videos of Your Mind:
Life's Greatest Videos

This exercise will help you review your day and adjust or correct any events you would like to see have a different outcome. This is a technique many athletes use to improve performance.

Take a comfortable position. Close your eyes and raise them slightly upward. Breathe slowly and deeply through your nose. Now take a deep breath and, while exhaling slowly, feel a wave of warm relaxation flowing gradually over your entire body from your toes to your head.

Follow your preferred technique for relaxation.

When you feel completely relaxed, imagine yourself comfortably seated in front of your TV and VCR. You have in your hand a videocassette entitled "Kaleidoscope of Colors." Insert this cassette into the VCR. Turn on your TV. The words BEST PATTERN will appear on your screen. This is your personal life screen. It can be used to view the past, present, and future. It is operated by an imaginary remote control with a master panel equipped to program and record events, store, erase, edit, and alter data. It is designed to put flexibility at your fingertips.

Adjust the "Focus" button until the words become large and clear. Once you are in focus, press "Fade" and see the words disappear from the screen, leaving a small red circle in the center of the screen.

Take a deep breath. As you slowly inhale, see the red circle expand to cover the entire screen with vivid red light. While holding your breath, pause briefly to absorb the color. As you exhale, see the red circle shrinking until it disappears into the center of your screen and is replaced by a small orange circle.

As you slowly inhale, see the orange circle expand, filling the screen with bright orange light. While holding your breath, pause briefly to absorb the color. As you exhale, see the orange circle shrinking until it disappears from the screen and is replaced by a small yellow circle.

As you slowly inhale, see the yellow circle expanding, flooding the screen with golden-yellow light. While holding your breath, pause briefly to absorb the color. As you exhale, see the yellow circle shrinking until it disappears and is replaced by a small green circle.

As you slowly inhale, see the green circle expanding, saturating the screen with brilliant emerald-green light. While holding your breath, pause briefly to absorb the color. As you exhale, see the green circle shrinking until it disappears from the screen and is replaced by a small blue circle.

As you slowly inhale, see the blue circle expand, filling the screen with clear blue light. While holding your breath, pause to absorb the color. As you slowly exhale, see the blue circle shrinking until it disappears into the center of your screen and is replaced by a small purple circle.

As you slowly inhale, see the purple circle expand, bathing the screen in a deep, rich purple color. While holding your breath, pause briefly to absorb the color. As you exhale, see the purple circle shrinking until it disappears from the screen and is replaced by a small, pulsing violet-pink circle.

As you slowly inhale, see the violet-pink circle expand, illuminating the screen with healing pink rays. While holding your breath, pause briefly to absorb the color. Exhale as the violet-pink circle fades from the screen. You are now relaxed and at a deeper and more powerful level of being.

Imagine that you have recorded your day on your mental camcorder.

Remove the previous videotape and load the VCR with the cassette labeled "A Day in My Life." Press "Play" and begin to review your day in a nonattached, objective manner. When you observe yourself handling a situation well, reinforce this action with self-praise.

When you observe an event where others have been helpful and offered you support, take a moment to feel gratitude.

When you observe an event that you perceive to be negative, press the "Pause" button. Study this frozen moment in time. Try to perceive the wholeness of the situation by moving beyond your initial reaction and view it with an understanding of both its positive and its negative aspects. Remember, for every problem there is a solution in your subconscious waiting to be discovered.

If you've allowed yourself to feel hurt or angry due to someone's words or actions, forgive them and release these disempowering feelings.

If your words or actions have contributed to someone else's discomfort or your own, forgive yourself and free yourself from feelings of guilt and remorse.

Erase all feelings of self-criticism and self-condemnation and criticism and condemnation of others.

If you have made mistakes during your day's activities, whether in business, sports, or on the home front, acknowledge them as valuable learning experiences, see them corrected, and move on.

If it is helpful, you can rewind and play back any portion of your tape to retrieve information or factors contributing to the problem.

Whenever you wish to make changes in your video of your day, simply stop the tape, visualize the preferred action, dialogue, and outcome, then press "Play" and continue.

When your day rolls to an end, acknowledge what you have learned from the experience, rewind your tape, press "Play," and enjoy your triple-star video.

When you are ready, let this scene fade from your imagination. Slowly return to your normal surroundings and to a more aware self. Open your eyes. Take several deep breaths. Stretch and feel energized and rested.

Inner-Weather Wizard

The object—to eliminate *in*-vironmental pollution caused by the negative spin of some old memories. By cleaning up your *in*-vironment, you have a second chance at the past. Clearing inner toxicity caused by stagnant memories will release new energy, boost health, and help you see things more clearly. Carrying around memories of incidents that got you really angry can increase the risk of heart disease, according to the *American Journal of Cardiology*. Studies conducted at Stanford University by Dr. C. Barr Taylor showed that memories of anger skyrocketed blood pressure and impaired the heart's pumping action. Other studies have shown a link to arthritis and other diseases from long-held anger.

Being a time-trekker gives you a chance to clear out any accumulated memories of resentment, guilt, fear, blame, disappointment, or hostility. Many people report the easing of physical problems after clearing out toxic memories. If some of the memories involving a parent, spouse, or other significant person are extremely deeply ingrained, it may take several memory sessions to experience major relief and release. The deeper the bruise, the longer it takes to come to the surface and dissipate. Haunting, or recurring memories are memories asking to be reviewed and released. You're the weather maker when it comes to "inner weather." You have the power to clear away the clouds and let the sun shine in.

Turn on your tape recorder with slow-tempo Superlearning Music or other visualization music.

Take a comfortable position. Close your eyes and raise them slightly upward. Breathe slowly and deeply through your nose. Now take a deep breath and, while exhaling slowly, feel a wave of warm relaxation flowing gradually over your entire body from your toes to your head.

Follow your preferred relaxation routine.

When you feel completely relaxed, imagine yourself seated comfortably in front of your TV and VCR. Slowly dim the lights until the only objects you are aware of in the safe, familiar surroundings are the TV screen, a shelf containing your "Personal Life Video Series," and the warm glow from a fireplace. Take a moment to observe the fireplace. Notice the steady, rhythmic movement of the slow-burning flames. Savor the pleasant aroma of the wood. Feel the gentle warmth radiating out from the soft golden-orange glow. The room is quiet. You feel a sense of complete privacy and deep inner peace.

Take from the shelf a videocassette marked "Kaleidoscope

of Colors." Insert it in your VCR and turn on the TV. BEST PATTERN will appear on the screen. This is your personal life screen which can be used to view the past. With the remote control in your hand, adjust the "Focus" until the words become large and clear. Once you are in focus, press "Fade" and see the words disappear from the screen leaving a small red circle in the center of the screen.

Take a deep breath. As you slowly inhale, see the red circle expand to cover the entire screen with vivid red light. While holding your breath, pause briefly to absorb the color. As you exhale, see the red circle shrinking until it disappears from the screen and is replaced by a small orange circle.

As you slowly inhale, see the orange circle expand, filling the screen with bright orange light. While holding your breath, pause briefly to absorb the color. As you exhale, see the orange circle shrinking until it disappears from the screen and is replaced by a small yellow circle.

As you slowly inhale, see the yellow circle expanding, flooding the screen with golden-yellow light. While holding your breath, pause briefly to absorb the color. As you exhale, see the yellow circle shrinking until it disappears and is replaced by a small green circle.

As you slowly inhale, see the green circle expanding, saturating the screen with brilliant emerald-green light. While holding your breath, pause briefly to absorb the color. As you exhale, see the green circle shrinking until it disappears from the screen and is replaced by a small blue circle.

As you slowly inhale, see the blue circle expand, filling the screen with clear blue light. While holding your breath, pause to absorb the color. As you slowly exhale, see the blue circle shrinking until it disappears into the center of your screen and is replaced by a small purple circle.

As you slowly inhale, see the purple circle expand, bathing the screen in a deep, rich purple color. While holding your breath, pause briefly to absorb the color. As you exhale, see the purple circle shrinking until it disappears from the screen and is replaced by a small, pulsing violet-pink circle.

As you slowly inhale, see the violet-pink circle expand, illuminating the screen with healing pink rays. While holding your breath, pause briefly to absorb the color. Exhale as the violet-pink circle fades from the screen. You are now relaxed and at a deeper and more powerful level of being.

Now you are prepared to take your trip down memory lane. Remove the previous tape from your mental VCR. Select a tape from "The Unsolved Memory Section" of your videocassette library. Load it into your mental VCR. You may consciously choose the memory you wish to review, or call upon your subconscious to select one for you. Press "Play" and see your memory emerge on the screen.

Ask your subconscious why this memory has been selected. Has it been triggered by a present situation or condition that has affected your emotional or physical well-being?

Review this memory in a nonattached, objective manner. Get a clear picture. Recollect in as much detail as possible, using all of your senses. Observe the physical surroundings of this memory. Where did it take place? Put it in a time frame. When did it take place? How long ago? How old were you? What time of the year is it? See it in Technicolor. What colors stand out in the setting? Are you indoors or outdoors? What are you wearing? Who else is present? What do they look like? Notice if there's any particular scent, fragrance or aroma attached to the memory. (For example, if the memory's about school, you might smell the chalk in a classroom.) Is there a familiar sound, noise, song, or some specific music linked to the memory?

What emotions were involved? How were you feeling? Did you feel embarrassed, ashamed, guilty, disappointed, angry? How did these feelings affect you or anyone else involved? What emotions were expressed by the other person or persons present? How did these feelings affect you? Take a moment now to turn your attention inward. How are you feeling about the incident now? Are your emotions the same, or have they changed? Are they as strong as they were, or have they dissipated with time? Is your perception of the memory the same, or have time and maturity brought new insights? Do a body check. Are you still holding any stored tensions from the event?

Search the memory for further information. Go back in time and recapture any data or past events leading up to this memory that may be helpful in understanding this situation. Study this frozen moment in time. Try to perceive the wholeness of the situation by moving beyond your initial reaction and viewing it with an understanding of its positive and negative aspects.

If you are reviewing a memory where your words or actions caused pain or discomfort to another person and left you with feelings of remorse or guilt, imagine yourself communicating with the other person. Calmly and clearly tell them how you felt and why you reacted the way you did. See the other person paying attention and understanding what you are saying. Tell the other person you're sorry for any discomfort you caused them. See the other person responding to your sincerity. See them smiling at you and you returning the smile. Feel a bond of mutual respect. Hear them tell you that they accept your apology and forgive you. Now forgive yourself and release this disempowering feeling.

If you are reviewing a memory where another person or person's words or actions have left you with feelings of hurt, anger, resentment, or a desire for revenge, give the other person an opportunity to explain how they felt and why they reacted the way they did. Hear them apologizing for the discomfort they have caused you and asking you to forgive them. Feel a sense of compassion for this person. Accept their apology and forgive them and wish them well. Smile at this person and see them smile back. Realize how blaming others for what has happened only disempowers you. Experience a feeling of relief as you release all these disempowering feelings and replace them with love and acceptance.

You might want to review a memory where you felt embarrassed or humiliated by the words or actions of others. It might be a time when someone laughed at you and ridiculed you when you were doing your best. Replace the laughter with smiles of approval. You see this person applauding your efforts and congratulating you. Your feeling of embarrassment melts away and you feel a sense of pride. If you're reviewing a memory where your own words or actions caused you or others embarrassment, imagine the other person forgiving you. Feel a sense of inner peace or relief as you forgive yourself.

You might be reviewing the memory of a job loss or financial-loss situation that was due to circumstances you perceived to be out of your control, leaving you with feelings of disappointment, bitterness, betrayal, powerlessness, worthlessness, or fear.

Imagine yourself talking to your past employer or any other person involved. Thank him or her for freeing you from your work obligations at that company and providing the opportunity for you to move forward to a better, more creative, and more rewarding job experience. Hear them expressing appreciation for your valuable services and wishing you well. Hear your former employer sincerely apologizing for the pain, discomfort, and upheaval this has caused you. Forgive and release your employer or the person involved with your financial loss. Forgive and release yourself. Feel a deep sense of relief as you release all disempowering feelings. Experience a surge of excitement, enthusiasm, and renewed optimism as you anticipate your bright new future.

When your memory review is complete, see a small pink dot appear in the middle of the screen and slowly expand outward. Visualize your memory dissolving into a spiral of pink color until the whole screen is flooded with pure pink light. Feel this pink glow from the screen radiating out into the room, surrounding you and enveloping you with its healing, loving energy.

Remove the videocassette from your mental VCR. Gently drop the video with its negative memories into the fireplace. See it melt and disappear in the glow of the flames and slowly disintegrate into ashes. With a "poof" see it vanish up the chimney.

If you're feeling a little weary from your mental memory workout, select a memory from your "Life's Finest Memories" videotape library and load it into your mental VCR. Press "Play."

Reenergize and revitalize by savoring one of your life's finest moments.

When you're ready, let this scene fade from your imagination. Slowly return to your normal surroundings and to a more aware self. Open your eyes. Take several deep breaths. Stretch and feel energized and rested.

Memory-Lane Garden

Do this visualization if a negative, angry, disempowering memory pops up during the course of your day evoked by a phone call or summoned back by a song, a fragrance, or other memory link.

Immediately picture the memory as a weed in an otherwise beautiful flower and vegetable garden. See yourself pulling the weeds out and placing them on the compost heap. Toxic-memory weeds will soon become mulch for the growth of beneficial new flowers and vegetables in the Memory Lane Garden.

The Possible You . . . *Now*

This exercise helps you create memories of the "future you." This technique has helped thousands of athletes reach the pinnacle of performance and receive coveted medals. It has also helped people build new skills. It can help you build an image of yourself as a successful, happy, healthy person with high self-esteem.

Take a comfortable position. Close your eyes and raise them slightly upward. Breathe slowly and deeply through your nose. Now take a deep breath and, while slowly exhaling, feel a wave of warm relaxation flowing gradually over your entire body from your toes to your head.

Follow your preferred technique for relaxation.

When you feel completely relaxed, imagine yourself in a natural setting—a lush forest, park, or garden—surrounded by all the beauty of nature. Recognize this to be your inner natural environment, a familiar place where you feel completely at ease, safe, and protected. This is a place with ideal growing conditions.

There is a pathway or road on which you have been traveling that stretches far ahead of you, farther than the eye can see. This is your life's journey.

See yourself standing on this pathway in the center of a great circle of light. Visualize yourself walking along this pathway guided by this circle of light that enfolds you and shines in front of you lighting the way. Your awareness expands, naturally engaging all your senses and allowing you to visualize in detail and safely experience all that is around you.

The sky is clear and blue, the air is clean and pure, the vegetation is green and lush. You feel the cool caress of the breeze and the gentle warmth of the sunlight as it filters through the branches of the trees. You are aware of the colors, scents, and sounds around you; flowers, trees, sounds of water, chirping of birds, whatever comes to you with pleasure.

Now imagine there is a person on the path ahead of you, walking where you have not walked, seeing what you have yet to see, and experiencing what you have yet to experience.

Separating you from this person is a stream of water. As you approach the stream, you are aware of a footbridge running over the water. It is a solid and sturdy little bridge. You move forward with certainty. You are aware of the natural rhythm and coordination between your footsteps and your breathing. With every step forward you acquire courage, wisdom, knowledge, confidence, strength, clarity, empathy, and tolerance.

At the middle of the bridge you meet the person you saw on the path. Pause and observe everything you can about this person. Notice that he or she is in good physical condition, at an ideal weight, healthy and attractive in every way. Sense that he or she is mentally alert, evolved, productive, energetic, strong, and serene—everything that you desire to be. This person is your future self.

Speak to this person. Converse with him or her. Seek advice on how you will achieve these attributes. Know that this person will work with you in every way to help solve any problems you have, meet challenges, and give you all the information, guidance, and support you require. This person will stay with you as an adviser and trusted guide into the future. At any time that you desire, you can meet again on this imaginary bridge.

Imagine yourself and your future self looking over the side of the bridge, gazing down into the water. Study the reflections that appear in the crystal-clear water. Notice that as you focus your attention, these reflections slowly merge into one.

Pause for a moment to integrate and internalize these aspects of your future self and your present self. Then continue across the bridge and continue on your life's path with a clear sense of direction, leaving behind tension, worry, guilt, fear, anxiety, resentment, and any undesirable feelings that have been disempowering you. Feel centered and calm and well prepared to move with ease into your future.

When you are ready, let this scene fade from your imagination. Slowly return to your normal surroundings and to a more aware self. Open your eyes. Take several deep breaths. Stretch and feel energized and rested.

Mind Designs: Concentration Patterns

This exercise enhances concentration abilities and helps build visualization skills by transferring outer patterns to your inner mind's eye.

Prosperity Pattern

When using this particular mind design for a concentration exercise or for the following exercise, "Prosperity Tree," the pattern can be "charged up" with sound to make it more effective. This prosperity pattern can be charged up by saying the word "aum" while looking at it or visualizing it.

Enlarge and attach the above pattern on a wall. It is a prosperity pattern handed down in ancient texts from India. As you focus your inner attention on it, the pattern invokes a state of consciousness focused on prosperity. As your concentration strengthens, creative ideas will surface that will help you manifest your desired goals.

1. Sit in a chair about three feet away from the pattern.
2. Get into a relaxed state by your preferred method.
3. Close your eyes and imagine a black screen in your mind.
4. Look at the prosperity pattern. Gaze at it for two minutes.
5. Move your eyes to the wall and gaze at an afterimage of the prosperity pattern.
6. Close your eyes and try to see the pattern on the screen of your mind.

Similar concentration exercises to strengthen concentration and develop photographic memory can be done with other geometric patterns: a star, square, or circle. Cut them out of white posterboard and mount them on a backing of black posterboard about 15 by 15 inches.

Prosperity Tree

Assume a comfortable position. Close your eyes. Take several slow, deep, even breaths. Feel a wave of relaxation roll over you and through you from your head to your toes, washing away all worries and tension, leaving you feeling physically relaxed and mentally calm, clear, and alert.

Picture yourself walking along a peaceful, tree-lined street or down a pathway in a beautiful park or garden. Become aware of the natural rhythm and coordination between the movement of your body and your breathing. As you stroll along enjoying all the pleasurable colors, sights, scents, and sounds of nature, your attention is particularly drawn to a bushy shade tree heavily laden with yellow foliage. It's so heavily laden, the branches gracefully slope down toward the ground.

Notice the rays of sunshine cascading across the leaves turning them a shimmering gold color. As you draw closer to this unusually beautiful tree, you observe that the branches are weighted down not with leaves but with gold coins. You go to the tree and reach for the coins. They are all within your reach. You pluck off a coin. You look closer. Each coin is clearly engraved with the special prosperity pattern. You run your fingers over the engraved design, sensing its energy. Notice that the coin is instantly replaced on the tree. Pluck off several more coins. They, too, are instantly replaced. No matter how many gold coins you take from the Prosperity Tree, more appear instantly. You are surrounded by an infinite supply of golden opportunities. The more you accept, the more become available to you.

Become aware of the infinite abundance of nature and the universe. Link with this source of infinite supply. Gratefully know, feel, and accept prosperity flowing to you.

Turn and walk slowly away from the tree, knowing that your opportunities are endless on this ever-blooming tree. You can return at any time. As you walk slowly away from the tree, take several deep breaths. Feel the cool air flowing through you.

When you are ready, let this scene fade from your imagination. Slowly return to your normal surroundings and to a more aware self. Open your eyes. Take several deep breaths. Stretch and feel energized and rested.

Section Four

Section Four

Resources

Section One

Superlearning Inc.
Suite 500
450 Seventh Avenue
New York, NY 10123
Phone: (212) 279-8450
Fax: (212) 695-9288
Mail-order tapes and books by the authors, selected materials from other experts; free brochure; discounts; special offers for the first *Superlearning* book and *Supermemory: The Revolution*.

To get in the right state for learning *plus* twenty minutes of special Baroque music: Tape 101.

An audio guide to producing your own Superlearning tapes, including a short demonstration lesson: Tape 102.

More Superlearning Music, a full forty minutes: Tape 103.

Superlearning Languages: three cassette programs (three hours) of travelers' phrases with booklet. Over one thousand vocabulary words. Spanish, French, German, Italian, Indonesian.

(Single tapes, $13.95 each. Language courses, $39.95. Shipping/handling $3.25 first item, $.75 each additional. U.S. funds.)

Also: relaxation and children's tapes, autogenics, sports, academic subjects, more music, subliminals, books, videos, and more.

In Canada for basic Superlearning materials: Ostrander & Associates,

1290 West 11th Avenue, Ste. #105, Vancouver, B.C. V6H 1K5. Phone: (604) 736-5287. Fax (604) 734-6909.

Superlearning Australia: Rafaele Joudry, P.O. Box A2237, Sydney South, New South Wales, 2000, Australia. Phone/Fax: 02-567-7941.

Professional Societies

Society for Accelerative Learning and Teaching (SALT), 3028 Emerson Avenue South, Minneapolis, MN 55408.

Society for Effective Affective Learning (SEAL), Forge House, Kemble, Gloucestershire GL7 6AD, England.

The Accelerative Learning Society of Australia (ALSA), 50 Emerald Place, Armadale, Western Australia 6112.

The Accelerative Learning Society of New South Wales (ALSN), 52 Saint Johns Avenue, Gordon, New South Wales 2022.

Deutsche Gesellschaft für Suggestopadagogisches Lehren und Lernen (DGSL). Blumenstr. 25, D-8011 Harthausen, Germany.

Society for Accelerative and Integrative Learning (SAIL) c/o Mori Accelerative Learning Center, 1180 Futoo-Cho, Kohoku-ku, Yokohama, Kanagawa-ken, 222 Japan.

Teachers and Trainers

Dr. Charles Adamson, Shizuoka Institute of Science and Technology, 2200-2 Toyosawa, Fukuroi 437 Japan. Accelerated learning and NLP training.

Dr. W. Jane Bancroft, University of Toronto, Scarborough College, West Hill, Ontario M1C 1A4, Canada. International consultant, lecturer, workshops.

Dr. Ivan Barzakov and Pamela Rand, *OptimaLearning*, Barzak Educational Institute, 885 Olive Avenue, Suite A, Novato, CA 94945. Language, business, teacher, and health training; workshops worldwide, learning materials.

Albert E. Boothby, 1254 Sunland Vista, Sacramento, CA 95831. Consultant, teaching, some one-on-one counseling.

Libyan Cassone, 21st Century Learning Systems, 3028 Emerson Avenue South, Minneapolis, MN 55408. Language, teacher, business training.

Lorne Cook, Sound Learning Systems, 32 Hedgewood Drive, Unionville, Ontario L3R 6J6 Canada. Workshops, teacher training, materials.

Dr. Lynn Dhority, Center for Continuing Development, 64 Mountain Street, Sharon, MA 02067. Courses, teacher training worldwide, books.

Mark Fletcher, English Experience, Brambletye, Woodland Road, Lyminge, nr. Folkestone, Kent, CT18 8EP, England. Language courses, teacher training for native and non-native speakers.

Peter Ginn, 301 Sycamore Street, Lake Jackson, TX 77566. Consulting, training, accelerated computer learning.

George Guthridge, International Institute of Reverse Instruction, University of Alaska Fairbanks–Bristol Bay, P.O. Box 1070, Dillingham, AK 99576.

Brian Hamilton, Apartment 2, 422 West 22nd Street, New York, NY 10011. Workshops, some one-on-one training, materials.

Dr. Mary Harris, 600 Peachtree Street, Suite 1550, Atlanta, GA 30308. Superlearning SAT tapes for the Defense Department, consulting.

Gail Heidenhain, Delphin, Partner für Seminare und Beratoung, Kampenwandstrasse 6, D-8011, Baldham, Germany. Training for Suggestopedia, industry, languages, self-coaching.

Ruth James, Ruben James Enterprises, 5607 Miners Circle, Rocklin, CA 95765. Language development specialist, Superlearning "Stress-free Success for the LDS" California exam tape.

Dr. Mary Lang, Creative Concepts in Learning, 621 Lynn Street, Moscow, ID 83843. Children's math and reading programs with video, audio, games; virtual reality.

Michael Lawlor and June McOstrich, Inner Track Learning, Forge House, Kemble, Gloucester, England GL7 6AD. Wide ranging courses, workshops, language training; materials.

LIND Institute (founded by Dr. Charles Schmid), P.O. Box 14487, San Francisco, CA 94114. Language courses and workshops; tape catalog.

Dr. Donald Lofland, Power Learning, 638 Escalona Drive, Santa Cruz, CA 95060. Workshops for students, teachers, business; books and tapes.

David Meiers, Center for Accelerated Learning, 1103 Wisconsin Street, Lake Geneva, WI 53147. Workshops and training.

Dr. Mayumi Mori, Mori Language Educational Institute, 1180 Futoo-cho, Kohoku-ku, Yokohama-shi. Kanagawa-ken, 222 Japan. Accelerated learning courses, materials, research.

Dr. Lyelle Palmer, Director, Office of Accelerative Learning, Winona State University, Winona, MN 55987. Consulting, lectures, workshops.

Dr. Allyn Prichard, 120 Sims Drive, Canton, GA 30115. Consulting, workshops.

Geoffrey Pullen, The Language Centre, Brighton Polytechnic, Falmer, Brighton BN1 9PH, England. Language courses and accelerated training.

Dr. Tatiana Radonjic-Matano, Speed Learning, 100 Overlook Terrace, Suite 19, New York, NY 10040. Courses; professional and business training.

Dr. Donald Schuster, Research into Mind, P.O. Box 8987, Welch Station, Ames, IA 50010. Teacher training, workshops, consulting worldwide. Books and tapes.

Dr. Hideo Seki, President, ALCR, Inc., 5113 Kamiuma, Setagaya, Tokyo, Japan. Courses, wide-ranging experiments in accelerating learning.

Bruce Tickell Taylor, Accelerative Tutoring & Transformations Institute, 45350 Ukiah Street, P.O. Box 451, Mendocino, CA 95460. International network of teachers and others interested in accelerating learning. Original accelerated learning materials.

Jenny Vanderplank, Chalet de Sixt, Maison Neuve, Sixt 74740, France. International workshops and teacher training.

Dr. John Wade, P.O. Box 20, Lyons, ACT 2606, Australia. Consulting, training, workshops worldwide, books and tapes.

Dr. Hartmut Wagner, SKILL Institute/SKILL Training, Schubertstrasse 3, W-6919, Bammental bei Heidelberg, Germany. Extensive business and teacher-training programs and materials, general workshops.

Dr. Rosella Wallace, P.O. Box 57, Anchor Point, AK 99556. Teacher training, workshops, consulting. Her books and tapes: *Rappin' and Rhymin'* and *Smartrope Jingles,* Zephyr Press, P.O. Box 13448-W, Tucson, AZ 86732.

Dr. Win Wenger, Project Renaissance, P.O. Box 332, Gaithersburg, MD

20884. Teacher, business, general training worldwide. Newsletter, books, papers, learning materials.

Jafni Zainal, Superlearning Educational Centre, 19 Jalan Layar Dua, 40000 Shah Alam, Selangor, Malaysia. Courses and business training.

Mindbody Specialists

Dr. Otto Altorfer, Center for Research & Education in Attitude Dimensions, 234 Alta Loma Drive, South San Francisco, CA 94080. Consulting, workshops for business and individuals to effect change. Catalog of papers and materials.

Eli Bay, Relaxation Response Ltd., 858 Eglinton Avenue West, Toronto, Ontario M6G 2B9, Canada. Consulting, stress management for individuals, corporations, government. Materials. In the United States, tapes available from Superlearning Inc.

Lisa Curtis, International Sophrology Institute, Suite 1519, 381 Park Avenue South, New York, NY 10016. "Turning Stress into Energy" lectures and workshops. Tape available from Superlearning Inc. Also information on Sophrology in English.

High-frequency Sound Therapy, Steele & Steele, P.O. Box 105, Lund, B.C., Canada VON 2GO. High-frequency tapes, books, and other materials.

Dr. Doe Lang, Charismedia, 610 West End Avenue, New York, NY 10024. International consultant individual and business for public speaking and charismatic presentation. Workshops and materials. Tapes and book available from Superlearning.

Dr. Monique Le Poncin, Institut National de Recherche sur la Prévention du Vieillissement Cérébral, Hôpital Bicêtre, 78, rue du General-Leclerc, 94275, Le Kremlin-Bicêtre, France. Help with memory loss and other problems of aging. Doctors can write for patient profiles and data; others for training programs.

Dr. Teri Mahaney, Supertraining, P.O. Box 10064, Sedona AZ 86336. "Change Your Mind" tapes, books, workshops.

Nizhoni, The School for Global Consciousness (director, Alex Petfi). Route 3, P.O. Box 50, Galesteo, NM 87540. International prep school training body, mind, spirit.

Bill Phillips, Patience T'ai Chi Association, 2620 East 18th Street, Brooklyn, NY 11235. Phone: (212) 332-3477. Classes, materials, and free referrals to t'ai chi teachers nationwide.

Karen Sands, Future Works, 57 Green Street, New York, NY 10012 Workshops dealing with midlife course correction and aging.

Dyveke Spino, c/o Superlearning, 450 Seventh Avenue, #500, New York, NY 10123. Sports training, whole-brain learning, and music. Tapes available from Superlearning Inc.

Dr. Deborah Sunbeck, c/o Infinity Press, 1764 East River Road, Rochester, NY 14623. Bodymind balancing, help with learning disabilities, research, and materials.

Sophrology

Dr. Raymond Abrezol, International College of Medical Sophrology, Avenue de la Gare 50, CH-1003 Lausanne, Switzerland. Sports training, clinical and social uses of Sophrology. International consultant and trainer. Tapes in English available from Superlearning Inc.

Sophrologie Caycédienne en Médecine et en Sciences Humaines (French Sophrology journal). Contact: Madame Danièle Raynal, Institut de Sophrologie Caycédienne de Bordeaux, 10 Place Pey Berland, Bordeaux 33000, France.

University Internationale de Sophrologie Caycédienne: Xalet Flor de Neu, Pal (La Massana), Principalité D'Andorre. Founded and directed by Alphonso Caycedo, M.D. Information on Sophrology courses, clinics, schools, training worldwide. In France computer net: Minitel: 3615 SOPHRO.

Bibliography

Music

Abrezol, Raymond. *Turning Sound* (tape). New York: Superlearning Inc., 1987.

Bancroft, W. Jane. "The Tomatis Method and Suggestopedia: A Comparative Study." *J. SALT* 7, no. 1.

———. "Yoga Factors in Accelerative Learning." *J. SALT* 8, no. 3.

Becker, Robert, and Gary Selden. *The Body Electric—Electromagnetism and the Foundation of Life.* New York: Morrow, 1985.

Bloom, Pamela. "Soul Music." *New Age Journal,* March–April 1987.

Bonny, Helen, and Louis Savary. *Music and Your Mind—Listening with a New Consciousness.* Port Townsend, WA: ICM, 1983.

Brown, Elizabeth, and Sherry Edwards. "Frequency Therapy." *Raum & Zeit* 3, no. 2, 1992.

Browne, Malcolm. "Ear's Own Sounds May Underlie Its Precision: Tiny Emissions May Be Central to the Mystery of Hearing." *The New York Times,* June 9, 1992.

Campbell, Don. *Music: Physician for Times to Come.* Wheaton, IL: Quest, 1990.

Chitouras, Jeff. "Esoteric Sound and Color." *Gnosis,* Spring 1993.

Clynes, Manfred. *Sentics—The Touch of Emotions.* New York: Anchor/Doubleday, 1977.

———. *Music, Mind and Brain.* New York: Plenum, 1982.

Cousto, Hans. *The Cosmic Octave—Origin of Harmony.* Mendocino, CA: Life Rhythm, 1988.

Edrington, Devon. "Binaurally Phased Sound in the Classroom." Tacoma, WA: 1984.

———. "A Palliative for Wandering Attention." Tacoma, WA: 1985.

Edrington, Devon, and C. Allen. "1984–1985 EEG Experiments with Binaurally Phased Audio Stimuli." Tacoma, WA: 1985.

Edwards, Sherry. *Psychotifics: The Hidden World of Sound.* Boulder, CO: Sounds True, 1988 (tape).

Fickett, David. "Sonic Bloom." *Fate,* March 1993.

Fideler, David. "Orpheus and the Mysteries of Harmony—Is the Universe Governed by the Same Laws That Rule the Harmonies of Music?" *Gnosis,* Spring 1993.

"French Research Links Hearing to Body Dynamics." *Brain/Mind Bulletin,* Theme Pack, Vol. 8—"Perception and Memory."

Gfeller, Kate. "Musical Mnemonics as an Aid to Retention with Normal and Learning-Disabled Students." *Journal of Music Therapy* 20, no. 4, 1983.

Gilmor, Tim. *About the Tomatis Method.* Phoenix, AZ: The Listening Center, 1988.

Goldman, Jonathan. *Healing Sounds—The Power of Harmonics.* Rockport, MA: Element Inc., 1992.

Halpern, Steven, and L. Savary. *Sound Health: The Music and Sounds That Make Us Whole.* San Francisco: Harper & Row, 1985.

———. "Tools for Transformation." *New Realities,* Summer 1985.

"Hearing Deficits May Be Source of Confusion That Causes Dyslexia." *Brain/Mind Bulletin,* Theme Pack, Vol. 8—"Perception and Memory."

Hoffman, Janalea; S. Summers; et al. "The Effects of 60 Beats Per Minute Music on Test Taking Anxiety Among Nursing Students." *Journal of Nursing Education,* Feb. 1990.

———. "Music and the Right Brain—A Case Study." *International Brain Dominance Review,* Fall 1984.

" 'Holophonic' Sound Broadcasts Directly to Brain." *Brain/Mind Bulletin,* Theme Pack, Vol. 8—"Memory and Perception."

Hunt, Roland. *Fragrant and Radiant Healing Symphony.* H. G. White, 1937.

Jenny, Hans. *Cymatics.* Basilus, 1974.

Joudry, Patricia. *Sound Therapy for the Walkman.* St. Denis, Sask.: Steele & Steele, 1984.

———. *Sound Therapy Documentary* (tape). Muenster, Sask.: St. Peter's Press.

Khan, Sufi Inayat. *Music.* New York: Weiser, 1962.

MacIvor, V., and S. LaForest. *Vibrations.* New York: Weiser, 1979.

Maleskey, G. "Music That Strikes a Healing Chord." *Prevention,* October 1983.

Mazie, David. "Music's Surprising Power to Heal." *Reader's Digest,* August 1992.

"MEG's Localize Vision, Epilepsy." *Brain/Mind Bulletin,* 9, no. 16 (Oct. 1, 1984).

Ostrander, Sheila, and Lynn Schroeder. *Supermemory.* New York: Carroll & Graf, 1991.

Pawelek, Y., and Larson, J. "Hemi-Sync and Second Language Acquisition." Fort Lewis, WA: Education Services Division.

Purse, Jill. "Healing Resonance." Re*VISION* 10, no. 1.

Rauscher, Frances; Shaw, G.; and Ky, K. "Music and Spatial Task Performance." *Nature,* Oct. 14, 1993.

Snider, Mike. "Mozart's Music May Sharpen the Mind." *USA Today,* Oct. 14, 1993.

"Sound and Nutrients in Agriculture." *Acres, USA,* Nov. 1984.

Stehli, Annabel. *The Sound of a Miracle.* New York: Avon Books, 1992.

Strauss, S. "Discovery May Spell End to Hearing Aids—Scientists Find Ear Cells Will Regrow." *The Globe and Mail,* February 16, 1993.

Tomatis, Alfred. *Education et dyslexie.* Paris: Editions ESF, 1978.

———. *The Conscious Ear.* Barrytown, N.Y.: Station Hill Press, 1991.

———. *L'oreille et le langage.* Paris: Éditions du seuil, 1978.

———. *L'oreille et la vie.* Paris: Éditions Robert Laffont, 1977.

———. see *Revue Internationale d'Audio-psycho-phonologie.* Paris.

———. *Vers L'écoute humaine.* Paris: Les Editions ESF, 1974, Vols. 1 and 2.

"The Noise/Disease Effect." *Frontiers of Science,* 4, no. 2 (May–June 1982).

Smart Food and Supernutrition

National Health Federation, P.O. Box 688, 4212 West Foothill Boulevard, Monrovia, CA 91016.

International Academy of Nutrition and Preventive Medicine, P.O. Box 5832, Lincoln, NE 68505.

The Academy of Orthomolecular Psychiatry—Huxley Institute for Biosocial Research, 900 North Federal Highway, Suite 330, Boca Raton, FL 33432 (information).
Smart Drug News, P.O. Box 4029, Menlo Park, CA 94026.
Megabrain Report, P.O. Box 2744, Sausalito, CA 94965 (information).
Overseas Sources for Smart Drugs: InHome Health Services, P.O. Box 3112, CH-2800 Delemont, Switzerland. Interlab, BCM P.O. Box 5890, London, WC1N 3XX, England.

References

Ahmad, Naseer. "Autism—One Man's Story About Overcoming an 'Incurable' Illness." *Ontario's Common Ground Magazine,* Fall 1990.
Asai, Kazuhiko. *Miracle Cure, Organic Germanium.* Tokyo and New York: Japan Publications, 1980.
Banderet, L. E., et al. "A Preliminary Report on the Effects of Tyrosine Upon Altitude and Cold-Induced Stress Responses." Natick, MA: U.S. Army Research Institute of Environmental Medicine, 1988.
Bland, Jeffrey. *Choline, Lecithin, Inositol and Other "Accessory" Nutrients—The Exciting New Uses of Powerful Nutrients for People with Special Needs.* New Canaan, CT: Keats, 1982.
Bell, Stuart. "Phosphatidyl Choline—Aids in the Fight Against Neurological Disorders and Aging." *Let's Live,* April 1982.
Cheraskin, E.; W. Ringsdorf; and A. Brecher. *Psychodietetics.* New York: Stein & Day, 1974.
Crook, William. "Yeast Can Affect Behavior and Learning." *Academic Therapy* 19, no. 5 (May 1984).
———. *The Yeast Connection.* Jackson, TN: Professional Books, 1986.
Davis, Adelle. *Let's Have Healthy Children.* New York: Signet, 1972.
Dean, Ward, and J. Morgenthaler. *Smart Drugs & Nutrients.* Santa Cruz, CA: B & J Publications, 1990.
DLPA in the Nutritional Control of Arthritis and Chronic Pain. Pomona, CA: *Nutrition News,* 1983.
Donsbach, Kurt. *Oxygen, Oxygen, Oxygen—$O_2O_2O_2$.* Rosarito Beach, Mexico: Wholistic Publications, 1991.

Fredericks, Carlton. *Eat Well, Get Well, Stay Well.* New York: Grosset & Dunlap, 1980.

———. "Nutrition for the Damaged Brain." *Let's Live,* May 1984.

———. *Nutrition, Your Key to Good Health.* Hollywood, CA: London Press, 1964.

———. *Psycho-Nutrition.* New York: Berkley Books, 1988.

Funfgeld, E. W. *Rokan—Ginkgo Biloba.* New York: Springer-Verlag, 1988.

Garrison, R. *Lysine, Tryptophan and Other Amino Acids—Food for Our Brains, Maintenance for our Bodies.* New Canaan, Conn.: Keats, 1982.

Gelenberg, A. "Tyrosine for the Treatment of Depression." *American Journal of Psychiatry* 147:622, May 1980.

Goleman, D. "Food and Brain: Psychiatrists Explore Use of Nutrients in Treating Disorders." *New York Times,* March 1, 1988.

Growdon, J. H., and R. J. Wurtman. "Dietary Influences on the Synthesis of Neurotransmitters in the Brain." *Nutrition Review* 37 (1979): 129.

Hobbs, Christopher. *Ginkgo—Elixir of Youth.* Capitola, CA: Botanica Press, 1991.

Hoffer, A. *Orthomolecular Psychiatry.* San Francisco: Freeman & Co., 1973.

Huerner, Richard. "Brain Food—Neurotransmitters Make You Think." *Let's Live,* Dec. 1981.

Kamen, B. *Germanium, A New Approach to Immunity.* Larkspur, CA: Nutrition Encounter, 1987.

Kulvinskas, V. "Spring Cleaning for Health and Vitality—Grass, Algae and Seaweeds Are *In!*" *Ontario's Common Ground Magazine,* Spring 1993.

McCabe, Ed. *Oxygen Therapies.* Morrisville, NY: Energy Publications, 1988.

Maleskey, Gale. "Boost Your Brainpower." *Prevention,* January 1985.

Mark, Vernon, and J. Mark. *Brain Power.* Boston: Houghton Mifflin, 1989.

"Medical Applications of Ozone." Norwalk, Conn.: International Ozone Association.

Mindell, Earl. *Vitamin Bible.* New York: Warner Books, 1981.

Murray, Michael. "Ginkgo Bilboa Extract: Is Europe's Most Popular

Medicine a Miracle Drug?" *Phyto-Pharmica Review* 3, no. 6 (November 1990).

————. "Ginkgo Bilboa: 'The Living Fossil.' " *Phyto-Pharmica Review* 3, no. 6 (November 1990).

Pearson, Durk, and S. Shaw. *Life Extension—A Scientific Approach.* New York: Warner Books, 1982.

————. *Mental Alertness.* Huntington Beach, CA: International Institute of Natural Health Sciences, 1981.

Pelton, Ross, and T. C. Pelton. *Mind Food and Smart Pills.* New York: Doubleday, 1989.

Pines, Maya. "Food *Does* Affect Your Brain." *Reader's Digest,* November 1983.

Rogers, L. L., and R. B. Pelton. "Effect of Glutamine on IQ Scores of Mentally Deficient Children." *Texas Reports on Biology and Medicine* 15, no. 1 (1957).

Salaman, Maureen. *Foods That Heal—Boost Memory; Sky Rocket IQ.* Menlo Park, CA: Maureen Salaman, 1992 (tape).

Sheinkin, D.; M. Schachter; and R. Hutton. *Food, Mind and Mood.* New York: Warner Books, 1980.

Stein, et al. "Memory Enhancement by Central Administration of Norepinephrine." *Brain Research,* 84: (1975) 329–35.

Thomson, Bill. "Do Oxygen Therapies Work? The AIDS-Ozone Connection." *East-West,* September 1989.

Williams, R. *Nutrition Against Disease.* New York: Bantam Books, 1971.

Yepsen, Roger, Jr. *How to Boost Your Brain Power, Achieving Peak Intelligence, Memory and Creativity.* Emmaus, Pa.: Rodale Press, 1987.

The High-Tech Mindpower Revolution

MegaBrain Report, P.O. Box 2744, Sausalito, CA 94965. Latest information and sources.

Supermemory, c/o Superlearning Inc., 450 Seventh Avenue, New York, NY 10123. Information and references.

ELF Cocoon International, Route 1, P.O. Box 21, St. Francisville, IL 62460.

Essentia, 100 Bronson Avenue, Suite 1001, Ottawa, Ontario K1R 6G8, Canada.

Tools for Exploration, 4460 Redwood Highway, Suite 2, San Rafael, CA 94903.

Aletheia Foundation, 1068 East Main Street, Ashland, OR 97520.

Electro-Medica, R.R. 2, Viking, Burnt River, Ont., Canada KOM 1CO.

Livewire Electronics Ltd., 54 Arco Road, Asheville, NC 28805.

All the above offer information and catalogs.

Bruce D. Baar, 1645 Farnham Lane, Downington, PA 19335, and The Heritage Store, P.O. Box 444, Virginia Beach, VA 23458-0444. Bio-batteries and information.

American Association of Acupuncture and Oriental Medicine, 50 Maple Place, Manhasset, NY 11030.

References

Beck, Robert. "BT 5—The Alternative." St. Francisville, IL: ELF Co-coon. 1985 (tape and pamphlet).

———. "Bibliography of Cranial Electro-Stimulation." Saint Francisville, IL: ELF Cocoon, 1985.

Becker, Robert. *The Body Electric.* New York: William Morrow, 1984.

———. *Cross-Currents: The Perils of Electropollution—The Promise of Electromedicine.* Los Angeles: Tarcher, 1990.

———. "Electromagnetic Fields—What You Can Do." *East-West,* May 1990.

Chang, S. *The Complete Book of Acupuncture.* Berkeley, CA: Celestial Arts, 1976.

"Cranial-Electrical Stimulation: Reduces Anxiety and Depression." *Focus on Alcohol and Drug Issues* (Hollywood, FL) 6, no. 1.

Ertl, J. P. "Electromechanical Therapeutic Apparatus." *Neuro Models Limited,* March 7, 1978.

———. "Louisiana Study of Learning Potential by Brain Wave Analysis." Louisiana State Department of Education, June 1976.

Grady, Harvey. "The Cayce Impedance Device—A Gift on the Doorstep." *Venture Inward,* May–June 1989.

Graham, D. J. "The Effects of the E.T.A. on the Electrical Activity of the Brain." Toronto: David John Institute.

———. Electromechanical Therapeutic Apparatus." Toronto: David John Institute.

———. "A New Model for Medicine—The Electro-Magnetic Man." Toronto: David John Institute, 1979.

———. "Summary of Findings: The Effects of the ETA on Brain Dysfunctioning." Toronto: David John Institute, June 1979.

Hooper, Judith, and Nick Teresi. *Would the Buddha Wear a Walkman?* New York: Simon & Schuster, 1990.

Hutchison, Michael, *Megabrain.* New York: William Morrow, 1986.

———. *Megabrain Power.* Los Angeles: Hyperion, 1994.

———. "Mind Expanding Machines: Can the Graham Potentializer Do for the Brain What Nautilus Does for the Body?" *New Age Journal,* July–August 1987.

Lerner, Fred. "The Quiet Revolution: Pain Control and Electromedicine." *California Health Review,* April–May 1983.

Llaurado, J. G., et al. "Biologic and Clinical Effects of Low-Frequency Magnetic and Electric Fields." Springfield, IL: Charles C. Thomas, 1974.

McAuliffe, Kathleen. "Brain Tuner: The Black Box—Secret Drug Treatment of Rock Superstars." *Omni,* January 1983.

———. "The Mind Fields." *Omni,* February 1985.

McGarey, William. *The Cayce Remedies.* New York: Bantam Books, 1983.

Maleskey, Gale. "Electricity's Healing Potential." *Prevention,* November 1985.

Patterson, Margaret. *Addictions Can Be Cured.* Berkhamstead, Eng.: Lion Publishing, 1975.

———. *Getting Off the Hook.* Wheaton, IL: Harold Shaw Publishers, 1983.

Shallis, Michael. *The Electric Connection: Its Effects on Mind and Body.* New York: New Amsterdam Books, 1988.

Taub, Harold. "Addicts Are Cured with Acupuncture." *Prevention,* September 1973.

Taubes, Gary. "An Electrifying Possibility—A Swedish Radiologist Posits an Astounding Theory: The Human Body Has the Equivalent of Electric Circuits." *Discover,* April 1986.

Wilson, Robert Anton, "Adventuring with Head Hardware." *Magical Blend,* July 1989.

General Bibliography

Abrezol, Raymond. "Sophrologie Caycedienne et Sport." *Sophrologie Caycédienne* 2, no. 1 (1993).

———. *Winning!* New York: Superlearning Inc., 1988 (tape).

———. *Sophrologie et Evolution—Demain L'Homme.*" Lausanne: Éditions du Signal; Paris: Chiron, 1986.

———. *Vaincre par la Sohrologie (Become a Winner with Sophrology).* Chene Bourg, Switz.: Diffusion Soleil, 1983.

Adamson, Charles. "Standardizing Student States." *Anchor Point: International Journal for Effective NLP* 5, no. 12 (December 1991).

———. "Suggestopedia." *The Language Teacher* 14, no. 6 (1990).

———. "A Suggestopedia Program in Japan." *Journal SALT* 13, no. 4.

Aldridge, Susan. "Reading, Writing, and Virtual Reality." *Omni,* August 1993.

Altorfer, Otto. "Mobilizing Reserve Energy at Work: A Composite of Common Learning Elements." *Journal SALT* 10, no. 4.

Arguelles, José. *The Mayan Factor: Path Beyond Technology.* Santa Fe: Bear & Co., 1987.

"Baby Moguls." *Inc.,* February 1985.

Bandler, Richard. *Using Your Brain—For a Change.* Moab, UT: Real People Press, 1985.

Barber, Larry. "Teaching with Love: An Interview with Marva Collins. *Science of Mind,* April 1993.

Berman, Phillip, and Connie Goldman. "The Ageless Spirit, Rollo May." *Guideposts,* July 1993.

Bittman, Barry. "A Breakthrough in Relaxation Training." *Pain-Free Newsletter* 2, no. 1.

Booth, Eric. "An Introduction to the Eakin School Project." Nashville Institute for the Arts, 1993.

Borysenko, Joan. *Guilt Is the Teacher, Love Is the Lesson.* New York: Warner, 1990.

"Breath Technique Selectively Activates Hemispheres." *Brain/Mind Bulletin* 13, no. 4; also see: *Brain/Mind Bulletin* 4, no. 17, and *Science* 204:1326.

Bryant-Tuckett, Rose, and Lloyd Silverman. "Effects of the Subliminal Stimulation of Symbiotic Fantasies on the Academic Performance of Emotionally Handicapped Students." *Journal of Counseling Psychology* 31.

"Canberra Teacher Shows How to Learn Quickly." *The Canberra Times,* August 1, 1992.

Caycedo, Alphonso. *Le Professeur Caycedo, Père de la Sophrologie Reconte sa Grande Aventure.* Paris: Retz, 1978.

Chamberlain, David. *Babies Remember Their Births.* Los Angeles: Tarcher, 1988.

"Children: Intelligence Is Improvable." *Aletheia, Discovery,* Winter 1993.

Croucher, Charles, and Hope Croucher. "Accelerated Learning in Japanese." *Incorporated Linguist,* 1981.

Diamond, Marian. *Enriching Heredity.* New York: The Free Press, 1988.

Dixon, Norman. *Preconscious Processing.* New York: Wiley, 1981.

Fletcher, Mark. "Superlearning 'An English Experience.'" *English Experience,* Kent, Eng.

Fryling, Vera. *Survival, Creativity and Transcendence.* New York: Superlearning Inc. 1986 (tape).

Galceran, Anne. "SALT for Theatre Actors." *SALT Newsletter* 12, no. 6.

Ginn, Peter. "Tell the Juggler." SALT International Conference Presentation, May 1989; also in *SALT Journal.*

Griscom, Chris. *Ecstasy Is a New Frequency.* Santa Fe: Bear & Co., 1989.

———. *Nizhoni: The Higher Self in Education.* Galesteo, NM: Light Institute Foundation, 1989.

Hallmark, C. L. "Superlearning Presentation." Document *OFO704 AT&T,* 1990.

Hartley, Robert. "Imagine You're Clever." *Journal of Child Psychology* 27, no. 3 (1986).

Holmes, Ernest. *The Science of Mind.* New York: Dodd, Mead, 1938.

Huey, John. "Managing in the Midst of Chaos." *Fortune,* April 5, 1993.

Huyler, Jean Wiley. "Game Show Winners Learn Computer Language." *A Review of the Alliance for Learning,* First Annual Symposium, Santa Fe.

"Implications of a Study of Transpersonal Memory." *Perspectives on Consciousness,* August 1987.

Joudry, Patricia. *Sound Therapy for the Walkman.* St. Denis, Sask.: Steele and Steele, 1984.

———. *And the Children Played.* Montreal: Tundra Books, 1975.

Juline, Kathy. "Making My Home My Heaven, An Interview with Maya Angelou." *Science of Mind,* November 1992.

Kataigorodskaya, Galina. *Intensive Language Teaching in the USSR.* Language Centre, Brighton Polytechnic. Available from SALT & SEAL.

Key, Wilson. *The Clam Plate Orgy.* New York: Signet, 1981.

Kiechel, Walter. "How We Will Work in the Year 2000." *Fortune,* May 17, 1993.

Lang, Doe. *The Charisma Book.* New York: Wyden Books, 1980.

Lawlor, Michael. "Suggestopedia in the Soviet Union." *SEAL Journal,* Spring 1992.

Le Poncin, Monique. *Brain Fitness.* New York: Fawcett Columbine, 1990.

———. "Imaging of Functional Brain in Aging—Clinical and Experimental Aspects," *IPA Psychogeriatrics Congress,* Chicago, 1987.

Liebling, A. J. *In Between Meals, An Appetite for Paris.* San Francisco: North Point Press, 1986.

Lofland, Donald. *Powerlearning.* Stamford, CT: Longmeadow Press, 1992.

Lorber, John. "The Disposable Cortex." *Psychology Today,* April 1981.

McGinley, L. "Uncle Sam Believes Message About Mom Helps Calm Nerves." *Wall Street Journal,* January 1, 1986.

MacLean, Paul. *The Triune Brain in Evolution.* New York: Plenum, 1990.

McOstrich, June. "Red Roses and Purple Asters to Perm." *SEAL Journal,* Spring 1992.

Mahaney, Teri. *Change Your Mind.* Santa Barbara: Supertraining Press, 1989.

"Memory: It Seems a Whiff of Chocolate Helps." *New York Times,* July 10, 1990. See also: *Journal of Experimental Psychology: Learning, Memory and Cognition,* July 1990.

"No First Grade Non-readers in Canadian School." *Brain/Mind Bulletin* 2, no. 21.

O'Regan, Brendan, and Thomas Hurley. "Multiple Personality." *Investigations, Institute of Noetic Sciences* 1, no. 3/4.

Ostrander, Sheila, and Lynn Schroeder. *Executive ESP.* Englewood Cliffs, NJ: Prentice-Hall, 1974.

———. *Psychic Discoveries Behind the Iron Curtain.* Englewood Cliffs, NJ: Prentice-Hall, 1970.

———. "Subliminal Report: What You Don't Know Can Help You— And Hurt You," Superlearning Inc., 1988.

———. with Ostrander, N., *Superlearning.* New York: Delacorte Press, 1979; Dell, 1981.

———. *Supermemory: The Revolution.* New York: Carroll & Graf, 1990.

Ostrander, Sheila, and Lynn Schroeder, eds. *The ESP Papers: Scientists Speak Out from Behind the Iron Curtain.* New York: Bantam Books, 1976.

Parker, Kenneth. "Effects of Subliminal Symbiotic Stimulation on Academic Performance: Further Evidence on the Adaptation-Enhancing Effect of Oneness Fantasiers." *Journal of Counseling Psychology* 21, no. 1.

Peters, Tom. "Thriving in Chaos." *Working Woman,* September 1993.

Phillips, William C. "T'ai-Chi Ch'uan as Meditation." *Full Circle,* Rocky Mountain T'ai-chi Ch'uan Foundation, Boulder, CO.

———. "The T'ai Chi Experience in Elementary Education." Patience T'ai Chi Association, 1985.

Prichard, Allyn, and Jean Taylor. *Accelerated Learning,* Novato, CA: Academic Therapy Publications, 1980.

Pullen, Geoffrey. "Professional Training of the Suggestopedia Teacher." *SEAL Journal,* Autumn 1991.

Reich, Robert. "Reclaiming Our Edge." *Working Woman,* September 1993.

Robbins, Anthony. *Awaken the Giant Within.* New York: Summit Books, 1991.

Rossi, Ernest. *Psychobiology of Mind-Body Healing.* New York: Norton, 1988.

Sacks, Oliver. "Neurology and the Soul." *New York Review of Books,* November 22, 1990.

Sandroff, Ronnie. "The Psychology of Change." *Working Woman,* July 1993.

Saunders, Melvin. "Ambidexterity." *Creative Alternatives Newsletter* 6, no. 1.

Schwaar, Pierre. "La Sophrologie Caycédienne et sa Practique. Sociale et Prophylactique en Suisse Pendant Plus de Vingt Ans." *Sophrologie Caycédienne* 2, no. 1, 1993.

Schuster, Donald. *How to Learn Quickly.* Ames, IA: Research into Mind, 1987.

———. *Huna: A Magic Way of Life.* Ames, IA: Research into Mind, 1992.

———. "Using Accelerative Learning in a Large University Class for Teaching Pascal Computer Language." *Journal SALT* 11, no. 4.

Schuster, Donald, and C. E. Gritton. *Suggestive Accelerative Learning Techniques.* New York: Gordon & Breach, 1986.

Schuster, Donald, and L. Schuster. "Educating the Children of Changing Cultures." *Journal SALT* 13, no. 1.

Schuytema, Paul. "Inside a Virtual Robot." *Omni,* September 1993.

Seki, Hideo. "Alpha Brain Wave Formation by Sine Wave Stereo Sounds." *Journal SALT* 13, no. 3.

———. "Application of SALT Method to a Large Number of Students." *Journal SALT* 6, no. 4.

———. "Speed Reading Improves SALT Achievement." *ALCR Inc.* (Tokyo), 1988.

Sheldrake, Rupert. *The Presence of the Past.* New York: Times Books, 1988.

Silverman, Lloyd. "A Comprehensive Report of Studies Using the Subliminal Psychodynamic Activation Method." *Psychological Research Bulletin* (Lund University) 20, no. 3.

Silverman, Lloyd; F. Lachmann; and R. Milich. "Unconscious

Oneness Fantasies: Experimental Findings and Implications for Treatment." *International Forum for Psychoanalysis* 1, no. 2.

Sinetar, Marsha. *Developing a 21st Century Mind*. New York: Villard Books, 1991.

Spence, Jonathan. *The Memory Palace of Matteo Ricci*. New York: Penguin Books, 1985.

Spino, Dyveke. *Tennis Flow*. Superlearning Inc., 1982 (tape).

———. *Creative Running*. Superlearning Inc., 1984 (tape).

———. *Creative Running II*. Superlearning Inc., 1986 (tape).

Sunbeck, Deborah. *Infinity Walk*. Rochester, NY: Infinity Press, 1991.

Taylor, Bruce, T. "An Attempt to Transform International Education." *Journal SALT* 11, no. 4.

Taylor, Eldon. *Subliminal Learning, An Eclectic Approach*. Salt Lake City: Just Another Reality Publishing, 1988.

Taylor, Peggy. "Mind, Body, and Beyond, an Interview with Joan Borysenko." *New Age Journal,* May–June 1993.

Van de Carr, Rene. *Prenatal Classroom*. Humanics Publishing, 1992.

Wade, John. "If You Can Do It in Timor." *SEAL Journal,* Autumn 1990.

———. *Super Study*. Melbourne: Dellasta, 1990.

Wallace, Rosella. "Active Learning: A Practical Application of Current Learning Theories and Recent Relevant Brain Research to Elementary Education," Ph.D. diss., Union Institute, 1989.

———. *Rappin' and Rhymin'*. Tucson: Zephyr Press, 1992.

———. *SmartRope Jingles and Smart Raps*. Tucson, AZ: Zephyr Press, 1993.

Wenger Win. *Beyond Teaching and Learning*. East Aurora, NY: United Educational Services, 1987. Updated 1993, available from Project Renaissance.

———. "Dual-Plane Awareness Techniques Other Than Lozanov's for Accelerating and Enriching Training & Learning." *Journal SALT* 12, no. 3/4.

———. *How to Be a Better Teacher, Today*. Gaithersburg, MD: Project Renaissance, 1991.

———. "A Proposal to Measure the Effects of Image-Streaming Upon Intelligence, Performance and Proficiency." *Journal SALT* 9, no. 1.

Wheater, Caroline. "The Power to Learn." *Here's Health* (England), September 1991.

Woodman, Marion. *Chaos or Creativity?* Pacific Grove, CA: Oral Tradition Archives, 1990 (tape).

Yates, Frances. *The Art of Memory.* Chicago: University of Chicago Press, 1966.

Bibliography for Sections Two and Three

Abrezol, Raymond. *Adventuring with the Brain.* New York: Superlearning Inc., 1987 (tape).

―――. *Sophrologie et Evolution—Demain L'Homme.* Lausanne: Éditions du Signal; Paris: Chiron, 1986.

―――. *Sophrologie et Sports.* Paris: Chiron, 1985.

―――. *Votre alimentation, symboles—energie.* Lausanne: Signal, 1990.

Bancroft, W. Jane. "Le Bien-Être à l'École: Relaxation Techniques in Paris Schools." *Journal SALT* 5, no. 2.

―――. "Civilization and Diversity—Foreign Language Teaching in Hungary." *Canadian Modern Language Review,* January 1973.

―――. "Discovering the Lozanov Method." *Journal SALT* 1, no. 4.

―――. "Foreign Language Teaching in Bulgaria." *Canadian Modern Language Review,* March 1972.

―――. "Interpretations of the Lozanov Method." *Journal SALT* 3, no. 3.

―――. *The Lozanov Language Class.* Arlington, VA: Center for Applied Linguistics (microfiche). *Journal SALT* 1, no. 1.

―――. "The Lozanov Method and Its American Adaptations." *The Modern Language Journal,* 1978.

―――. "Sophrology and Suggestology." *Journal SALT* 4, no. 2.

―――. "Suggestology and Suggestopedia: The Theory of the Lozanov Method." *Journal SALT* 1, no. 3.

―――. "Yoga Factors in Accelerative Learning." *Journal SALT* 8, no. 3.

―――. "Unconscious Assimilation in Foreign Language Learning."

New Approaches to Foreign Language Methodology (15th AIMAV Colloquium). Nijmegen: University of Nijmegen, 18–24, 1984.

Bandler, Richard, and John Grinder. *Frogs into Princes: Neuro-Linguistic Programming.* Moab, UT: Real People Press, 1979.

Bay, Eli. *Maximizing Performance.* Toronto: Relaxation Response, 1984.

———. *Progressive Relaxation and Basic Autogenics.* Toronto: Relaxation Response, 1983 (tape).

Belanger, Bagriana. *La Suggestologie.* Paris: Retz, 1978.

Biallo, Horst. "Superlearning—Sanftes Buffeln." *Wertschafts Wuche,* November 8, 1989.

Bochow, Peter, and Hartmut Wagner. *Suggestopadie—Superlearning.* Speyer, Ger.: GABAL, 1986.

Brown, Randall. "SALT in Special Education." *Journal SALT* 11, no. 1.

Brownlee, Phyllis. "Suggestopedia and Its Application to the Education of Children with Learning Disabilities." *Journal SALT* 6, no. 1.

Bush, B. "A Comparison of Innovative Training Techniques at the Defense Language Institute Foreign Language Center." (Research Report #1426, 74 p.) *ERIC Documents,* ED281384. 1986.

Carter, John, and Harold Russell. "Description and Results of a Field Study Using the Relaxation-Handwriting Improvement Program with Learning Disabled and Emotionally Disturbed Children." *Journal SALT* 9, no. 4.

Caycedo, Alfonso. *L'aventure de la sophrologie.* Paris: Retz, 1978.

———. *Dictionnaire abrégé de Sophrologie et relaxation dynamique.* Barcelona: Ed. Emege.

"Chemistry Teacher with 'Brain-Based' Methods Featured in Book." *Arizona Education Assn. Advocate,* December 1991.

"Computers Help the Blind Go It Alone, by Giving Them Jobs as Operators." *Your Health,* April 2, 1985.

Cooter, Stephan. "Teaching English Grammar and Punctuation Rules and Practice: A Five-Year Study of SALT and Suggestopedia Methods." *Journal SALT* 11, no. 2.

———. "WHY YOU didn't Learn and how you CAN." *Journal SALT* 6, no. 3.

Croucher, Charles and Hope. "Accelerated Learning in Japanese." *Incorporated Linguist,* 1981.

Curtis, Lisa. *How to Turn Stress into Energy with Seven-Minute Stress Breakers.* New York: Superlearning Inc., 1989 (tape).

Davrou, J., and F. LeClerq. *The Astonishing Possibilities of Your Memory Through Sophrology.* Paris: Retz, 1982 (French).

———. *Sophrotherapy: Psychotherapeutic Application of Sophrology.* Paris: Retz, 1982 (French).

DePorter, Bobbi, with Mike Hernacki. *Quantum Learning.* Dell, 1992.

Dhority, Lynn. *The ACT (Acquisition Through Creative Teaching) Approach: The Artful Use of Suggestion for Integrative Learning.* Bremen, Ger.: PLS Verlag, 1991.

Dineen, Janice. "Superlearning: Relaxation, Baroque Music Key to New Teaching." *The Toronto Star,* November 22, 1988.

Dong, Paul, and Aristide Esser. *Chi Gong—The Ancient Chinese Way to Health.* New York: Paragon House, 1990.

Erskine, Ron. "A Suggestopedic Math Project Using Nine Learning Disabled Students." *Journal SALT* 11, no. 4.

Fryling, Vera. *Autogenics and Success Strategies.* New York: Superlearning Inc., 1983 (tape).

———. *Optimal Health.* New York: Superlearning Inc., 1984 (tape).

———. *Stress-Free Learning and Super Performance.* New York: Superlearning Inc., 1982 (tape).

Gassner-Roberts, Sigrid. "Suggestopedia Research in the GDR: A Personal Report." *Journal SALT* 11, no. 2.

Gawain, Shakti. *Creative Visualization.* San Rafael, CA: New World Library, 1978.

Gerber, Richard. *Vibrational Medicine—New Choices for Healing Ourselves.* Santa Fe: Bear & Co., 1988.

Gilmor, Timothy. *About the Tomatis Method—Transformation Through Enhanced Listening.* Barrytown, NY: Station Hill Press, 1992.

Grassi, John. *The Accelerated Learning Process in Science: A Handbook for Teachers.* Framingham, MA: A.L.P.S. Method, 1985.

Hallmark, C. L. "Superlearning Presentation." OFO704 AT&T, 1990.

Hegels, Wolfgang. "Superlearning, eine Lernmethode mit Zukunft." *Personalführung.* 1/89.

Held, Dean. "Case Study—Now Johnny *Can* Read." *Journal SALT,* 4, no. 3.

———. *The Intuitive Approach to Reading and Learning Disabilities: A Practical Alternative.* Springfield, IL: Charles C Thomas, 1984.

Held, D., and R. Mason. *Magic for Everyone: Alternative Reading Activities for the Disabled Reader (A Holistic Approach).* Superior, WI: Superior Educational Press, 1985.

Huttenrauch, Helmut. "Ein Feuerwerk aus Kreativitat und Lernfreude." *Q-Magazin,* 1/92.

Ilpola, Peija. "Suggestopedia in Finland." *Journal SALT* 9, no. 4.

Jaehrling, Dieter. "Suggestopedie und mentales Training in der betrieblichen Bildung bei Audi." *Personalfuhrung,* 1/89.

Kettlewell, David. "A Postcard from Europe." *SEAL Journal,* Spring 1992.

Keller, Bess. " 'Superlearning' Helps Put the Blind to Work." *The Montgomery County Sentinel,* November 16, 1984.

King, Serge. *Mastering Your Hidden Self—A Guide to the Huna Way.* Wheaton, IL: Theosophical Publishing House, 1985.

Klein, Joachim. "Mit ganzheitlichen Methoden Spass am Lernen erzeugt." *Congress & Seminar,* 11/90.

Kotlowicz, Alex. *There Are No Children Here.* New York: Anchor, 1993.

Lang, Doe. *Anger—Fire in the Boiler Room.* New York: Superlearning Inc., 1989 (tape).

———. *How to Conquer Stage Fright of All Kinds.* New York: Superlearning Inc., 1985 (tape).

Lenz, Linda. "It's 'Superlearning' Era Here." *Chicago Sun Times,* November 30, 1986.

Lofland, Don. *Powerlearning.* Stamford, CT: Longmeadow Press, 1992.

Lozanov, Georgi. "Problems of Suggestology." *Proceedings of the First International Conference on Suggestology.* Sofia, Bulgaria, 1971.

———. *Suggestology and Outlines of Suggestopedy.* New York: Gordon & Breach, 1978.

Mahaney, Teri. *Change Your Mind.* Santa Barbara: Supertraining Press, 1989.

Nelson, Wally. "Experimentation with the Lozanov Method in Teaching Word Retention to Children with Learning Disabilities." *Journal SALT* 4, no. 4.

Ostrander, Nancy. *Superlearning Guided Imagery for Children*. New York: Superlearning Inc., 1983 (tape).

Ostrander, Sheila, and Schroeder, Lynn. *Psychic Discoveries Behind the Iron Curtain*. Englewood Cliffs, NJ: Prentice-Hall, 1970.

———. *The ESP Papers: Scientists Speak Out from Behind the Iron Curtain*. New York: Bantam Books, 1976.

———. *Superlearning*. New York: Random House Audio, 1984.

———. *Learn How to Learn*. Los Angeles: Audio Renaissance, 1990.

———. *Superlearning Video*. Superlearning Inc., 1986.

———. *Succeeding*. New York: Superlearning Inc., 1987 (tape).

———. *Power Concentration*. New York: Superlearning Inc., 1987 (tape).

———. *Supermemory*. New York: Carroll & Graf, 1991.

———; with Ostrander. N. *Superlearning*. New York: Dell, 1981.

Pillai, Patrick. *Sonapuncture—Acupuncture Using Intrasound*. Toronto: Electro-Medica, 1990.

Prichard, Allyn. "Adapting the Lozanov Method for Remedial Reading Instruction." *Journal SALT* 1, no. 2.

———. "College Developmental Mathematics." *Journal SALT* 2, no. 3.

———. "Lozanov-Type Suggestion Techniques for Remedial Reading." *Journal SALT* 1, no. 4.

———. "SALT Applied to Remedial Reading: A Critical Evaluation." *Journal SALT* 5, no. 2.

———. "A SALT Remedial Reading Class: An Experimental Update." *Journal SALT* 11, no. 1.

———. *Superlearning Basic Mathematics*. New York: Superlearning Inc., 1982 (booklet and tape).

———. *Superlearning Geometry and Trigonometry Review*. New York: Superlearning Inc., 1983 (booklet and tape).

———. *Superlearning Vocabulary*. New York: Superlearning Inc., 1982 (booklet and tape).

Prichard, Allyn; D. Schuster; and J. Gensch. "Applying SALT to Fifth-Grade Reading Instruction." *Journal SALT* 5, no. 1.

Prichard, Allyn, and J. Taylor. *Accelerating Learning: The Use of Suggestion in the Classroom.* Novato, CA: Academic Therapy Press, 1980.

"Le Professeur Caycedo crée l'Université Internationale de Sophrologie Caycedienne." *Bulletin de la Fondation Alfonso Caycedo,* Andorra: 1993.

Rose, Colin. *Accelerated Learning.* New York: Dell, 1985.

Saferis, Fanny. *Une revolution dans l'art d'apprendre.* Paris: Robert Laffont, 1978.

Scheele, Paul. "Photo Reading." *SEAL Journal,* Spring 1993.

Schmid, Charles. "Language in New Dimensions." *Journal SALT* 3, no. 3.

Schuster, Don, and C. E. Gritton. *Suggestive Accelerative Learning Techniques.* New York: Gordon & Breach, 1986.

Schwarz, Jack. *Human Energy Systems.* New York: Dutton, 1980.

———. *Voluntary Controls.* New York: Dutton, 1978.

Seki, Hideo. "Alpha Brain Wave Formation by Sine Wave Stereo Sounds." *Journal SALT* 13, no. 3.

———. "Application of SALT Method to a Large Number of Students." *Journal SALT* 6, no. 4.

———. "Final Form of the SALT Method Suitable for Engineering Education in a Large College Class." *Journal SALT* 9, no. 3.

———. "Influence of Music on Memory and Education and the Application of Its Underlying Principles to Acupuncture." *International Journal of Acupuncture and Electro-Therapeutics Research* 8, no. 1 (1983): 1–16.

———. "Japanese Language and SALT." *Journal SALT* 12, nos. 3/4.

Sperling, J., and W. Wolensky. "Superlearning: Can It Be Effectively Adapted to Technical Education?" IBM *Technical Report,* 00.3014.

"Suggestopadie in der Weiterbildung—Gemeinsames Projekt der Universität München und der Siemens AG." *CBT Aktuell,* no. 12.

Takahashi, Masaru, and Stephen Brown. *Qigong for Health—Chinese Traditional Exercise for Cure and Prevention.* Tokyo and New York: Japan Publications, 1986.

Taylor, Bruce T. "Low-Budget Introduction of Elementary Accelerative Mathematics." *Journal SALT* 9, no. 2.

Taylor, Jean. "Teaching Remedial Reading with SALT." *Journal SALT* 3, no. 3.

Thorstad, H., and W. Garry. "Suggestopedia, An Advanced Simulation Technique." Norfolk, VA: U.S. Atlantic Fleet Training Center, 1977.

Tohei, Koichi. *Book of Ki: Co-ordinating Mind and Body in Daily Life.* Tokyo and New York: Japan Publications, 1979.

————. *Ki in Daily Life.* Tokyo: Ki No Kenkyukai H.Q., 1978.

Tomatis, Alfred. *The Conscious Ear—My Life of Transformation Through Listening.* Barrytown, NY: Station Hill Press, 1988.

Turnbow, A. W. *Sleep-Learning: Its Theory, Application and Technique.* Sleep-Learning Research Association. 1956.

Vannan, Donald. "Adapted Suggestology and Student Achievement." *Journal SALT* 6, no. 2.

Ventura, Jose Anadon. *La Relajacion Colectiva del Dr. Caycedo.* Barcelona: Editorial Andes Internacional, 1977.

Wade, John. *Accelerative Learning.* Canberra, Aus.: Community Education, 1987 (video).

————. *Quick 'N'Easy QUERTY.* ACT, Aus.: Tonal Typing, 1991.

————. *Superstudy.* Lyons, ACT, Aus.: Dellasta, 1990.

————. *Teaching Without Textbooks.* Carlton Victoria, Aus.: CIS Educational, 1992.

Wagner, Hartmut. "Auswertungsbericht uber den Schulversuch 'Ganzheitliches Lernen.' " *Quelle: Management Wissen,* December 1984.

Walker, Ann. "Implementing Whole-Brain Methods for Reading Instruction." *Journal SALT* 13, no. 3.

Wexu, Mario. *The Ear: Gateway to Balancing the Body—A Modern Guide to Ear Acupuncture.* Santa Fe: Aurora Press, 1975.

The Wonders of Qi Gong—A Chinese Exercise for Fitness, Health and Longevity, China Sports Magazine, Los Angeles, Wayfarer Publications, 1985.

(Note: *SALT Journals* are available from SALT, 3028 Emerson Avenue South, Minneapolis, MN 55408; and the national ERIC System, Center for Applied Linguistics, 3520 Prospect Street, NW, Washington, DC 20007.)

Index